Premigration Legacies and Immigrant Social Mobility

Premigration Legacies and Immigrant Social Mobility

The Afro-Surinamese and Indo-Surinamese in the Netherlands

Mies van Niekerk

LEXINGTON BOOKS
Lanham • Boulder • New York • Oxford

LEXINGTON BOOKS

Published in the United States of America
by Lexington Books
A Member of the Rowman & Littlefield Publishing Group
4720 Boston Way, Lanham, Maryland 20706

PO Box 317
Oxford
OX2 9RU, UK

Copyright © 2000 by Het Spinhuis, Amsterdam
Translation copyright © 2002 by Lexington Books
Originally published under the title *De krekel en de mier* by Het Spinhuis, Amsterdam

Cover photograph copyright © by Merlijn Michon

All rights reserved. No part of this publication may be reproduced,
stored in a retrieval system, or transmitted in any form or by any
means, electronic, mechanical, photocopying, recording, or otherwise,
without the prior permission of the publisher.

British Library Cataloguing in Publication Information Available

Library of Congress Cataloging-in-Publication Data

Niekerk, Mies van.
　　[Krekel en de mier. English]
　　Premigration legacies and immigrant social mobility : the Afro-Surinamese and Indo-
Surinamese in the Netherlands / Mies van Niekerk.
　　　　p. cm.
　　Includes bibliographical references and index.
　　ISBN 0-7391-0431-4 (alk. paper)
　　　　1. Immigrants—Netherlands—Social conditions. 2. Creoles—Netherlands—Social
conditions. 3. Hindus—Netherlands—Social conditions. 4. Suriname—Emigration and
immigration. I. Title.

JV8152 .N53513 2002
305.891′41—dc21

2002066880

Printed in the United States of America
♾ ™ The paper used in this publication meets the minimum requirements of American
National Standard for Information Sciences—Permanence of Paper for Printed Library
Materials, ANSI/NISO Z39.48–1992.

Contents

List of Tables

Foreword

Surinam, a small country on the coast of South America, gained its independence from the Netherlands in 1975. Culturally, Surinam belongs to the Caribbean, and like other Caribbean nations, it has suffered serious economic and political problems. As a result, a large percentage of its population has emigrated. In this book, anthropologist Mies van Niekerk examines the social and economic adjustment of two groups of emigrants from Surinam to the Netherlands: the Afro-Surinamese or Creoles and the Indo-Surinamese or Hindustanis. The former are descendants of African slaves initially brought to the Caribbean to grow sugar for European landowners. The latter are descendants of indentured laborers from India brought to grow sugar after the Dutch government abolished slavery. Van Niekerk asks: in what ways are Afro-Surinamese and Indo-Surinamese in Holland similar and in what ways are they different?

All knowledge results from comparison. In psychology, much useful knowledge comes from comparing individuals who have been assigned to a control group with individuals who have been assigned to an experimental group. In anthropology, experiments are rare. Social scientists never have complete control over their subjects; even if they did, cultural influences operate not at the level of individuals but at the level of groups, communities, and states. To study these effects, anthropologists engage in crosscultural comparison. By comparing individuals in more than one culture, society, or state, they hope to learn how culture affects human behavior.

Unfortunately, the number of causal influences on human behavior is larger than the number of contexts available for study. Hence, at best, cross-cultural comparisons render hypotheses about human behavior plausible. Still, some crosscultural comparisons are more informative than others. For students of ethnic attainment, this book should rank at the top of the list. A more compelling crossnational strategy cannot be constructed. Van Niekerk compares two groups of immigrants who hail from the same source country, many of whom arrived in Holland at roughly the same time (the 1970s). Previous studies of immigrants have compared peoples from different sending countries who settle in the same receiving country and people from the same sending country who settle in different receiving countries. But, to my knowledge, no scholar has ever compared culturally different immigrants from the same sending country who settle in the same receiving country.

Not only do these two groups share sending and receiving countries, but the native Dutch barely distinguish between them. Research on Dutch attitudes toward minorities suggests that Creoles and Hindustanis rank in the middle of an ethnic hierarchy in which immigrants from Turkey and Morocco are the most stigmatized. American readers may have some difficulty imagining this scenario; other English speakers should have less of a problem. The difficulty for Americans is that, in the United States, people of African descent generally suffer the most stigma. But in countries where Africans did not undergo a prolonged period of enslavement, the public's view of blacks is less pernicious. In Britain and Canada, for instance, studies show that whites rank Afro-Caribbeans more favorably than they rank South Asians.

These considerations heighten the practical relevance of this volume for Americans. But this book also makes an important theoretical contribution. Recent scholarship on immigration to the United States suggests that some national origin groups are adapting in new ways. This perspective, known as "segmented assimilation theory" was initially formulated by Herbert Gans, Alejandro Portes, and Min Zhou; it challenges many of the predictions of classic assimilation theory. According to the classical view, immigrants arrive with values and customs that originate in their homelands and, partly as result, they are at a disadvantage. This disadvantage is evident in the major institutions of the host society: schools, the economy, the polity, and so on. Over time, however, immigrants, and/or their children and grandchildren acculturate; they exchange these premigration repertoires for the values and customs prevalent in their new environments. Partly as a consequence of this change, their disadvantage dissipates. That is, in the economy, the polity, etc., they reach parity with natives. In other words, they have assimilated.

Segmented assimilation challenges this causal order, arguing that two other immigrant adaptations are emerging. One adaptation involves refusing, or at least delaying, acculturation. Of particular importance are values that put the family before the individual, favor ethnic undertakings over popular pastimes, and endorse self-control rather than self-indulgence. Immigrant groups following this trajectory usually come from "traditional" societies, cultures where individuals have less freedom than in the contemporary West. The young typically defer to the old, the female to the male. The labor force of these groups is disproportionately self-employed or employed by coethnics, a situation that reinforces their isolation from the attractions of competitive individualism. Children raised in these circumstances are believed to do well in school, to exhibit few social problems, and to experience upward occupational mobility in adulthood.

Another adaptation involves adopting the norms of lower-class, disadvantaged "involuntary" minorities. Initially developed by the anthropologist John Ogbu, the term "involuntary" minorities refers to subordinate groups that have been introduced to a nation involuntarily, through slavery, colonization, or conquest. In the United States, the largest such groups are African Americans and Mexicans. Members of such groups have experienced discrimination and disadvantage for so long that some "conclude that they are worse off than they ought to be for no other reason than that they belong to a subordinate and disparaged minority group. . . . Unlike immigrants, they do not see their situation as temporary; on the contrary, they tend to interpret the discrimination against them as permanent and institutionalized" (Ogbu 1991: 14). In order to maintain their self-esteem, some segments of these populations have developed a set of alternative norms, values, and survival strategies. Among the latter are "rioting . . . sports, entertainment, hustling, drug dealing and the like" (Ogbu 1991: 14-15). In short, the values and behaviors of lower-class members of involuntary minorities are the polar opposite of the values and behaviors promoted in "traditional" societies. Unlike immigrants, involuntary minorities feel "that it requires more than education, individual effort and hard work to overcome the barriers against them" (Ogbu 1991: 14). According to segmented assimilationists, a significant fraction of first- and second-generation Caribbean and Hispanic youth have adopted this stance.

Van Niekerk's methodology offers a unique way of testing segmented assimilation theory. There are no African Americans in the Netherlands. Thus, the adaptation of the Afro-Surinamese reveals how immigrants of African descent adapt in the absence of a preexisting oppositional subculture. Furthermore, as readers will discover, it turns out that very few Indo-Surinamese are self-employed. Thus, the adaptation of the Indo-Surinamese reveals how immigrants of Indian descent adapt in the absence of an ethnic economy.

In the main, van Niekerk finds very little difference in the socioeconomic attainment of Afro-Surinamese and Indo-Surinamese immigrants. However, educational patterns within the second generation lead her to predict that, in the long run, the latter will pull ahead of the former. Moreover, her qualitative research indicates that the proportion of males gravitating toward an oppositional subculture, and the proportion maintaining such an outlook into adulthood, is larger among Creoles than Hindustanis. If these admittedly preliminary observations turn out to be correct, then the key causal mechanisms of segmented assimilation theory are misspecified. In the first places, some members of a black immigrant group may adopt an oppositional stance even in the absence of an indigenous black underclass. In the second place, some members of an East Indian immigrant group may retain a traditional, collectivist orientation even in the absence of an ethnic economy.

One way to explain these disparities would be to argue that, in this era of globalization, values and lifestyles are diffused without the benefit of face-to-face contact. The media and the communications industry transmit stereotypical messages all over the world, leaving little room for inter- or intranational disparities. Van Niekerk takes a different approach. Drawing on the historical legacies of Africans and East Indians in Surinam, she shows how the colonial situation affected the value system of both Creoles and Hindustanis generations before their departure for the Netherlands. Familiarity with this legacy takes much of the surprise out of their present adaptations. This is not to say that, after arriving in Holland, the two groups' values remained static or immutable. On the contrary, the post–World War II situation in Surinam, as well as contemporary Dutch society, has shaped the outlooks of both Indo-Surinamese and Afro-Surinamese. Still, the cultural baggage with which the two groups arrived was not the same. As a result, even though the social and economic conditions that they have encountered in Holland are similar, their responses to those conditions are different.

In recent years, students of ethnic attainment have been reluctant to incorporate culture into their theories. To do so, they fear, implies that the cultures of more successful groups are superior to the cultures of less successful groups. From this perspective, less successful groups become morally responsible for their condition. In this book, Mies van Niekerk accords culture a central explanatory role, but she never "blames the victim." Students of ethnic attainment would do well to consider her example.

Suzanne Model
Professor of Sociology,
University of Massachusetts at Amherst

Acknowledgments

This book on Caribbean immigrants in the Netherlands is the result of my research on the differential social mobility of immigrant groups. Since the 1980s I have been involved in research on Caribbean immigrants and their children in Dutch society, particularly immigrants from Surinam or the former Dutch Guiana. In this book the focus is on the two main groups from this Caribbean country, the Afro-Surinamese and the Indo-Surinamese. The public images of the two groups are very different and resemble the stereotypes of "The Grasshopper and the Ant"—the title of the original Dutch version of this study that appeared in 2000. The research was financed by the Netherlands Organization for Scientific Research (NWO), which also funded the English translation.

The research this book recounts was conducted at the University of Amsterdam, first at the Department of Anthropology and Sociology, later at the Institute for Migration and Ethnic Studies (IMES). My study was part of a research program entitled "The Interrelation between the Socioeconomic and Cultural Position of Immigrants in Dutch Society" that was supervised by Hans Vermeulen, to whom I am especially grateful. First as a student, later as a researcher, for years I was amply able to benefit from his knowledge and research experience. I would also like to express my gratitude to Rinus Penninx, whose comprehensive knowledge of minority research and loyal and critical guidance were a great support.

There are numerous other people who helped make this book possible. In the first place, I would like to thank all the Surinamese families and respondents who took part in the study. I had known some of them for years and only got to know others in the course of the study, but I have fond memories of the interviews and talks with many of them. I would also like to thank my colleagues at the IMES and my fellow researchers and friends in the study group that met regularly for years under the supervision of Hans Vermeulen. I would like to make special mention of some of the people who—in a wide range of ways—contributed toward this book: Toon Pennings, Flip Lindo, Maurice Crul, Heleen Ronden,

Marlene de Vries, Tijno Venema, Livio Sansone, Ruth Vreden, Bob Sanches, Jair and Randall, Wonnie and Julia Sanches, Suzanne Heezen, Pien van Niekerk, the Naipal family, and the Kanhai family. Lastly I would like to thank Sheila Gogol for her fine translation.

Mies van Niekerk

Chapter One

Introduction

In the public image of Surinamese immigrants in the Netherlands, the Afro-Surinamese do not come off nearly as well as the Indo-Surinamese. They are often in the news in a negative light, and they are more frequently associated with poverty and deprivation and, at any rate in the past, with crime and drug use. The Indo-Surinamese, however, tend to be in the spotlight as successful immigrants who work themselves up the social ladder by being so diligent. Comparisons are readily made with Asian immigrants in the United States, and there is often a strong Indo-Surinamese identification with "Asian success." These ideas on social success and failure are not a Dutch invention for that matter. Even in Surinam itself, stereotype notions on the two groups still persist.

This book is about the social mobility of immigrants and their descendants in the Netherlands from the former Dutch colony of Surinam or Dutch Guiana on the northern coast of South America. I focus particularly on the Afro-Surinamese, called *Creoles* in Surinam, the descendants of African slaves and people of mixed European and African descent, and the Indo-Surinamese, called *Hindustanis* in Surinam, the descendants of indentured East Indians from the former British India.[1] Together, these two groups constitute the majority of the Surinamese population.[2] Most of the Surinamese immigrants came to the Netherlands shortly before and after Surinam became independent in 1975. Up until 1980, they could freely enter the former mother country. The question is how they did in Dutch society and whether there was really a difference in the social position and mobility of the two groups. In other words, are the stereotypes about them accurate, or are we dealing here with an ethnic myth (Steinberg 1989)? If it is a myth, how did the Afro-Surinamese get such a negative image and the Indo-Surinamese such a positive one? If it is not a myth and the Indo-Surinamese really are that much more successful than the Afro-Surinamese, how can this be accounted for?

I focus in this book on the possible differences in the social mobility of two ethnic groups. In classic immigration countries like the United States, ample attention is always devoted to differences in the social mobility of various groups of immigrants, but the issue always gives rise to heated discussions and controversies.[3] The old culture-of-poverty debate and more recently the debate on the emergence of a black underclass are the clearest illustrations.[4] There are also the success stories of the Jews or Asians like the Chinese or Koreans. In the case of groups that are successful, explanations are often proposed in terms of culture or ethnic resources, whereas in the case of less successful groups references are made to the opportunity structure of the society and to discrimination or racism.

So in essence, this debate on differential social mobility is about the importance of *structure* and *culture*. It is not a debate untouched by controversy. After all, research into differential social mobility does imply comparing groups, which in turn is quick to evoke moral judgments. Some authors try to avoid this by turning the very criteria social success is measured by into the topic of debate. Economic criteria such as income, education and occupation are said to be too one-sided, too Western, and too culturally specific (Werbner 2000). This might seem to be a convenient way to sidestep morality tales (Steinberg 1989: 86), but the question is how warranted this kind of relativism is. The goals immigrants aspire to when they leave home are generally the same: they are looking for a better life and social security. In this sense, there would seem to be a growing transnational consensus as to the value of a number of products of the modern world (Roosens 1989a: 157).

The central comparison here is relevant to this structure-versus-culture debate. The Afro-Surinamese and Indo-Surinamese are from the same country in the Caribbean and most of them came to the Netherlands in the same period. This means they were confronted with similar socioeconomic conditions in terms of the labor market, housing, education, and government policy. Since a number of factors were more or less the same for both groups, the emphasis in this study is less on the opportunity structure of the receiving society and more on aspects related to the groups themselves, their history and culture. This does not mean the opportunity structure plays no role at all, it just did not differ much for the two groups.

This emphasis on the history and culture of immigrant communities focuses on aspects of the immigrants in the Netherlands that have largely been overlooked in the research. Until recently, much of the emphasis was on the poor socioeconomic position of ethnic minorities.[5] Particularly in quantitative studies on the position of minorities, the "ethnic factor" is often treated as a residual factor, covering anything that can not be explained by SES variables.[6] This unexplained variance in comparisons between groups defined according to ethnic origin is often referred to as culture or ethnicity (Vermeulen 1992: 27). Other authors cite discrimination as a potential cause for a poor position in society, or at any rate leave it open as a possibility after an explanation in terms of SES variables has proved inadequate.[7]

A great deal of information is already available on the socioeconomic position of immigrants in the Netherlands as well as the underlying structural factors of social disadvantage. It is not as clear, though, exactly what influence is exerted by the "ethnic factor" in processes of social mobility and indeed what this factor entails. It has been repeatedly observed in sociology of education studies that the effect of ethnic background on school performance is strongly interrelated with the effect of the socioeconomic position of parents, though there is very little clarity as to the meaning of this relation (Driessen 1995). The need is emphasized for new research approaches to investigate this relation in greater depth.[8] A similar observation is made in research on the labor mobility of immigrants: the usual labor market theories prove inadequate when it comes to explaining the entire difference between the various immigrant groups and the Dutch population (Dagevos 1998). The aim of this study is to gain insight into what is referred to as the ethnic factor.

At the beginning it was *not done* to distinguish between the various ethnic groups in the Surinamese population. Especially in the 1970s and 1980s and certainly in progressive nationalistic circles, ethnic differences were not supposed to be referred to at all. This was quite understandable in view of the political aspiration of forging a unified nation in newly independent Surinam. Research conducted in the 1980s nonetheless suggested that there definitely were differences between the Afro-Surinamese and the Indo-Surinamese, particularly in the fields of education (Koot et al. 1985; Tjon-A-Ten 1987) and entrepreneurship (Boissevain et al. 1984). However, no systematic survey has been conducted yet of the social positions of the two groups. My study describes the development of the social positions of the two Surinamese groups in the Netherlands and aims to show how the differences might be interpreted.

Ethnic Background and Social Mobility

In this study, I examine the differences in the social mobility of two immigrant groups of different ethnic background who moved into more or less the same socioeconomic context. The emphasis is consequently on the relevance of their history and culture in relation to various contextual factors. In this section, I briefly address this issue and describe the points of departure of my research and the central concepts of this study. I come back to this issue in greater detail in chapter 9, but then it is on the basis of the research results.

Structure and Culture

In its simplest form, the discussion on which factors are relevant to the differences in the social mobility of various immigrant groups is often reduced to a debate on the primacy of *structure* or *culture*. Some authors believe the class position of immigrants and the opportunity structure of the host society are of decisive significance, though others hold that the cultural resources immigrants bring with them are more important than class factors or discrimination.[9] The academic structure-versus-culture debate seems to rely strongly on the points of view held beforehand. It might be wiser to take an approach that focuses on the interaction between the two.[10] However, there are not many empirical studies that demonstrate this interaction.

One example of this approach is the historical study by Perlmann (1988) on the differences in the schooling and economic attainment of various immigrant groups and African Americans in the late nineteenth and early twentieth centuries in the United States. Perlmann refers to three factors generally cited to explain the differential social mobility of immigrant groups: (1) the premigration history and the conditions of immigration; (2) the extent of discrimination the immigrant group is faced with in the new environment; and (3) the group's position in the economy and class structure there.

The importance of discrimination and class as factors is not disputed in Dutch studies nor anywhere else for that matter. There is not much difference of opinion about either of these factors, though it is far more difficult to empirically demonstrate the presence and the effect of discrimination than it is to show the effects of class factors.[11] The premigration heritage factor is not only the most controversial, it allows the most scope for multifarious interpretations. Perlmann (1988: 5-6) sums up what this heritage is generally thought to entail and distinguishes two clusters of factors. The first cluster pertains to the occupational skills of immigrants resulting from their positions in the social structure of the country of origin. The second cluster pertains to various sorts of cultural attributes more or less related to the socioeconomic structure of the country of origin. It includes the immigrants' beliefs, attitudes, habits, and values (e.g., work ethic, attitude to learning and schools), features related to family relations and gender roles (e.g., attitudes to the employment of women, attitudes to the education of girls, the strength and nature of family ties) and to community relations, and worldviews. Many of these cultural attributes are clearly related to the economic and social structure of the country of origin, though others are less directly tied to it.

In this study, I take a rather wide view of the premigration heritage. I see it as including all the nonmaterial baggage immigrants take with them when they move to a new country, and this baggage can be more or less directly linked to their structural position in the country of origin. I work from the assumption that only an analytical distinction can be drawn between *culture* and *structure*. Empirically, they are inextricably connected.[12] In this study, I nonetheless try to disentangle the importance of culture in social mobility processes.

Culture, History, and Ethnic Origin

What exactly do I mean by culture in this study? In anthropological literature alone, there are any number of definitions. It would be pointless to even try to define it in an all-inclusive way. What I mean by culture is the knowledge, skills, and values that people share. This study focuses on what Barth calls the distinctive background of experience of immigrants and the fund of knowledge, skills, and values they bring with them (1994: 14). In this sense, culture is the product of the experiences of past generations. However, culture becomes very static and non-historical if we leave it at that. Culture is constantly developing in a concrete social context on the basis of the experiences of the individuals in question. "[T]hough we learn it largely from others as a basis for interpretation and action in the world, it accumulates in each of us as a precipitate of our own experience" (Barth 1994: 14).

Thus I view culture as the result of adaptations to the circumstances of the present based upon a heritage from the past.[13] Individuals are socialized in a certain social setting and presented with certain behavioral models, but at the same time they are also the actors in the construction of culture. However, they are not completely free in this connection. Culture is partially unconscious, and not something people can always consciously manipulate. What is more, individuals always operate within the limitations of a given period of time and within certain societal relations. As a well-known saying in anthropology goes, "Men make their own history, but they do not make it just as they please" (cited in Wolf 1994: 6).

This concept of culture does manage to escape what is known as the culturalist fallacy, namely, conceiving of cultures as sharply delineated, homogeneous, and relatively unchanging entities (Vermeulen 2000). This kind of concept of culture says more about the historical period when the concept was formulated than about today's reality. More than ever before, transnational connections and intercultural worldwide influences develop. Also within specific societies or social groups, culture is differentially distributed and there is cultural amalgamation.[14] So there is no reason to assume that the differences between ethnic or immigrant groups are any larger than the ones within groups. If culture is generated in part by the experiences of individuals in certain social circumstances, there are clearly also cultural differences that crosscut ethnic boundaries. Obviously, the experiences of different individuals just differ, if for no other reason than because they belong to different social classes, sexes, or generations. So not all culture is ethnic culture. Just as we can speak of the culture of ethnic groups, we can speak of class cultures, occupational cultures, youth cultures, or girls' cultures. Depending on the positioning of individuals in the social structure, overlapping cultures occur, for example, ethnic youth cultures or male occupational cultures.

So obviously culture and ethnic group do not always totally coincide. With this internal variation in mind, it is still possible to speak of ethnic cultures. I concur with Eriksen, who comments on the differences between the populations of Indian and African descent in Trinidad and Mauritius that "It would be foolish to pretend that such differences do not exist, but it would be equally untenable to treat them as givens" (1992: 121).

Ethnic Origin and Ethnic Identity

Ethnic background has to do with people's descent. Compared with ethnic identity, it is more objective, as is sometimes underscored by a common language or religion. Though this does not necessarily have to be the case. Later generations of immigrants can be culturally assimilated into the host country without losing sight of their origin. In the United States, millions of people can still trace their Irish or Italian descent even if they see themselves as Americans or hyphenated Americans and are also viewed as such by the people around them. In fact it is the loss of ethnic culture that often makes people want to grasp at the last remnant of it as a symbol of their shared origin. Steinberg speaks in this connection of the "dying gasp" (1989: 51), the last spark of ethnic culture before the stage of total assimilation.[15] In this context, the concept of ethnicity or ethnic identity is more applicable.[16]

The concept of ethnic identity differs from the concept of ethnic origin by the *belief* in a joint ancestry, history, and culture. So, unlike ethnic origin, it is subjective. Regardless of who someone's ancestors are or what cultural background they come from, ethnicity has to do with how people identify in ethnic terms. Vermeulen (1984) draws a clear distinction between ethnicity and culture. Ethnicity is not about objective cultural differences, it is about the meaning people attribute to these differences.

In this study, the focus is on relatively recent immigrants to the Netherlands who are still the first or the "1.5" generation. This is why the culture they brought with them can still be assumed to be more important to them than to third or fourth-generation immigrants like the Irish Americans or Italian Americans referred to above. If Surinamese youngsters see themselves as Dutch, it does not necessarily mean they are completely assimilated in a cultural sense. In *Apache-Indian*, author Anil Ramdas describes the dilemma of Indo-Surinamese youngsters who would love to be "modern" but still feel very much at home in the Indo-Surinamese setting. "They can't stand anything associated with 'coolie,' but they still like the atmosphere. . . . The problem is that what they want to reject because it reeks of disdain is precisely what the soul won't let go of" (1996: 142, 143-44). This is the opposite of what I observed above about third- or fourth-generation Irish Americans or Italian Americans. Whereas these Americans cherish the last remnant of their ethnic culture because in essence they have become so totally American, the Indo-Surinamese youngsters in the story by Ramdas are still Indo-Surinamese in everything they do and say, and they are trying as hard as they can to leave it behind.

For research on social mobility, ethnic origin is far more important that ethnic identity. This point is also made by Perlmann and Waldinger (1997), though they note that interethnic marriages sometimes make it difficult to specify the exact ethnic origin of third-generation immigrants. They criticize researchers who in a case like this essentially just pass the question on to the respondents by asking them what group they identify with. However, if the aim is to gain insight into the social mobility of immigrant groups, these authors feel we need to know the actual ethnic ancestors, not the subjective identities of the present generation (1997: 899). Berthoud et al. (1997: 14) are of the same opinion. They draw a distinction between ethnic origin (family origin) and ethnic self-definition. They call origin a *matter of fact*, and self-definition a *matter of opinion*. It is clear from the study by Berthoud et al. that in most cases, there is not that much discrepancy between the two, except when it comes to people from the Caribbean.[17] Studies conducted in the Netherlands produce the same result. The discrepancy between ethnic origin[18] and ethnic self-identification is relatively great among the Surinamese and Antillean populations, both Caribbean immigrants. They are more apt to identify as Dutch than immigrants from Turkey or Morocco would be (Verweij 1997: 8-9).

Which aspects are relevant to this study? I have noted above that ethnic origin is more relevant than ethnic identity or self-identification. I am primarily concerned here with the history of two Surinamese populations and how it has influenced their position in Dutch society. The question then is how to determine their ethnic origin. This is no problem as regards the Surinamese population as a whole, since the usual criteria of where they were born or where their parents were born will suffice. It is a problem though as regards Afro-Surinamese and Indo-Surinamese immigrants in the Netherlands, especially in quantitative studies. In the official statistics, Afro-Surinamese and Indo-Surinamese descent can not be traced and in survey research only approximated. I return to this point in the next section in connection with the quantitative data used in this study.

The Study

In this section, first I address the central research question. Then I present the research method that was used and describe the research population.

Central Research Question

The research addressed the development of the social position of Afro-Surinamese and Indo-Surinamese immigrants in the Netherlands, the social mobility
differences between them, and the explanations for these differences. Since the
socioeconomic context has been approximately the same for the two groups, the
emphasis is on the factors that supplement the structural explanations. These additional explanations pertain to aspects of the culture and history of the two
groups. Some theoretical comments are made on these explanations in the previous section. On the basis of these comments, the central research question can
be formulated as follows:

> How has the social position of Afro-Surinamese and Indo-Surinamese immi-
> grants in the Netherlands developed and to what extent do their culture and his-
> tory provide an additional explanation for differences in their social mobility?

This focuses attention on the historical dimension of immigration and social mobility. Immigrants do not arrive in a new country with a totally clean slate. In
addition to material possessions, they bring sociocultural baggage as well. This
means that upon arrival in a new country, different categories of immigrants
start from different positions depending on their history in the country they
come from. So to what extent are differences in social mobility based on their
premigration social position and the role they played in the economic structure
of the country of origin? In the first instance, this refers to the knowledge and
skills that are closely linked to their socioeconomic position in the country of origin. The question, however, is to what extent the nonmaterial baggage of immigrants is also derived from their premigration class position? As is noted in the
previous section, research elsewhere has shown that the premigration heritage is
more comprehensive. This study focuses on the premigration heritage in the
broadest sense.

How the social position of immigrants and their children develops after migration is not only the result of the sociocultural baggage they have brought with
them. To a large extent it is also shaped by the socioeconomic structure of the
society they have moved to. This structural context was more or less the same
for the Afro-Surinamese and Indo-Surinamese immigrants who came to the
Netherlands in the period of mass migration. So differences in social mobility
can barely be attributed if at all to the opportunity structure of the receiving society. This does not mean this structural context did not exert any influence in
this case, but it does mean the role was more or less the same for the two
groups. It is important to see how—given the structural context—the specific
immigration history of Afro-Surinamese and Indo-Surinamese immigrants influenced the development of their social position after their immigration.

The premigration heritage cannot be assumed to have been the same for all the members of each ethnic group. After all, culture is not evenly distributed within immigrant groups. What is more, culture is not simply a legacy from the past, it is the result of adaptation to the present on the grounds of this heritage. There will consequently be differences in how individuals and subgroups from the two ethnic groups adapt to these new circumstances on the basis of new experiences. This means attention has to be devoted to the internal variation within ethnic groups.

Starting from these considerations, the general problem addressed here can be posed in three questions:

1. What is the premigration history of Creoles and East Indians, in particular as regards their role in the economic structure of Surinamese society and their social position?
2. What differences in social mobility are there between Afro-Surinamese and Indo-Surinamese immigrants in the Netherlands, and how should these differences be viewed in the light of the premigration history? What is the role of culture in this connection and what changes occur in this respect in the Netherlands?
3. What changes have occurred within the two ethnic groups regarding the questions posed in numbers 1 and 2 and how can they be explained?

Design and Methods

As regards the premigration history (research question 1), I have examined the historical development of the Afro-Surinamese and Indo-Surinamese social position, the mobility patterns that were exhibited, and the economic sectors the two groups were active in. To explain the differences in their social positions, I focus on the economic and political conditions on the one hand and on how the two groups have adapted to them on the other. This historical aspect of the study is based upon the relevant literature as well as anthropological fieldwork, the core of this research. During my fieldwork, I asked people at length about their own history and the history of their family before the move to the Netherlands. In later 1995 and early 1996, I went to Surinam to delve deeper into this issue.

The second question pertains to the postmigration history. How did the social position of Afro-Surinamese and Indo-Surinamese immigrants develop in the Netherlands? At the start of my study, the information available on the social position of the two groups in the Netherlands was extremely limited and fragmentary. There was adequate information about the total Surinamese population, but no clear separate data on the Afro-Surinamese and Indo-Surinamese segments. It was possible though to get a clear impression of the two groups from the data files of a representative survey (SPVA-1994)[19] conducted by the Institute of Sociological and Economic Research (ISEO) at Erasmus University Rotterdam. It provided statistical data that had not been published yet, which I analyzed in greater detail for this study.[20] As is noted above, it is problematic in survey studies to ascertain the ethnic origin of Afro-Surinamese and Indo-Surinamese immigrants in the Netherlands since, in this case, the place of birth is not a useful criterion. This is why the SPVA used a combination of a subjective and an objective criterion, namely, self-definition and language use. Ethnic self-definition as a criterion might be contradictory to what I have noted above about the need for an objective criterion to ascertain ethnic origin, but in this case no better method was available. Moreover, it is important that the method is primarily focused on ethnic origin and not on all the conceivable ethnic self-definitions, and that this approach seems to have produced a good result. For more detailed information on ascertaining ethnic origin in the SPVA, I refer the reader to appendix 2.

My objective with the quantitative data from the SPVA was to see if there were any differences between the Afro-Surinamese and Indo-Surinamese social positions in the Netherlands. I have focused on their positions as regards education and the labor market, since this is how social mobility is usually measured.[21] A more detailed analysis of the mobility routes was needed to show the positions the immigrants and their children had come to occupy in the Dutch school system and labor market. Compared with large-scale quantitative studies, qualitative research is better suited for showing how social conditions affect the way individuals think and act and how in turn the way they think and act influences their social position.[22] This was the underlying idea behind my anthropological fieldwork. Though the quantitative material did provide a picture of the two Surinamese groups as a whole, the fieldwork focused on immigrants with a lower-class background. They constituted the majority of the immigrants who came to the Netherlands at the time. The goal of this study, after all, is to examine the postmigration process of social mobility, which is why people who were already in the upper classes in Surinam are less interesting.

In the first instance, the empirical research focused on the family background and the influence it had on the social careers of the younger generation. For this purpose, I recorded individual and family histories. What I was mainly interested in was the aspects of the histories connected to the socioeconomic position in Surinam and the Netherlands, and the causes underlying them. As far as possible, I tried to talk to various individuals from one family, preferably from two or even three generations. Even in the cases where I just spoke to one individual, I always focused on the family of origin. I hoped these histories would provide insight into the role of the family background, and in particular the sociocultural influence it had on the school and occupational careers of a younger generation. Actually, I was interested in family background features directly connected with the schooling and labor market position of the parents (educational level, occupation, and job experience), sociocultural features (family structure and gender roles) and the intergenerational transmission of social legacies or, more simply, the messages parents conveyed to their children.[23]

The histories illustrate objective and subjective aspects of intra- and intergenerational mobility. They provide insight into the various mobility routes of different generations and of men and women. Family and life histories thus constitute an important source of knowledge about social reality.[24] In addition, this intensive research method enabled me to gain insight into the respondents' own interpretation and perception of their situation. This is an aspect of social mobility that usually remains invisible in survey research but nonetheless plays an important role, as will be demonstrated.

In the second instance, the empirical research focuses on the various sociocultural contexts individuals operate in. I am referring here to the direct social environment outside the family, that is, the social networks of relatives and peers, the neighborhood and ethnic community. The social embeddedness of individuals in various contexts influences how they think and act and the access they have to knowledge, information, and other resources.[25] In this sense, social embeddedness contributes to shaping social careers.

In periods of varying intensity, my fieldwork was conducted from late 1994 to late 1996. It took place in the cities of Amsterdam and The Hague for the simple reason that large Surinamese communities live there, mainly Afro-Surinamese in Amsterdam and Indo-Surinamese in The Hague. The decision to do fieldwork in Amsterdam was stimulated by the fact it is where I live, I know the city well, and I did not have to travel very far. What is more, I had conducted research in the Surinamese community in Amsterdam in the past.[26] I did not confine myself to either of the two groups in each city, though the emphasis in Amsterdam was on Afro-Surinamese and in The Hague on Indo-Surinamese informants. I consulted a wide range of secondary sources on the local situation ranging from city publications to local research reports and periodicals of organizations in the local Surinamese communities. In both cities, I came into contact with my informants in any number of ways. In the first place, I made contact via third parties, key informants who I consulted because of their knowledge and insight into the local Surinamese community, acquaintances who had contact with potential informants, and informants I had interviewed in the past. One of the risks of this approach, also known as the snowball method, is that the composition of the research group becomes one-sided if too many informants are recruited through a limited number of networks. This is why I made sure of a certain distribution of the entrances or starting contacts; there were a total of thirteen of them. In addition, I used other methods as well. A second way to come into contact with potential informants was by going to places or gatherings where I felt there was a good chance of meeting people who belonged to the research population I had in mind. A third approach was less conventional. I got into touch with several Afro-Surinamese girls who I knew from an earlier study in Amsterdam and interviewed them again. The advantage was that I already knew a great deal about their situation at an earlier point in time and was able to supplement this information now—fifteen years later. The girls had been teenagers at the time and were now in their thirties. The fourth way to make contact was via Surinam. At the end of 1995 and the beginning of 1996, I spent almost two months in Surinam and spoke to the friends and relatives of my informants in the Netherlands.[27] When I returned to the Netherlands, I spoke to the relatives of people I had met in Surinam. Photographs and letters were instrumental in this whole process in much the same way as I had been asked to bring money and presents for the relatives in Surinam. This made me part of the flow of money and goods crossing the ocean at such a high frequency between Surinam and the Netherlands.

By far the bulk of the research material is from the interviews, which varied from more formal interviews to extremely informal conversations. In addition, participant observation was a major source of research data. Going to places and gatherings was not only a way to come into contact with potential informants, it provided a context for informal conversations and participant observation. I attended weddings and birthday parties, temple services, informative meetings, and social workers' consultation hours. I regularly spent time at the meeting places of Surinamese organizations and had a look at various "Surinamese" schools. I went to some places quite regularly or even frequently and repeatedly spoke to people there. On some occasions I was able to do all kinds of favors for them. In part at the locations referred to above, I interviewed key informants, people I knew or assumed would be familiar with the subjects I was interested in. These key informants included school principals, social workers, board members of self-help organizations, welfare workers, and local politicians.

Based on this combination of research methods, I gained as much insight as I could into the problems at hand. The core of my study is qualitative, but the quantitative survey data and my examination of the historical literature on Surinam provide important supplementary information. The strong point about the quantitative material is that the findings are representative and can be generalized. This is not usually the strongest aspect of anthropological research. However, quantitative research also has its limitations, since in many cases it only produces statistical connections in response to quantitative questions. In this sense, perhaps my anthropological fieldwork can supplement the survey because it demonstrates the context, complexity, and interrelatedness of certain phenomena, something that is not easy to do solely on the basis of statistics.[28] According to Bertaux and Thompson, the survey as research method on social mobility is even "condemned to remain blind to core aspects of the very processes it aims to investigate" (1997: 6). To put it simply, quantitative material can give a good impression of the extent of social mobility, but qualitative research sheds light on its nature and the underlying factors that shape it. Thus I do not strive to present a quantitatively representative picture, though I have tried to make the research population as varied as possible. Instead, the main aim of my study is to detect relations that are often largely overlooked in quantitative studies and provide a theoretical interpretation for them.

Research Population

The study focuses on immigrants from the lower socioeconomic class in Surinam. As criterion for belonging to this class, I took the educational and occupational level at the time of their move to the Netherlands. I used the same categories Venema did in his study on Afro-Surinamese social relations and the Afro-Surinamese religion winti in Amsterdam (1992: 23). Venema divided the population into lower class, higher lower class, and middle class. He used various criteria for this purpose, and I used one of them, a combination of educational and occupational level. People who did unskilled work and had not attended more than a two-year postprimary school or vocational school were categorized as belonging to the lower class. The higher lower class consisted of people who did skilled work or lower level office work and had attended no more than a four-year secondary school. It is true that this approach is mainly suited to an urban or urban Creole pattern of social segmentation, but this classification does also seem to be useful as indication of the class distribution of immigrants with a rural background. I view the lower socioeconomic class as including everyone in either of the lower-class categories. This includes the majority of the Surinamese immigrants. In 1985, 88 percent of the Surinamese immigrants in the Netherlands had not attended more than a two-year postprimary school or four-year secondary school before leaving Surinam (CBS/UvA 1988: 23). In 1979, 77 percent of the Surinamese immigrants in the Netherlands were unskilled or skilled workers and lower level employees. If the self-employed are included, most of whom presumably fell under these educational criteria as well, then the figure was 86 percent (Reubsaet et al. 1982: 54).

However, the seemingly simple criteria of the first generation's educational and occupational level at the time of the move to the Netherlands did entail certain complications. It was not always easy to draw such strict distinctions. Sometimes the criteria did not apply to everyone in a given family. Even the parents in one and the same family were sometimes in different classes, for instance a woman who was a teacher and a man who was a street vendor. It also happened that families in one family network were of very different socioeconomic levels, and that via a lower-class family I came into contact with a middle-class family in the same family network. I also met well-educated youngsters or university students who had come to the Netherlands without their parents, but who were originally from a low socioeconomic background. In these cases, there was not much point to strict adherence to the criteria, especially since my aim was to examine the nature, underlying causes, and mechanisms of social mobility. This is why the exceptions were so significant and useful, though none of the cases involved anyone from an established middle-class background. Even if the immigrants did personify upward social mobility themselves, they were from lower-class backgrounds. At most, they belonged to what has been referred to in earlier studies as the emerging middle class (Vermeulen 1984: 39-42).

My study not only focuses on the immigrants themselves but also includes their children, at any rate insofar as they were young adults. The point of departure was that there had to already be some idea of their career prospects. This excluded children and adolescents from the study. As class criteria, I took the educational and occupational level of the parents or grandparents regardless of the education or occupation of the children or grandchildren themselves. In other words, they were the children or grandchildren of the first generation of immigrants from the lower socioeconomic class.

As regards the moment of arrival in the Netherlands, most of my Surinamese respondents came in the period of mass immigration in the 1970s and 1980s. My study also includes people who came before 1970 and newcomers who did not arrive in the Netherlands until the 1990s, but in much smaller numbers. In this sense, my research population resembles the total Surinamese population in the Netherlands. Although their numbers are much smaller, the history of the early and recent immigrants adds some contrasting details to the picture of the social mobility of the majority of the respondents.

As regards their ethnic origin, the research population consists mainly but not completely of Afro-Surinamese and Indo-Surinamese immigrants. Ethnic origin is not only simpler to ascertain in qualitative than in quantitative studies, the results are more valid and reliable.[29] In my study, I did not include any respondents of mixed Surinamese and Dutch descent. This second generation of mixed descent constitutes a certain selection of the children of Surinamese immigrants. They are often children of the early immigrants who were mainly of Creole origin. In part this is why I adhered to the limited definition of foreign origin here and only included the children of *two* Surinamese parents in my study. The population does include a small number of informants of mixed Surinamese descent. Their ethnic background is a mixture of Creole and East Indian or other mixtures, such as East Indian and Javanese or East Indian and Amerindian.[30] My research method automatically brought me into contact with these people. Their history, which was often very different from that of other Surinamese immigrants, provided interesting extra information.

All things considered, I examined the history of sixty-four extended families, many of which consisted of various nuclear families and households. One way I collected my material was from the interviews I had with 102 informants. By asking these informants about other members of their families, I gathered information about a total of 288 individuals. Of course the information was not always equally extensive or in-depth, and sometimes it was even extremely limited. The nature and amount of material thus varied greatly from one family to the next. In some cases I spoke to various people, had numerous interviews and telephone conversations, went to family parties, and visited relatives in Surinam, and in others I only interviewed one person and asked for some crucial information about the other members of the family. However, even the more superficial information contributed toward presenting a socioeconomic profile of the family. I view twenty-five of these sixty-four families as core cases, since the information I gathered about them is more extensive and in-depth.

The number of Indo-Surinamese and Afro-Surinamese families is more or less the same, thirty and twenty-eight families, respectively ten and thirteen of which are core cases. Measured according to the number of people however, the Afro-Surinamese research population is smaller as regards the number of men, though not as regards the number of women. This is due in part to the frequent absence of the fathers in Afro-Surinamese working-class families, and in part it is because the men are not as easily accessible to outsiders.[31] A less family-oriented approach by a male researcher who spent more time on the street and at public places might have produced more male informants. This does not mean the category of Afro-Surinamese men with a low educational level were left out of my study altogether, it just means I collected much of the information about them indirectly from their girlfriends, wives, mothers, and sisters.

As is noted above, the fieldwork was not confined to these families and informants or to the interviews I did. Much of the knowledge and insight were acquired in other contexts and in the course of talks with numerous other Surinamese informants in Surinam as well as the Netherlands. It is difficult to quantify these talks, but there were twenty-two key informants I had more formal interviews with. Many of them were early immigrants to the Netherlands, and about half of them were Afro-Surinamese and half Indo-Surinamese. For more extensive information about the research population, I refer the reader to appendix 1.

Notes

1. As was the case elsewhere in Latin America and the Caribbean, the term *Creole* originally referred to Europeans born in the colonies. It gradually came to include Africans born in the colonies, so that it pertained to everyone born there whose parents came from overseas. With the arrival of Asian immigrants, the term Creole came to have a specific meaning in Surinam, pertaining to the descendants of African slaves as well as people of mixed African and European descent (van Lier 1971: 2). Nowadays, the term Creole is predominantly used there to refer to the urban population as distinct from the Maroons, the descendants of runaway slaves who mainly live in the inland regions of Surinam. The term Afro-Surinamese is becoming increasingly popular among the Creoles themselves. Depending on the context, I use both these terms in this book. The East Indians, referred to in Surinam as Hindustanis, are descendants of contract workers from the former British India who were recruited from 1873 to 1917 to come and work on the plantations (see chapter 3). In the case of Surinam, the term Indo-Surinamese is somewhat misleading, since it would also include another segment of the Surinamese population, the Javanese. They are from the former Dutch East Indies, now Indonesia, and they were recruited as contract workers for the plantations in much the same way as the East Indians. In this book though,

I use the term Indo-Surinamese, which is clearer for a non-Dutch reading audience, to refer to East Indians or Hindustanis in the Netherlands. Unlike the term Afro-Surinamese for Creoles, Indo-Surinamese is not a term Hindustanis use to refer to themselves. In Surinam as well as the Netherlands, they are referred to in Dutch as Hindustanis, which can be viewed as the Surinamese equivalent of the term East Indian, as is used in the Caribbean and elsewhere. I concur here with the English use of the term East Indian, at any rate for the Surinamese context. For the Dutch context, I use Indo-Surinamese.

2. In addition to Creoles and East Indians, there are other ethnic groups in Surinam. Amerindians are the only native group there. The arrival of all the other groups is linked to the colonial history of Surinam as a plantation society. The Javanese are the third largest group in Surinam. There are also the Maroons and smaller groups such as the Chinese, Lebanese, and Europeans (see, e.g., van Lier 1971 and Dew 1978).

3. See Lieberson (1980); Light and Gold (2000); Perlmann (1988); Portes and Rumbaut (1996); Sowell (1981); Steinberg (1989); Waldinger (1996); DeWind et al. (1997).

4. On the culture of poverty, see Lewis (1966). For criticism and comments, see Leacock (1971); Valentine (1968). For the debate on the underclass, see Gans (1990 and 1992); Steinberg (1997); Wilson (1987, 1991, 1996, and 1999).

5. This largely has to do with the fact that in the first instance, research into ethnic minorities was government funded. Only recently did the funding sources became more diverse, and consequently the research field wider and more varied (van Niekerk 1993b; Penninx 1988b).

6. SES stands for socioeconomic status.

7. See Dagevos (1998).

8. See Fase and Kleijer (1996).

9. See in this connection the frequently cited studies by Steinberg (1989) and Sowell (1981).

10. See, e.g., Boissevain et al. (1984); Boissevain and Grotenbreg (1986); Sansone (1992); Waldinger et al. (1990).

11. See the Ph.D. dissertation by Dagevos (1998) and the review of it by de Beer (1999).

12. Cf. Vermeulen (2000).

13. Cf. Hannerz (1969 and 1996).

14. See, e.g., Barth (1986); Hannerz (1992 and 1996).

15. Cf. Roosens (1989a).

16. In social science literature on ethnic groups, the terms ethnic identity and ethnicity are usually used as synonyms (Vermeulen 1984: 15).

17. This discrepancy is evident as regards Black Caribbeans as well as Indian Caribbeans (Berthoud et al. 1997: 14-15).

18. The criterion here is the country of birth or the parents' country of birth.

19. This 1994 survey, called The Social Position and Use of Provisions by Ethnic Minorities (*Sociale Positie en Voorzieningengebruik Allochtonen*, SPVA), was prompted by the lack of data on immigrant groups. In 1986 the Dutch government had the ISEO develop a monitoring system to periodically assess the living conditions of the largest

immigrant groups in the Netherlands. Up to now the survey has been held in 1988, 1991, 1994, and 1998. The SPVA survey is considered representative on a nationwide basis regarding the groups studied.

20. The ISEO has since devoted separate attention itself to the two immigrant groups from Surinam and the SPVA-1994 findings in this connection have been published (Martens and Verweij 1997). Wherever it is relevant, I refer here to this publication, and not just to the unpublished SPVA data.

21. See Dronkers and Ultee (1995).

22. Cf. Perlmann (1988: 215); Wilson (1991).

23. Cf. Brinkgreve et al. (1994); Brinkgreve and van Stolk (1997).

24. Cf. Bertaux and Thompson (1997).

25. See, e.g., Coleman (1988); Fernández Kelly (1995); Portes (1995); Portes and Rumbaut (1996: 232-68); Zhou (1997).

26. See van Niekerk (1984); van Niekerk and Vermeulen (1989); see also Vermeulen (1984).

27. I spoke to a total of sixteen nuclear families there who were part of nine extended families. The nuclear families included a total of more than forty adults plus a number of children.

28. Cf. Bertaux and Thompson (1997); Savage (1997).

29. In qualitative and intensive studies, ethnic origin is ascertained in a logical and very natural way. Spontaneous verbal statements, the place of the meeting or the context of the conversation usually make it obvious what someone's ethnic descent is. Let me give an example from my own research. I was talking to an eighteen-year-old girl who told me she saw herself as Dutch Surinamese. "I was born and raised here," she explained, "but my roots are Surinamese." When I asked her whether there were a lot of Surinamese pupils at her school, she said, "Not at all. Most of them are Dutch. Well actually it is kind of divided. Maybe less than five percent of them are black, the rest are Moroccan, Hindustani and Dutch." So although in the first instance she defined herself as Dutch Surinamese, in another context she saw herself as Surinamese as distinct from Dutch. Then she used the term Surinamese to refer to blacks and was distinguishing them from people of East Indian descent, whom she called Hindustanis. So strictly speaking, hers was an ethnic self-definition that varied according to the situation, as is usually the case. It was clear though from the whole context of the interview, and from other contexts where I came across this same information, that she was a girl born in the Netherlands of Afro-Surinamese descent.

30. In Surinam, in this case in Paramaribo, the country's capital, this ethnically mixed category mainly consists of people of Creole and some other ethnic origin. The mixed category includes far fewer people with no Creole origin who are, for example, a mixture of Hindustani and Javanese (Schalkwijk and de Bruijne 1997: 34). The mixed category is quite small in Surinam (Paramaribo), where it constitutes about 10 percent of the total population (Schalkwijk and de Bruijne 1997: 34; see also Hassankhan et al. 1995: 257).

31. Cf. Sansone (1992: 27).

Chapter Two

The Surinamese in the Netherlands

More than two decades after the exodus from Surinam, it is clear that many of the immigrants and their children have settled for good in the Netherlands. Even though the Surinamese still have strong ties with their country of origin, actually returning is not a realistic option for most of them. It is even less the case for the second generation, by now more than a third of the Surinamese population in the Netherlands. The Dutch in turn would seem to be growing accustomed to the Surinamese presence. The stereotypes have become less negative, and at a local level, relations with the Dutch reached a kind of turning point around 1980.[1] In other fields as well, the integration of the Surinamese is making good progress.[2] An extensive ethnic infrastructure has developed, ranging from organizations directly promoting Surinamese interests to schools and social work agencies, all focused on improving the position of the Surinamese in the Netherlands.

In comparison with other immigrant groups in the Netherlands, from the start the fact that they possessed Dutch nationality gave the Surinamese a stronger legal position. Many Surinamese were already Dutch nationals before they arrived, at any rate up until Surinam became independent in 1975. In fact up until 1980, Surinamese immigrants to the Netherlands could choose to opt for Dutch nationality. During this period, emigration from Surinam assumed dramatic proportions for the homeland. A considerable percentage of the relatively small Surinamese population (now about 400,000) left the country.

From the mid-1970s onward, there was a sharp rise in the Surinamese population in the Netherlands, certainly if we count the children born in the Netherlands. At the moment, there are almost 300,000 people of Surinamese origin in the Netherlands. They constitute 2 percent of the total Dutch population and are thus one of the largest immigrant groups. There is a strong Surinamese residential concentration in the Randstad, the most urbanized western part of the Netherlands, and within this urban agglomeration most of them live in Amsterdam, The Hague, and Rotterdam. More than half the Surinamese population in the

Netherlands lives in these three large cities, where they constitute 8 to 10 percent of the population.

The majority of the Surinamese in the Netherlands belong to the first generation (182,000). If we define the second generation as the children of at least one parent born in Surinam, it has 115,000 members, that is almost 40 percent of the Surinamese in the Netherlands. If we use a more limited definition of the second generation as the children of two parents born abroad, it has almost 80,000 members.[3] This second generation is still relatively young.

In a socioeconomic sense, the Surinamese are extremely heterogeneous. On the average, they do still lag behind the Dutch, but their position in society is better than that of other large immigrant groups such as Turks and Moroccans. Less information is available about the positions of the Afro-Surinamese and Indo-Surinamese. Is it indeed true that the Indo-Surinamese are more successful in Dutch society than the Afro-Surinamese, as their public image seems to have it? In this chapter, I present a picture of the positions held by these two Surinamese groups, in particular in the fields of education and employment. First I describe the development of the social position of the Surinamese in general.

Starting Position after Immigration

Who moved from Surinam to settle in the Netherlands in recent decades? What was their starting position in Dutch society, and what baggage relevant to their social career did they bring with them? It is typical of the Surinamese immigration that in various periods, different categories of the population joined the exodus. The Surinamese population in the Netherlands consequently became increasingly varied in an ethno-cultural as well as a socioeconomic sense. This is why, based on the history of this migration, I examine who the Surinamese people were who settled in the Netherlands in the course of time.[4]

There is a long tradition of migration from Surinam to the Netherlands, but up until after World War II it was confined to small numbers of people who predominantly came on leave or to study or retire. The students were mainly Afro-Surinamese, and the highest social classes in Surinam were overrepresented (Sedoc-Dahlberg 1971). In the nineteenth century, there had already been evidence of this kind of student migration. Following the example of the former colonial elite, the indigenous elite sent their children to the Netherlands to complete their education. From then on, studying in the Netherlands became a reason for emigration that was to gradually expand to larger segments of the population. Emigration to the Netherlands came to be widely viewed as synonymous with a better life and social and economic advancement. "Studying" became a kind of collective rationale, a standard reason for leaving (Bovenkerk 1975: 45).

In the 1960s, for the first time there was emigration on a larger scale. The Surinamese economy was not doing well at the time, whereas the Dutch economy was booming. This promoted emigration, which was less and less restricted to the elite. In addition to the group of students, now including East Indians, there were Surinamese emigrants from various occupational groups: skilled workers, nurses, and office personnel. The number of unskilled workers remained limited. These emigrants were from a more widely varied social background than the students, but most of them were still of Afro-Surinamese descent.[5] Although very few of them had been recruited by Dutch companies or agencies, they came to the Netherlands to look for a job. In part, however, these immigrants were also crossing the ocean to get a better education or learn a trade (Bayer 1965). On the other hand, there were more students who had to get a job to support themselves, so the borderline between students and labor migrants was no longer as clear as it had been in the past (van Amersfoort 1968). During this period more and more Surinamese immigrants came as a family or had their families follow them.[6]

With the independence of Surinam approaching, the nature of the migration exhibited a drastic change in the 1970s and a mass exodus began. The new immigrants increasingly came from all the classes and ethnic segments of the population. The majority were still from Paramaribo, but they gradually began to come more frequently directly from the countryside.[7] This flow of migration expanded in part because the anticipated economic development was not taking place in Surinam, and more and more people left for the Netherlands in an effort to improve their living conditions and prospects for the future. The uncertain future of Surinam after independence in 1975 also played a role. Many people felt they had to take advantage of the opportunity before the Netherlands restricted the immigration flow. In addition, there was the fear of Afro-Surinamese domination and ethnic conflicts, as had been the case just across the border in Guyana, after the Netherlands withdrew altogether from the Surinamese political stage. Encouraged by their leaders to do so, now many East Indians and Javanese were also leaving the country. In short, unsure about what independence would bring, many people decided to play it safe and left in a hurry for the Netherlands. There was a veritable "departure madness" (Reubsaet et al. 1982: 47). In 1974 and 1975, more than 50,000 people left Surinam.

Another important moment in the migration history was the introduction of the visa requirement in 1980. There was a transitional arrangement in the period from 1975 to 1980 pertaining to the migration from Surinam to the Netherlands. As had been the case when independence was declared in 1975, the Dutch policy once again gave the impression that soon it would no longer be possible to move to the Netherlands (van Amersfoort and Penninx 1993: 67). Just to be sure, many people left for the Netherlands before the end of the transitional arrangement and thus secured Dutch nationality.[8] Although the Dutch policy was focused on restricting immigration from Surinam, the short-term effect was precisely the opposite, and in 1979 and 1980 another 30,000 Surinamese immigrants came to the Netherlands.

After the sharp fall in immigration immediately after 1980, there was a slight rise in the 1980s due in part to the political developments in Surinam.[9] In general though, immigration from Surinam remained at a stable and rather low level (between approximately 4,000 and 6,000 people a year; van der Heijdt 1995: 20) throughout the 1980s.

Starting in 1990, immigration rates rose again and, in the first few years of the decade, fluctuated at this higher level with a small peak of 9,000 immigrants in 1993 (van der Heijdt 1995: 20). The main reason for this increase in the early 1990s was the rapidly worsening economic situation in Surinam, with unprecedented inflation and sharp price rises. Surinamese immigration rates began to fall again starting in 1993, probably due to the stricter admission policy (van der Heijdt 1995: 20). Regardless of the formal restrictions, however, there are still people coming from Surinam to the Netherlands.[10] The Surinamese community is relatively large and most newcomers have relatives, friends, or acquaintances in the Netherlands who can put them up until they find a place to live. Obviously no figures are available on how many Surinamese are in the Netherlands without a residence permit. It is presumably a relatively small group compared with other groups of undocumented immigrants. At any rate, this was the conclusion of a study conducted in Rotterdam (Burgers and Engbersen 1996).[11]

Thus the general conclusion is that as regards its socioeconomic features, in the course of time the Surinamese population in the Netherlands became increasingly varied. Initially it was a relatively well-educated group that came to the Netherlands, but at the time of the mass migration the average educational level was considerably lower. A 1985 study shows that 71 percent of the immigrants who came to the Netherlands in 1975 had no more than a primary school education (see table 2.1).[12] On the average, the later immigrants were once again better educated, but there was still a large percentage of poorly educated ones. In 1985, the large majority of the Surinamese community (88 percent) had at most a four-year secondary school diploma.

The occupational level of Surinamese emigrants when leaving Surinam exhibited a great deal of diversity. The majority of the Surinamese in the Netherlands in 1979 (68 percent) had worked in Surinam as lower-level employees or skilled workers (see table 2.2). The category of unskilled workers was relatively small, although there were probably also numerous people with low educational levels in the self-employed category.[13]

By Dutch standards, the educational and occupational level of the Surinamese immigrants who arrived in the Netherlands in the course of time was relatively low. Compared, however, with many of the labor migrants from southern Europe, Morocco, and Turkey, the Surinamese had relatively high educational and occupational levels. From the beginning, this gave them a more favorable starting position in the Netherlands.[14]

Table 2.1 *Educational level of Surinamese immigrants aged 18 or older when leaving Surinam in periods of departure up to 1985 (in percentages)*

	primary school	four-year secondary school	five- or six-year secondary school	college or university	total absolute (=100%)
up to	50	32	10	8	184
1971-1974	61	27	11	1	227
1975	71	22	5	2	192
1976-1979	59	29	8	4	184
1980-1985	54	29	10	7	111
total	60	28	9	4	n=898

Source: CBS/UvA (1988: 23).

Table 2.2 *Occupational level of Surinamese immigrants in the Netherlands in 1979 at the time of departure from Surinam (in percentages)*

unskilled worker	9
skilled worker	27
lower-level employee	41
self-employed	9
middle-level employee	13
higher professions	1
absolute total (=100%)	487

Source: Reubsaet et al. (1982: 54).

The Surinamese: Employment and Education

In this section, I examine where the Surinamese immigrants wound up on the Dutch labor market and how their position developed in the course of time. Then I describe the present position of Surinamese immigrants with respect to education.

The Surinamese and the Dutch Labor Market

Unlike the case of the labor migrants from the Mediterranean countries, the arrival of the Surinamese was not triggered by the Dutch labor market's need for unskilled workers. In the 1960s, Dutch companies and agencies did recruit personnel in Surinam, but only on a very limited scale. Moreover, it was mainly skilled workers such as technicians or nurses who were recruited. These early immigrants, recruited or otherwise, arrived in a period of economic expansion. There were plenty of jobs. For the Surinamese who came in the 1960s, the problem was not so much how to find a job, but how to find an apartment or even a room to rent.[15]

The situation was quite different for many of the later immigrants. Bovenkerk once commented that the tragic thing about the mass Surinamese migration was that it took place at the "wrong time" (1983: 160). And indeed it was in the 1970s, just when so many people were arriving from Surinam, that economic growth slackened and unemployment rates rose. This economic recession clearly manifested itself after the first oil crisis in 1973, and even more so after the second one in 1979. From then on, there was more and more of an unemployment problem. The two largest immigration peaks in 1975-75 and 1979-80 thus coincided more or less with the oil crises. If for no other reason, from the start the chance of finding a job was very limited for the Surinamese newcomers.

In addition, the Surinamese were not the only ones entering the Dutch labor market in large numbers at the time. As a result of the postwar baby boom and the increased labor participation of women, the Dutch population itself was generating a growing supply of labor (de Vries 1994: 13). The declining number of jobs and the simultaneous growth in the labor supply resulted in rapidly rising unemployment rates. The percentage of unemployed people in the labor force rose from 4.3 percent in 1974 to 17.4 percent in 1984 (de Vries 1994: 14). The Surinamese unemployment rate was higher than the Dutch. In 1979 a quarter of the Surinamese labor force was out of a job, and this was almost five times as high as the unemployment rate for the entire Dutch labor force (Reubsaet et al. 1982: 128).

According to the study by Reubsaet et al. (1982: 120-21), this relatively higher Surinamese unemployment rate in the 1970s could largely be attributed to the sharp rise in the number of new immigrants. They concluded that the figures on the registered labor reserve did not give any indication that, as a category, the Surinamese were more affected by the increasing unemployment. In 1979 and 1980, the average annual total unemployment and total Surinamese unemployment figures in the Netherlands rose to more or less the same extent (Reubsaet et al. 1982: 121).

In the 1980s, all this changed. The whole Dutch economy had to be restructured, and this reduced the number of industrial jobs. Unemployment mushroomed and since it did not end, so did long-term unemployment. The Dutch unemployment trends did not, however, develop the same way as the Surinamese. At the beginning of the 1980s, the Dutch unemployment rates rose more rapidly than the Surinamese (Langbroek and Muus 1991: 24), but the Dutch were the first to benefit from the upswing in the economy starting in 1983. Though there were fewer poorly paid jobs in the industrial sector, there were more and more similarly poorly paid jobs in the service sector (Kloosterman and Elfring 1991: 149). The people who benefited most from the rising number of jobs were the Dutch newcomers on the labor market, youngsters who had just left school and women, though to an increasing extent in various forms of flexible labor. There was less unemployment among the total labor force starting in 1983, but unemployment became even more widespread among immigrants from Surinam (Langbroek and Muus 1991: 24). There are no exact figures on this period, but Reubsaet and Kropman estimate the Surinamese unemployment in the mid-1980s at anywhere from 35 to 40 percent and presume that youth unemployment rates even exceeded 50 percent (1983: 14). Long-term unemployment became particularly prevalent among Surinamese youngsters, especially in the large cities.

The tide did not turn for the Surinamese until 1988. There was a rapid fall in unemployment rates. More than a quarter of the Surinamese labor force had been unemployed in 1991, but by 1998 it was only true of 10 percent.[16] There was thus a spectacular decline in Surinamese unemployment within a matter of one decade, and it was even somewhat more rapid than among the entire labor force in the Netherlands. There was also a considerable fall in long-term unemployment in this period. Nonetheless, Surinamese unemployment rates are still two and a half times as high as Dutch ones. In comparison with Turks, Moroccans, and Antilleans, however, the Surinamese are doing much better (Martens 1999: 47).

Explanations for Unemployment

The question to be examined is why Surinamese unemployment rates did not keep pace with the ones for the Dutch population as a whole. Why did Surinamese unemployment rates continue to rise in the 1980s and why were the Surinamese apparently far less able to benefit from the expanded job market?

First, there was the continuing immigration. It greatly increased in the 1970s and to a large extent influenced the Surinamese unemployment rates. The immigration did continue into the 1980s, but at a rather low and stable level. There was, nonetheless, a more rapid proportional rise in the Surinamese than in the total Dutch unemployment rates in the 1980s. This might mean immigration became less of a factor in the explanation of unemployment. Later developments would seem to confirm this. Although there was once again a sharp rise in the immigration figures in the early 1990s, it was precisely during this period that Surinamese unemployment continued to decrease. In other words, immigration would seem to have become less important as a cause of the high Surinamese unemployment rates.

Second, there are the specific features of the Surinamese labor supply. Langbroek and Muus (1991: 52-59) cite a number of specific features of the

Surinamese unemployed that do not enhance their position: their relatively low educational level, especially of the men, their less relevant job experience or lack of any job experience at all, once again especially of the men, and the Surinamese concentration in the large cities, where unemployment is so widespread.

Third, the expanded labor supply gave employers a stronger position of power. They could afford to select more strictly. So in addition to the general process of people with more education displacing people with less, it is very probable that multifarious selection mechanisms and discrimination also played a role on the labor market that was detrimental for the Surinamese.[17] This was demonstrated with respect to the Surinamese as far back as the 1970s and was recently once again confirmed.[18]

Another factor that played a role, but this time in reducing the unemployment rates, was government policy. One instrument the authorities used to combat the widespread ethnic minority unemployment was the Plan for Ethnic Minorities as Civil Servants. In the first stage of this plan, half the jobs went to Surinamese applicants (Tesser 1993: 91). In the second stage, the Surinamese similarly took far more advantage of this policy than other ethnic minorities (Dagevos 1995). Surinamese job-seekers also used the Municipal Employment Offices more often than in the past to find jobs. It is true that they still lagged behind the native Dutch population, but their outflow chances were more favorable than those of other ethnic minorities. In Amsterdam, the situation was even somewhat more advantageous for Surinamese than for native Dutch job-seekers. And Surinamese and other ethnic minority college and university graduates had an excellent chance of finding a job through the Municipal Employment Office (Tesser et al. 1996: 134).

It is impossible to say exactly to what extent this government employment policy has contributed to reducing Surinamese unemployment as compared with other factors. The fact that the younger Surinamese generation has a higher educational level probably plays a role as well, as does the growing number of jobs in the service sector, especially in the care sector (Kloosterman and Elfring 1991: 195).

The Employed

From the start, the Surinamese were less confined to industrial jobs than the labor migrants from the Mediterranean countries. This is particularly true of the Surinamese immigrants who found their first jobs in the Netherlands in the second half of the 1970s (Dagevos 1998: 28). They may well have worked more often in the industrial sector than Surinamese immigrants who entered the labor market during other periods, but in general the Surinamese have always been strongly represented in the service sector. As regards this point, they do not differ much from the native Dutch. In 1998 the Surinamese were generally as strongly represented in the sectors where the native Dutch work, though there was a slight overrepresentation in the fields of health care and social work (Martens 1999: 51).

The job level development of the Surinamese who are employed is a reflection of the migration history (Dagevos 1998: 32-33). The Surinamese who entered the labor market in the 1970s started relatively more frequently at a low level than the earlier immigrants. As is also the case with the native Dutch, there was a higher percentage of low-level jobs among the recent starters, perhaps as a result of changing trends in the economy (Dagevos 1998: 33). In general, however, there is evidence of upward mobility (Dagevos 1998: 40).

At the moment, the Surinamese nonetheless lag behind the native Dutch as regards their job levels: they are overrepresented at the lower occupational levels and underrepresented at the higher ones; there is no difference at the middle level (Martens 1999: 50).

This then is the situation of regular employees. They constitute the large majority of the Surinamese labor force, though there has been a sharp rise in the number of self-employed people in the Surinamese community—and indeed among the rest of the Dutch population—since the mid-1980s. In 1997, more than 5 percent of the labor force consisted of independent entrepreneurs (van den Tillaart and Poutsma 1998: 40).[19] The Surinamese self-employed are fairly evenly distributed over the various sectors, and they bear a resemblance to Dutch entrepreneurs in this sense. In either case, approximately a fifth of the entrepreneurs work in producer services. For the rest, the Surinamese are relatively active as merchants in the commercial sector and in the hotel, restaurant, and café sector (van den Tillaart and Poutsma 1998: 48-49).[20]

Even if judging from the figures, entrepreneurship does not seem that significant a channel for upward mobility, this does not tell us everything there is to know about the economic potential of immigrants. Many economic activities are conducted in the informal or semi-informal circuit. Some authors assume this to be a question of concealed unemployment or poverty, but others are of the opinion that it is an economic potential that never surfaces in the official statistics.[21]

Educational Position

What educational position do the Surinamese occupy at the moment? Ever since their arrival in the Netherlands, there has been an undeniable rise in their average educational position. In comparison with their parents, Surinamese youngsters stay in school longer and get more advanced diplomas. There might still be many Surinamese in the Netherlands who never finished or even attended primary school (9 percent), a category that is nonexistent among the native Dutch (Martens 1999: 40), but the longer the Surinamese are in the Netherlands, the smaller this poorly educated category becomes.

The important point is that there has been a considerable improvement in the Surinamese educational position since the 1980s. At the time, Surinamese pupils lagged behind their Dutch peers at the primary school level (Koot and Uniken Venema 1988), there was a level and an age lag at the secondary school level (Reubsaet et al. 1982), and Surinamese pupils were overrepresented at schools for children with learning problems (Autar 1990). A great deal has changed since then. In 1998 a third of the Surinamese still had no secondary school diploma of any kind, but this category is becoming smaller.[22] For the rest, the percentage of Surinamese with only a diploma from a four-year secondary or vocational school decreased considerably in one decade, and there has been a clear increase in the number of college and university graduates.[23]

A comparison between the Surinamese and the Dutch shows that in 1998 there were no longer any sizeable differences at the middle levels. The greatest differences were at the highest and lowest educational levels. In 1998, 15 percent of the Surinamese who were no longer attending school full-time had a college or university degree, as compared with 28 percent of the Dutch. At the lowest level as well, there was still a considerable difference between the Surinamese, 29 percent of whom had not finished any secondary or vocational school, and the Dutch, only 18 percent of whom had not (Martens 1999: 40).

So for the time being, the average Surinamese educational level is still lagging behind the Dutch, although in some senses the differences are getting smaller. There is not much difference now between the percentage of Surinamese youngsters who immediately go on to a five-year or six-year secondary school after they complete primary school (40 percent) and the percentage of Dutch children who do (44 percent) (Martens 1999: 39). There is also a decline in the dropout rate.

For a number of reasons, the longer the Surinamese are in the Netherlands, the better their educational position. Most of them have already been through the first stage of getting settled. This means there are fewer adjustment problems than at the start.[24] Parents and children alike have improved their mastery of the Dutch language and increasingly use it at home.[25] In addition, more and more schoolchildren have been born or at any rate brought up in the Netherlands. Children who have been in the Dutch school system from the start have a better start than children who came at a later age and interrupted their school career in Surinam to move to the Netherlands. Thus the remaining educational lag can be explained less and less by conditions directly related to moving to and settling in the Netherlands. To a certain extent, though, these migration-related factors do continue to play a role. I get back to this in chapter 6. A second cluster of factors that explain the differences pertains to the socioeconomic position of the parents, the classical explanation for an educational disadvantage. The parents' position in society, in particular their educational level, can explain the lag at least in part, though there is no consensus about the extent to which this is the case.[26] I go into this in greater detail in chapter 7.

Although the educational position of the Surinamese is thus less linked to migration-related factors and more to the parents' socioeconomic position, there is still an unexplained remainder. Sometimes referred to as "the ethnic factor," this unexplained remainder has been approached in very different ways by various researchers.[27] They refer to the specific factors that play a role in the educational performance of immigrant pupils, which can have either a favorable or an unfavorable effect. One frequently cited factor is the ethnic composition of the student body.

If a school is "black," it is assumed to have a negative influence on the performance and social integration of immigrant schoolchildren.[28] However, research findings about the correlation between the ethnic composition of the student body and the school performance of schoolchildren do not always point in the same direction. Some researchers feel certain there is a correlation, though others can barely find any evidence of it. What is more, education experts have made some rather critical comments about the studies conducted on this topic (Meijnen and Riemersma 1992: 80-81; Tesser et al. 1995: 266-69). As yet, there is no consensus as to the conclusion that the ethnic composition of the student body has an unfavorable effect on the school performance of pupils at "black" schools. Nor is it an undisputed fact that "black" schools (i.e., with large ethnic minority concentrations) impede social integration (Teunissen 1996).

Ethnic relations in society at large and at schools in particular constitute another factor. It has been suggested that these influences can unintentionally have a negative effect on Surinamese schoolchildren. This has to do with the behavior and expectations of teachers as regards Surinamese schoolchildren, interethnic relations among the classmates, and the monocultural nature of the curriculum (Dors and Sietaram 1989). However, up to now very little empirical research has focused on whether and, if so, how institutional discrimination and racism influence school performance and school careers (Fase 1994: 86; Penninx 1988a: 236).

Lastly, the home environment of immigrant schoolchildren can influence their school performance. The idea is that the parents' socioeconomic position does not sufficiently account for children's school performance, and that ethnic and cultural factors play a role as well. There is, however, no consensus among educational sociologists about whether and, if so, to what extent ethnic background can be viewed as a special factor in explaining school success in addition to socioeconomic status (Driessen 1995). One problem is that in quantitative studies, it is difficult to distinguish the effects of socioeconomic position and the effects of ethnic background. In this study, I devote extensive attention to this question.

The Position of the Afro-Surinamese and Indo-Surinamese

What position do the Afro-Surinamese and Indo-Surinamese occupy in the Netherlands? Are there differences between their social positions, and if so, how do they manifest themselves? In this section I present a picture of the socio-economic positions of these two Surinamese groups. More differentiated data on gender and generation or age are cited in the following chapters. The data here are based on the 1994 survey referred to in chapter 1, The Social Position and Use of Provisions by Ethnic Minorities (SPVA-1994, ISEO/EUR). Although the most recent SPVA survey conducted in 1998 did contain data on the entire Surinamese population in the Netherlands, there were not yet separate data on the Afro-Surinamese and Indo-Surinamese segments. At the time, the aim of the quantitative material was to outline the social positions of the Afro-Surinamese and Indo-Surinamese segments of the population, since no clear picture had been presented yet when I launched my study. This material consequently served as the basis and guideline for the qualitative research to be conducted. This is why it is quite acceptable that the 1994 figures are presented here for the two Surinamese groups separately. For that matter, a preliminary nonstatistical description of the results of the 1998 SPVA survey (Martens 1999: 143-44) shows that as regards several main points, the trends continued along the same lines. The only point that is known beforehand to have changed a great deal is the unemployment rate, which witnessed a drastic fall in recent years. For the data described here, I refer the reader to the tables in appendix 3.

To what extent are the negative image of the Afro-Surinamese and the positive one of the Indo-Surinamese confirmed by the figures? Up until recently, very little information was available about the real differences between the two groups on the labor market. A few things can, however, be said about the recent past. Ever since the 1970s, ample attention has been focused on the unemployment rates of young Afro-Surinamese men.[29] As I noted above, in this period of mass immigration, the chances of finding a job were extremely limited for people without much education. Employers could afford to be more selective in recruiting personnel, which definitely had not been the case in the 1960s. The fact that the labor supply was so large created more leeway for discrimination. Bovenkerk and Breuning-van Leeuwen (1978) did indeed discover a link at the time between discrimination and the relation between supply and demand on the Amsterdam labor market. More recent research shows that it is mainly Afro-Surinamese men with a low educational level who have less of a chance of getting a job than native Dutch applicants with the same qualifications (Gras et al. 1995).[30] Since their chances on the regular labor market are so limited, many of them resort to alternative survival strategies in the informal sector.

The Indo-Surinamese segment of the population can also be assumed to have included unemployed unskilled workers, but researchers and the media have always devoted far less attention to this category. This might be because of the greater visibility of certain subgroups among Afro-Surinamese men and their appearance and lifestyle that were so conspicuous at the time (Biervliet 1975; Buiks 1983). Whatever the reason, a great deal of research has been focused in the past few decades on the Afro-Surinamese and far less on the Indo-Surinamese.

Even though there is no way of knowing how realistic the impression was that unemployment was more widespread among the Afro-Surinamese at the time, we can get an idea of the two groups' unemployment rates in 1994. Contrary to what the focus on the Afro-Surinamese suggested at the time, there was virtually no difference between the unemployment rates of the two groups. The registered unemployment amounted to 20 percent of the Indo-Surinamese and 21 percent of the Afro-Surinamese labor force. Although these figures pertain to 1994 and unemployment has decreased considerably since then, they do show that, up until recently, there was little difference in the unemployment rates.

As regards other aspects as well, the Afro-Surinamese are not in the lowest position. Afro-Surinamese labor market participation (69 percent) is higher than Indo-Surinamese (51 percent). What is striking instead is the relatively large nonparticipation of the Indo-Surinamese on the labor market. This is also evident from data on the main source of income. The Afro-Surinamese far more frequently have an earned income, whereas the Indo-Surinamese are relatively often disabled or housewives (see tables 3 and 4, appendix 3).

The labor forces exhibit another difference: on the average, the Afro-Surinamese are employed at a higher job level, which is not surprising in view of their higher average educational level. The Indo-Surinamese are more frequently employed at an elementary job level. A relatively high percentage of the Indo-Surinamese have no secondary or vocational school diploma (42 percent as compared with 26 percent of the Afro-Surinamese), whereas there are nearly twice as many college and university graduates among the Afro-Surinamese (13 and 7 percent, respectively). Lastly, the average Afro-Surinamese income is higher, as is only to be expected since they more often have an earned income and their average job level is higher (see tables 5, 7 and 8, appendix 3).

In short, the Afro-Surinamese socioeconomic position is better than the Indo-Surinamese in a number of crucial ways. Does this mean there is no factual basis for the negative image of the Afro-Surinamese? Not quite. If we take a closer look at the figures and distinguish between males and females, differences emerge that make this image easier to understand. Afro-Surinamese men are the most frequently unemployed, more frequently than women and more frequently than the Indo-Surinamese (see table 2, appendix 3).

Another difference that is similarly unfavorable for the Afro-Surinamese pertains to the duration of unemployment (see table 9, appendix 3). Among the Indo-Surinamese, the duration of unemployment is usually short, but for the Afro-Surinamese it is more apt to be long, and in fact a quarter of the Afro-Surinamese unemployed have been registered at a municipal employment office for five years or more. This similarly coincides with the picture of persistent unemployment among Surinamese men in Amsterdam and Rotterdam that earlier studies have presented.

The question of labor mobility in the course of time can be addressed by comparing the job levels of the first and last job in the Netherlands. They are, however, only random indications of the situation of the two groups as a whole, and they do not necessarily reveal anything about the careers of individuals.[31] This comparison nonetheless shows that as a whole, the two groups did witness a certain upward mobility. A picture of the labor mobility of individuals can also be obtained in another way (see table 6, appendix 3).[32] These data indicate that there are barely any labor mobility differences between the two groups. At any rate relatively speaking, since the percentages of individuals who moved to higher or lower job levels were approximately the same in both groups (17 and 9 percent, respectively), and approximately three-quarters of both groups remained at the same job level. In an absolute sense, the Afro-Surinamese still occupy a higher position on the labor market.

Lastly, is there any truth to the public notion that the Indo-Surinamese are more frequently independent entrepreneurs than the Afro-Surinamese? This notion cannot be confirmed on the basis of the SPVA figures: in both groups, only small percentages of the labor force are entrepreneurs, 3 and 2 percent respectively.[33] According to sources other than the SPVA, in Amsterdam the Indo-Surinamese are, however, more frequently independent entrepreneurs (Boissevain et al. 1984; Choenni 1997). Choenni estimates that in Amsterdam, 2.5 percent of the Afro-Surinamese and 5 percent of the Indo-Surinamese labor force are independent entrepreneurs (1997: 104). This overrepresentation in Amsterdam might well explain the Indo-Surinamese image as entrepreneurs. This is certainly the case in The Hague: in certain parts of the city, the Indo-Surinamese are immediately visible as entrepreneurs.

The Surinamese in Amsterdam and The Hague

There are more than 110,000 Surinamese residents in Amsterdam and The Hague together, in other words, 38 percent of the entire Surinamese population in the Netherlands. Amsterdam has the largest Surinamese population: it is the home of more than 24 percent of all the Surinamese in the Netherlands. The Hague is home to 14 percent of the Surinamese population in the Netherlands. The percentage of Surinamese residents is much higher in these two cities than in the rest of the Netherlands. In Amsterdam, the Surinamese are 10 percent and in The Hague 9 percent of the population.[34] Approximately 70 percent of the Surinamese population in Amsterdam are of Afro-Surinamese origin. In The

Hague, the Surinamese of Indo-Surinamese origin are in the majority, constituting approximately 80 percent of the city's Surinamese population.[35]

Generally speaking, the Surinamese in both cities are less concentrated in the older districts than Turks or Moroccans, and if they do live there, it is often in better housing. Most of the Surinamese have moved on to the better flats for rent in the social housing sector and often live in renovated or new flats. Especially in Amsterdam Southeast (Bijlmermeer), they often rent rather expensive flats in the subsidized sector, which the middle classes for whom Bijlmermeer was initially built for proved to be less and less interested in.[36]

There is a difference in the extent to which the two Surinamese groups own their own homes. The Indo-Surinamese are almost three times more apt to own their own homes than the Afro-Surinamese (22 and 8 percent respectively).[37] In view of the distribution of the two groups over the two cities, there are relatively more property owners among the Surinamese in The Hague than in Amsterdam. Since The Hague has a higher percentage of homeowners than Amsterdam (Kruythoff et al. 1997: 9), to a certain extent, the difference in home ownership between the two ethnic groups coincides with the difference between the two cities.

Other dissimilarities between the Afro-Surinamese and Indo-Surinamese are indicative in part of a difference between the two groups and in part of a difference between the two cities. This holds true for the size and composition of the households. Indo-Surinamese households are usually larger, whereas Afro-Surinamese households consist almost as frequently as native Dutch households of only one person. Similarly like the Dutch, the Afro-Surinamese are less apt to live in a household consisting of a husband and wife and their children (and possibly others) than the Indo-Surinamese. In this sense, Afro-Surinamese households bear more of a resemblance to Dutch ones.

If we compare the two cities, however, it is obvious that Indo-Surinamese households in Amsterdam are not only smaller than in The Hague but also that, relatively speaking, three to four times as many single Indo-Surinamese live in Amsterdam. In this sense, the Indo-Surinamese in Amsterdam bear more of a resemblance to the rest of the Amsterdam population (including the Afro-Surinamese), whereas the Indo-Surinamese in The Hague exhibit a more traditional household pattern.[38] In other words, there are either apparently city-wise differences between one and the same ethnic group, or such a thing as the local nature of an ethnic community.

One aspect in which no local dissimilarities emerge and in which both Surinamese groups do differ from the indigenous Dutch pertains to the percentage of single-parent families. Contrary to what is generally assumed, the single-parent family is just as common among the Indo-Surinamese as the Afro-Surinamese. Nationwide, this type of family is seven times as common among the Surinamese than the Dutch. The background and history of the Afro-Surinamese and Indo-Surinamese one-parent family are, however, completely different. I go into this in greater detail later in the book.[39]

Lastly, there are no sizeable differences between the socioeconomic profiles of the Afro-Surinamese and Indo-Surinamese in the two cities. In other words, the Indo-Surinamese and Afro-Surinamese in The Hague do not differ that much from the two groups in Amsterdam.[40] Nationwide trends generally also pertain to the Surinamese in both cities. For example, the Indo-Surinamese generally have a lower income than the Afro-Surinamese, even if we only examine the income from paid employment. As regards the unemployment rates, there are similarly no sizeable differences between either the Afro-Surinamese or the Indo-Surinamese in Amsterdam and The Hague. In other words, as regards the matter of socioeconomic position, the ethnic differences are more striking than the city-wise ones.

This last conclusion is confirmed if we compare the Afro-Surinamese and Indo-Surinamese communities in Amsterdam and The Hague with those in other Dutch towns and cities. The SPVA-1994 does not show any differences in these respects that systematically point in any specific direction. As regards the matter of socioeconomic position, the Afro-Surinamese and Indo-Surinamese communities in Amsterdam and The Hague can be assumed to be representative of the entire Surinamese population in the Netherlands.

In Closing

In social science literature, the poor position of immigrants is often explained by referring to the discrepancy between the demands of the labor market and the features of the labor supply. In part there definitely was a discrepancy of this kind among the Surinamese immigrants who came to the Netherlands in the mid-1970s and around 1980. Their educational and occupational levels were often not in keeping with the demands of the labor market, where there was a trend at the time toward fewer jobs in the industrial sector and more jobs in the service sector. It was unfortunate that there was so much unemployment on the Dutch labor market in precisely the period when so many new immigrants were arriving from Surinam. This would largely seem to explain the disproportionately high Surinamese unemployment rates, especially since there was thus also more leeway for direct or indirect discrimination. And then when the job situation gradually improved, the Surinamese had to compete with new categories of immigrants joining the labor market in large numbers. The Surinamese were initially at a disadvantage, but ultimately they too benefited from the expanding employment opportunities in the service sector. Nowadays the Surinamese labor force is largely active in the same sectors as the Dutch and there is far less Surinamese unemployment. So in part, the Surinamese have thus caught up with their native Dutch counterparts.

The figures cited in this chapter show that, contrary to expectations, the Indo-Surinamese are no more successful than the Afro-Surinamese in the sense that they occupy a better position in society. In fact the opposite is the case: the measurements on several important features (educational and occupational levels and income) show that the Afro-Surinamese are in a better position. What is more, the Afro-Surinamese are not more frequently unemployed and their labor market participation is greater.

If we differentiate the general picture, though, the figures do provide some basis for the public images referred to earlier. Afro-Surinamese men are relatively the most frequently unemployed. The fact that the total Afro-Surinamese unemployment rate is lower is the Afro-Surinamese women's doing. For the rest, the long-term unemployment rates are similarly highest among the Afro-Surinamese.

However, the entrepreneurial image of the Indo-Surinamese is not confirmed by the SPVA figures, which indicate that they are not independent entrepreneurs any more frequently than the Afro-Surinamese. As was demonstrated earlier and will be illustrated even more clearly later in this study, there are some reservations about these figures. What is more, in view of the general trend I do not exclude the possibility that entrepreneurship has also recently increased among the Indo-Surinamese.

How should the differences be interpreted that have been observed between the Afro-Surinamese and the Indo-Surinamese? On the grounds of the relatively low educational level of the Indo-Surinamese, they might be expected to be more frequently unemployed. Yet that is not the case: the unemployment rates of the two groups are approximately the same. And what explains the low labor market participation of the Indo-Surinamese as compared with the Afro-Surinamese? These differences do not completely result from the labor market situation in the Netherlands, but they are apparently indicative of differences between the two groups that were already there when they first came to the Netherlands.

One limitation of the figures presented here is that they depict only the group average, which is in essence the net result of the upward and downward mobility of individuals and subgroups and of migration movements.[41] In itself, this does not grant insight into either the mobility trajectories or the social mobility of parents and children. Survey research generally gives a statistical description, not an explanation of social mobility (Bertaux and Thompson 1997; Savage 1997). With this qualitative study, I hope to address a few of these restrictions. My aim is to provide insight into the mobility process of individuals (intragenerational) and families (intergenerational) and the factors that shape it.

In this book I describe the various mobility trajectories of the Afro-Surinamese and Indo-Surinamese, men and women, and the children of the first-generation immigrants. In chapter 3, I focus on the history of the Afro-Surinamese and Indo-Surinamese in Surinam. This history helped shape their starting position in Dutch society and the social and cultural resources they had at their disposal. In chapter 4 I return to the Dutch situation.

Notes

1. Cf. van Niekerk et al. (1987 and 1989).

2. See for a more comprehensive overview van Niekerk (1994 and 2000a); see also van Niekerk (1997 and 2000b).

3. The figures cited here date back to 1 January 1999 and are from Statistics Netherlands (CBS 1999). *Allochtonen* or "immigrants" are defined as people who were born abroad and at least one of whose parents were also born abroad (the first generation), and people who were born in the Netherlands, at least one of whose parents were born abroad (the second generation). In other words, immigrants are defined as people with at least one parent who was born abroad (CBS 1999: 48).

4. See for the Surinamese migration history van Amersfoort (1987); Bovenkerk (1973, 1975, and 1976).

5. See Reubsaet et al. (1982: 321).

6. Cf. Lamur (1973: 130).

7. Of the Surinamese people who lived in the Netherlands in 1979, 17 percent had come directly from the countryside. Virtually all the others came from Paramaribo or the immediate vicinity (Reubsaet et al. 1982: 53).

8. In principle, the Surinamese who were in Surinam in 1975 at the moment when independence was declared lost Dutch nationality.

9. One of the developments was the "December murders" in 1982, when the military authorities had fifteen prominent Surinamese shot summarily, and another was the internal war that was raging during this period (see Vocking 1994).

10. Ever since 1980, the grounds for a residence permit include: reuniting or forming a family, having a job, attending a course of study or undergoing medical treatment that would not be possible in Surinam. In the course of time, there has been a gradual shift from reuniting to forming a family, and relatively more and more single people and people in the fifteen-to-forty age group have come to the Netherlands (Sprangers 1994; Tas 1994: 9).

11. The researchers do note though that no statements can be made in this connection with absolute certainty. At any rate, there are fewer Surinamese without a resident permit in the police records. The researchers cite two reasons. Surinamese people without resident permits do not wind up in the criminal circuit as frequently as other undocumented immigrants. What is more, the police are less apt to associate them with illegality (Burgers and Engbersen 1996).

12. Table 2.1 pertains to the majority of the Surinamese who were in the Netherlands in 1998, approximately three-quarters of whom had arrived in the Netherlands before 1986 (Martens 1999: 29).

13. Table 5 in appendix 3 gives an overview of the occupational level of the last job in Surinam of immigrants who were living in the Netherlands in 1994. This more recent information presents a more complete picture. The categories are, however, not the same ones that were used by Reubsaet et al. (1982), so that the two tables are not comparable.

14. Cf. Vermeulen and Penninx (2000).

15. See, e.g., Bayer (1965).

16. These two figures are based on The Social Position and Use of Provisions by Ethnic Minorities (SPVA) surveys conducted in 1991 (Martens et al. 1992: 32) and 1998 (Martens 1999: 47), respectively.

17. For a concise overview of research on the selection practices of employers, see Veenman (1994: 90-92). See also Tesser (1993: 82-85), who devotes attention to interpretation problems in research of this kind.

18. See Bovenkerk and Breuning-van Leeuwen (1978); Gras et al. (1995).

19. According to the SPVA survey, the percentage of self-employed people was only 3 percent in 1998. This is barely higher, if at all, than the percentage in the SPVA-1994 survey, although mention is made elsewhere of a sharp rise (van den Tillaart and Poutsma 1998). This is also noted in a publication on the SPVA-1998 survey (Martens 1999: 34, 60).

20. Cf. Choenni (1997: 102).

21. See Kloosterman et al. (1997).

22. See Martens (1999: 20); Martens and Verweij (1997: 20).

23. The percentage of youngsters who only graduated from a four-year secondary or vocational school decreased from 40 to 31 percent in the decade from 1988 to 1998. In the same period, the percentage of college and university graduates increased from 7 to 15 percent (Martens 1999: 40; Tesser et al. 1996: 156).

24. Cf. Koot et al. (1985).

25. Cf. Martens (1999: 85).

26. See, e.g., Dagevos et al. (1996: 36); van 't Hof and Dronkers (1993). See for an overview Fase (1994); Meijnen and Riemersma (1992: 68-72).

27. See, e.g., Fase (1994); Fase and Kleijer (1996); Meijnen and Riemersma (1992: 67-82).

28. See, e.g., Dors et al. (1991).

29. See Biervliet (1975); Buiks (1983); Sansone (1992).

30. The study referred to above (Gras et al. 1995) demonstrates that Surinamese applicants with a low educational level have less of a chance of getting a job than those with a higher educational level, and that men have less of a chance than women. The difference between applicants with a high and a low educational level is greater, however, than the one between men and women. There was no evidence of discrimination in the case of well-educated women. Nor for that matter was it explicitly stated anywhere beforehand that the Surinamese involved in this research were Afro-Surinamese. It is clear from the context, however, that this was the case. The applicants with a low educational level in this true-to-life experiment had to have a slight Afro-Surinamese accent (1995: 133), since they applied for the jobs by telephone, and it was not clear from their names (Creole pseudonyms) that they were from Surinam. It was only in the conclusion (1995: 162) that an explicit reference was made to Afro-Surinamese respondents.

31. The first jobs in the Netherlands of the people in the 1994 survey may have started that year, but they might well have started much earlier. What is more, the first and the present job in the Netherlands can be one and the same job (see table 5, appendix 3).

32. Table 6 in appendix 3 gives an impression of the Afro-Surinamese and Indo-Surinamese labor mobility measured according to the level of their first and last jobs in the Netherlands. Since in many cases the numbers are too small, this table gives absolute numbers rather than percentages. I only calculated the percentages of the total number of individuals who stayed at the same job level or went to a lower or higher one. A total of 73 percent of the Indo-Surinamese and 75 percent of the Afro-Surinamese remained at the same level. In both groups, 9 percent went to a lower level and 17 percent to a higher one (since they have been rounded off, the percentages do not add up to exactly 100 percent). So there are barely any differences between the mobility of the two groups. Three-quarters of the Indo-Surinamese and of the Afro-Surinamese moved to neither a higher nor a lower job level. The percentages of individuals who moved to a higher or lower level were virtually the same for both groups. So in general both the groups did improve their position, since almost twice as many people moved to a higher than to a lower level.

33. These percentages do not include people who work free-lance. If we combine the categories of independent entrepreneurs and people who work free-lance, the Afro-Surinamese score even higher: a total of 5 percent of the Afro-Surinamese and 4 percent of the Indo-Surinamese belong to this combined category (SPVA-1994 survey). It should be noted in this connection that the figures are from 1994, and there has since been a considerable expansion in entrepreneurship (van den Tillaart and Poutsma 1998).

34. These are Statistics Netherlands figures from 1 January 1999 (CBS 1999; Martens and Weijers 2000: 18-23).

35. The percentages of Indo-Surinamese and Afro-Surinamese residents of these two cities are based upon the SPVA-1994 survey.

36. See van Amersfoort and Cortie (1996); de Klerk and van Amersfoort (1988).

37. These figures are from the SPVA-1994 survey. Unless otherwise specified, the data cited in this section are also from this survey.

38. In the SPVA-1994 survey, the absolute number of Afro-Surinamese residents of The Hague is too small to warrant any conclusions. It is nonetheless clear that there are no sizeable differences between the Afro-Surinamese in the two cities.

39. See chapter 5.

40. As is noted above, however, in the SPVA-1994 survey the absolute number of Afro-Surinamese in The Hague is small so that it is difficult to draw a comparison of this kind.

41. Cf. Robinson (1990).

Chapter Three

Premigration History: Creoles and East Indians in Surinam

There are still traces today of the ethnic division of labor that developed in colonial times in Surinam. Although the distinctions did fade in the course of time between the separate positions long held in society by Creoles and East Indians, they were clearly visible for quite some time after World War II.[1] Most Creoles had urban occupations, often as civil servants, whereas East Indians were more apt to work in the private sector, and more often than Creoles in various jobs in the agrarian sector. As time passed, however, Creoles and East Indians came to exhibit less difference as regards the economic sectors they worked in, their occupations, and the level of the positions they held.

No data is available on the present-day distribution of Creoles and East Indians over various economic sectors and occupations. The last national census to draw a distinction between the ethnic groups was taken in 1971. However, it is the 1964 census that grants us more insight into the economic activities of each of these groups.[2] At any rate it enables us to see the roles Creoles and East Indians played in the economic structure of Surinam about a decade prior to the exodus to the Netherlands. The 1964 census shows that at the time, Creoles were largely employed as civil servants. This held true for no less than 40 percent of the Creoles, and only 15 percent of the East Indians. A total of 44 percent of the East Indians worked in the agrarian sector, as did little more than 7 percent of the Creoles. For the rest, Creoles clearly worked more frequently in the mining and service sectors (Dew 1978: 15). In general, Creoles were more evenly distributed over the various economic sectors. In virtually all the sectors, Creoles held more of the positions. It was only in the agrarian and transport sectors that they were second to East Indians (Dew 1978: 16).

If we take a more detailed look at the various occupational groups and occupations, it is striking that Creoles worked much more frequently than East Indians in academic, executive, and managerial occupations, and women to an even greater extent than men (Lamur 1973: 162). Many Creole women (37 percent) worked in the service sector. De Bruijne (1976: 62, 103) notes that this mainly pertained to domestic work, medical care, and teaching.[3] By far the largest group of East Indian women (60 percent) worked in the agrarian sector (Lamur 1973: 162). The ethnic specialization was even more marked if we look at specific occupations. Typical Creole occupations around 1964 were shoemaker, welder, domestic servant, and nurse, and East Indians typically worked as cart drivers, tailors, and pedlars (de Bruijne 1976: 103-4).

A great deal has changed since then and the ethnic division of labor has become considerably less marked. What I am interested in here, though, is how this ethnic division of labor developed. First, I examine the specific positions of Creoles and East Indians in Surinamese society and show how they developed in the course of time. Second, I try to explain why this ethnic division of labor developed as it did.[4]

The Development of an Ethnic Division of Labor

If we want to see why so many Creoles came to work in the town of Paramaribo and East Indians mainly worked in the rural areas for so long, we need to go back to when the first East Indians arrived in Surinam, in other words the period shortly after the abolition of slavery.

Free and Unfree Labor

From 1873 to 1917, more than 34,000 people from what was then the British colony of India were shipped to Surinam (de Klerk 1953: 73).[5] There were two reasons why. First, the colonial authorities and planters were afraid there would be no one to work on the plantations after the abolition of slavery, or more precisely after the period of State Supervision (1863-1873), when the government was still seeing to it that ex-slaves signed a labor contract. Second, the authorities and planters felt a need to reduce the labor costs so as to keep the old plantation system in operation. Now that the planters no longer had free access to the labor of ex-slaves, who could also earn a minimal living outside the plantations, there was the danger of wages rising (Kruijer 1968: 48). So Asian contract workers were not only brought in to provide the plantations with labor but also to keep the costs of labor down. If the ex-slaves did not leave the plantations of their own accord, they were thus ousted and replaced by Asian laborers. There were still more than 28,000 ex-slaves on the plantations at the end of the State Supervision period, but by the end of 1876 this figure had been reduced to less than 9,000 (Heilbron 1982: 111).

In addition to importing contract workers, there was a second more indirect way to provide labor for the plantations, namely by control over the land. Besides working for wages on a plantation, owning a plot of land was another way for ex-slaves to earn a living. Heilbron (1982) shows how control over the land became a way for planters to gain control over labor. In some cases, they even took over fallow land just to keep ex-slaves from settling there as independent farmers. Planters also set aside land for emancipated slaves so they would have extra hands to help with the harvest. The colonial authorities saw to it that workers settled in the vicinity of the plantations by leasing land to them at special government settlements, which were old deserted plantations or plantations the government had bought and divided up into plots. The size of the plots of land was deliberately kept to a minimum, so that the people who lived there had no choice but to work part of the time on the plantations.[6] Many of them were thus unable to earn a living on their own and remained dependent on the plantation. A wide range of mixtures of wage labor and small independent farming thus gradually developed in the agrarian sector. According to Heilbron (1982), this was a result of the small farmers being in a lasting relation of dependence on the plantations. Only in a few districts (Coronie, Upper Surinam, and Para) were ex-slaves able to remain independent by acquiring the ownership of plantations themselves.

In principle, ex-slaves were nonetheless also in a position to settle independently. According to an official measure passed in 1863, it was possible to become the owner of a small plot of land.[7] Ex-slaves were, however, initially excluded, and this did not change until 1888, when they were also able to become the owners of demesne land (Heilbron 1982: 118). Willemsen (1980: 122) also notes the nontransparency, arbitrariness, and inequality in the application of the rules. Requests for deeds to property were frequently rejected. What is more, there were all kinds of conditions connected to this land distribution method that were difficult for small farmers to meet (1980: 124-25).

Another way for ex-slaves to settle independently as small farmers was to start cultivating a plot of new land themselves. Many people settled on the shores of the large rivers and took to producing cacao. The people who exported their produce were particularly apt to reach a reasonable level of prosperity. Initially it was these Creole farmers who developed the small farming sector (van Lier 1971: 229-30). Around the turn of the twentieth century, though, many of these cacao farmers left the countryside and moved to the city. The crisis in the cacao sector caused by severe diseases in the cacao plant was not the only reason for their moving. There were starting to be more lucrative ways to earn a living outside the agrarian sector. The gold and balata industries generated new sources of income. Many people moved to Paramaribo, and from there they periodically worked in the interior in the gold and balata industries. Although the earnings were not bad, it was still a lifestyle without any security since the contracts were always temporary.

In general, Creole small farming was characterized by various waves of migration to and from the city (van Lier 1971: 233). Periods of industrious activity in the city alternated with periods of recession and mass unemployment. The shuttling back and forth between the countryside and the city is mainly attributable to the economic structure of Surinam, which long remained a raw material producer without much industrial development (Heilbron 1982; Kruijer 1968). This meant the job structure was extremely unstable, and it was largely the Creoles who suffered as a result. To an important extent, the geographic mobility of the Creole lower class also has to do with this economic instability (Buschkens 1974).

From Large to Small Farming

Unlike Creoles, East Indians long remained dependent on farming. Starting in 1863, a modest official policy stimulated settling in the countryside. The government settlements referred to above were founded for this purpose. Starting in 1895, however, the government adopted an active settlement policy to promote small farming. Up until then, the policy of government settlements had mainly been focused on providing labor for the plantations. With the decline of the plantation economy, the need arose to further develop the small farming sector. The year 1895 is generally viewed as the year of the transition from large to small farming.

The government clearly had an interest in preserving the East Indian ties with the land, and, adopted a positive attitude to them to further this. There was also a special condition pertaining to East Indians. They had the protection of British Indian authorities, who acted to promote the interests of their subjects abroad. All this resulted in a settlement policy being implemented by the Surinamese government that was more attractive for East Indians.[8] Former contract workers would not forfeit the right to freely return if they settled as small farmers at one of the government settlements. If they did choose to give up their right to freely return, they would be given a hundred Dutch guilders, which was a considerable sum of money at the time. Later the favorable settlement conditions were expanded even further, and they could also get the hundred-guilder premium if they settled outside the government settlements (van Lier 1971: 235).

This is what East Indians preferred to do. In fact if they could, they settled outside the government settlements altogether. The disadvantage of settling independently was that they had to cultivate the barren land themselves, whereas at government settlements the necessary infrastructure was provided. The forests were cut down, and there was a drainage system and roads. The advantage was that after two years, they became owners of the land. This had an enormous appeal for East Indians, coming as they did from overpopulated regions in India. They soon came to view the government settlements as a temporary stop on the way to an independent life (Speckmann 1965: 41). Especially at the time of the cacao crisis, many East Indians left the government settlements to settle independently outside them. In many cases, they took over plots of land from Creole cacao farmers who were moving to the town.

The increasing number of independent farmers coincided with a growing demand for locally grown food (Heilbron 1982: 221). It was predominantly East Indians who supplied these products. The farmers around Paramaribo focused on supplying food for the city. They soon attained a level of relative prosperity and became increasingly engaged in the transport to the consumer. But it was mainly the shift to rice cultivation that led to the East Indian success in the agrarian sector, where they were able to greatly expand and modernize the production of rice. This was feasible in part because of the excellent natural conditions and sales possibilities and the stimulating official policy. After beginning as self-sufficient farmers, they were soon producing for the national and later the international market. Especially at the time of the two world wars, there was an enormous rise in the rice production figures.

Urban Employment and Education

For a long time, more or less up to World War II, East Indians continued to mainly work in agriculture, whereas Creoles had long been engaged in any number of nonagrarian occupations. The Creole segment of the population was also far more heterogeneous than the East Indian one as regards the aspect of social class. In fact the very word *Creole* is a term par excellence designating an economically and culturally extremely heterogeneous population.

The Creole occupational differentiation originated in the period before emancipation. In addition to a higher middle class mainly consisting of Europeans, in the nineteenth century there was also a large middle class of free mulattos and Africans in the city of Paramaribo.[9] What is more, at the time many slaves had already ceased to work in the agrarian sector. Van Lier notes that by the mid-nineteenth century, no fewer than 35 percent of the productive slaves were working as artisans and domestic servants (1971: 163). At the time of the abolition of slavery, some slaves were already in the city and some moved there then to look for a job. It was from these groups that the lower middle class and urban proletariat emerged.[10]

In Surinam, unemployment in the city was a growing problem that had been there since emancipation. The large category of artisans was particularly hard hit by the problem, as were people who aspired to social advancement via education. Many of the better educated Creoles would have liked to become civil servants, but there were not enough jobs in the government apparatus for them (van Lier 1971: 249-51).

The unemployment rate among these urban middle groups had always been high, but starting in 1924 it was high among the lower class as well (van Lier 1971: 248), due in part to the recession in the balata and gold sectors. The unemployment rate in Paramaribo fell during World War II, primarily as a result of the bauxite industry and the presence of American troops stationed there.

Except in the bauxite industry, many of the jobs were only temporary (van Lier 1971: 402-3). Since then, the city has had a great deal of overt and hidden unemployment and a large informal sector.[11] It is true that the economic situation of the Creole middle class has not been constantly poor, but it is characterized by considerable instability and insecurity (Buschkens 1974).

Education has always been the most important instrument for Creole upward mobility. The advantage Creoles had for a long time over East Indians was largely a result of their early participation in the school system. There has been compulsory education ever since 1876, but it is perhaps even more important that, from the start, Creoles were oriented toward a Western lifestyle, including the value attributed to education. From the very start of the nineteenth century, mulattos were attending school and, like the children of the Dutch colonists, some were continuing their studies in the Netherlands (van Lier 1971: 111). East Indians, however, were initially not particularly interested in educating their children, and since they were only in Surinam temporarily, the rules pertaining to compulsory education were applied to them with great leniency (de Klerk 1953: 128-29).[12] All this was, however, soon to change.

At the beginning of the twentieth century, especially as of the 1920s, a certain extent of occupational differentiation also began to emerge among East Indians. For them, the move to the city was linked to the food supply for the urban population. Agriculture was flourishing around Paramaribo, and this was accompanied by a growing East Indian role in commerce (markets and shops) and transport. In addition, more and more East Indians were working as artisans in the city. In these sectors, they began to compete directly with the Creoles (van Lier 1971: 248; Speckmann 1965: 230). The economic revival during World War II once again attracted many East Indians to the city. From that time on, education began to play a role of increasing importance in the upward social mobility of East Indians. According to van Lier, the poor secondary school attendance of East Indians largely accounts for the small size of the East Indian middle class up until World War II (1971: 221). However, the position East Indians had attained in the agrarian and trade sectors was a good starting point for further occupational differentiation via education.[13] Nowadays East Indians work in virtually all the sectors of the economy.

The Ethnic Division of Labor: In Pursuit of an Explanation

Why did this ethnic division of labor develop as it did? Why did Creoles leave farming? Did they have an aversion to the work, as is sometimes claimed? Did they think cultivating rice was typical "coolie" work? Why were the East Indians the ones to go in for farming? How is their success at it to be explained? Was it related to their diligence and frugality? In explaining the underlying reasons for this ethnic division of labor, I devote attention to three clusters of factors: (1) the government policy and economic circumstances that generated different opportunities for the two groups; (2) the role of the ethnic ideology prevalent at the time; and (3) the different ways the two groups took advantage of the economic possibilities.

Differential Opportunities

The limited Creole participation in the agrarian sector is sometimes explained by their general aversion to farming.[14] Of course the possibility should not be excluded that Creoles had an aversion to the work in the fields they had done in the past as slaves. It would be unwarranted, however, to view this as characteristic of an entire segment of the population, besides which there is no call to provide any explanation at all. This is all the more so since there is ample evidence of precisely the opposite. After the State Supervision period, there was a relatively prosperous class of Creole farmers. Van Lier notes that it was the result of the individual initiative and efforts of the ex-slaves themselves (1971: 229-30). It is true that many ex-slaves fled the countryside even before emancipation in 1863, but in a comparable society like British Guiana, many ex-slaves did remain in the agrarian sector (Kruijer 1968: 163; Lowenthal 1960: 793). In other words, there would seem to have been other factors besides the alleged aversion to farming.

Various conditions played a role in most of the Creoles leaving the agrarian sector. First, there was the policy of the planters and the authorities for providing labor at the plantations. Although many ex-slaves did voluntarily leave the plantations, there was also a policy focused on replacing them by Asian contract workers. The Asians were not only cheaper, as newcomers they were easier to control than the ex-slaves.

Second, there were more and more opportunities for earning a living elsewhere in the agrarian as well as other sectors. Ex-slaves were thus no longer dependent on the plantations. Many settled as independent farmers outside the government settlements or on demesne land. Others were attracted by the higher wages in the balata or gold industries. The attraction of these rural industries was reinforced later when so many people had to look for new ways to earn a living at the time of the cacao crisis.

Third, conditions were different in the period when Creoles were settling as independent farmers than in the later period when East Indians were. Up until 1895, the government settlement policy was extremely restrictive and it was difficult to settle independently outside the government settlements. What is more, ex-slaves were initially discriminated against in the land grant system involving demesne land or even excluded altogether. It was not until 1895 that conditions became more favorable because small farming was then given priority over the plantations. By then, though, Creoles were already turning away from agrarian life.

Fourth, there was the attraction provided by the educational and employment opportunities in the city. The lure of the city dates back to colonial times and did not only begin after emancipation. Whoever lived outside the city on a plantation only did so because there was no other choice. So it should not be surprising that Paramaribo continued to work like a magnet. In addition to the economic opportunities, there was also the urban lifestyle that attracted Creoles (van Dusseldorp 1963: 40; Kruijer 1951).

Conversely, there are certain circumstances that might explain in part why East Indians stayed in the agrarian sector so long and so successfully. In the first place, there was the very simple reason that although the contract workers had come of their own free will, once they were under contract they were no longer free to leave the plantation. Their situation differed from that of the Creoles in that they had no alternatives. Even after their contract was over, they were still not completely free to come and go as they pleased. For quite some time, they were prohibited, for example, from working in the gold or balata sectors. The only economic openings for them were to produce food for their own consumption or for the market (Heilbron 1982: 214). In other words, for a long time farming was pretty much the only option East Indians had.

Second, with the expansion of the settlement policy after 1895, in their efforts to promote small farming and tie East Indians to the land, the authorities made the settlement conditions more attractive for them.[15] The role played by the British Indian authorities is important in this connection. It was in part under their influence that the Surinamese government changed its policy with respect to East Indians in 1895. De Klerk notes that, in effect, the immigration system had become a colonization system (1953: 165). As a result of this official policy, the small East Indian farmer was able to set up shop as it were under far more favorable conditions than the Creole farmer in the past.

A third factor in the East Indian success in the agrarian sector was the shift to growing rice. The excellent natural conditions helped make this feasible. In addition, for reasons to be dealt with below, East Indians were well able to supply the labor needed for growing rice.

The good marketing opportunities constituted the last factor. Increasing the production of rice was in keeping with the government goal of replacing imported products and improving the local food supply. This soon meant relative prosperity for these rice growers. This also holds true of the farmers who had settled in the vicinity of Paramaribo and were producing food for the city. They also started to take more and more responsibility for transporting and marketing their farm products themselves, which led to an important new source of income.

The significance of these second and third factors is illustrated by the relatively limited success of the East Indian farmers in Saramacca. Without good sales possibilities or good drainage, they did not do nearly as well as the rice growers in Nickerie or the farmers around Paramaribo (van Lier 1971: 236).

Ethnic Ideology

Agriculture might have been the main advancement route for East Indians, but for Creoles it was urban employment and education. As was noted above, the policy adjustment in 1895 was accompanied by a change in the ethnic composition of the agrarian population. Was this an unintentional effect of the policy or a deliberate effort to favor East Indians to keep them in the Surinamese agrarian sector? In part a number of developments just happened to coincide, and the need to develop small farming came in precisely the period when many Creoles were leaving the agrarian sector and more and more East Indians were available to settle independently. It is no coincidence, though, that it was East Indians who were favored by the new farming policy. A link has been drawn between the differential treatment of these two segments of the population and their alleged suitability for farming, in that Creoles were simply viewed as being less suitable for it than East Indians (Willemsen 1980: 126-27).

A notion like this was mainly an expression of the power relations prevailing at the time.[16] The social relations between the planters and ex-slaves did not suddenly change after emancipation. The hostile attitude of the ex-slaves to the planters was understandable, since so many forms of overt and covert resistance had developed during slavery (Hira 1982). However, the planters' tendency to view ex-slaves as unmanageable and unreliable after the State Supervision period had less to do with these alleged character traits than with a number of concrete conditions, namely, the higher wages the ex-slaves wanted to earn, and could earn elsewhere, the low wages the contract workers had to accept, and the planters' fear of labor unrest and conflicts that would be caused by the presence of ex-slaves on the plantations.[17]

Whether overt or covert, the Creole opposition to the planters in the post-slavery period was thus directly related to the way they had previously been forced to supply labor. The cultural mechanisms they had developed to cope with oppression resulted in behavior patterns that were not unexpectedly interpreted very differently by the planters than by the ex-slaves themselves. The behavior ex-slaves viewed as a legitimate way to cope with a life of slavery was viewed by planters as unreliable conduct. The two interpretations were not, however, attributed with the same significance, since the planters' interests were to dominate the political scene for a long period of time. The interests of the country were equated with the continuation and prosperity of the plantations. According to van Lier (1971: 239), up until 1920 the ideas of the planters far outweighed all the other perspectives on the situation in Surinam. The ideas held by the planters also shaped the stereotype of the Creole role in the Surinamese economy. The exodus from the agrarian sector that the planters expected after the termination of State Supervision over the ex-slaves was initially belied by the facts. The later inflow to the city seemed, however, to confirm the notion of "negroes" commonly held by the planters. Although the Africans had originally been brought to Surinam because they were thought to be well suited for farm work, now the idea prevailed that "negroes" were not much good at farming and in fact were not very motivated to work at all (van Lier 1971: 239-44). Of course there was a labor problem, according to van Lier, since nationwide unemployment was accompanied by a shortage of plantation workers. But Creoles simply were not willing to continue working like slaves, and this is what led to the myth of "the lazy negro" (Kruijer 1968: 122). The contents of this myth could easily change. The heavy labor Creoles were doing in the inland regions necessitated a revision of the idea that "negroes" were not willing to work hard. Now the myth had it that because of their adventurous nature, they needed to do work with a lot of variation (van Lier 1971: 243). Van Lier counters these racist notions by noting that the way the Creoles behaved was totally understandable in view of the social context of the period: "The conduct of the Creole and the peculiarities which he shows as a laborer can be explained from clearly perceptible social and economic motives" (1971: 244).

The more favorable way East Indians were treated had to do in part with this ethnic stereotyping and ideology. This does not necessarily mean the image of East Indians was all that positive. In the beginning they also exhibited forms of resistance or even outright rebellion.[18] Their prospects were not as grim as those of the ex-slaves, though, if only because they still had the option of returning to India after the expiration of their contract. What is more, East Indians were under the protection of the British Indian authorities, who acted on their behalf with the Surinamese colonial government. As a result of this protection and state supervision of the adherence to the contract conditions, the treatment of contract workers gradually improved. In general, as they proved their worth as farm laborers, they began to be treated more benevolently. The ethnic stereotyping kept pace with these developments. Heilbron cites the view that certain ethnic groups were more suitable for cultivating certain crops than others (1982: 222-23). In this view, Asian immigrants were more suitable than other segments of the Surinamese population for small farming in general and rice cultivation in particular. Heilbron rightly refutes the notion that this had to do with their innate nature.

The question remains though as to why Creoles did not shift more from cacao to food crops for the local market as East Indians did. And to the extent that Creoles did make an effort to do so, why were they less successful than East Indians? And what accounts for the success of East Indians in the rice sector? Questions like these cannot be completely answered by referring to the economic and political situation. East Indians were apparently able to take better advantage of the opportunities the agrarian sector was presenting. After refuting the idea of a natural disposition, some authors then simply ignore the possibility of any social or cultural explanations. To what extent did East Indians have specific resources that gave them a more favorable starting position as small entrepreneurs in farming and commerce? And why was the route via education and urban employment apparently more suitable for Creoles? I go into all these questions in the following section, where I devote special attention to two aspects that are important in this connection, namely, family structure and economic conduct. Both these aspects are often referred to in social science literature on Surinam to help explain the differential social success of Creoles and East Indians.

Differential Adaptation

The rapid social advancement of East Indians in Surinamese society is often linked to their family structure. In farming as well as commerce, or more generally in entrepreneurship, it is thought to put them at an advantage.[19] The family system of the Creole lower class, however, is usually linked to an unstable social position and poverty.

The patriarchal East Indian extended family does indeed seem to have had certain advantages for their position in the agrarian sector. Ideally, the families of fathers and sons constituted an economic unit under the leadership of the father. This provided a good basis for the organization of labor and financial management. Thus family interests coincided with the interests of the business enterprise, which stimulated the loyalty of individual members of the family. In addition, there was no need to hire outside labor. All this enabled East Indian family businesses to acquire a good competitive position. By the beginning of the twentieth century, East Indian farmers were even competing successfully against the Dutch farmers who had been brought in to provide the city's food supply (Speckmann 1965: 43).

In the cultivation of rice, East Indians similarly appeared to be at an advantage. Despres (1967: 89) explains why the availability of members of the family as laborers promoted scale enlargement and boosted profits, so that rice could be produced as a cash crop.[20] Wherever capital is scarce, family labor is a good investment, and this is all the more so in branches as labor-intensive as the cultivation of rice. Heilbron (1982: 213) suggests that this is one reason why Creole farmers did not switch to the cultivation of rice after the cacao crisis. In Coronie, which even today is still a Creole farming district, they primarily switched to coconuts as the main crop. Like cacao, coconuts entail a much less labor-intensive form of farming than rice. In World War I, however, they switched to growing rice there as well, but due to the poor organization and irrigation coordination, there were numerous problems (van Renselaar 1963a: 476).[21]

It has similarly been repeatedly noted that the East Indian family system provided a good starting position for entrepreneurship outside the agrarian sector.[22] This was the case in multifarious related economic activities such as the transport and sale of farm products. Another factor that played a role in the agrarian sector was the ownership and inheritance of land. Among East Indians, it was traditionally the sons who inherited the family property. Among Creoles, all the children had an equal right to the land, but property often was not divided up. This meant heirs who lived somewhere else continued to have a claim to the use or proceeds of the land. What is more, since it was usually unclear who the actual owners were, this made it difficult to get credit. This failure to divide up the property is one of the reasons why the Creole role in small farming remained so limited (Egger 1995: 182-83).

The more diffuse Creole kinship system had advantages as well as disadvantages. Since Creole farmers predominantly continued to operate at a subsistence level, many of them periodically left to spend some time wherever the earnings were better. The ones who left were mainly the young men and the older people stayed behind, which meant the loss of much of the family labor (Heilbron 1982: 273).[23] Despres (1967: 88) notes that the people who stayed behind in the agricultural sector were easily able to keep the production going because the tree crops and other products were not labor-intensive. They were less lucrative than rice, but they could still be produced for the farmers' own consumption or the local market, while the men supplemented the income with their wage labor. The Creole family system thus made it possible to respond flexibly to whatever the conditions were. But there were also disadvantages. The claims of relatives who lived somewhere else to the use or proceeds of the land were a constant burden for those who remained behind. The same held true for the money income earned outside the agrarian sector, since the men had numerous obligations to the relatives who remained behind. Van Renselaar (1963a: 478) notes that the obligations family members and fellow plantation dwellers had to each other had a strongly leveling effect on the prosperity differences in the community. In this sense, these mutual obligations also constituted a good social safety net. The family system facilitated the constant migration movements, since people in the rural as well as urban settings could always fall back on their relatives (Despres 1967: 85).[24] There was also evidence in the urban context of the leveling effect of Creole social networks, as is noted by Pierce (1973) in a study on the poorer districts of Paramaribo.

A second common explanation for the differential social position has to do with the economic conduct and lifestyle of the groups in question. In short, East Indians are thought to owe their upward social mobility to their diligence, sober lifestyle, and frugality. Creoles, however, are not thought to have the right attitude for improving themselves and getting ahead. Their poor work ethic and consumerist lifestyle are thought to serve instead as obstacles to social advancement. Particularly in the earlier literature on Surinam where the concept of the pluralist society still plays a prominent role, references are regularly made to differences in the "economic mentality" of the various segments of the population.[25] The question is to what extent the attribution of characteristics of this kind to these two ethnic groups is warranted, and to what extent do they constitute an explanation for the differences in their social positions.

There is no denying a number of clear differences between the Creole and East Indian lifestyles. The extremely sober lifestyle of the East Indian immigrants and their ability to save money, even with the meager amounts they were earning, were striking at the time.[26] East Indians had long been accustomed to living at a near subsistence level, but Creoles were more oriented toward the lifestyle of Europeans. Their isolated life in the countryside enabled East Indians to preserve their sober lifestyle for quite some time and ignore the status symbols of Creoles (Speckmann 1963a: 463, 465). The urbanization process took place among Creoles much earlier, and reinforced their aspirations and focus on urban consumer patterns. However, East Indian urbanization and social mobility were to change their lifestyle as well. Speckmann noted in the 1960s that the needs and spending patterns of young East Indians in the city were changing. Compared with their parents they had much more of a consumer mentality (1963a: 466). In other words, the East Indian frugality and sobriety sometimes thought to be "ethnic" features were not immutable. Apparently the contrast between Creole and East Indian lifestyles had much to do with the difference between urban and rural living.

Differences in economic conduct do not, however, only influence social position, they are also a reflection of it. The economic situation of the Creole lower classes was one of periodic unemployment, geographic mobility, and irregular earnings. This is why a life pattern characterized by strong income and expenditure fluctuations was more typical of Creoles than East Indians.[27] This would seem to have been truer of men than women. Unlike Creole men, Creole women were thought to have little choice but to adopt an attitude more focused on the future for the simple reason that they bore the permanent responsibility for the children.[28]

Despres's findings on the saving patterns of Creoles and East Indians in nearby British Guiana are interesting in this connection (1967). He shows that Creole villagers saved less than East Indian villagers, but Creole bauxite workers saved more than East Indian sugar workers. In the first case, the Creoles were poorer than the East Indians, and in the second it was the other way around: East Indian sugar workers were poorer than Creole bauxite workers. In other words, the difference in the saving patterns reflected their different economic positions (1967: 94). Thus the idea of the frugal East Indian and the spendthrift Creole is merely a stereotype. Despres (1967: 95) nonetheless holds that ethnic stereotypes of this kind are not simply generated by misconceptions of the different economic positions of Creoles and East Indians, nor can they be totally explained away by the economic activities of the two groups. According to Despres, the two groups did exhibit striking consumer patterns, but the patterns were inspired by the different values they held. Creoles tended to immediately spend their money on what they viewed as the pleasant sides of life. East Indians preferred to set aside their money for long-term expenditures, particularly for religious practices.

In addition to the differences in their lifestyle and saving patterns, Creoles and East Indians were thought to have a different work ethic. East Indians were thought to mainly owe their success in society to their own permanent diligence. "The reputation of the groups was in conformity with the facts: they were generally regarded as hard-working people" (Speckmann 1965: 52). Although no one is apt to refute the idea that East Indians are generally hard workers, they did not earn this reputation until after they settled independently on their own land (de Klerk 1953: 138).[29] According to van Renselaar, the small Creole farmer, however, never lost his farmhand mentality and was always willing to give up farming as soon as he could find a job somewhere else that would pay more (1963a: 479). Given the fact that Creole farming predominantly remained at a subsistence level, it is not surprising so many people left if they could earn more somewhere else. The relatively great Creole geographic and labor mobility can also easily give the impression they had no predilection for a regular job. Perhaps Creoles associated a regular, boring job with slave labor. If so, this was only reinforced in a later historical period by the economic structure of Surinam, which was not in any way geared toward a large category of "free" workers.[30] Later, when industries did start to flourish, particularly the lumber and bauxite industries, they were largely dependent on the labor of Creole workers.

Conclusion

From a historical perspective, Creoles and East Indians each had their own routes and rates of social mobility. The typical social mobility routes of each group can be accounted for on the basis of the differential opportunities in certain periods in Surinamese society, and the groups' responses to them based on their specific background and history. However, neither factor alone can explain the different patterns of social mobility. It was mainly the interaction between the opportunity structure and the adaptation to it that played a role. In this connection, ethnic stereotyping and ideologies would seem to have played an intermediary role. In part the stereotyping of the two groups shaped the economic functions attributed to them. However, the ethnic stereotyping colonial policy was based upon was not neutral. It was spawned by the point of view of a colonial elite that gave high priority to agriculture. This meant a different policy was in effect for each of the groups, or that one and the same policy had differential effects. In other words, ethnic stereotyping is always embedded in power relations.[31]

Ethnic stereotyping and ideologies are, however, not set in stone. In the course of time, the ideas about Creole ex-slaves kept changing with the changes in the economic functions they served. The image people had of East Indians, which was initially not unmitigatedly positive, similarly altered as they played their allocated role in the agrarian sector to satisfaction. Ethnic stereotypes exhibit a certain persistence, but they are apparently also open to change. With the

differential adaptation of Creoles and East Indians to the changing social context, apparently the stereotypes about them changed as well. So the images
people have of ethnic groups not only influence their position in society but also
they are a reflection of it.

In Closing

Ever since they first arrived, East Indians exhibited a considerable and relatively
rapid rise in Surinam society. For quite some time, they were in an inferior position to Creoles, but this is definitely no longer the case. Since World War II,
they also increasingly became part of the urban population.[32] As a result of migration to the city, greater educational participation, altered aspirations, and occupational differentiation, East Indians gradually entered the fields once domi-
nated by Creoles (Egger 1995; Hassankhan et al. 1995). Since the 1960s, East
Indians were not only able to further reinforce their economic position but also
to become a numerical majority (Dew 1978: 5).

In the 1960s and 1970s, Creoles also benefited from the economic prosperity
in Surinam. After independence, any number of plans and projects were launched
that initially generated ample jobs. In the long run, though, the actual reality of
the situation failed to meet the expectations and, especially for Creoles, not
much changed (Egger 1995: 192). In the least productive and ultimately the
most vulnerable sector of the labor market, the number of jobs increased. This
was precisely where Creoles were so overrepresented. They played only a very
minor role in the fields that did flourish, such as the rice sector, but mining and
industry, where Creoles were relatively frequently employed, were stagnating
(1995: 192-93).

This then was the situation in Surinam up until the mass migration to the Netherlands. How are the historical developments referred to above related to the description given in chapter 2 of the social position of the Afro-Surinamese and
Indo-Surinamese in the Netherlands? This brief survey of the history of the two
groups in Surinam makes it understandable why the Afro-Surinamese population had a better starting position in the Netherlands and is still doing better on
average than the Indo-Surinamese population.

However, the socioeconomic differentiation within both these communities
plays a significant role. This is a more recent development in the Indo-Surinamese community. Around 1900, East Indians all started at more or less the same
low position in Surinamese society as contract workers, but the position of the
Creole population had been extremely heterogeneous since colonial times. In
other words, the Creole population is essentially a melting pot of various social
strata in Surinamese society. This is why the class distribution in the Afro-Surinamese population in the Netherlands is so sizeable. It is difficult to estimate the

extent to which it is more sizeable than the class distribution in the Indo-Surinamese population in the Netherlands, and consequently whether it might in part explain why the Afro-Surinamese are doing better.

Notes

1. Here I use the term Creole rather than Afro-Surinamese to distinguish the Creoles from another Afro-Surinamese group, the Maroons. What is more, the term Afro-Surinamese came into use more recently, and it is consequently less appropriate in this historical context.

2. In addition, more has been published on the basis of the 1964 census and there are more detailed data available about it.

3. These data from the study by de Bruijne solely pertain to Greater Paramaribo and not to all of Surinam, as do the data referred to earlier.

4. This chapter is a revised version of two articles published in the past (see van Niekerk 1995 and 1996).

5. In addition to British Indians, after 1891 Javanese workers were also brought in from the Dutch East Indies.

6. See also de Klerk (1953: 163); Willemsen (1980: 123-24).

7. This measure stipulated that the allocation of demesne land was possible, for which no land tax or personal duties had to be paid for a period of six years. After two years of regular cultivation, the right to free ownership would be granted. Based on this decree, small landowners could also get small advances (van Lier 1971: 226).

8. See, e.g., de Klerk (1953: 162-63); Speckmann (1965: 38-42).

9. In Surinam at the time, these segments of the population were referred to as *coloured people* and *negroes*, respectively, both of whom are categorized as *Creoles*.

10. See van Lier (1971: 96-116).

11. See van Gelder (1985).

12. From 1890 to 1906 there were special "coolie schools" to encourage East Indian children to attend school. They were taught there in their own language. Once it was clear, however, that East Indians were in Surinam to stay, more importance came to be attached to education in Dutch (de Klerk 1953: 129-30).

13. See also Speckmann (1962/63).

14. See, e.g., Speckmann (1965: 46).

15. See van Lier (1971: 235); Speckmann (1965: 38-42).

16. Cf. Williams (1991: 147-54).

17. Cf. Heilbron (1982: 97); Kruijer (1968).

18. See Hira (1982: 196-215).

19. Cf. Benedict (1979).

20. Although Despres's analysis pertains to the position of East Indians in British Guiana, I feel it is just as applicable to the Surinamese situation (see also Despres 1970).

21. Cf. Despres (1967: 48).

22. See, e.g., Benedict (1979).

23. Cf. van Renselaar (1963a: 477).

24. Cf. de Bruijne (1976: 48-49).

25. See, e.g., van Renselaar (1963a and 1963b); Speckmann (1963a and 1963b).

26. See, e.g., de Klerk (1953: 138).

27. Cf. Brana Shute (1979); Pierce (1973).

28. Cf. Benedict (1979: 320-21); Buschkens (1974).

29. De Klerk notes that the reputation of contract workers could differ from one transport or category of immigrants to the next. Some shipments of imported workers were known for their fine work performance, whereas others had a poorer reputation and were called *lesiman jahāz* or ships of lazy men (1953: 138-39).

30. Cf. Heilbron (1982); Kruijer (1968); Willemsen (1980).

31. Cf. Williams (1991).

32. A survey conducted in 1992 among heads of households in Greater Paramaribo shows that Creoles and East Indians constituted 35 and 31 percent of the population respectively (de Bruijne and Schalkwijk 1994: 13). The urbanization level was high, with only 20 to 25 percent of the working population in Surinam employed in the agrarian sector (de Bruijne 1995: 5).

Chapter Four

Mobility Trajectories

How did the legacy of premigration history influence the position of the Surinamese in Dutch society? In only a few generations, the Indo-Surinamese experienced a double migration. To what extent were they able to continue the upward mobility that had begun in Surinam after they arrived in the Netherlands? As is noted above, in various ways the starting position of the Afro-Surinamese was more favorable. The question is whether these differences persisted after migration to the Netherlands. Did the differentiation become deeper, or did the move make the two groups more similar?

This chapter focuses on the mobility trajectories of first-generation Afro-Surinamese and Indo-Surinamese immigrants. I use the term first-generation immigrants to refer to the ones who no longer attended school full-time after they arrived in the Netherlands. I draw a distinction between the early immigrants who came in the 1950s and 1960s and the later ones of the 1970s and 1980s.

Early Immigrants of the 1950s and 1960s

Most of the Surinamese who came to the Netherlands settled in the large cities. What accounts for the fact that Amsterdam attracted so many Afro-Surinamese and The Hague so many Indo-Surinamese? Some of my respondents suggest it might have to do with the nature of the two cities. Perhaps the Amsterdam nightlife and swinging, cosmopolitan atmosphere is more in keeping with the urban Afro-Surinamese lifestyle, and the more conservative sedateness of The Hague more suited to the Indo-Surinamese. Since there is little I can add to these conjectures, I would now like to take a brief look at the settlement history of the earliest Surinamese immigrants.

The First Surinamese to Settle in Amsterdam and The Hague

The Surinamese who came to the Netherlands before World War II were either on leave or youngsters from the Creole elite who came to complete their education at the universities in Amsterdam or Leiden. A completely different group of sailors, adventurers, or stowaways also arrived at the harbor in Amsterdam and simply stayed on. They earned a living doing odd jobs and some wound up in the entertainment world. Surinamese musicians played at jazz clubs, bars, and nightspots in Amsterdam and were just as popular as the well-known American performers before them (Kagie 1989; Oostindie 1986). In clubs like Negro Palace and The Cotton Club, it was jazz that they played and not Surinamese music, because that was what the audience was familiar with. Surinamese entertainers adopted stage names with an American sound: Theodoor Kantoor became Teddy Cotton and Arthur Lodewijk Parisius was known as Kid Dynamite (Openneer 1995). Others earned a less honest living in Amsterdam's underworld.

It is true that Amsterdam was not the only city where Surinamese immigrants were settling at the time, but in various ways it was the center for what was still predominantly an Afro-Surinamese community. The universities in Amsterdam and Leiden attracted students, and the harbors in Amsterdam and Rotterdam laborers. But when it came to the nightlife, the world of music and entertainment, and the political and cultural organizations, Amsterdam did occupy the central role. In the historical overview that Oostindie (1986) wrote about the period up until 1955, Rotterdam plays much less of a role than Amsterdam, and The Hague barely any role at all. Amsterdam was traditionally the city where most of the Surinamese came to live (Reubsaet and Geerts 1983: 25). The Royal Netherlands Maritime Company (KNSM) ran a passenger line from Paramaribo to Amsterdam, where friends and acquaintances came to welcome newcomers at the pier. Most of the first Surinamese small entrepreneurs also settled in Amsterdam. They opened cigar shops, sold tropical products, and had their own bars (Oostindie 1986).

As far as I know, less information is available on why so many Indo-Surinamese settled in The Hague. Some authors suggest that Indo-Surinamese students who went to Leiden University settled in nearby The Hague. With its hustle and bustle, Amsterdam was associated with the negative aspects of nightlife and the world of hustlers. The Hague, however, was known as a quiet town for decent people, which is what people returning to Surinam told prospective emigrants there.[1] A certain ethnic antagonism around the time Surinam became independent might have played a role in this connection. The Indo-Surinamese, who started coming to the Netherlands at a later stage than the Afro-Surinamese, simply chose to go to another city. This does not mean two ethnically separated circuits developed. There were also some Indo-Surinamese, be it in limited numbers, in Amsterdam's student world and more politically oriented organizations. There were probably also some Indo-Surinamese who deliberately chose Amsterdam at the very start or moved there later. It was, nonetheless, The Hague that consistently had a special attraction for the Indo-Surinamese. Once a small group had settled there, The Hague soon became the city newcomers were likely to opt for as well.[2]

As a result, even before the mass exodus began from Surinam, there was already a kind of ethnic division between Amsterdam and The Hague. No statistics are available on this period, but the Surinamese emigration figures for the year 1971 do give a good indication of what was going on (Zielhuis 1973). In that year 22 percent of the Creoles settled in Amsterdam, 17 percent in Rotterdam, and 8 percent in The Hague. In that same year, 29 percent of the East Indians settled in The Hague and 19 percent in Amsterdam.[3] Once this geographic distribution of the two ethnic groups had become a fact, the process was only reinforced.

Not only did more and more people from Surinam come to the Netherlands after World War II, it was now different categories who were coming. In addition to students and people on leave, various occupational groups came as well: laborers, civil servants, office workers, nurses, and teachers. This was increasingly the case in the 1960s, and they soon numerically exceeded the students. They came from all the segments of Surinamese society, but mostly the better educated or well-to-do classes. After the predominantly male students, more and more women and children started to come as well. In the first instance they were not coming to the Netherlands to complete their education but to get a job, though they did sometimes combine working with studying. The general desire for a better life was at least as important, and this was something you had to go to the Netherlands for.

In the rest of this section I do not discuss the people who came to the Netherlands to complete their education, except when I describe the early Indo-Surinamese immigrants who didn't start coming in numbers of any size to speak of until this period. I concentrate on the ones who constituted the bulk of the newcomers up until the 1970s. There is only a limited number of respondents from this period, but their history contrasts in an interesting way with the later immigrants. Wherever possible, I consult the literature from this period, limited though it may be. Therefore, this section is set up in a different way than the following one about the immigrants of the 1970s and 1980s.

Afro-Surinamese Laborers

Young men started coming from Surinam to the Netherlands around 1950 looking for jobs as laborers. Not that they had any special aim in mind, as one of them relates in retrospect, "it was just the time when people started going to Europe."

My earliest respondent arrived in the Netherlands in 1949. His father told him he had to learn a trade before he left Surinam. "Once you have a trade," his father said, "you can leave and earn a living anywhere in the world." He went to a vocational school and after he got some practical experience working for different employers, at the age of twenty-one he was ready to embark on the big adventure. So it was not poverty or unemployment that made him want to come to the Netherlands, but he did have high expectations of what life there was going to be like.

A later immigrant who arrived in 1965 says much the same thing. He had a good job working for "the Americans," in this case the Surinam Aluminium Company (Suralco), a bauxite company, so there was no urgent reason for him to leave. "But the way it was in Surinam then, you know, everyone was talking about it, all the guys wanted to go to Holland. Scores of young men were on the move." When a friend of his who also worked for the Surinam Aluminium Company left, he decided to go too.

When these Creole labor immigrants, now retired, first arrived, they were met by the older Surinamese people who had come before World War II and now "showed them the ropes." Some became active in the circles around the Surinamese political and cultural organizations in Amsterdam, and came into contact with Surinamese intellectuals and students. Others were confined to the help and support they got from friends, relatives, or acquaintances. In those days, long before social work agencies started to be subsidized by the government for this purpose, newcomers had to rely on whatever private help was available. Some of them feel the later immigrants had a much easier start. As one respondent puts it, "The people who came on the Bijlmermeer[4] Express had it made."

Finding a place to live was no simple matter back in those days. In the postwar Netherlands with its huge housing shortage, most of the young Surinamese newcomers had to rent a room, often an attic room, from a landlady.

In Mr. M.'s case[5] it was a room in the part of the attic where coal was stored, and he had to turn off the light at ten o'clock. In the postwar period of reconstruction, it was a frugal life. "You didn't have much light, twenty-five Watts and if you were lucky forty Watts. That was all anyone had, people used to all sit around a big table under the lamp."

No heating, barely any place to cook, and strict supervision of visitors, this was the situation awaiting many of the young men who came to the Netherlands at the time. Finding a job was, however, relatively simple in the 1950s and 1960s. Within a few days after they arrived, the respondents had a job. One of the men says his boat arrived on Sunday, he went to the Labor Office on Monday, and by Tuesday he had a job. Another respondent simply got a job at the gate of a shipyard he happened to be passing by on the way to a job interview somewhere else. It happened within a week after he arrived.

"This old guy from North Amsterdam was standing at the gate," Mr. G. (67) relates, "and he shouted 'What are you looking for?' I said, 'Sir, I am looking for a job.' 'What can you do?' the man asked. 'Sir, I am a blacksmith.' So he said, 'Come with me, come in, they can use people here.' And then I was introduced. I kept thinking maybe I have to do something to show him what my work is like, but the man said, 'There is no need for that.' He just asked me 'When can you start?' I think it was a Tuesday and I said, 'tomorrow.' But he said 'No, that is not the way we do things because you just got here. Come back on Monday next week.' So that is the way it went."

The study Bayer (1965) conducted on Surinamese laborers in the Netherlands shows that except in the period right after they arrived, most found a job suited to their educational level. As regards skilled and unskilled workers alike, the notion that the Surinamese were working at much lower levels than their education warranted proved to be untrue (Bayer 1965: 54). This seems quite plausible considering the labor shortage at the time. Surinamese job-seekers probably met with less discrimination than in later years, which does not necessarily mean the early immigrants did not meet with any discrimination at all. Once they got jobs, all kinds of problems arose on the shop floor. The problems were caused by the adjustment problems they were experiencing, and the uncooperative or outrightly hostile attitude of their Dutch coworkers. They had to cope with racist jokes and sometimes felt they didn't have the same promotion opportunities. It also sometimes happened that Surinamese laborers were dismissed because they were felt to be poorly adjusted or not suited for the work. They were usually quick to find a new job, though, and some of them, still according to Bayer, even frequently changed jobs.

There were also very different interpretations of the problems at the time in the interaction with Dutch co-workers.

In retrospect, Mr. G. (67) pretty much took it all in his stride. He had to adjust at first to how the Dutch treated each other, which was something he was especially confronted with at work. It was not always easy to get the jokes the Amsterdammers used to make. "But as time went on you learned to deal with people, and you learned that they didn't mean to offend you or make you feel you weren't accepted. It was part of how those people are with each other and the kind of jokes they make with each other."

Not everyone had the same experience. Bayer suggests a link with the length of time they had been in the Netherlands. The people who felt discriminated against at work were usually the ones who had not been in the country long. On the other hand, it was possible, at any rate according to Bayer, that in the course of time people became resigned to the inevitable, even to discrimination (1965: 59). It is not clear whether it was a matter of becoming accustomed to discrimination or whether a period of adjustment was needed to be able to put alleged discrimination into perspective.

Apart from these problems with interpersonal contact, there is the more or less organized resistance Surinamese laborers came up against at the workplace. It sometimes happened at companies where Surinamese laborers were recruited as a group. In a number of cases, steps were taken against their coming (Bayer 1965: 65ff.). Since Surinamese laborers were only very rarely recruited, resistance of this kind was confined to a few incidents.

Discrimination in the sense of unequal access to scarce goods was more frequent at the time on the housing than the labor market. Bayer suggests that the scarcity of good housing was more of a problem for the Surinamese than the native Dutch (1965: 42ff.). In view of the housing shortage at the time, this seems very plausible. The Surinamese were sometimes openly refused access to housing, even if it was clearly vacant.[6]

The study by Bayer (1965), one of the few sources on these early postwar Surinamese immigrants, does not describe a homogeneous group solely consisting of laborers. Bayer uses the term "worker" in the broadest sense. His research population includes students working their way through school, workers who attended classes, and people who alternated between manual labor and office work. It was not always easy to draw a sharp distinction between people who were working and people who were studying.[7] Laborers, even the ones who had had a certain amount of education, were continuing their training in the Netherlands. Welder, fitter, and electrician were typical Afro-Surinamese occupations. Some of them had day jobs and then took courses in the evenings. The career of Mr. R., who is quoted above, is a good illustration.

Mr. R. (53) was twenty-one when he came to Amsterdam in 1965 with his brother on the *Willemstad*, a KNSM ship. He got a cheap larboard berth for 333 guilders. He continued on to Rotterdam, where a friend was going to help him get settled. He wound up in an attic room without any heating, any place to cook, or a shower. All it had was a cold water faucet. Although it was already May, he can still remember how cold it was. That first winter, he was horribly homesick. He had some friends who helped him through it. They came to pick him up so he didn't spend all his time alone in his room, especially on the weekends. He got to know some other people from Surinam, and one of them, whose wife had joined him, took him in as a lodger.

Mr. R. did not have to leave Surinam. In fact he had quite a good job as a welder there. But like so many young men at the time, he wanted to go off and seek his fortune in Holland. In fact you had to have a pretty good job in Surinam, otherwise you would not even be able to pay the fare. As a young boy, he always wanted to be a sailor. At school he had finished the third year of a four-year secondary school when he decided he didn't want to go on with it. He would walk around town and often go to the harbor, where he loaded and unloaded cargo if they could use an extra hand. What he was dreaming of though was to leave on a ship himself. A couple of the neighborhood boys had already become sailors. "They would come back on the KNSM ship in nice jeans and shoes. They would tell stories about how they had been in Denmark and China and Japan. They had traveled the world. So I wanted to be a sailor too and I would go to the harbor to see if I could sign up for one of those ships." His efforts were not very successful. Once he tried to go along as a stowaway, but that didn't work either. It looked like his dream wasn't going to come true.

After his "adventure as a sailor," as he calls it himself, he got a job in a match factory. After about two years, he wanted to learn welding and got a job as an apprentice welder at a construction company. They made balcony fences and oil tanks for Shell. Then he worked for Suralco in Afobaka until he went to the Netherlands. It was a good job because it paid well. Everyone wanted to work for the foreign companies, "those were the best jobs."

In the Netherlands, first Mr. R. worked for the Rotterdam Dry Dock Company, and then for Wilton-Feijenoord in Schiedam. In the meantime, he was improving his skills as a welder. Altogether it took four or five years, because he was taking one course after the other. And he was taking the courses in the evening after working all day. In the end, he had all the welding diplomas.

At the end of the 1960s he went to Germany once, selling door to door. A lot of young Surinamese men were doing that at the time. They were especially recruited by German publishers to go door to door and try to get people to subscribe to their magazines. Mr. R. still remembers the sentence they were taught to start with: "Gutentag Mutti, ich bin ein brasiliener Student." (Good afternoon, Madam, I am a Brazilian student).

After his shipyard jobs, Mr. R. worked as a welder for various subcontractors all across the Netherlands until he was classified a few years ago as physically unfit for that kind of work. He has since found a subsidized job in burglary prevention, and lives in Amsterdam with his Dutch partner.

The combination of working and taking courses required a great deal of perseverance and left very little leisure time. Bayer (1965: 62) notes how attractive the Amsterdam nightlife was with all the bars and clubs. This made it all the more difficult to attend evening classes. You had to be willing to make enormous sacrifices if you wanted to get ahead, according to the earliest immigrant in my study, and it was not something many people managed to do.

The respondents Bayer spoke to had at most completed four-year secondary school. They were part of what I refer to above as the Surinamese lower class, the part that led a regular life working or studying or combining the two. Some of them did often change jobs or had various temporary jobs, but it was still a different category from what Bayer calls "the underworld." Not that the circuits were totally separate, since people did sometimes know each other or go to the same bars or dance clubs (Bayer 1965: 79, 96). There was a difference in their lifestyle, though, and a certain distance was maintained. "Look, there have always been criminals," one respondent says, "they were there, but you just minded your own business." The important thing was not to be associated with that world. This was all the more true of the students. There was a world of difference between the lifestyle of a university student and a *wakaman* or hustler. The respondents in Bayer's study and the laborers in my own study occupy a position somewhere between the two extremes. The same is true of the white-collar workers who also arrived in the 1950s and 1960s. They were a group that gradually came to include more and more women.

White-Collar Workers

The white-collar workers were also mostly Creoles from Paramaribo. Many were teachers, nurses, and office workers. The office workers had various levels of education and experience (van Amersfoort 1968: 30). Nurses and a number of the laborers were among the few categories of employees who were recruited in Surinam. They were hired to work in the Netherlands while they attended courses. This is how one of my respondents came to the Netherlands at the age of nineteen in 1962.

During their training period in the Netherlands, the group of thirteen girls Mrs. W. (51) was part of lived on the grounds of a home for the mentally ill somewhere outside the Randstad.[8] Mrs. W. had not completed the four-year secondary school she was attending, and had worked for three years at an office. Like so many civil servants, she was taking evening courses for officials at the Surinam Law School. It was especially her mother who put pressure on her to go to the Netherlands. She had heard from her boss about opportunities for girls to be trained as nurses in the Netherlands. "I was young and there were other things on my mind, so my mother thought it would be better for me to go to the Netherlands and live in somewhere so there would be some supervision. She thought I would be able to study better that way." That was the underlying idea of her well-intentioned mother. There was no financial need for her to leave, the family was doing nicely with the two parents both employed. "At the time you really had to have a lot of money if you wanted to go and study in the Netherlands. You had to come here on a ship or a plane, and your parents had to pay your way. You didn't have anyone to stay with, you had to go to a boarding school and for that your parents had to be very well-to-do." This also held true for another daughter from the same family, who went to a boarding school in the Netherlands run by the Church of the Moravian Brethren.[9]

Mrs. W. never did complete her training. After working for two and a half years at the home for the mentally ill, she decided to leave and move from this rural environment to Amsterdam. She had already spent a lot of her time off there, going out and meeting other people from Surinam. She wasn't the only one. The girls from Surinam had been accustomed to the urban environment in Paramaribo and missed city life. In this sense, they differed from the Dutch girls at the training course, "real provincials" who didn't have any need to spend their evenings going out in a city. In Amsterdam, at first Mrs. W. stayed with a girlfriend, and it was hard but she managed to find a room for herself. Finding a job was much easier. "Jobs were a dime a dozen at the time." She applied for a job at a home for the aged and was hired immediately. She worked there for a year and a half and then applied for the same kind of office job she had had in Surinam. Once again, she had no trouble finding a job. After three and a half years, she decided to quit. By then she had a second child and had broken up with the father of her children. She started getting welfare benefits. She stayed home with the children for a couple of years, and when they were old enough to go to school alone, she went back to work. She didn't want to stay on welfare, but it was the late 1970s and times had changed. She had to apply for one job after another. In the end, she did get an office job, which she still has today.

In addition to nurses, teachers and office workers were coming to the Netherlands in this period, most of them still Creoles. Most of the female office workers I spoke to did clerical work, and the male ones were often bookkeepers. In the evenings, the men often enhanced their skills by taking courses in bookkeeping, accountancy, or economics. Studying was important to many of them, and was in fact the main reason they had come to the Netherlands. In three of the Afro-Surinamese families in my study, the husband studied, sometimes in addition to a job, and the wife worked.

Family immigration was becoming more common in this period. Husbands and wives would come together or one after the other with their small children. In the 1960s, housing was a problem for these families. Mrs. S. arrived in 1963 and lived with her husband and two children in one room. "Hardly anyone had relatives here at the time," she remembers. "I was the first of my family to come." In the beginning Mrs. E., who came to the Netherlands in 1967, had to live with her husband and four children in two rooms they sublet. Yet these immigrants had less of a problem finding housing than the single men who came to the Netherlands. Like students, the single men met with more resistance from potential landlords.[10] At any rate, the families' accounts of how they found a place to live are less distressing than those of the young men who had no choice but to rent a room in someone else's flat. Not that it was easy to find an appropriate flat, nor was it indeed easy for anyone at the time, but they came up against fewer outright refusals. "Even Dutch people couldn't find a place to live," Mrs. E. remembers. In this period, most of the Surinamese in Amsterdam were still living in the center and the older districts. The period when so many Surinamese newcomers lived in Bijlmermeer had yet to begin. Unlike the immigrants of the 1970s, most of the Surinamese who came in the 1960s lived as the only ones in all Dutch neighborhoods.

It was relatively easy for these immigrants to find a job. In the families of the few respondents who arrived in this period, the husbands and wives both worked. Their careers generally exhibit upward social mobility. Of course, there were obstacles to surmount, certainly in the beginning. The move to the Netherlands often interrupted the careers they had started in Surinam. After a certain amount of time, though, the situation usually improved and they clearly felt they were doing better. In retrospect, most of them have had a more or less stable employment career, and it is no exception for them to have held the same job for lengthy periods of time. The history of the E. family is a good example.

Mr. E. came to the Netherlands in 1966 at the age of thirty-five. He made preparations for the arrival of his wife and four children, who came a year later. They didn't have any relatives in the Netherlands yet, so they were on their own. At first they rented two rooms from a Dutch woman.

The most important reason to come to the Netherlands was that Mr. E. wanted to further his education. He had attended a four-year secondary school in Surinam and earned a living doing bookkeeping. He wanted to continue studying in the Netherlands. He got a bookkeeping job and studied for his State Practical Business Administration Diploma, which he got. He ultimately became the head of the financial division at a nonprofit organization, where he continued working until he retired.

The family had only come to the Netherlands temporarily, at least that was the idea at the time. "I just came to stay for a couple of years," Mrs. E. (60) says, "and as soon as my husband was finished studying we were going to go back. But then my oldest daughter went to the university, and the other children went on too. So then you think: Let's let the children graduate first. That is how we wound up staying. And the situation nowadays in Surinam, with all the politics and the goings on, it makes me prefer to be here. Because look, if we had gone back, who can guarantee we would have found a job? I still have a house in Surinam, so I can get up and go any time I want. But what about my children?"

Mrs. E. was a schoolteacher in Surinam. Her father had a shoe shop and he had his children continue their education after primary school. She was at a Catholic secondary school run by nuns. She was very good with little children, and they asked her to come in the afternoons after school and help with the kindergarten. Her father gave her permission, and as a schoolgirl of fourteen, she was earning forty guilders a month. After she finished the four-year secondary school, the nuns encouraged her to attend the teacher training school, which she completed at nineteen. Later, when she was already working, she went on to get her teaching certificate.

Mrs. E. comes from a family of eleven children. Her father was a good trades-
man and his shop did good business. He was not rich, but he could afford to send
his children to school. "Look, those poor people, the poorest of the poor, they
could not afford it. Even if the children were good at school, if there was not any
money for it they couldn't go to school. They had to get a job or clean houses. So
they could never get very far." The older children in the family made it easier for
the younger ones to go to school too. Mrs. E. was one of the older children in the
family, and she was already making a financial contribution when the younger
ones were still at school.

In the Netherlands, her husband didn't feel it was necessary for Mrs. E. to start
working right away. But they were living in two rooms and she had enough of
being at home all day, so she got a job. She asked a friend if she didn't know of
something for her to do, and her friend suggested cleaning work, which was
something she could start doing right away. She took her advice, and was soon in
charge of a team of workers.

When they got their first flat and Mrs. E. wanted to earn some money to make
life more comfortable, she applied for a teaching job. She didn't keep the job for
long, since it was outside Amsterdam and traveling back and forth was too much
for her. She had four children to take care of, and her husband was studying. She
had several other jobs that were not in the teaching field and were below her educational level. She was a hard worker and often had a couple of jobs at the same
time. She didn't mind working in the evenings or on the weekend either. She ultimately got a job in Surinamese youth welfare work, which she held quite happily
until she had to stop a few years ago for health reasons.

Except regarding housing, these immigrants barely made any mention of discrimination. It might have to do with their polite and favorably disposed attitude
to the host country, but this was not the sole factor. The period of arrival also
plays a role, as is evident from their references to the later immigrants or their
own children who entered the labor market at a later stage: they had a much
harder time of it. In this sense, the experiences of these immigrants are similar
to those of the laborers described above, be it that the laborers also might have
had a harder time at the work site itself. The experiences of these immigrants
also confirm the conclusion of earlier studies that the experiences of discrimination of the Surinamese vary according to the period of time and the circumstances (Vermeulen 1984).

The First Indo-Surinamese Immigrants

No exact figures are available on the Indo-Surinamese in the Netherlands in
the 1950s and 1960s. However, we know that they were a very small part of
the total Surinamese population in the Netherlands at the time. Van Amersfoort

conducted a study in the late 1960s on the early Indo-Surinamese immigrants in Amsterdam. In 1968 he estimated the Surinamese population in the Netherlands at 18,000, only 10 percent of whom were Indo-Surinamese (1970: 113).

Like the Afro-Surinamese, the first Indo-Surinamese immigrants came to complete their education in the Netherlands. Only they came in a much later period. Juglall (1963), one of the first prewar Indo-Surinamese students in the Netherlands himself (Oostindie 1986: 37), refers to "a few dozen" Indo-Surinamese youngsters who came to the Netherlands after World War II to study. There were to be more and more of them after 1955. In 1963, Juglall estimates the number of Indo-Surinamese students in the Netherlands at 660 (1963: 88). They were nonetheless still strongly underrepresented in the total Surinamese student population. In 1967, the Indo-Surinamese were only 14 percent of the total number of Surinamese students registered at Dutch universities (Sedoc-Dahlberg 1971: 20-21). It was not until later that more Indo-Surinamese students began to attend Dutch colleges and universities. The Indo-Surinamese had, however, already started their educational progress. It is striking that in the 1960s, a larger percentage of Indo-Surinamese than Afro-Surinamese university students were from a poor background, as is evident from the Ph. D. dissertation by Sedoc-Dahlberg (1971: 181). She examined the backgrounds of various ethnic groups of Surinamese students registered at Dutch universities in 1967. Table 4.1 is based on data from her study.[11]

Table 4.1 *Backgrounds of Afro-Surinamese and Indo-Surinamese students registered at Dutch universities in 1967 (in percentages)*

	Afro-Surinamese	Indo-Surinamese
higher class	26	10
middle class	54	40
lower class	21	50
absolute total (=100%)	535	112

Source: Sedoc-Dahlberg (1971: 181).

No fewer than half the Indo-Surinamese students in the Netherlands at the time were thus from the lower class, which was only true of 21 percent of the Afro-Surinamese students. The higher class was two to three times as strongly represented among the Afro-Surinamese students.

Based again on what my respondents say, upward mobility was already witnessed within this first generation of early Indo-Surinamese immigrants.

Mr. U. came to the Netherlands in 1966 at the age of twenty-six. Already trained as a schoolteacher, he wanted to continue his education in the Netherlands. He studied at the University of Leiden and went on to teach at a technical college. He was from a large simple East Indian family that lived on the outskirts of Para-maribo. The family worked hard and was able to support itself, often by doing all kinds of farm work. There were sizeable occupational and educational level differences within the family. An older brother of Mr. U. had very little schooling and became a tailor, a common occupation in the East Indian community at the time, but a younger brother of his went on to become a medical specialist.

That is often the way it went. The older children had to help the family make ends meet, and thanks in part to their efforts, the younger ones could continue their education.

Sheila (33), who came to the Netherlands as a child in 1975, remembers how things went in her family. Her father was the oldest in a large family and never had a chance to get an education. But the whole family supported his youngest brother, Sheila's uncle, when he went to the Netherlands in the 1960s to study medicine. His return to Surinam as a doctor made so much of an impression on everyone who stayed behind that Sheila still remembers: "Oh it was such a grand event when he came back, the whole family stayed up because he came late at night. Not just the family, the people from the neighborhood too. Oh what a celebration! He had been away for I don't know how long. He was the first to go to the Netherlands. It was really something special at the time. They sent him whatever he needed, rice and things like that. Because you didn't have it yet in the Netherlands, they didn't know about good rice. So my parents supported him from Surinam, they really stimulated him. It wasn't like he was gone and we didn't have anything to do with him any more. My parents did everything because my father was the oldest, so all the money came from him. Of course we wanted my uncle to get his medical degree. Back in those days, things were hard for the Surinamese in the Netherlands. Very hard. Now you can get anything you want in the supermarket around the corner, but it was not like that then. Now any vegetable you can think of is on sale at the market. But then there were just potatoes, and it was so cold. You had to do without the simplest things. And he was all alone and had to take care of himself. All alone in a room, and freezing! But he made it and he came back! What a grand day that was!"

Unlike the Creole elite and middle class, East Indian families were still not accustomed to sending their sons to study in the Netherlands. As Sheila relates, it was a grand event that involved the whole family. After they graduated, East Indians were more apt than Creoles to return to Surinam, where they had better opportunities for upward mobility. This had to do with the pillarized way Surinamese society was organized, and the fact that the East Indians were still lagging behind in the field of education (van Amersfoort 1970: 129).

The early Indo-Surinamese immigrants were not all students. Like the Afro-Surinamese, some of them also came to work and not just to study but very little is known about them. We do have some information though on how many Indo-Surinamese were living in Amsterdam at the time. Van Amersfoort (1970) estimates that 450 of the total of 9,000 Surinamese living in Amsterdam in 1968 were Indo-Surinamese, and notes that about half of them were civil servants and schoolteachers. They were often young people who had attended a four-year secondary school and wanted to advance by attending courses. They often considered themselves "students." The other half, according to van Amersfoort, were laborers as well as students, though there were far fewer Indo-Surinamese than Afro-Surinamese laborers.

Like the students, the laborers in this first generation of immigrants moved up from the low social position they had occupied in Surinam. The children of these early immigrants thus started their school careers from a relatively favorable position, since their parents had a good education or a good social position. This category was certainly evident as well among the early Afro-Surinamese immigrants, as is noted above, but among them there was already more of a distribution as regards social class than among the Indo-Surinamese.

Immigrants of the 1970s and 1980s

The large majority of Surinamese immigrants arrived in the 1970s and 1980s. The two largest waves of immigration brought approximately 80,000 newcomers from Surinam to the Netherlands. They have now been here for twenty to twenty-five years. In this section, I examine how they settled in the Netherlands, how they have done on the Dutch labor market, and the mobility patterns evident there.

Migrating and Settling

There are repeated references in the literature on Surinam to the fact that the move to the city virtually always preceded the move to the Netherlands. This whole process was closely linked to the emancipation of various segments of the Surinamese population. The Creoles went first, and they were followed by the Asians and other groups. There was somewhat of a change in this multistage pattern at the time of the mass exodus in 1974 and 1975, when more and more East Indians also left the country directly from the countryside. By the mid-1970s, almost a quarter of the total number of emigrants were leaving directly from the Surinamese countryside to the Netherlands (Reubsaet et al. 1982: 53).

Thus the two groups have different geographical origins. Most of the East Indians did come from Paramaribo or the immediate vicinity, but they had settled more recently in the city than the Creoles. The Creole residence in Paramaribo covered more generations than the East Indian residence there,[12] and there is clear evidence of this in my research population. With only a few exceptions, all the Afro-Surinamese families are from Paramaribo. They had lived there for generations. Only a few of the older respondents were not born in the city. They are from the districts of Coronie or Para. Most of the East Indian families also come from Paramaribo or the semi-urban areas around it. Many of these families had not, however, lived there that long; approximately half the older people were not born in the city. They come from several districts, including Saramacca and Nickerie. So within a relatively short period of time, these families had moved twice, once from the countryside to the city of Paramaribo, and once from there to the Netherlands. Only a minority of the Indo-Surinamese families in my study moved directly from the countryside (in this case from the districts of Surinam and Nickerie) to the Netherlands. The history of the S. family is an example of the multistage migration of many Indo-Surinamese families.

The father of Mrs. S. (41) moved from the interior of the country (Para) to the city and settled near Lelydorp. His major means of support was the sale of milk. Initially he only sold the milk of his own cows, but later he also bought and sold the milk of other people's cows. He did it all by bike. He managed to save up enough from buying and selling milk to buy a plot of land on the outskirts of the town for 70 or 80 guilders in the 1950s. So he made a second move further in the direction of Paramaribo. In addition to the sale of milk, he began to sell other products such as rice and oils. At first he sold them on the market, but after he saved up enough, he had a little shop built for 90 guilders. Saving and then investing further, according to his daughter this was how he kept on expanding his business. "My father was very clever," she recounts. "He was very business-like. He did not have much education, he just went to primary school up until the sixth grade, but he had a good business sense." He earned quite a bit of money when the city expanded and bought up part of his property. Mr. S. started out as a very poor man, but left his children quite a bit. As an extended family, they continued to live on the family property, where a number of houses had since been built. A number of his children and grandchildren left for the Netherlands in the 1970s.

This account illustrates how geographical mobility was accompanied by socioeconomic mobility.

Compared with the Afro-Surinamese, the Indo-Surinamese had far fewer relatives to rely on when they arrived in the Netherlands in this period. Although most of the Surinamese immigrants who arrived shortly before Surinam gained independence had to rely on the Dutch government to help them out when they first arrived, this was more true of the Indo-Surinamese. The Afro-Surinamese immigrants, at least the ones in my study, were more apt than the Indo-Surinamese to go directly to the large cities. A number of Indo-Surinamese families originally settled outside the Randstad, sometimes as far away as the provinces of Limburg or Friesland, and later moved to the Randstad.

Many of the immigrants have improved their housing situation since their arrival in the Netherlands. The conduct of the Indo-Surinamese on the housing market is striking in this connection. Although they generally do not occupy a better labor market position than the Afro-Surinamese, nor are their incomes any higher, they nonetheless more frequently own their own homes. Perhaps the fact that they had fewer relatives to put them up when they first came to the Netherlands put more pressure on them to purchase property. Reubsaet et al. (1982: 80) note that the Surinamese in The Hague purchased homes relatively frequently; in 1979 almost half of them lived in homes that belonged to them personally or to the head of the household they were part of. In Amsterdam this was only true of 5 percent. The researchers conclude that the Surinamese in The Hague viewed the purchase of a home as a way to solve their housing problem, and not necessarily as something they wanted to do. Since The Hague had less subsidized housing than Amsterdam, this certainly sounds plausible. The question is whether it completely explains the differences between the purchasing patterns of the Surinamese in The Hague and Amsterdam. Among the Indo-Surinamese, there also seems to be a continuation of a property ownership pattern that already existed in Surinam; there too, the East Indians were more apt to own their own homes than the Creoles. In part, this has to do with the difference between urban and rural living; in the countryside, people often own their own homes. Even in the towns, though, the East Indians are more apt to own their own homes than the Creoles. If the East Indians do rent a flat, it is almost always in the nonsubsidized sector. There are barely any East Indians living in the subsidized housing projects funded by the authorities (Schalkwijk and de Bruijne 1997: 92-93).

When they left Surinam, the East Indians frequently sold all their possessions just to be able to pay the fare and then buy another home in the Netherlands. Sometimes a few families did it together. Several of the families in my study purchased a large house and shared it with the families of their brothers. The Indo-Surinamese not only more frequently own their own homes, but also they more frequently act as landlords. At any rate, this is something I came across among my Indo-Surinamese and not my Afro-Surinamese respondents. In Surinam as well, the East Indians are more commercially minded than the Creoles as regards owning and renting out property.[13]

A number of the Creole families who did own their own home in Surinam kept it after they left. It is often family property that has not been divided up among the legal heirs for generations. There is often some close or distant relative living there, who usually pays a small amount of rent. The idea is not so much to make money as to have someone looking after the house. Ever since the enormous inflation of the early 1990s, it has not been much of a money-earning proposition anyway, since after it is converted into Dutch currency, the rent in Surinamese guilders would not amount to much. This is why nowadays a house in Surinam is viewed more as a burden than an asset, certainly if the tenant expects the owner to be responsible for the upkeep. In these cases, it is more for emotional than financial reasons that people keep a house in Surinam.

However, the high inflation also created lucrative opportunities for the Dutch Surinamese. With hard Dutch currency, they were at a great advantage on the Surinamese housing market. Homes were purchased from the Netherlands to live in later or just to have as an investment. I heard about several cases of Dutch Surinamese homeowners having Surinamese locals rent out their property for them there, and in Dutch guilders.

Unemployment and Decline in Status

How did the first generation from Surinam do on the labor market in the Netherlands? What were their skills and job experience worth in the Dutch context? We know many members of this first generation did not have much of an education, often little more than primary school, and had a hard time getting started. This generation included numerous Indo-Surinamese immigrants whose rural background and relatively recent move to the city were largely to blame for their poor starting position. Not only was the quality of the schools in the countryside poorer, the quantity was limited as well. For further education, you had to go to the city. East Indians in the countryside thus either had to have relatives in Paramaribo who they could live with or had to go to a boarding school. So there were any number of obstacles that anyone who wanted to get a better education had to surmount. For a long time, the Catholic Church played an important role in this connection,[14] a role somewhat comparable to the role the Church of the Moravian Brethren played for the Creoles. Various older Indo-Surinamese respondents received their entire education from members of the Catholic clergy. The other side of the coin was that they were often expected to convert to Catholicism. In general, however, members of the older Indo-Surinamese generation had not had much education at all, even if they did come from the city.

Apart from the limited opportunities, a good education was not always necessary to earn a living or even reach a certain level of prosperity. This held true in the traditionally most important East Indian economic niches, farming and trade. Especially in Nickerie, which was reasonably prosperous, an uneducated rice farmer could have a business that earned him a relatively high status and good income. Material prosperity did not necessarily require a good education. The same held true in other branches of entrepreneurship, for example, for people who worked as street or market vendors, shopkeepers, and craftsmen. Craftsmanship was often acquired on the job, and a formal education was not always called for. It also meant it was easy to switch from one line of work to another. A sixty-year-old East Indian in Surinam told me he had been working as a carpenter and tailor as well as a fisherman and painter. In other sectors of the labor market, however, training was more important. Anyone who wanted a job with the government, the police, or the school system had to have certain diplomas.

The jobs the Indo-Surinamese men in my research population had in Surinam can be divided into four categories: farming, skilled crafts (e.g., tailors, carpenters), commerce, and teaching. I use the term commerce in the widest sense; I define the sector as including people who sold their own farm products on the market as well as the retail and wholesale trade, street vendors, and representatives and buyers for chain stores The people in the farming sector did virtually all their farm work part-time. They also had other jobs, mainly as shopkeepers or market sellers, but also as assistant schoolteachers, police officers, civil servants, or chauffeurs. Once they arrived in the Netherlands, their skills and job experience did not always prove to be relevant. As a result, many of them could not work in their old field or at the same occupational level, that is if they could find a job at all. They were mainly self-employed people who worked in the farming or trade sectors and artisans.

Mr. M. (54) came from a poor peasant family. His father had only a small plot of land and could not leave enough behind for his children to live on. This is why in addition to doing farm work on his plot of land, Mr. M. had to work as a chauffeur for a large-scale farm. From the moment he arrived in the Netherlands, though in 1975, he never worked again. Nor did his wife. She too came from a peasant family and started helping to plant and harvest rice when she was young. She was able to finish primary school and then got a sewing certificate. After she was married, she helped out with the farm work, did the housework, and sometimes made clothing and sold it to a little shop, thus supplementing the family income. Mr. and Mrs. M. were both musical and would get paid for singing at weddings and religious occasions. In the Netherlands, the family got welfare benefits and supplemented them with what they earned doing the same things they had done in Surinam.

Mr. H. (47) was from a large peasant family in the district of Saramacca. In addition to doing farm work, his father sold car parts and lumber. In Paramaribo, Mr. H. earned a living as a tailor. He only finished primary school, but he acquired the required skills on the job. In 1978 he came to The Hague with his wife and children. He could not work as a tailor there without the appropriate diplomas. He would make something for someone now and then, but he could not officially do this work. If he had any job at all, it was a temporary one through an employment agency. At the time of my study, he had been classified as unable to work for some time. His wife (40), also from a peasant family in Saramacca, got married when she was seventeen and never worked outside the home in either Surinam or the Netherlands.

These two families are no exception. Many of the immigrants never worked again after they came to the Netherlands. The ones who did manage to find a place on the labor market often had to accept a job of a completely different kind or at a lower level than in Surinam. Self-employed people without any credentials usually had no choice but to do unskilled work.

In Surinam Mr. L. (73) did farm work in the district of Saramacca. He rented a six-hectare plot of land, cultivated rice and vegetables there and had some cows. He also did some work for the Ministry of Agriculture, Cattle Breeding and Fishing. He feels he had a good life in Surinam, and he was quite happy living there. But things went downhill after Surinam became independent, which is why he left in 1979. One of the first things he did when he arrived was respond to an advertisement in the newspaper. He got the job, but he soon discovered he did not meet with the requirements. He had to drive a fork-lift truck, something he had never done before. It was not long before he found a job at a dairy product factory that did not require any special skills. Mr. L. was fifty-one at the time, and worked at the factory until he qualified for early retirement.

Mr. S. came from what was originally a farming family that, like so many others, had switched from farming to the market and retail trade. He came to the Netherlands in 1975 with his wife and children. Since he had not had much more than a primary school education, he had no choice but to accept a job doing unskilled work. In the Netherlands he earned a living as a stockroom clerk, whereas in Surinam he had been a respected man with a responsible job in the family business.

The situation these two men found themselves in was much the same for many of their peers who had been petty farmers or self-employed entrepreneurs in Surinam. Once they got to the Netherlands, they had to accept jobs doing unskilled work like stocking shelves, cleaning, packing, or driving. It often meant a painful decline in status.

An occupational change was not, however, invariably perceived as a decline in status. Depending on the circumstances, many farmers had already worked for wages in Surinam. If the proceeds from their farm produce were barely enough to live on, working for wages often meant some necessary extra income, and thus a material improvement. At any rate quite a few Indo-Surinamese immigrants started out by working in the Dutch industrial sector, as did so many of the Surinamese who arrived in the second half of the 1970s (Dagevos 1998: 28). Various of my respondents initially worked at one of the factories in Twente or Brabant, and they didn't move to The Hague until later. Their jobs almost always involved unskilled work. Many of these people later lost their jobs, qualified for disability benefits or left of their own accord. In general, disability rates are relatively high among Indo-Surinamese men (see tables 3 and 4, appendix 3).[15] Although many Indo-Surinamese immigrants have probably also since disappeared from the industrial sector, they are still slightly overrepresented there in comparison with the Afro-Surinamese (Martens 1999: 143).

The transition to the Netherlands was not as great for the Afro-Surinamese as it was for many Indo-Surinamese. On the average, the Afro-Surinamese were not only better educated, they often had occupations it was easier to continue working at. Starting in the 1960s, the lower-class Afro-Surinamese predominantly worked in three Dutch sectors: the industrial sector, especially the steel industry, the administrative sector, and the care sector.

In the 1970s, more than half the male Surinamese labor force had factory jobs or worked as artisans (Reubsaet et al. 1982: 143). This also held true for the city of Amsterdam separately (Gooskens et al. 1979b: 66). The steel industry occupied an important position in this sector. I have noted that many Afro-Surinamese men had been steelworkers and welders in Surinam. In the 1960s, there were plenty of job opportunities in the steel and shipbuilding industries in the Netherlands, but this was less and less the case in the 1970s and afterward. Many steelworkers lost their jobs, and in Amsterdam this even occurred to the extent that it affected the entire unemployment picture. At the time of the mass Surinamese influx into Amsterdam in 1975, unemployment rates in the steel industry were mushrooming (Gooskens et al. 1979a: 99).

Some of the Afro-Surinamese men in my research population had been skilled or unskilled laborers in Surinam, either with a permanent job or a temporary one in the informal sector. In a number of cases, skilled laborers could continue working at more or less the same kind of job, though it did not always mean an improvement in their position.

> Mr. V. had worked as a welder for the Surinam Aluminium Company for about ten years in Surinam. After he came to the Netherlands in 1971, he continued in this line of work, but at various jobs. After two periods of time spent back in Surinam, he returned to the Netherlands in 1988. Ever since then he has been working "here and there," and at the moment he has a harbor job in Amsterdam.

> Mr. N. (75) used to work on a ship as a first mate. After his wife died, he had to come ashore to take care of the children. First he worked in various technical occupations in Surinam and then, starting in 1979, he did the same in the Netherlands. His last job was on the maintenance staff at a factory.

It was not possible for all the Afro-Surinamese laborers to continue working in their former occupation or find a related job. The unemployment rates rose, even among skilled workers, and for the growing category of unskilled workers, it was extremely difficult to get a job. Like Indo-Surinamese men, Afro-Surinamese men often had to do unskilled work, or they too would be out of a job. In this sense, immigration to the Netherlands had a leveling effect. Despite their totally different positions in Surinam, once they got to the Netherlands the Indo-Surinamese petty entrepreneurs and Afro-Surinamese laborers sometimes found themselves in much the same situation.

In addition to the men who did or didn't have a job, there was a category of women who disappeared from the labor market after the move and became housewives or qualified for welfare benefits. The group included Indo-Surinamese as well as Afro-Surinamese women, although for different reasons. In Surinam, especially near the city, farming was only a part-time activity for many East Indian men. It was mainly the women who stayed behind to do the farming.[16] In Surinam they could combine their domestic chores with the farm work or a job in some other capacity in the family business, but in the Netherlands there was no way for them to continue their work or occupation. Unaccustomed as they were to working for wages outside the home, in the Netherlands they withdrew into the household.

Some of the poorly educated Afro-Surinamese women also found it impossible to continue doing the work they were used to after they came to the Netherlands. Some of them had worked in the informal sector in Paramaribo, doing sewing, ironing, or laundry, and some had sold their wares at the market. Many had been housekeepers and cleaning ladies for middle-class families, a practice dating back to colonial times when they worked in the homes of the European or Creole elite. This domestic work was often done by self-supporting female heads of households, and to a lesser extent by married women (Buschkens 1974: 149). In their absence, these single mothers had to have someone watch their children. If the grandmother was not able to take care of the children, other arrangements had to be made. This required a great deal of organizational skill, and sometimes there was no solution but to leave the children alone. So it is no wonder that once the absolute need to go out and earn a living was alleviated after the move to the Netherlands, many women no longer gave a job outside the home such a high priority.

This is, however, only one side of the coin. The rules and regulations on mothers with young children who are on welfare constitute the other side. At the time, these women were not under any obligation to look for a job; this was supposed to give them the opportunity to tend to their family. What is more, employers were not eager to hire women who had the sole responsibility for looking after a family (Lenders and van Vlijmen-van de Rhoer 1983: 31ff.). As a result, employment agencies had a hard time placing single mothers with young children. This not only had to do with the prevailing notion that women with children ought to stay home (up until recently, the labor market participation of Dutch women was relatively low),[17] it was also linked to the widespread unemployment of the 1970s. The criteria determining whether or not people were hard to place had to do with the relation between the labor supply and demand (Gooskens et al. 1979a: 100). On the one hand, these women were more or less forced to stop working once they got to the Netherlands, but on the other they were only too happy to take advantage of the opportunity to devote their time to taking care of their family. The shortage of babysitters and child care facilities and the relatively low wages in comparison with the welfare benefits, especially for poorly educated women who—as single parents—preferred to only work part-time, were factors that made matters even more complicated.[18]

The relation between the labor supply and demand influenced the position of poorly educated Afro-Surinamese men in much the same way. Men from the Creole working class often had some technical skills, but many had little formal education (Buschkens 1974: 146-47). They were the ones who had done odd jobs in Surinam, often in the informal sector. The structure of the job market in Surinam was such that there was a shortage of skilled workers, but very little place for the unskilled. However, it was not only their lack of training and relevant job experience that made it so hard for these male immigrants in the Netherlands. The official agencies in Amsterdam alluded to the "maladjusted" or "deviant" behavior of Surinamese workers that made them less appropriate for the local labor market or hard to place. Some employers even told the official employment agencies they were not willing to hire any workers from Surinam (Gooskens et al. 1979a: 100). A number of these poorly educated young Afro-Surinamese men were unemployed for lengthy periods of time, others started receiving welfare benefits and disappeared in essence from the labor market. For many of them, long-term welfare dependency was the result.

So in sum, despite their urban background, higher average educational level, and more relevant job experience, some of the Afro-Surinamese in the Netherlands wound up in much the same position as the Indo-Surinamese at the lowest ranks of the labor market. What is more, for the Indo-Surinamese, the transition from the work they had done in Surinam to their jobs in the Netherlands often meant a decline in status. But many members of both these groups found jobs requiring only very elementary skills, if any, became unemployed, or disappeared from the labor market altogether. At the end of the 1970s, the poorly educated Afro-Surinamese men and the formerly self-employed Indo-Surinamese men constituted what was referred to as the hard core of the Surinamese unemployed (Reubsaet et al. 1982: 154).

Occupational Continuity and Upward Mobility

To what extent could Afro-Surinamese and Indo-Surinamese immigrants in the Netherlands continue to work at the same occupations as in Surinam, and to what extent did they have to switch to new kinds of work? On the basis of my research data, I conclude that at any rate in a number of occupations, there was a striking continuity. This was more often the case among the Afro-Surinamese than the Indo-Surinamese, and more among the women than the men of both groups. The occupations with the greatest continuity were in the administrative sector, the care sector, and the educational sector.

In the 1970s, approximately a third of the Surinamese in the Netherlands in general and Amsterdam in particular were employed in the administration, financial, organization and management sector (Gooskens et al. 1979b: 66; Reubsaet et al. 1982: 143). In my research population, this pertains to Afro-Surinamese men and women and Indo-Surinamese women who had also done office work in Surinam. Indo-Surinamese men had far less frequently been employed in this sector in Surinam.[19] In Surinam office jobs, particularly civil service jobs, were traditionally the realm of the Creoles, although this has changed in recent times.[20] A civil service job might not have been very lucrative, but it did provide a certain degree of security and you didn't have to work very hard. This was quite different from the private sector, where there was less security and you had to work harder, but the earnings were also higher.[21] At any rate, office work had quite a high status, and apparently was a route many immigrants took in the Netherlands. And there were ample opportunities to do so at the time. In a sense, the prospects for Surinamese immigrants were better in this sector than in the industrial sector. In view of the structure of the Dutch labor market with so many government institutions and service industries, it is not surprising that numerous Surinamese immigrants were employed in the administration, financial, organization, and management sector (Reubsaet et al. 1982: 144). It was even true that immigrants who had not worked in this sector in Surinam did so after they came to the Netherlands (1982: 143). They usually held lower-level jobs that did not require more than a four-year secondary school diploma. In the course of time, however, the prospects at this level became less favorable when computer technology led to the disappearance of many simpler jobs. So although the administration and financial sector did account for numerous jobs in the 1970s, many of the lower-level jobs in the sector later disappeared.

Another sector that allowed for a large extent of occupational continuity was the care sector with jobs in the social and medical field. Virtually exclusively the realm of women, it was traditionally a field where many Creole women had worked, though this later changed. The Afro-Surinamese women in my study who had worked in this sector in Surinam cared for the aged and the ill and worked as nurses. The overrepresentation of Surinamese women in the care and nursing sector in the Netherlands in the 1970s (Reubsaet et al. 1982: 142-43) is probably largely based on the role of Afro-Surinamese women. However, Indo-Surinamese women also increasingly worked in this sector in the Netherlands, at any rate the ones in my study did. Women who had worked in the care sector in Surinam could not completely carry on as before, but the changes were not that sizeable, as is illustrated by the careers of two Afro-Surinamese women.

Mrs. T. (42) had a nurse's aide certificate and had done that work in Paramaribo. She came to the Netherlands in 1978 and worked at various nursing homes. Via an employment agency, she was employed at a hospital in the section where plaster casts were made. From there, she applied for another job at the same hospital on a nursing ward, which is where she continued to work.

Mrs. F. (52) only finished primary school. Before she left for the Netherlands in 1973, she worked in the homes of two Dutch families. She took care of the children and did domestic chores. In the Netherlands, at first she worked in the kitchen at a home for the aged. Then she started helping with the care of the aged, which is what she still does.

As is clear from both these examples, it was possible for women to build up a stable career and even make some progress. Since then, the prospects in this sector have only gotten better because the number of jobs increased sharply (Kloosterman and Elfring 1991: 195). It is relatively common for Surinamese immigrants to work in the care sector.[22]

Another occupational sector in Surinam that employs relatively many though not exclusively women is the kindergarten and primary school system. Teaching there used to be a predominantly Creole occupation. In the early 1970s, it was still true that more Creoles than East Indians were teachers in Surinam, and more Creole than East Indian women (Volkstelling [Census] 1971/1972). According to various respondents, teaching also gradually became an approved profession for East Indian girls that provided an income and a certain status. In my research population, the teachers came from the lower socioeconomic circles in Surinam. In his study on the Creole lower class, Buschkens (1974: 149) concludes that despite their education, in part teachers can be classified as belonging to the lower class. Most of them have a lower-class background and the salaries of young teachers are lower than those of skilled laborers.

In Surinam, education was one of the few routes to upward mobility. However, there were considerable differences in the quality of the various teachers' training programs. Some of my respondents worked in the countryside as teaching assistants even though they themselves had little more than a primary school education.[23] What is more, there were different levels in the official teachers' training courses.[24] In other words, there were differences between the quality of the teachers' training, which were reflected in the chances they had on the Dutch labor market. In general, they had a hard time finding teaching jobs in the Netherlands. Teachers who were not qualified to teach in the Netherlands had to either switch to another line of work or first get additional training. Due to the high unemployment rates among teachers in the Netherlands at the time, even the ones with the right qualifications often had a hard time finding a job.[25] In addition, the Surinamese job experience and teaching style did not always meet the Dutch requirements. This is why some teachers decided to leave the profession. All things considered, teaching was not a sector where it was easy for first-generation immigrants to continue doing the same kind of work they had done in Surinam, although a number of them certainly did succeed. For others, an advanced teaching certificate could give them a good start in a different career, sometimes at a higher level.

The way first-generation immigrants had to switch from one occupation to another cannot be simply explained in general terms. The following account of an Indo-Surinamese couple illustrates the occupational mobility that was often experienced, due in part to the circumstances. Mr. and Mrs. R. both had lower-level teaching certificates and had worked in Surinam at a rural school.

Mrs. R. (48) came to the Netherlands in 1979 with her husband and two small children. They initially moved in with her parents-in-law in Oldenzaal. Via her brother, her husband could get a job doing unskilled work at a fuse box factory there. "The hours were irregular," Mrs. R. relates, "and he really had to get used to it. It was hard work, and he had to wear those rubber gloves and boots and goggles . . . He wasn't eating properly. You know life was very different here, and there was the climate. And we were living with all those relatives in one house." But they didn't have any choice. All they had was a three-month visa and they still had to get their residence permit. "You had to start somewhere," Mrs. R. says. "If you don't have a job, you don't get a residence permit, and without a residence permit you don't get a house!" And after the Foreigners Act was passed, a work permit was required. This meant trouble for her husband. The company couldn't keep him on without getting fined, so they let him go. Mr. and Mrs. R. both kept applying for any job they could get until they were at their wits' end and were already considering going back to Surinam. "Because I couldn't stand living in fear that one day they would pick you up and put you on the boat or . . . I didn't want that, because I didn't deserve it. No, the way I felt was that I had not done anything to deserve that." But she preferred not to think about going back to Surinam, because they would have had to start from scratch there. Fortunately something happened that saved them just in time. Via an acquaintance, Mr. R. could get a job in Leiden at a typewriter factory. They rented a room in The Hague, and a company bus took him to Leiden every day. For the time being, they left the children with their grandparents in Oldenzaal. To Mrs. R., that was the worst part of it. Not that the children were not being properly taken care of, not at all, it was just that she had never had to leave them with anyone else before, "and it happened here of all places!"

At any rate, it gave them "a break," as Mrs. R. calls it. "Then at the end of the month we thought that as soon as he gets his first wages, we'll be able to go visit the children." The job Mr. R. now had also enabled them to get a residence permit and start looking for a flat. They found a tiny overpriced flat in the Schilderswijk, an old inner-city neighborhood in The Hague. They felt 500 guilders was an exorbitant rent they had to pay, but at least they could have the children living with them.

Things did not go well for Mrs. R. Unable to find a job, she was home all day and soon started seeing a doctor. He took one look at where she was living and decided to do something about it. He advised her to register at the Labor Office and though it did take some time, in the end she found a job doing secretarial work at one of the ministries.

By then her husband had found a better job as a conductor for the Netherlands Railroad. He took a training course and was later promoted to chief conductor. He was suffering from fatigue at the time and did not look well, and a social worker helped the family get a better place to live. There were two salaries coming in now, which meant a big step forwards. They could rent a good flat in a better neighborhood. The worst times were over. A year later, they were even able to move to a single-family home in a small town outside The Hague, where they lived happily for several years. In the course of time though, it became hard for Mrs. R. to travel back and forth to work, so they moved again to a house they rented in Rijswijk on the outskirts of The Hague. By then Mr. R. had been classified as no longer able to work. Mrs. R. was still working at the ministry, but ever since a reorganization there she was now working as a receptionist.

Up to now, I have examined the mobility between various occupations or sectors. To what extent was there also a change in the occupational *level*? In other words, how much job level mobility was there? After they came to the Netherlands, in the first instance many immigrants, the Indo-Surinamese more than the Afro-Surinamese, would seem to have experienced a job level decline. However, in the course of time, there was a certain increase again. I draw this conclusion based on my qualitative research data. There is some support for it in the quantitative material if I compare the job level of the last job in Surinam with the level of the first and present job in the Netherlands (see table 5, appendix 3).[26]

The most striking pattern among the first-generation immigrants is a process I refer to as resource accumulation. There is a considerable difference between the Indo-Surinamese and Afro-Surinamese immigrants as regards the nature of these resources. Whereas the accumulation of economic resources is more characteristic of the Indo-Surinamese, the accumulation of educational qualifications is typical of the Afro-Surinamese.

In Surinam, many East Indians were already accustomed to engaging in various economic activities at the same time. As is noted above, East Indian farm workers often did this work only part-time and were engaged in various other activities as well, usually in the trade and transport sectors. In the city, it was not unusual to combine a regular job as a teacher or civil servant with working "for yourself." In the Netherlands, an adaptation of this same pattern has emerged. The F. family, consisting of a father, a mother, a son, and a daughter, is a good example. After they arrived in the Netherlands, the parents began with a combination of jobs, a small restaurant, and cleaning work.

Mr. and Mrs. F. came from Paramaribo to the Netherlands in 1974 with their two small children. Mr. F. (46) had been a textile salesman at Kirpalana, one of the two large department stores in Paramaribo. He finished primary school and that was pretty much all the education he had. The same is true of Mrs. F. She is from Nickerie, where as a young girl she helped out in her mother's grocery shop until she got married. Her father was a rice farmer. In the Netherlands, Mr. F. worked as a stockroom clerk at a department store, where he was later promoted to stockroom manager. Two years later, his wife got a job at the same department store, first serving in the canteen and later as a cashier. She worked there for a total of nine years.

In addition to their jobs, Mr. and Mrs. F. opened a small restaurant, where they worked in the evenings. As soon as she was finished with her day's work at the department store, Mrs. F. would get started at the restaurant. They did this for some time, until a fire broke out and the restaurant was closed down. Then the couple took a cleaning job together for the evenings, while they were both still working at the department store. It was "key work," in other words they were responsible for cleaning an entire building, in their case a bank. Every day there was eight hours of cleaning work to do, four hours for each of them. But they could finish up in two hours if they worked hard. Not that they didn't do a good job—there were never any complaints—they just worked well and quickly. And if one of them was sick, their son or daughter had to help out. This way they kept the cleaning job for themselves. Their double income soon enabled them to buy their own home in the Netherlands.

After a reorganization at the department store, they both lost their jobs. Then Mrs. F. had a job serving coffee for six months, but her contract was not renewed. After she had worked for some time as a substitute at a supermarket in the neighborhood, she was able to get a permanent job there. When their son started his own business, they gradually both started working there, as did their daughter.

It is not that unusual in the Indo-Surinamese community to have a job and a business of your own at the same time. People also sometimes have two jobs, or generate double incomes in other ways.

Mr. C. (47) came to the Netherlands in 1975. He took a short technical training course and found a job as a mechanic. He has since had the same job for seventeen years. When the company moved, he and his family stayed in The Hague, so he now has to travel quite a distance every day. He leaves at six o'clock in the morning and gets home at four-thirty. He still manages to have a cleaning job for two evenings a week. He and his wife and four children live in a flat they rent from the city, but he also owns another flat that is too small for his family, which he rents out. He would like to buy the six-room flat he now lives in from the city, but it is not possible.

So Mr. C. has three sources of income: a regular job, the cleaning work in the evenings, and the flat he rents out. Mrs. S., to cite another example, has four sources of income: she has a regular job, works as a seamstress and makes clothes for people, grows vegetables, and rents out flats.

I did not see any evidence among my Afro-Surinamese respondents of this pattern of various economic activities and sources of income, at any rate not in these forms. Some early immigrants did have two jobs, but I did not speak to anyone who had a job and a business of his own or who had a job and rented out flats. What I did see more evidence of among the Afro-Surinamese respondents was an accumulation of educational qualifications: people who had not had much education past primary school, but compensated for this later by gradually advancing to a higher educational level, usually in combination with a job. I illustrate this with two typical trajectories, one of a man and one of a woman. Both of them came to the Netherlands as young adults, but they did not attend school in the daytime here. I would like to note in advance that the trajectory taken by the man is one I came across far less frequently than the one taken by the woman.

Mr. B. came to the Netherlands in 1980 at the age of twenty. Although he had no more than a vocational school diploma when he arrived, he is now a mathematics teacher at a comprehensive school. Mr. B. is from a Creole family with eight children that lived in a lower-class neighborhood in Paramaribo. His mother earned a living doing two cleaning jobs, one in the morning at the Health Department and the other in the afternoon at a shop.

In the sixth grade of primary school, Mr. B. failed the entrance exam for the local four-year secondary school, but he passed the one for the vocational school. However, his mother wanted him to go to "one of the best and strictest two-year secondary schools in Surinam." It was a Catholic school. After that he would be able to switch to the four-year school. He completed the two-year school, but he preferred to go on from there to a vocational school. He decided he wanted to be a lathe operator. He was good at all the subjects at school, but "a total flop" at draftsmanship. He says he had enough discipline though to do the final examination in three years. He decided not to go on to the more advanced technical school, and applied for a job at the Surinam Aluminium Company (Suralco). He was hired, but he didn't realize until later that they didn't hire just anyone. At Suralco, they already knew he was "a boy who was extremely well-disciplined." A representative from Suralco would regularly come to the vocational school and ask about the performance of the pupils in their second year there. Mr. B. knows for example that one of the boys in his class who was very good in the practical subjects but had a poor attendance record did not have a chance to be hired at Suralco. It was where everyone wanted to work, because you earned such good wages there. At the age of eighteen, Mr. B. was earning much more there than a schoolteacher. He was also earning more than his mother, who got 124 guilders a month as a cleaning lady at the Health Department, whereas he was earning 300 guilders every two weeks. Even civil servants didn't earn that much. So he would strut proudly around the neighborhood in his hard hat from Suralco. He could afford to buy brand name jeans for more than thirty guilders. Other boys would wear cheap pants made by the local tailor.

Influenced by his brother, who had already emigrated, and due to certain developments at Suralco, he nonetheless left for the Netherlands in 1980. At first he did work requiring little or no skill at various firms and the Dutch Post Office. He began to take technical courses in the evening, but he still wasn't satisfied. He decided he would like to teach and switched to a teachers' training college. Via a special preadmission trajectory, he was admitted to the college. He completed the preliminary training in one year instead of the usual two. He had no trouble with mathematics and physics. The lower-level technical school he had attended in Surinam was comparable to a middle-level technical school in the Netherlands.

Mr. B. attended the teachers' training college in the evenings and taught in the daytime. He began teaching adults and later continued at a lower-level technical school. He did not have his teaching certificate yet, but the school was still happy to hire him (the school got special permission from the ministry). In 1988 he got a job teaching at a comprehensive school outside Amsterdam. In the meantime, he had started taking courses in policy and management in the school system, though he has now stopped for the time being because it was too much. After all, he does have a time-consuming job and a family with two children; his wife also works.

Mrs. A. came to the Netherlands alone in 1978 at the age of nineteen. She did have a few brothers and half-brothers already living here. Her mother had always wanted to move to the Netherlands, but her father hadn't. This is why her mother did not object when she followed her brothers and half-brothers to the Netherlands. After she arrived, first she stayed with an aunt and then with a half-brother and sister-in-law, but within half a year, she had her own place. Mrs. A. is from a large family in a lower-class Creole neighborhood in Paramaribo. Her mother has thirteen children. The oldest ones are Mrs. A.'s half-brothers and half-sisters. Her father was a civil servant and worked now and then as a "salesman," as she calls it. He sold everything from watches to electrical equipment. Her mother has always been a housewife. She had to leave school at an early age because she was pregnant.

Mrs. A. never got any further in Surinam than a two-year secondary school and a typing certificate. She was not a good pupil, she says herself. She was left back a couple of times at primary school. So after she arrived in the Netherlands, she had little choice but to do unskilled work. She found a job at an envelope factory, but it was not work she could continue doing for more than two months. In the meantime, she applied for a training position as a nurse's aide, and was accepted. It took her a bit longer than usual to complete the training, but two and a half years later she did get her certificate. She worked as a nurse's aide at the same place for another three years, and then started studying for a new certificate; she did a middle-level vocational training in institutional work. She took the courses in the evenings, and her employer gave her one day a week paid leave to study. After a conflict at work, she decided to leave. She found another job in a family-style home outside Amsterdam but also left that job after two months, once again in connection with a conflict. By then she had her middle-level certificate and was able to get a job at an institution for children with auditory disorders. She worked there for six months, but it was "too strict, too hierarchic" for her. Before she submitted her resignation, she had already found a new job at a youth care center. It was more to her liking, and she worked there for five years. In the meantime, she completed a higher-level vocational training in social and didactic care. She felt this warranted a better job. "There was a good reason why I put so much energy into my education. To be quite honest, I would like to have a management position." In two months, she is going to start working at a project for teenagers who cut classes or are at risk of dropping out of school altogether. She is now taking a one-year management course.

I frequently came across the kind of trajectory Mrs. A. followed among Afro-Surinamese women. This career pattern is a good illustration of the "risers" among the first generation of Afro-Surinamese women. Not only is the gradual rise in the educational and occupational level striking in the career of this respondent, so is the way she easily went from one job to the next. Despite the high unemployment rates in the 1980s, it was apparently not that difficult to find a job in the care and welfare sector. In part, her ethnic background was an advantage in this connection, since various of the institutions where she worked were happy to have someone of foreign or Surinamese descent on their staff.

Formal and Informal Entrepreneurship

My research population includes a number of entrepreneurs, most of whom are Indo-Surinamese rather than Afro-Surinamese. There is a great diversity in the kinds of businesses they were involved in. If I also count the economic activities my respondents' relatives engaged in, then among the Indo-Surinamese I observed a clothing business, an accountancy office, a video rental shop, street market selling, and a consultancy firm. My Afro-Surinamese respondents referred to their relatives having a barber shop and running a coffee shop, and twice to relatives selling at a street market.

Two patterns of entrepreneurship can be observed among the Indo-Surinamese. The first involves a founder of a business who is poorly educated and starts selling at a shop or market and gradually develops a prosperous business with the help of his wife and children. In my study, this is a business that began around 1970, before the mass Indo-Surinamese influx in The Hague. A good example is the shop run by the K. family.

The K. family's shop is on a busy shopping street in downtown The Hague. They sell a wide range of merchandise, from domestic utensils to religious articles and music tapes. The shop clearly caters to a predominantly Indo-Surinamese clientele. Mr. K. first started by selling groceries, but his business has since expanded into a large shop that occupies a prominent position on a street lined with immigrant-owned shops. Mr. K. does the buying, and he takes regular trips to India or the United States for this purpose. His wife and his son (17) serve customers in the shop, and sometimes their daughter (21) does as well. The son completed a four-year secondary school, and he is in charge of transferring merchandise from the warehouse to the shop. He proudly tells me he is the sales manager. The daughter is attending business school and helps in the shop in her free time and on the holidays. Some of Mr. K.'s other relatives are also retail or wholesale entrepreneurs in The Hague, Amsterdam, or Rotterdam. Up until recently, a brother of Mr. K. also worked in the business, but he has now started his own business.

In this more classical family business trajectory, experience in entrepreneurship plays more of a role than education. The K. family is part of a family network that also includes a number of other entrepreneurs.

A completely different pattern involves the better educated immigrant who starts a business in addition to having a job, like Mr. B. did. He is from a peasant family. His father wanted a better life, and he also opened a grocery shop. Mr. B. himself had no entrepreneurship ambition at the time. Like many of his peers, he opted for education as a route to upward mobility. However, once he was in the Netherlands, in addition to his regular teaching job he too started a business of his own. I give quite a detailed account of his career below. In a sense, he is not typical of my research population because he already had a good education before he arrived in the Netherlands. In another sense, though, his situation does typify the lives of children from poor peasant families who exhibit strong upward mobility. In his case, however, the rise already began in Surinam.

Mr. B. (55) came to the Netherlands with his family in 1975. Little more than two decades later, he is a teacher at a vocational college for immigrants and the manager of a company law and tax consultancy firm. In order to get this far, he took a long route requiring a great deal of perseverance and ambition.

His parents, as he puts it himself, were poor. The family lived in a remote spot in the rural district of Surinam and since the nearest school was five kilometers away, in the beginning he did not go to school at all. It was not until he was nine years old that he started attending primary school and learned Dutch. The family moved closer to Paramaribo a few years later. Mr. B.'s father sold a plot of land so he could start a shop. Later he sold a second plot of land to be able to build a new shop. This is how he made the transition from peasant to shopkeeper.

The new school Mr. B. switched to was better than the one in the countryside. After primary school, he attended a two-year secondary school and then combined a job with studying for his certificates as assistant teacher, teacher and then headmaster. He was working as the head of a school in the countryside when he decided to go to the Netherlands in 1975.

After making every effort and holding various temporary jobs, he finally found a regular job in the Netherlands in the field of adult education for immigrants.

But he did not stop there. He worked informally as a tax consultant and studied company law and tax law at the Open University. He started simply by helping people fill in their tax forms, but soon expanded his activities and began doing the commercial administration for small businesses. He initially worked from his own home, but soon made it more formal. He registered with the Chamber of Commerce and rented a floor that he furnished as an office. And he did all this while he still had a day job teaching. His family helped him out if he had too much work to do. He asked his son, who was still at school, to help him on the weekends and his wife, who worked as a radiology technician at a hospital, in the evenings. His brother, who had a bookkeeping certificate and was now studying for the State Practical Business Administration Diploma, also helped him.

The office has since expanded into a full-fledged company. Mr. B. not only purchased a building that he totally converted into a modern office, he also started working more and more professionally. His son (28) and daughter (25) both work for the company, and another daughter, who is an executive secretary at the Post Office, is also considering coming to work there. His son has a Master's in Business Administration and his daughter is studying to become a tax consultant. One heads the bookkeeping department, the other the tax department. In addition to his wife and children and a niece of his wife (part-time), there is one Indo-Surinamese and one Dutch employee at the company. The company has expanded from predominantly Indo-Surinamese to Turkish and Moroccan and recently Dutch clientele as well. So Mr. B. no longer caters solely to clients from his own ethnic community.

It is clear from this account of Mr. B.'s career that in the first instance, he did not choose to be an entrepreneur. In essence, it was the route that his father took a generation earlier. His father rose from peasant to shopkeeper, and the son moved up to become a teacher by getting an education. It was only in the second instance that he set up his own company, but without giving up his teaching job. A second conclusion is that Mr. B. did not start his own company for lack of other opportunities or because he was unemployed. Although he feels he was better able to satisfy his ambitions via his own company than in the school system, he added a successful business to an already reasonably successful teaching career. In this case, the decision to start his own business represents a deliberate preference for entrepreneurship. The desire to "be your own boss" or "start something for yourself" is also evident among people with a job, and it can also be observed in the better educated younger generation.

I note in chapter 2 that, contrary to what was expected, the Indo-Surinamese did not engage in entrepreneurship any more frequently than did the Afro-Surinamese. What is more, only a small percentage of the total Surinamese labor force engaged in entrepreneurship at all. So the question is whether the Indo-Surinamese have abandoned their traditional upward mobility route. Will entrepreneurship come to play less of a role than it did in Surinam? There entrepreneurship served as a stepping stone for the educational career of the next generation. Even before they came to the Netherlands, the East Indians had chosen the route of education and urban occupations. According to Choenni (1997), in Surinam entrepreneurship was already an "incorporation trajectory in the final stage." Although a conclusion of this kind is still premature, it is conceivable that in the future the entrepreneurship trajectory might be replaced by other forms of upward mobility.[27] According to my respondents, young people do indeed have less interest in the more traditional branches their fathers are in (the retail trade, for example, in tropical products and other groceries). It remains to be seen though whether—especially in view of the general growth of entrepreneurship in the Netherlands, especially in producer services (van den Tillaart and Poutsma 1998)—a younger generation of better educated people isn't going to go into new branches of trade and industry. For the time being, however, the question is whether Indo-Surinamese entrepreneurship is as insignificant as the SPVA survey figures indicate. First, Choenni's own study and other research show that the Indo-Surinamese are overrepresented among the Surinamese entrepreneurs in Amsterdam.[28] Second, there is the question of whether the SPVA survey figures cover the whole picture. A survey might simply categorize people like Mr. B. described above, with a job as well as a business of their own, as employees. Perhaps it is more important that the figures pertain to the position of entrepreneurs in the formal economy; they do not necessarily cover the entire range of informal economic activities the Indo-Surinamese also engage in. As is illustrated in the previous section, entrepreneurship is also an activity people with a job engage in, and it is precisely the combination of various sources of income that is more characteristic of the Indo-Surinamese than the Afro-Surinamese. In this sense, the Indo-Surinamese are more frequently entrepreneurs than the official figures show. We should also bear in mind that activities that were quite formal in Surinam may very well be informal in the Dutch context. The strict regulations in the Netherlands change the immigrants' income-generating activities into something informal. Thus the institutional context of regulations determines whether or not their entrepreneurship activities are formal or informal.[29] Moreover, the borderline between formal and informal entrepreneurship is not as strict in Surinam as in the Netherlands, and the threshold for starting a business is lower. In this sense, the formal requirements that pertain to businesses in the Netherlands were quite an obstacle for the poorly educated immigrants, certainly in the early days (Boissevain et al. 1984). This is probably one reason why there was more informal entrepreneurship.

In addition, perhaps the importance is underestimated of Indo-Surinamese entrepreneurs as employers. After all, some entrepreneurs do have personnel working for them. The number of formal employees might be quite low (Choenni 1997: 102), since relatives who work for a family business often are not formally included. Relatives who only work part-time or are not formally on the company payroll often remain invisible. For the rest, entrepreneurs can also employ other people, often newcomers with Surinamese nationality who do not have a work permit. They certainly cannot be found in the official figures.

> Ram (30) came to the Netherlands, where a few of his brothers and sisters were already living, in 1994. His formal reason for coming was to study at a business college, but in fact, the real reason was that his move to the Netherlands was prompted by the poor economic situation of his family. His prior schooling was, however, inadequate to enable him to successfully complete the first year, and this meant his residence permit was no longer valid. The only way for him to stay in the Netherlands legally was to marry a girl with a Dutch passport. Up until then, he had been supported by his relatives; he could not get a job because employers were not willing to hire an undocumented immigrant. Just to earn some kind of a living, he started working for an acquaintance in Rotterdam who sold heavy equipment in Surinam. He accepted the risks that working illegally entailed because he had nothing to lose. Anything was better than going back to Surinam.

In the official statistics, transnational entrepreneurship also probably often remains invisible. In Surinam as well as the Netherlands, I came across people who did business with one foot in the Netherlands as it were and the other in Surinam. They would deal in second-hand cars and tires, for example, or second-hand durable consumer goods (refrigerators and stoves) and parts for them. They would do their buying in the Netherlands and selling in Surinam. Some immigrants are also known to have earned quite a bit in foreign exchange dealings in the 1990s. In addition to money and material equipment, in all these cases know-how and contacts in the two societies play an instrumental role. After all, it is their know-how and contacts that made it possible for these people to act as intermediaries, and it is precisely this role that generates their income.

I have the impression the Indo-Surinamese engage in this kind of trade more than the Afro-Surinamese. Of course, this does not necessarily mean the Afro-Surinamese do not have any informal income at all. What they do is usually referred to as *hosselen*, a Dutch word derived from the English hustling,[30] but it is hard to draw a borderline between informal entrepreneurship and "hustling." In Surinam, hustling was usually associated with abject poverty. In a situation of scarcity, hustling was a way to earn a little something. In the Dutch context, this concept has been expanded and in certain circles, it is taken to mean dealing drugs.[31] The people who hustle in the Netherlands though are often on welfare and simply have to earn something on the side to be able to survive. Perhaps hustling and informal entrepreneurship might best be viewed as two extremes of a wide range of income-generating activities.

Although the term hustling is traditionally associated with urban unemployment and consequently with the Afro-Surinamese, they certainly do not have a monopoly on it in the Netherlands. Sooner or later, many of the people in a situation of long-term welfare dependency feel a need to supplement their meager incomes. According to several of my Surinamese respondents whose profession brings them into contact with this conduct, there is no difference in this connection between the various groups of Surinamese immigrants. At most, or so they say, the Indo-Surinamese are smarter about it or better at concealing it. In essence, it is a survival strategy in the Dutch welfare state in much the same way as it is for many native Dutch people.[32]

Single mothers on welfare are one group that spends a lengthy period of time at the minimum income level. The economic situation of one of my respondents is a good example of the numerous welfare mothers who have a hard time making ends meet.

Mrs. U. (51) lives in a high-rise in Bijlmermeer with her two teenage daughters. She does not have a job, and owes money to the Welfare Department and the National Health Service. In the past, she used to work as a cleaning lady at two hospitals in addition to receiving a welfare benefit. Ever since the Welfare Department found out about it, they have been deducting a certain sum of money every month to pay off her debt. So she is chronically short of money. Her two daughters are still at school and receive a small monthly student benefit from the state. They also sometimes earn a little but not too much, otherwise they would lose their right to child benefits. The mother and daughters help each other financially if necessary, but it is never easy to make ends meet. Usually it is not even feasible. Mrs. U. makes every effort to earn a little extra money, otherwise they really cannot get by. She is very inventive this way, and apparently has the right contacts.

Mrs. U. sews clothes for people in her immediate vicinity. She also sometimes works for a shop, where she dresses the mannequins in different winti[33] styles and makes hammocks. She and her older daughter also work as hairdressers, and can straighten, wave, braid, and knot hair. She also cooks food and sells it, she makes pickles, bakes cakes, and fills special orders. She can also cook Javanese and East Indian delicacies. "I bake a lot. Someone just called me yesterday. Tomorrow I have to bake some things for a birthday party. And then on Friday I have to make some special Surinamese dishes for another birthday party. I get plenty of orders!" Her latest activity is selling complete meals in a room under one of the apartment buildings; she does not have to pay rent for the room. She cooks the meals at home in the afternoon, and after she and her daughters have had dinner, she takes the meals to the informal basement restaurant in another apartment building where they are sold. "But I didn't do any cooking today," she says when I come to see her, "I'll do it tomorrow, I'll make something simple because I don't have much money." She shows me the contents of her purse. "Maybe twenty guilders, that's it." Later she tells her daughters to go get some French fries because she didn't do any cooking today.

Mrs. U. is not the only one in the high rise Bijlmermeer to earn much of her income in the informal circuit. I did not conduct systematic research on this point, but there is certainly no denying the existence of an entire network of overlapping informal economic activities. This case of Mrs. U. alone is a good illustration. She buys batik material from a Surinamese man who makes regular purchases in Indonesia. This is the material she uses to dress the mannequins for the shop window. When she brings the meals she cooks at home to the basement restaurant to sell them, she usually walks, but at the end of the evening she has a driver take her home with all her pots and pans, so he also gets part of her informal earnings. And officially, Mrs. U. and the traveling salesman she buys her material from are both registered as being unemployed.

From the Surinamese perspective, there is nothing unusual about earning a little on the side. In Surinam it was quite normal to have a couple of jobs at the same time, or engage in various economic activities. In the Netherlands men and women of all ages, Indo-Surinamese and Afro-Surinamese alike, continue to do so. A young man might sell drugs, and an elderly woman home-made cooking or clothing. From the windowsill of her downstairs flat in the Schilderswijk in The Hague, even Mrs. D., a seventy-year-old Indo-Surinamese woman, sells the *tulsi* plants she cultivates herself to people passing by. Ever since he finished a four-year secondary school, Krish (32), a musician who went to India several times to improve his mastery of the *tabla*, has been living on welfare and what he earns playing.

So in this sense as well, immigration has a certain leveling effect. As a result of their move to a welfare state, the high unemployment rates in the period of immigration and the inadequacy of their prior training and diplomas, the Afro-Surinamese and Indo-Surinamese at the bottom of the socioeconomic ladder find themselves in much the same position. However, the Indo-Surinamese more frequently engage in various economic activities at the same time and in addition to a job. Whereas earning a little on the side in addition to a welfare benefit might well be viewed as a "modern poverty" phenomenon that occurs in both groups, the accumulation of sources of income reveals an entrepreneurial approach that is far more characteristic of the Indo-Surinamese. The question is whether this more entrepreneurial and business-like mentality of the Indo-Surinamese is an advantage in their efforts to achieve upward mobility in Dutch society. I discuss this point in detail later in this book.[34]

Conclusion

In the chapter, I focused on the social mobility trajectories of Afro-Surinamese and Indo-Surinamese immigrants in the Netherlands. The period of arrival appeared to play a significant role. In the 1950s and 1960s, when most of the Surinamese immigrants were still Afro-Surinamese, it was much easier for them to find jobs than in the 1970s and 1980s. They more frequently found jobs in keeping with their educational level, and they experienced less discrimination on the labor market than in a later period. This does not mean there was no discrimination at all in the 1950s and 1960s, but it was more prevalent in the field of housing, which was scarcer at the time than jobs.

In addition, the background of the immigrants themselves helped determine the position they were to occupy on the labor market. For the time being, though, Afro-Surinamese and Indo-Surinamese immigrants were both having a hard time getting started in the 1970s and 1980s. Despite their extremely heterogeneous premigration history, in the Netherlands laborers with little or no marketable training wound up in the same unfavorable position at the bottom of the labor market or became dependent on welfare. So immigration had, as it were, a leveling effect on the differences between the lower-class immigrants of the two groups.

In addition to this leveling trend, there were also premigration differences between the two groups that continued to play a role after their arrival in the Netherlands. From the perspective of their specific history in Surinam, it is not surprising that the Afro-Surinamese should still have a higher educational and occupational level than the Indo-Surinamese and thus a higher average income. In view of their urban experience, it is also understandable that after their migration, the Afro-Surinamese were better able to maintain a certain occupational continuity. It was far more difficult, however, for the Indo-Surinamese to pursue their former lines of work, especially in entrepreneurship. In other words, the premigration occupational and employment history of the two groups did not meet the requirements and specifications of the Dutch labor market in the same way or to the same extent. As a result, the Indo-Surinamese experienced more of a status decline on the labor market than the Afro-Surinamese and—be it often unintentionally—more occupational mobility. It is true that many Afro-Surinamese laborers such as steelworkers or welders also had to switch to other occupations, but to a lesser extent than the Indo-Surinamese. Moreover, in the case of the Afro-Surinamese it was more frequently a result of structural changes in the Dutch occupational structure than a direct effect of immigration, as was the case with the Indo-Surinamese. Although the Indo-Surinamese are not formally entrepreneurs any more frequently than the Afro-Surinamese, they do appear to be more enterprising. I frequently came across an accumulation of educational qualifications or a combination of working and studying, but the combination of various sources of income is more characteristic of the Indo-Surinamese. In other words, in addition to a job or a business of their own, they engage in a wide range of formal or informal economic activities. I drew a distinction between these activities and the informal economic activities the long-term unemployed or welfare recipients often engage in. In their case, it is more what the Surinamese refer to as "hustling," and in this sense there is barely any difference between the Afro-Surinamese and the Indo-Surinamese. Whether formal entrepreneurship will turn out to be of minor importance in the near future or, in accordance with the general trend, increase in importance and to what extent, still remains to be seen.

Notes

1. Bloemberg (1995: 46), based on the MA thesis by G. J. Tornij: "Invloed van persoonlijke relaties op migratie van Hindoestaanse Surinamers naar Den Haag" (Influence of personal relations on immigration of East Indians from Surinam to The Hague), Amsterdam, Free University, Geography and City Planning Institute (1975).

2. Cf. Cottaar (1998).

3. My own calculations based on data gathered by Zielhuis (1973: 27).

4. The Bijlmer or Bijlmermeer is a high-rise residential area built about thirty years ago on the city outskirts where many newcomers have settled.

5. This is a pseudonym, as are all the other respondents' names in this book.

6. Bayer notes that a study conducted by the General Students' Association of Amsterdam (Algemene Studenten Vereniging Amsterdam) shows that 40 percent of the landladies refused to rent a room to "colored people." The Social Advisory and Information Bureau (Maatschappelijk Advies en Inlichtingenbureau) estimated that this percentage was as high as 80 percent. According to this last source, the percentage of landladies who refused to rent rooms to *university students* was even higher, namely, 95 percent (Bayer 1965: 104-5).

7. Cf. van Amersfoort (1968).

8. The Randstad is the urban agglomeration in the west of the Netherlands including Amsterdam, Rotterdam, The Hague, Utrecht and the surrounding area.

9. The family itself belonged to the Reformed Church, a Protestant church known as *bakra kirki* or white church. Many of the congregation's members had a somewhat better social position. whereas the Church of the Moravian Brethren was more of a church for the lower class.

10. See also note 6.

11. Unlike Sedoc-Dahlberg, I solely cite the figures for the Afro-Surinamese and Indo-Surinamese students, and not for the students from other ethnic groups, and I calculated the percentages on the basis of absolute figures.

12. Cf. de Bruijne (1976: 95-96).

13. See Schalkwijk and de Bruijne (1997: 114).

14. For example, Paramaribo had a Catholic boarding school for East Indian children from the countryside.

15. It also struck me during the study that various Indo-Surinamese men worked or had worked at a sheltered workshop for the disabled. This was not something I witnessed among the Afro-Surinamese.

16. Cf. de Bruijne (1976: 62, 76).

17. See, e.g., van der Lippe and van Doorne-Huiskes (1995).

18. Cf. van Niekerk (1992).

19. See also Volkstelling (1971/1972: 40).

20. In the mid-1960s, there were still more than three times as many Creoles as East Indians working in the government sector (Dew 1978: 16). Since then, the percentage of East Indians working for the government has increased, but it is still lower than the percentage of Creoles. In the 1960s and 1970s, there was a sizeable expansion in the number, not so much because there was more work but just to be able to give more people a job. The provision of civil service jobs was an important instrument in the hands of political parties, which could thus increase their following. In essence, this greatly oversized government apparatus concealed much of the unemployment in the capital (de Bruijne 1976: 64).

21. De Bruijne, quoted in Gooskens et al. (1979a: 140).

22. In 1995, 37 percent of the immigrants employed in this sector were Surinamese. This information is from a study conducted by the Temporary Support Center for Immigrants in the Care Sector called *Aanpak arbeidsdeelnamebeleid allochtonen in de zorgsector* (Approach to labor participation policy on immigrants in the care sector, n.d.).

23. In fact they were called teaching assistants. As soon as they themselves had completed primary school, they would start working in the daytime as a class aid while attending more advanced classes in the evening. So they did not have any formal teaching credentials. A few of my respondents had done this kind of work.

24. The lower certificate (A) qualified teachers to teach kindergarten and the first two grades of primary school, and the higher one (B) qualified them to teach all the other grades of primary school.

25. Cf. Reubsaet et al. (1982: 144).

26. Only with certain reservations can the three items in this table be compared. What we have here is an impression at an aggregated level at three moments in time. So the figures do not necessarily say anything about the mobility of individuals within the groups.

27. However, this might well change if well-educated young people choose entrepreneurship in response to discrimination and the shortage of jobs, as was the case for example with the Sikhs in Great Britain (Gibson and Bacchu 1988).

28. Cf. Boissevain et al. (1984).

29. Cf. Kloosterman et al. (1997: 19).

30. See van Gelder (1990).

31. See Sansone (1992).

32. See, e.g., Engbersen (1990).

33. Winti is the Afro-Surinamese religion.

34. See chapter 7.

Chapter Five

Careers of Afro-Surinamese and Indo-Surinamese Men and Women

There have been just as many African-American and Caribbean objections to the image of the strong black woman as Asian ones to the notion of the passive and docile "Asian" woman.[1] These stereotypes are gross exaggerations of reality and overlook other important dividing lines such as social class. What is more, they suggest that things are as they are and are not apt to ever change.

The fact remains that historical and cultural differences affect the labor market participation of women from different immigrant groups. In essence, these differences have to do with the family structure and the division of labor between men and women that has developed in the course of time. In this chapter, the focus is on gender differences. If we examine men and women separately, the ethnic differences become all the more significant. This is particularly visible on the labor market as regards labor market participation. To a certain extent, these differences were also evident in chapter 4, but there the focus was on differences in ethnic background. Here attention is explicitly devoted to gender as well as ethnic background.

Labor Market Participation and the Role of the Breadwinner

Afro-Surinamese and Indo-Surinamese men and women advance via different trajectories of mobility. Traditional gender roles still play a clear role in this connection, as is most clearly illustrated by their labor market participation in the Netherlands. As has been noted earlier, Indo-Surinamese labor market participation is lower than Afro-Surinamese. If gender as well as ethnic background is taken as the point of departure and four categories are thus included in the analysis, Afro-Surinamese men with the highest and Indo-Surinamese women with the lowest level of labor participation emerge as the two extremes (see table 5.1).

The active role of Afro-Surinamese women is striking. Their high labor participation (63 percent) compensates for the low level of Indo-Surinamese women

(43 percent) to such an extent that the average level of Surinamese women is the same as that of native Dutch women (53 percent).[2]

Table 5.1 *Labor market participation* *of Afro-Surinamese, Indo-Surinamese, and native Dutch men and women in 1994 (in percentages)*

	Afro-Surinamese	Indo-Surinamese	native Dutch
women	63	43	53
men	77	60	72

Source: SPVA-1994, ISEO/EUR; Martens and Verweij (1997: 32).
*   Number of individuals in the labor force expressed as percentage of the total number of people in the 15 to 65 age group.

The question is how these relatively large labor market participation differences can be accounted for. In part they are generated by premigration conditions. As in the Netherlands, in Surinam men's labor participation was higher than women's. In the early 1970s, more than two-thirds of the male Creole and East Indian labor force (67 and 69 percent) was active in the production process.[3] Women were far less active on the labor market, though Creole women were more active than East Indian women (28 and 12 percent).[4] The figures only pertain, however, to the position on the formal labor market. In particular, this means the labor of East Indian women is underestimated. In Surinam they were often working members of the family in the farm work, at the market, or in the shop. They did this work in addition to their domestic chores. These women worked short or long hours in the family business, depending on what was needed. This had to do with the size of the plot of land or the family business and the extent to which their husband also had a job somewhere else. So the low percentage of working East Indian women conceals the fact that they often did engage in productive labor, but in the informal circuit and frequently in the context of a family business.

In comparison with men, the percentage of working Creole women (28 percent) was not high either, but, as in the case of East Indian women, more Creole women had paying jobs than the official figures indicate. In one way or another, virtually all the Creole women in my study who had already left school in Surinam were engaged in paid labor. It could be a regular job, but it could also be in the informal sector. Women from the Creole lower class in Paramaribo generally had a higher educational level than East Indian women from the lower class or from the countryside. They consequently had easier access to regular jobs, for example, as civil servants, secretaries, or nurse's aids. Of course there were also East Indian women in occupations like these, but in Paramaribo East Indian women with little or no education were less apt to work outside the home at the time than Creole women.

Although the official figures thus underestimate the labor market participation of East Indian as well as Creole women, there is nonetheless a difference between the two groups in this respect. It can be traced back to a difference in the family structure between the two groups and the role of the man as breadwinner.

The Cultural Ideal of the Male as Breadwinner

It is true that the ideal of the male as breadwinner is not unknown among Creoles, but it does play a far more significant role among East Indians. The ideal is most prevalent among the older generation, immigrants from the countryside, and the groups with the lowest educational level. In the course of my fieldwork, numerous women told me that as far as their husbands were concerned, they didn't have to work. Regardless of whether or not they had jobs outside the home in the Netherlands, they liked to tell me they didn't *have to* as far as their husbands were concerned. This was apparently something to be proud of. The other side of the coin is that in fact husbands are sometimes very much against their wives going out to work. The Organization for Hindu Media (OHM) devoted a radio program (14 October 1996) to women's labor market participation and to whether educated women have a harder time finding an Indo-Surinamese husband. The fact alone that special attention was devoted to this question illustrates the changing ideas about working women in the Indo-Surinamese community. The whole situation is apparently in a state of flux and fewer people see the male breadwinner as the ideal than in the past. This kind of discussion on women's right to a career of their own would be inconceivable in the Afro-Surinamese community, where women have traditionally been the breadwinners themselves.[5]

The question remains as to where this ideal comes from among the Indo-Surinamese. Why do Indo-Surinamese women as well as men consider it inappropriate for women to work outside the home? It seems to have to do with the family honor women are traditionally supposed to uphold. A woman's conduct in public could cause her family to lose face. It also has to do with the family's economic position, since a man whose wife does not have to work can show the outside world that he is well-to-do. He is perfectly capable of taking care of his family by himself. This is in keeping with his status as head of the family. The opposition to working women mainly pertains to women who work outside the home. Doing her share of the family's farm work was quite normal in Surinam. In addition to doing the domestic chores and taking care of the children, women often used to tend the livestock and work with the men in the fields. Especially in the busy periods in the rice fields, during the planting and harvesting, as many people as possible had to help out and this included women. Women of the first generation still remember how they used to take turns working on each

other's land when the rice had to be planted, which was extremely labor intensive at the time and had to be done within a short period of time. Sometimes
women would be paid to do this work on adjacent plots of land. But working on
someone else's land was essentially just an extension of the daily agrarian activities at home. It was also customary for women to play a role in selling their
own farm products or help in the shop.

If farming alone did not enable a family to support itself, members of the
family would have to look for a job or earn an extra income some other way. It
was often the men who did so while their wives remained behind to do the farming. Men worked as chauffeurs for example, and in Nickerie they engaged in
wage labor in the agro-industry. In some cases, peasant families resembled
working-class families in that the men engaged in wage labor and their wives
devoted almost all their time to working at home. So it was the husband who
went out to earn the money. It was something of a disgrace if a husband let his
wife go out to earn an income.[6] A woman could earn an extra income by doing
some supplementary work at home, for example, as a seamstress. But even in
these cases, the women say that as far as their husbands were concerned, they
did not *have to* work, they were only doing it "to help him out." Apparently the
male breadwinner was the norm, even if in actual practice, it was definitely not
a norm all the men were always able to fulfill.

With the move to Paramaribo and the increased educational participation, a
lot of things changed. Women became better educated and were more frequently
earning money. Daughters would contribute to their father's household, and
wives to their husband's household. It was generally true that the younger the
women, the better educated they were. Whether or not women worked outside
the home depended on the social class of the family of origin and their own individual educational level.

> Mrs. F. (45), who helped out at her parents' shop until she got married, made this
> clear in so many words: "Women only went to work if they were teachers or had
> a good job. Or they were women from the poorer families. But the normal thing
> was for a woman to get married and stay home."

Despite the exceptions, the norm was for married women not to work. Since
there was a growing trend for educated women to have a job, this norm gradually changed. What is more, these women had better chances on the marriage
market; their education meant an investment in the future. This obviously affected the traditional ideal of the male as breadwinner.

Yet the traditional division of labor between men and women did not completely disappear. It still persists in the Netherlands as well, be it in an altered
and weakened form. It is still common practice in many Indo-Surinamese families for men to be the breadwinners, at any rate the main ones. More conservative men oppose the idea of their wife working outside the home, or only allow

her to have a small part-time job. There are two sides to the reasoning about this. First, the men feel they ought to be able to earn a living themselves so their wives can devote all their time to the children. They see it as their obligation to support their wives and children, and they are afraid that if their wives have a job outside the home, it will be at the expense of the family. The second argument in the perception of many Indo-Surinamese, especially women, is that men want to earn a living themselves so they don't have to be dependent on a woman. They are "jealous" and want to protect their wives from the outside world. They are also afraid that as soon as their wives start working outside the home, they will no longer be willing to accept everything. Some men suffer from a kind of emancipation anxiety; the classical role patterns are changing, and they do not know yet where this will lead. Men sometimes say Indo-Surinamese women become too self-reliant in the Netherlands, and before you know it they want to have a say about everything at home. They feel this leads to marital conflict and divorce. Essentially these men are often afraid of losing their power and authority at home. Of course this fear is not unjustified, since the better educated women are, and the more they work and earn their own income, the stronger their position in the family. So the point is not just that women have jobs, it is also that men feel the decisionmaking about this is no longer in their hands and their role as head of the family is affected.

Of course, not all women are equally interested in their own emancipation, nor do all men feel the same way about their role as breadwinner. I address these differences later. Let it suffice here to conclude that clear traces can still be found among the Indo-Surinamese in the Netherlands of the ideal of the male breadwinner. But the days when a wife who didn't have a job was viewed as a sign of prosperity do seem to be fading further and further into the past.

Women's Financial Independence

I have noted above that the Creoles in Surinam certainly were not unfamiliar with the idea of the male as breadwinner. It might be more accurate, though, to say that it was an ideal many of them had a hard time putting into effect, so that alternatives became quite customary. This mainly holds true for the Creole lower class of Paramaribo, and far less for the middle class. Matrifocality is characteristic of the lower class. It means in short that women are often the head of the family, and that alternative relations between men and women are very common.[7] Women not only play a central role in the family in an emotional sense but also as authority figure and breadwinner. A man's relation to his family has a great deal to do with his financial input in the household. Unemployment or inadequate earnings consequently weaken his position in the family —he loses respect and loyalty. The more or less marginal position of men in the family that gradually emerged in the course of time is linked to the economic instability the Creole lower class of Paramaribo periodically experienced.[8] At the same time, an urban environment does give women a wide range of ways to earn money, and they are less dependent on men there than women in the countryside (Buschkens 1974: 205). This economic independence of women in the Creole lower class has since become common practice. Even if the man is there or acts as breadwinner, women often still play a central role, in which case it is referred to as latent matrifocality.

This central role played by mothers served as the basis for the image of the strong black woman. The idea that lower-class Creole women in Surinam were self-reliant and not dependent on men is nonetheless somewhat misleading. As was the case with East Indian women there, having a regular breadwinner or husband gave a woman a respectable status, and part of it was that she no longer went out to work or no longer did certain kinds of work (Buschkens 1974). Economic self-reliance and independence were definitely not always viewed as the ideal. Independence was usually not a matter of choice and it often implied poverty. What is more, women usually did remain dependent on the financial support of a man. Most women could not do without the material support of members of their immediate family, or without their help as babysitters. Young mothers often continued to live with their parents or mother.

The situation of July and her mother, who I met in Surinam, is an illustration of this. July is a nurse. When she goes to work, she leaves her four-year-old son with her mother. July makes a considerable financial contribution to the household, and in part her mother, who is retired, depends on it. July in turn depends on her mother for the care of her son and for a place to live, since she would never be able to pay for a place of her own. So in this case there is a certain reciprocity in the mother-daughter relation.

In general, women in the family formation stage were dependent on their mothers or other female relatives. When a woman left her mother's household and moved in with a man, she was dependent on him if there were young children to care for. In that case, she had less of a chance to work outside the home. But if necessary, in other words if her husband didn't come through, a woman would have to go out and work. This was obviously problematic if she didn't have anyone to mind her children. One of my respondents remembers how as a child, she would be shut up in the house with her little brothers and sisters when her mother went to work. Her mother didn't have a babysitter, and didn't want to leave them outside the house without any supervision. But there often were relatives or neighbors around who could babysit. In the Netherlands, where informal networks are weaker, there is less of this kind of help available. Many women use institutionalized childcare or combine formal with informal care.

So on the one hand, lower-class Creole women were extremely vulnerable and financially dependent on men, especially if they had young children. But on the other, they were constantly aware of the need to be able to earn a living themselves, and if necessary they did so. In this sense, they became accustomed to having to be financially independent. In the Netherlands, many women exchanged financial dependence on a man for another kind of dependence, that is, on welfare. If the situation made it necessary, they had a right to benefits here. Marital problems had often even been what stimulated their move to the Netherlands, since they knew that here at any rate they would be able to have an income of their own. As was noted above, a variety of reasons kept quite a few single mothers in the Netherlands from going out and working at the time. What few Afro-Surinamese housewives I came across in my study were all welfare mothers. I will go into this later. Suffice it to say here that Afro-Surinamese women have been traditionally familiar with having to earn a living themselves, although in Surinam this was often an involuntary kind of independence.

Afro-Surinamese and Indo-Surinamese Women

The extent to which Afro-Surinamese and Indo-Surinamese women are financially independent or differ in this respect are not issues I can address on the grounds of my own qualitative research material. We can, however, gain insight into this question by examining some of the quantitative SPVA data. Housework is more frequently the main activity of Indo-Surinamese than of Afro-Surinamese women. This is the case for 35 percent of Indo-Surinamese women and 20 percent of Afro-Surinamese women (see table 4, appendix 3).

Another indication of the role of women is the degree to which they earn their own income. When asked about their main source of income, almost twice as many Indo-Surinamese as Afro-Surinamese women report having no income of their own (27 and 15 percent). In this respect, Indo-Surinamese women are very like native Dutch women (26 percent of whom have no income of their own). What is more, Afro-Surinamese women far more frequently have earnings than Indo-Surinamese women (52 and 36 percent) and are similar in this way to native Dutch women (53 percent of whom have earnings).[9] In this respect Afro-Surinamese women also differ less from men than Indo-Surinamese women. These data indicate that gender differences are smaller among the Afro-Surinamese than the Indo-Surinamese in this respect (see table 3, appendix 3).

It is clear from these data that Afro-Surinamese women are financially more independent than Indo-Surinamese women; they more frequently have an income of their own, and it is more often an income from paid employment. To a certain extent, there is thus a continuation of a difference already in evidence in Surinam. This still does not reveal the extent to which women in the Netherlands have become dependent on income sources other than paid employment, whether their own or a breadwinner's. After all, once they moved to the Netherlands, there was now the possibility of applying for welfare. This will be addressed below, where I also devote attention to the role of the breadwinner and financial independence in relation to the family structure and household composition.

Family Structure and Economic Position

As is evident from my qualitative study, there are multifarious types of households and breadwinner roles, ranging from married couples with a male breadwinner to two-income households and single-parent families headed by a female. In this section, I mainly focus on single-parent families and examine the relationship between the family structure and the financial dependence or independence of women.

In examining the types of Afro-Surinamese and Indo-Surinamese households, the equally high percentage of single-parent families in both groups is immediately evident. Contrary to the expectations, there is barely any difference between Afro-Surinamese and Indo-Surinamese households in this respect: 22 and 24 percent of all the Afro-Surinamese and Indo-Surinamese households are single-parent families (see table 10, appendix 3). Both these Surinamese groups differ markedly in this respect from the native Dutch, where only 3 percent of the households are single-parent families. It is true though that the percentage of two-parent families is higher among the Indo-Surinamese than the Afro-Surinamese (and the native Dutch). If we solely examine households with children, then the Afro-Surinamese have a higher percentage of one-parent families. A total of 38 percent of the Indo-Surinamese and 45 percent of the Afro-Surinamese households with children are single-parent families.[10] What is striking about these data is the sizeable difference between the Surinamese and the Dutch as regards the prevalence of single-parent families, and the fact that the Afro-Surinamese and Indo-Surinamese differ much less from each other in this respect than was expected.

Afro-Surinamese Single-Parent Families

Surinamese single-parent families differ in that the Afro-Surinamese ones are mainly headed by unwed mothers and the Indo-Surinamese ones by divorced women. As was extensively noted above, the matrifocal type family has long been characteristic of the Creole lower class in Surinam. And not only in Surinam, but among black populations throughout the Caribbean and the United States. There are various ways of looking at the persistence of this traditional type of family. Some theories view matrifocality as a legacy of the African past or of slavery. Other theories emphasize the present-day socioeconomic conditions and see matrifocality as an adaptation to poverty.[11] The notion is generally accepted that matrifocality is an adaptation to a poor or unstable socioeconomic position, on the basis of historical and cultural legacy. Neither cultural traditions nor the socioeconomic context alone can explain the development of the African-American family system.[12] The discussion nonetheless often focuses on the primacy of either "culture" or "structure." The question then arises of how to explain the fact that some groups develop matrifocality whereas others in similar socioeconomic conditions do not.[13]

This matrifocal tradition did not disappear in the Netherlands. It was noted above that a combination of circumstances led to the disappearance of poorly educated Afro-Surinamese women from the labor market. In the 1970s, welfare mothers were not under any obligation to look for a job if they had children under the age of twelve to take care of. The even more prevalent norm at the time that mothers did not work outside the home at all, combined with the high unemployment rates and the way employment agencies operated at the time, to stimulate many women to withdraw from the labor market altogether.[14] This trend continued among the younger generation in the 1980s.[15]

A great deal has since changed, first and foremost because of the sharp fall in unemployment. The norms as regards working women and the way employment agencies operate have changed in such a way as to promote women's increasing labor market participation. There is a stricter obligation to look for a job, and there are more training and retraining options for women wishing to reenter the labor market. All things considered, the socioeconomic context welfare mothers find themselves in today is quite different from that in the 1970s or 1980s.

However these changes have not necessarily benefited all women. Single mothers sometimes experience the obligation to apply for a job as a pressure that makes it even harder to deal with their difficult situation.

Mrs. H. (37) is the mother of five children. She had been on welfare for years, but the Welfare Department recently informed her that she had to pay back what she had earned off the books, so she had to look for a job. She now has a state-subsidized job linked to a compulsory training course. However, she is having some problems with two of her teenaged children and the supervising family guardian has advised her to spend more time with her children. But how is she supposed to do that? Without the training there won't be a job, and without a job there won't be an income and there won't be any money to pay her debts.

The more favorable employment situation has also influenced the prospects for the younger generation. It is nonetheless still the case that a great deal depends on other factors. One of them is education. Girls' prospects are still shaped by their educational level. The better educated girls are, the greater the priority they usually give their training and chances for a good job. Judith (22) for example is studying at a college. Her boyfriend wants them to move in together and have a child, but for the time being, she is putting it off. She wants to graduate from college and have a job before she starts thinking about a baby. Girls with less education are less apt to postpone motherhood. They get pregnant because their boyfriend wants them to or because they want to make sure he will stick around. Others want to have their own place and live there with a baby so they can get welfare. Sometimes this is not only how girls strive for independence and a certain status as an adult, they also want to be able to wear brand-name clothes, which is something they need an income of their own for.

For young welfare mothers, dropping out of school or leaving the labor market are not irreversible. There are female respondents in my study who once spent some time as welfare mothers, but they have since started working again. Some went back to work more or less involuntarily, pressured by the activating labor market policy, others did so because they wanted to. The younger generation carries on the tradition of women working outside the home, often regardless of whether or not they can rely on the income of a man. Younger women are more ambitious, they want to get ahead, get an education, and have a good job.

Gina (34) had been on welfare for years. She has two children, and in the past she could rely on her partner for financial support even though they were not living together. A few years ago, Gina started working again even before she and her partner broke up. She used to earn something off the books or work as a temp for an employment agency. But now she has a regular job caring for elderly people and has started a part-time vocational training. When I met Gina in the course of a study in the early 1980s, she was in much the same situation as the teenaged girls I interviewed for my present study. Gina was nineteen at the time, had just left school where she was training to care for the elderly, and she was pregnant. After the baby was born at her mother's house, she went to a home for single mothers because it would make it easier for her to get a flat of her own. Not that her mother liked this idea at all. Once she started living on her own, she was on welfare and only worked very irregularly. Anyone who didn't know better would think Gina's situation was hopeless, and she had no prospects for the future. Nonetheless, she did manage to improve her situation in the end, thanks to a number of circumstances: it was not hard to get a job at the time, especially in the care sector, she had good relations with her grandmother, mother and sisters, who all helped take care of each other's children, and a sister who stimulated her to go back to school.

The more women like Gina advance in their work and training, the less apt they are to be financially dependent either on a partner or on welfare.

The crucial question is whether girls or young women with children only temporarily drop out of school or withdraw from the labor market and are thus only temporarily dependent on welfare, or whether they have landed for good in a situation it is not easy to ever get out of. In other words, is it a question of a family stage or of poverty? I cannot make any quantitative statements in this connection, but both these aspects do seem to play a role. An important difference between the situation today and in the 1980s is that the employment situation is better. There are more jobs and more opportunities for women who want to reenter the labor market. Furthermore, the educational level of the woman in question is an important factor (as in the case of Judith), and so is the support a woman gets from her network of relatives (as in the case of Gina).

It is not only the economic context or financial aspects that may reinforce the Creole tradition of single-parent families. The sociocultural context of Dutch society is also a contributing factor. Single Afro-Surinamese women are less and less of an exception, certainly in the urban context. Nowadays the obsolete-sounding concubinage referred to in the literature on matrifocality is simply called living together or living apart together. So there is a certain convergence between Creole patterns of how men and women relate and the new relations between the sexes that have developed in the Netherlands in the past few decades. It is a cultural convergence underpinned by women's greater financial independence.

Indo-Surinamese Single-Parent Families

As I have noted, Indo-Surinamese single-parent families are mainly headed by divorced women. Divorce was also quite common in Surinam—almost one-third of the marriages ended this way (Speckmann 1965: 169).[16] It is difficult to say whether the divorce rate rose or fell after migration to the Netherlands. The Dutch context does give women more survival options after a divorce. After all, they always have the possibility of an independent income in the form of welfare. Some Indo-Surinamese view "Dutch society" as the cause of divorces.

> Mr. D.'s wife left him and he thinks it would never have happened to him in Surinam. "If we had stayed in Surinam, there was hundred-ten percent chance nothing like this would have happened!" He admits that men might misbehave there, they might drink or be unfaithful, but still, in Surinam a wife stays with her husband. Here in the Netherlands, Mr. D. says, women just leave their husband or tell him to leave.

The question, however, is whether divorces have increased or merely become more visible, perhaps because there are so many shelter options for women in Dutch society (Eldering and Borm 1996).

What is more, since the figures do not accurately reflect the actual situation it is difficult to see whether the divorce rate is higher or lower in the Netherlands than in Surinam. Mungra (1990: 45-46) discovered that the official number of single-parent families is higher than the actual number. In his study on Indo-Surinamese families in the Netherlands, there appeared to be a considerable discrepancy between the official number of single-parent families in his random sample from the Registry and the actual number. Whereas his sample of fifty families officially included twenty-nine single-parent families, in reality there were only eighteen. It is common knowledge in the Indo-Surinamese community that people get divorced just to become eligible for welfare.[17]

As far as I know, there are very few Indo-Surinamese unwed mothers. One might, however, get a different impression, since many women with children have not had a civil marriage. Sometimes they are only married "East Indian style." In other words, they have only had a religious Hindu or Muslim ceremony without being married by law. In Surinam, under certain conditions a religious ceremony could be valid as a civil marriage. This is not the case in the Netherlands. Here Muslims and Hindus often consider an East Indian style marriage a legitimate form of living together; you are not officially married by law, but live together in a socially accepted fashion. Some people find this hypocritical, but others often think it is a very good compromise. There are also practical reasons not to get officially married, since it can make it impossible to get or keep welfare benefits. Divorced women who live with a second man also often do so after just a religious ceremony, as was customary in Surinam.

Unlike the Afro-Surinamese single-parent family, the Indo-Surinamese one is thus mainly a result of divorce. But as in the Afro-Surinamese case, various postmigration circumstances have influenced the prevalence of single-parent families. They have to do with the sociocultural context in the Netherlands and changes in the Indo-Surinamese community itself in combination with the social security provided by the Dutch welfare state.

Convergence and Divergence

The emergence of single-parent families might have different underlying reasons in the Afro-Surinamese and Indo-Surinamese communities, but there is also a certain extent of convergence insofar as there is a relation between this phenomenon and poverty or economic instability. Buschkens (1974: 177) noted that, contrary to public opinion, relations between men and women who lived together, whether officially married or not, were no less stable among the Afro-Surinamese than the Indo-Surinamese. Based on the figures cited by Speckmann, Buschkens concluded that in both cases, approximately one-third of the relationships were terminated. He also showed that although the percentage of illegitimate children might have been much higher among the Afro-Surinamese than the Indo-Surinamese, this had to be viewed in the proper perspective. The percentage of Afro-Surinamese children born out of wedlock also includes the children of unmarried parents who lived together, whose fathers had legally acknowledged them. If these acknowledged children are not included, there is very little difference between the percentages of illegitimate children among the

Afro-Surinamese and Indo-Surinamese (Buschkens 1974: 189, 193). So it is definitely erroneous to view Afro-Surinamese marriages or relationships as being more unstable than Indo-Surinamese ones.

In theoretical discussions on matrifocality, a relationship is repeatedly observed between poverty and the single-parent family. R. T. Smith, one of the protagonists of the structural approach, has suggested a relationship between matrifocality and an unstable socioeconomic position or poverty (in Buschkens 1974: 15). Matrifocality is also thought to be more prevalent in urban than rural settings, and more common in the countryside among wage laborers than peasants.[18] In the latter case, the status of the man in his family is relatively strong because he is also in charge of the labor the members of his family provide for the family farm.[19]

As I have noted, divorce and desertion were frequent among the Indo-Surinamese. Speckmann (1965) observed this in the 1960s, but it had also been the case in an earlier period. The life stories of the oldest Indo-Surinamese women in the Netherlands that were recorded by Lalmahomed (1992a) include repeated references to desertion, men with extramarital relations, women who get married for the second or third time, and men and women with illegitimate children. These are family patterns that bear a very strong resemblance to what Buschkens describes in the Creole lower class of Paramaribo. They would seem to be mainly linked to the poor conditions people lived in during the first period after their migration to Surinam. In later periods as well, economic instability among the Indo-Surinamese marginalized the role of the male as breadwinner. The poorest people often had to engage in wage labor, sometimes to supplement the work they did farming their own land.

Consequently, some of my Indo-Surinamese respondents had unpleasant childhood memories. Mrs. C. (49) came from a farming family with thirteen children. Her father was a lumberman and was away from home a lot. Sometimes he was away for months on end. "My mother was left to do all the work." Together with the children, she worked hard doing all kinds of farm work. They had a coconut field, vegetables and fruit, and a rice field. They also had chickens and ducks and milk from a couple of cows. So they could have had a pretty good life, especially since her father earned a nice salary as foreman. But most of the money never reached the home. He would go out with his friends and spend most of the money on himself. "My mother had to work her fingers to the bone," Mrs. C. recalls, "and if she didn't sell things, there wouldn't be any food in the house." Mrs. C. could get along better with her mother than her father. Whenever he came home, he would hit her. She decided not to wait and see whether her father was going to arrange a marriage for her like he did for her sister when she was fifteen. Before it was her turn, she left home and went to stay with some people she knew in Paramaribo. She definitely did not want to lead the same kind of life as her mother. She worked very hard to make sure she got a good education. The price she had to pay for it was high though: she couldn't go back home again, because her leaving meant so much disgrace for her family and shame for her parents and older brothers.

Problems of this kind are still very much in evidence among Indo-Surinamese immigrants in the Netherlands.[20] Divorce, living together without being married, extramarital relations, and excessive drinking are topics that came up again and again in the stories my respondents told me. Besides the numerous single-parent families, there are Indo-Surinamese families very similar to "the latent matrifocal family." There is a man in the family, but compared with the woman he only plays a relatively marginal role. The woman is the one with the authority at home, she manages the household budget, and in fact she is often the breadwinner. The men often get disability benefits and do some odd jobs, either paid or unpaid jobs, sometimes in Surinam. In a number of cases, the wife has an outside job and the husband stays home.

> The experiences of Carla, a second-generation Indo-Surinamese girl, are a good illustration. Via her Indo-Surinamese boyfriend, she came into contact with people very different from her own family. "If I look at my boyfriend's friends, they are the kind of guys who are going to stay home and have their wives go out and work. They get together and have a fine time. I see the same thing happening at my boyfriend's home. His father stays home and does the housework and takes care of the children and the mother goes out and works. And I see that happening a lot in his friends' families, their mothers have jobs and their fathers are at home. And those men, those guys, they are not the least bit ashamed about it. They don't even try and hide the fact that they stay home and their wives go out and work."

The same family patterns are thus found among the Afro-Surinamese and Indo-Surinamese alike with little or no education and without a job. Due to circumstances, behavioral patterns also sometimes develop in lower-class Indo-Surinamese families that deviate from what is essentially viewed as desirable. The ideal of the male breadwinner who supports and protects his wife and children is still very much in evidence in this lower class, but due to the circumstances, people cannot always live up to it. In certain senses, the emerging middle class or stable lower class seem to be more able to meet with the prevailing norms in the Indo-Surinamese community. They are "more East Indian" as it were: they get married twice, once at City Hall and once with a Hindu or Muslim religious ceremony, the youngsters do not leave home until they get married and certainly do not live together without being married, and the man acts as the main breadwinner and is the authority figure at home.

A relationship between a vulnerable economic position and the prevalence of single-parent families could be derived from the proportion of welfare mothers.

However, there are no data on the number of welfare mothers in either group. We do know, though, how many women have welfare as their main source of income. The percentages for the two groups were the same in 1994 (see table 3, appendix 3). It is clear from more recent data that whether or not they have a job, on the average single Afro-Surinamese mothers less frequently have low incomes than single Indo-Surinamese mothers (SCP/CBS 1999: 155-56). In this sense, single mothers of both groups coincide with the general Afro-Surinamese and Indo-Surinamese profile.[21]

Despite the converging trends cited above, there is also a certain degree of divergence, that is, differences in how family patterns described above are socially accepted. The Creole tradition of single-parent families has not only been in existence for a long time but single motherhood has been legitimated and institutionalized. The pressure to conform is stronger among the Indo-Surinamese, as will become clear later in this book.[22] This is also evident from the status of divorced women among the Indo-Surinamese. Divorced women do not have an easy position in the Indo-Surinamese community. Although they are not an exception to the rule, they are still often viewed that way. As a divorced woman, you are unprotected and "open game" for men, as one respondent put it. "Anyone can come on to you." In addition, a second marriage is more problematic for a woman than for a man. Parents consider it somewhat of a disgrace for their daughter to marry a divorced man. This is something that can play a role in the negotiations preceding a marriage.

Another indication of the extent to which single-parent families are accepted in the Afro-Surinamese community is the relation between fathers and children. Afro-Surinamese children from single-parent families often have their mother's surname. Even if they do have their father's surname, it does not automatically mean the grandchildren will as well. One Afro-Surinamese father jokingly said to his daughter, "Don't get married, just give your children my name." It is striking how negative the Afro-Surinamese can be about their father, especially the ones whose father was barely if ever there.

Monica (17) thinks her father does not have to appear out of the blue and start helping her out. He never thought twice about her or spent a penny on her. "He never bought one single diaper for me. My mother did everything for me, she always took care of me. That is why I have so much respect for her."

Children from two-parent families also, however, often have more loyalty and respect for their mothers than their fathers. Children often barely know their father's side of the family or feel less close than they do to their mother's relatives. This is inconceivable in Indo-Surinamese families, where children are primarily part of the father's family. This might explain why I came across several Indo-Surinamese (and no Afro-Surinamese) families in my study consisting of a father and his children.

From a historical perspective, the marginal role of men with regard to the family[23] is a reaction to a marginal socioeconomic position with a clear cultural component in the Afro-Surinamese case. Among the Indo-Surinamese, the leaning toward matrifocality is weaker and less institutionalized. The long-term practice of adaptation to socioeconomic conditions has given the single-parent family a more socially accepted status among the Afro-Surinamese.

Women's and Men's Careers

What course do women's and men's careers take and what differences can be discerned between the two ethnic groups in this respect? In the following section, I address these questions from the perspective of the past in Surinam and the present-day reality in the Netherlands.

Women: Marriage, Family, and Career

Getting married and having children often means more of a change for Indo-Surinamese than Afro-Surinamese women. In the Indo-Surinamese community, marriage is one of the major life events that marks a status transition for men and even more so for women. In Surinam, East Indian girls were traditionally expected to be virgins when they got married, which meant they had to be protected and supervised by their father and brothers. Girls were a "fragile possession," as one of my respondents put it, because they could bring shame upon the family name. This is why marriages were arranged for them when they were still very young, before "anything could happen." East Indian girls were often not expected to go any further than primary school, but this depended in part on the financial capacity of the family. Girls who had to get married could no longer attend school, and girls who no longer attended school had to get married. In very simple terms, this was the prevalent attitude in the period when the oldest of my respondents were growing up. In other words, attending school and getting married were the two alternatives. If a girl was given an opportunity to get an education, it was strictly prohibited for her to have even the slightest contact with boys.

One of my respondents, who is now fifty-two, remembers very well how she asked her father for permission to go on with her education after primary school. He allowed her to continue attending school under one condition: she would no longer go out on the street and talk to people there, certainly not to boys. In an effort to keep up with the other girls at school, she saved her money, penny by penny, for a compact and powder puff. When her father discovered this, he questioned her very strictly. Did she want to get an education or did she want to get married? As a young girl, another female respondent had been caught by her brother when she was talking to a boy. At home she got a beating, she was taken out of school and had to get married. Having even the slightest contact with a boy could mean a girl would have a marriage immediately arranged for her.

In Surinam, East Indian girls were mainly brought up with a view to their future role as wife and mother. Their schooling was barely relevant. When girls got married, they would leave their family and as daughter-in-law, primarily become part of their husband's family. So even if a family could afford it, there was no point to making too much of an investment in a girl's education. There were also fathers who arranged marriages for their daughters at a later age and did allow them to attend secondary or vocational school first. In the period before her marriage, the daughter would thus often make a financial contribution to her father's household by working outside the home. This was more common in the city than in the countryside. It gradually became more common for girls to also get more of an education, and they gradually reached the marriageable age later and later. Yet the notion did not disappear altogether that by a certain age, girls were supposed to be married.

Among Creole women in Surinam, it was not so much the wedding ceremony as the birth of the first child that marked the transition to adulthood. For them, a pregnancy was more often the reason to discontinue their education. It was not so long ago that girls who got pregnant were automatically expelled from school in Surinam. But for Creole women in Surinam, having to take care of a family generally coincided much more with having to earn an income of their own, and a diploma was very important in this connection. This was especially the case for female heads of families. Married women were much less apt to work outside the home. Women who were the sole breadwinner had no choice but to earn a living themselves, and having an income of their own only reinforced women's independence. Girls were brought up with this idea and encouraged to get an education, at any rate to assume they were going to have to be able to earn a living. In the Creole lower-class culture, it was and still is not customary to think in terms of either getting married or earning a living. In the lower class, people often do not get married until they are older. First a man has to achieve a certain level of prosperity before he can think about marriage. Marriage at a later age also meant Creole women did not view marriage nearly as much as an alternative for a career. Being married and leading the life of a housewife was at most something they hoped to do at some later stage in life (Buschkens 1974).

For East Indian women in Surinam, the perspective of a life as a housewife was much more common. They not only got married much younger, there was the certainty that a married woman would be taken care of. When a man got married, he knew that at a certain point he would have to start earning a living if he wanted to become independent from his parental family. This idea is still prevalent today in the Netherlands. If an Indo-Surinamese man gets married, he has to be able to support his wife and children. Sometimes this also keeps men from continuing their own education.

Vyay (30) felt that at the time, he was already too old to be a student. After a long school career, he graduated from secondary school and went to the university. He changed his major once, but failed to complete his studies. "That is a pity," he thinks in retrospect, "it still bothers me. But at a given moment you are just too old. You have to start earning a living and building something up for yourself." He did a short college training, found a job via an employment agency, and got married. But he won't really be happy until he has a regular job and some finan-cial security.

Anil (27) feels much the same way. He was studying at a technical university but he got married young and studying would have taken too much of his time. "As a man you are the one who has to go out and earn a living." So he switched to a shorter training course.

I am not completely excluding the possibility that age is sometimes also used as an excuse to justify having failed as a student, but there is still the prevailing idea that married men bear the main responsibility for the family.

All this is true much more for girls than for boys. From about the age of six-teen, an Indo-Surinamese girl in the Netherlands can expect to be getting mar-riage proposals. In certain circles, parents like their daughters to be married off before they are twenty. These are the parents who never had much of an educa-tion themselves and don't see any need for their daughters to either. In one Indo-Surinamese family, the parents did not see any need for their daughter to attend a five-year secondary school, even though the primary school advised her to. Her parents felt a four-year school would be enough for her, and after that she would be old enough and educated enough to get married.

Girls who choose to go on studying after they are twenty get married later —between the age of twenty and twenty-five. If they wait any longer than that, there is apt to be a problem finding an appropriate groom. Boys can marry at a later age, but still preferably by the time they are twenty-five, and definitely no older than thirty. More and more girls want to postpone marriage, and certainly if they are still studying, their parents often agree. There are parents who po-litely turn down all the marriage proposals for their daughters until they are fin-ished with their studies. Girls want to build a life for themselves first, with a good education and then a job. They want to be independent before they get married. "Because if you marry young," says Jenny (27) "and you get divorced when you are thirty or forty, suddenly you are on your own and you have no way of earning a living." The pressure to get married often comes more from the rest of the family or the immediate social environment than from the parents.

In the Indo-Surinamese community, getting married and getting an education are thus still two competing elements, even though the balance does seem to be gradually changing. Women are increasingly aware that an education is a good investment in the future because you never know what can happen. The longer Indo-Surinamese youngsters continue studying, the more of a need they feel for independence and the more apt they are to want to live on their own before they get married. Youngsters who attend a college or university develop a lifestyle that is sometimes difficult to reconcile with their parents' ideas. Many parents have a hard time accepting it if their children, particularly their daughters, want to move out before they get married, and in some circles it is a disgrace for the family. There are nonetheless youngsters who do manage to come up with a compromise. Students who would like to live on their own but don't want to do so without getting married simply get married, move out of their parents' home, and complete their studies. It is a creative way to meet with the norms and at the same time be young and have a good time. In the presence of her husband, no matter how young she is a married girl can go out until all hours of the night. It is far more problematic for an unmarried girl, and in some circles totally out of the question. Youngsters have thus found a way to make being married and studying two alternatives that no longer necessarily exclude each other. I have the impression, however, that this is feasible only for a small minority.

There are no clear rules of this kind for Afro-Surinamese girls as regards leaving home. It is not such a problem for them, and is not something they are apt to disagree with their parents about. The main problems Afro-Surinamese mothers have with their daughters have to do with their relations with boys and trying to make sure they don't get pregnant. If a girl does get pregnant, it does not necessarily have to mean the end of her school career. A lot depends on whether her mother is willing to take care of the baby and encourages her daughter to stay at school, and on whether the girl herself wants to continue living with her mother or would prefer to live on her own. These are crucial questions.

Marcia (30) was pregnant at the age of 18 and wanted to stop the course she was taking to work as a hospital orderly. Her mother didn't agree and felt she should finish the course. She did so, and lived with her mother until the baby was six months old. In retrospect, she is glad she finished the course, because it gave her the basis for the more advanced part-time courses she later completed, in addition to the job she still had when her second child was born a few years later.

In other cases, though, having a baby meant terminating a girl's education, at any rate for the time being.

Sandra (17) was nearing the end of her pregnancy when I first met her. She had completed a four-year secondary school a few months earlier. She was planning to stay home and take care of her baby until the beginning of the next school year. Then she wanted to go back and attend a senior secondary commercial school. I spoke to her again more than a year later, when the next school year had already begun. Sandra had not carried out her plan. She was still living with her parents, but was going to get a place of her own soon and was focusing her attention on that.

As I noted above, however, quitting school doesn't have to mean stopping for good. It can be a temporary stage in the family cycle. Some of the girls I knew from a previous study did indeed go back to school. Several of my respondents opted for this route. It often means a combination of working and studying, and the courses of study are often vocational. One of my Indo-Surinamese respondents teaches at a college and told me it was striking that Afro-Surinamese students are so motivated to study at a later age. The Indo-Surinamese do not so easily start studying something new when they are older. This is illustrated by the statistics. In the above-twenty-five-age category of Afro-Surinamese women, 14 percent are day students, and this is only true of 5 percent of the Indo-Surinamese women in this age category (SPVA-1994; Martens and Verweij 1997: 78).

In general, Afro-Surinamese women do not view getting married, living together, or having children as obstacles to their career. Whether or not women work outside the home depends in part on the family stage they are in, but in all the age categories the labor market participation of Afro-Surinamese women is considerably greater than of Indo-Surinamese women (SPVA-1994; Martens and Verweij 1997: 80). This combination of raising a family and working outside the home is a tradition Afro-Surinamese women brought to the Netherlands from Surinam. It is not generated by a feminist perspective or the ideals of women's liberation, but rather, it is born of necessity as it were. Many women would prefer a different kind of life. In the first instance, they do not view the absence of a man in the house with whom they can share all the responsibilities (from child-care and domestic chores to earning a living) as a positive thing. They view it as something normal—it is simply what men are like. The emancipation notion that is associated with the self-reliance and independence of Afro-Surinamese women is merely an ad hoc explanation. It is true that their arrival in the Netherlands in the 1970s did coincide with a tendency toward greater labor market participation among native Dutch women. In this sense, a certain extent of convergence was evident between what Creole women had always been accustomed to doing in Surinam, and what native Dutch women were increasingly aspiring to.

Rapid changes are also taking place among Indo-Surinamese women in the fields of education and labor market participation. It is obvious that the more education they have, the greater their labor market participation. Among the women with a secondary school education or more, there is barely any difference any more between the labor market participation of Indo-Surinamese and

Afro-Surinamese women (SPVA-1994; Martens and Verweij 1997: 81). It is the less educated Indo-Surinamese women who lag behind Afro-Surinamese women in this sense.

Men: Jobs, Unemployment, and Alternative Careers

The public image of Afro-Surinamese men, particularly in the period of increased immigration, definitely was not good. They were repeatedly in the news in a negative way and soon attracted the attention of researchers. Popular notions on Afro-Surinamese men suggested that they were more frequently unemployed than Indo-Surinamese men. I noted earlier in this book that there was not much difference between the Indo-Surinamese and Afro-Surinamese unemployment rates in general, but that differences did exist when the unemployment rates of men and women were considered separately. Afro-Surinamese men seemed to be more frequently unemployed than Afro-Surinamese women, and also more often than Indo-Surinamese (men and women, see table 2, appendix 3).

Yet unemployment figures are only one side of the coin. Afro-Surinamese men might be unemployed more often, but the number of working men among them is also relatively large. This seems contradictory, but becomes clearer if we bear in mind that the proportion of nonactive members of the labor force is relatively high among the Indo-Surinamese. We can thus conclude that the absolute proportion of working people among Afro-Surinamese men is higher than among Indo-Surinamese men (cf. tables 1 and 2, appendix 3).

More than among the women, there would seem to be a polarization among Afro-Surinamese men. There are those who are well educated, employed, and earn a reasonable to a good living, but there are also the long-term unemployed who are poorly educated. Paid employment is the main source of income for 59 percent of Afro-Surinamese men (see table 3, appendix 3). In fact a quarter of the Afro-Surinamese men earn a relatively high income. It is mainly the ones with an extremely low educational level who are relatively often unemployed (SPVA-1994; Martens and Verweij 1997: 48, 82). So the actual labor market position of Afro-Surinamese men is more varied than the stereotyping would tend to suggest.

The fact cannot be denied though that, in the large cities, there definitely is a category of poorly educated, unemployed young Afro-Surinamese men whose survival strategies have come to be increasingly entrenched in the drug trade. In response to their poor chances on the regular labor market, in essence they have moved further and further away from the customary channels for upward social mobility. Sansone (1992) refers in this connection to the interaction between processes of exclusion and self-exclusion.

In some senses, Afro-Surinamese women would seem to be advancing more than men from the same background.

When I spoke to one of my respondents from a previous study and asked her how her male and female friends were doing now, she told me the girls she knew back then were doing fine, but the boys were not. She mentioned two boys by name who she still sees nowadays on the street; they are drug addicts.

This might sound anecdotal, but examples like these are not isolated cases. The same differences between men and women even occur within one and the same family. I repeatedly came across families where the women have fine positions and the men only marginal ones.

Mrs. A. (36) is from a large family from one of the lower-class neighborhoods in Paramaribo. She only had very little schooling when she came to the Netherlands, but has since been able to achieve a considerable level of upward social mobility. Her sisters still live in Surinam and have all gotten an education and have become a primary and a secondary school teacher and a sociologist. Her brothers in the Netherlands did not do nearly as well. One of them has never really settled into any occupation, and one is a construction worker. Her two younger brothers in Surinam do not do anything at all. One of them dropped out of school and is being supported by his girlfriend, another one is barely an adult and already has a child with a sixteen-year-old girl.

Creole women in Surinam have traditionally been more focused on a regular career, since they are the ones who take primary care of the children. Due to the absence of men or their marginal position as husband and father in the family, women bear more of a responsibility for earning the family income, choosing the children's schools, keeping in contact with their teachers, and so forth. They are more apt to come into contact with the various institutions and agencies that deal with their children. They cannot sit back and wait, they have to play an active role. "My father talks a lot, my mother does what has to be done," is how a young respondent described the roles played by her parents. "My father was the one who decided what had to be done," another respondent said, "but my mother was the one who did it."

Creole lower-class men in Surinam are not known as loving and devoted husbands and fathers. Instead, they earn a reputation by proving their masculinity to their friends (Brana Shute 1979). These men spend a lot of time on street corners and with their friends, and the dividing line is often hard to see between simply hanging around and trying to earn a little bit of money. Their reputation depends more on the world outside the family than on how much they help with the housework or the children. Comparable behavioral patterns, but adapted to big city life in a welfare state and with new money-making options like dealing drugs, are evident among young Afro-Surinamese men in Amsterdam (Sansone 1992). Roughly speaking, Afro-Surinamese women are more oriented toward a regular career, but many of their male counterparts seem to be more focused on an alternative career.

This does not necessarily mean there is no evidence at all of behavioral patterns of this kind among the Indo-Surinamese. On the contrary, boys from Indo-Surinamese families that originally came from Paramaribo exhibit behavior very similar to that of young Afro-Surinamese men. Especially in the period immediately after 1975, boys of the in-between generation seemed to be having a difficult time. They dropped out of school, came into contact with the drug scene or started gambling, and unbeknownst to their parents, had girlfriends or even illegitimate children before they got married.

Robby (35) was one of these boys. He had been going to a four-year secondary school in Surinam, but he couldn't keep up at the same kind of school in the Netherlands and switched to a vocational school. He was going to go on to a more advanced vocational school, but it didn't work out. He loved sports, he was a disc jockey, and was very popular with the girls. He started gambling, got into debt, and did some shoplifting. He got into real trouble twice. How was he going to tell his parents he had gotten his girlfriend pregnant? And what was he going to do when it came out that he had debts in the name of his family? It seemed as if there was no way to solve these dilemmas. But he was from a close-knit family that was not about to let him down. In the end, he shaped up. The whole period when he was sowing his wild oats turned out to be a temporary stage in his life. Robby got married, got a regular job, and is now the father of three children.

In essence, these are behavioral patterns of lower-class young men that do not differ much from the ones prevalent among the Afro-Surinamese. They are presumably more common there than among the Indo-Surinamese because they are inherent to an urban lifestyle that developed in a situation of poverty that, in the Creole case, lasted for generations. There is another difference as well. It is not uncommon for the Indo-Surinamese to abandon a "deviant" career as soon as they reach the marriageable age. I only heard of a few men who did not get married or lead a more regular kind of life once they reached that age. In one family there was a man who had never been married and had what the Indo-Surinamese consider an extremely deviant lifestyle. He lived with an older woman and they were not married. The family knew about it, but pretended they didn't. The man visited his relatives, but they never visited him.

The Afro-Surinamese do not have this kind of turning point in their lives when a man is expected to permanently accept the responsibility for a family. It is more common for Afro-Surinamese men to continue their old lifestyle until a later age.

A respondent told me about her brother (42), who was in prison again and again. His family put a great deal of pressure on him to finally stop using drugs. For a while it looked as if he was going to better his ways. He was doing a training course to work as a caretaker, but it didn't work out in the end. He felt it was too much for him, and he wanted to "take it easy." Nowadays he does not get up on time in the morning, he does not go to classes any more, and he does not do his homework.

There is an existing pattern of Afro-Surinamese boys assuming a more regular lifestyle when they start living together, but it is less common than among the Indo-Surinamese. The central importance of marriage and the obligation every Indo-Surinamese parent feels to make sure their child "marries well" keeps Indo-Surinamese boys from going astray. As is discussed in greater detail in chapter 8, after a certain age they have more of a tendency to exhibit "proper" behavior.

Conclusion

Whatever differences there are between the Afro-Surinamese and Indo-Surinamese become more marked if a distinction is drawn between men and women. There is a considerable change in the picture of the labor market participation of the two groups if we examine the male and female categories separately. There then appears to be a relatively large difference between Afro-Surinamese and Indo-Surinamese women as regards labor market participation, and between Afro-Surinamese and Indo-Surinamese men as regards unemployment. The low labor market participation of Indo-Surinamese women is striking, as is the relatively high unemployment rate among poorly educated Afro-Surinamese men.

It is difficult to explain these differences on the basis of the differential opportunities that Dutch society provides. Gender differences in the labor market position have to do with the family structure and gender roles, which date back to premigration times. The family structure and division of labor between men and women that developed under certain socioeconomic conditions in Surinam still play a role in the process of social mobility in the Netherlands. The economic independence of Afro-Surinamese women in the Netherlands is greater than that of Indo-Surinamese women, just as it was before migration. The matrifocal family structure that developed among the Afro-Surinamese and the central role of women are still very much in evidence and have perhaps even been reinforced in the Netherlands. The patriarchal East Indian family structure is still evident in the cultural ideal of the male breadwinner still adhered to in the Indo-Surinamese community, though it does seem to have become a bit weaker.

A definite convergence between the Afro-Surinamese and Indo-Surinamese can be observed among families in both groups who occupy a similarly low socioeconomic position. The men in both groups sometimes experience long-term dependence on welfare or other benefits, be it that unemployment prevails among the Afro-Surinamese and disability is relatively more common among the Indo-Surinamese. One important difference, however, is that the Afro-Surinamese exhibit more of a continuation of alternative career patterns that were also in evidence in Paramaribo, whereas alternatives of this kind are less institutionalized among the Indo-Surinamese and are often of a temporary nature.

In the Afro-Surinamese as well as the Indo-Surinamese community, multifarious changes are taking place, particularly as a result of the increased financial self-reliance and independence of women. The changing patterns are related to the altered social context after the migration to the Netherlands. As a result of the social security provided by the welfare state and the favorable job situation in the 1990s, there are ever more economic opportunities in the Netherlands. An additional specific condition plays a role for Afro-Surinamese women. The matrifocal patterns they brought with them when they immigrated increasingly coincided with the latest trends in Dutch society, namely, the growing labor market participation of women and the alternative family formations and interaction patterns between men and women. Changes also occurred in this connection among the Indo-Surinamese, but not so much as a matter of course and they often clash quite severely with the prevailing ideas in the community. Any number of changes are now nonetheless affecting the lives of the Indo-Surinamese. For a younger generation of women, getting married and having children are less of an obstacle to getting a good education and having a professional career than they were for their mothers. Afro-Surinamese women were always aware of the need to be able to be financially independent, and getting an education was part of this. However, the relatively rapid emancipation of Indo-Surinamese women might well be one reason why there is more of a debate and more conflict in the Indo-Surinamese community about the traditional roles of men and women. In this respect, there would seem to be a rapid reduction in the gender differences regarding Indo-Surinamese educational and labor market participation. Among the Afro-Surinamese, there was always less of a difference between the sexes. In this sense, the Afro-Surinamese exhibit more continuity in the role of women than the Indo-Surinamese.

Notes

1. Cf. Warrier (1994).

2. It is true that the figures presented here date back to 1994, but the observed trends were also evident in the SPVA-1998 (see Martens 1999: 143).

3. See Volkstelling (1971/1972: 39). This is the percentage of the employed in the total population above the age of fourteen.

4. The figures pertain to the percentage of working people, so they do not include the job-seekers. As regards the percentage of job-seekers, there are similarly barely any differences between Creole and East Indian men (9 and 8 percent) The difference between the women is greater: 7 percent of the Creole women are looking for a job, as compared

with 1 percent of the East Indian women. The Census (Volkstelling 1971/1972) report that this information is taken from, though, notes that these figures present an overly positive picture.

5. See also the following section.

6. Cf. Lalmahomed (1992a: 29).

7. See Buschkens (1974).

8. See chapter 3.

9. See for a comparison with native Dutch women: Martens and Verweij (1997: 44).

10. These figures were calculated on the basis of data from the SPVA-1994 as published by Martens and Verweij (1997: 74).

11. For an overview of the theories on matrifocality, see, e.g., Buschkens (1974: 10ff.) and Venema (1992: 30ff.).

12. Cf. Mintz and Price (1992: 64-65).

13. See, e.g., Hoetink (1961).

14. See also chapter 4.

15. Cf. Sansone (1992).

16. The figures pertain to divorces as well as cases of disowning or desertion without an official divorce (see Speckmann 1965: 167).

17. This was also alluded to by the Organization for Hindu Media (OHM) in its radio program on this topic on 26 May 1996 called "Divorce for extra social assistance."

18. Frazier, who conducted research in the United States on the influence of slavery on the black family, noted the difference between peasants on the one hand and the urban lower class and plantation workers on the other. The former were thought to have more stable marriages, whereas the latter had more "matricentric" families. This is also felt to apply to Surinam (in Venema 1992: 31).

19. This is the idea postulated by R. T. Smith and cited by Hoetink (1961: 92). Hoetink defends, though, the importance of cultural factors here in an effort to arrive at a synthesis between the "functional" and "historical" explanations.

20. See also Eldering and Borm (1996).

21. Cf. chapter 2.

22. See chapter 8.

23. To avoid any misunderstanding, let me state clearly that Afro-Surinamese men are not marginal in family life as such. The role of men with regard to their parental family is not the least bit marginal. If men play a marginal role, then it is as husband and father, but not as son, brother, or uncle (see also Venema 1992: 41). One of my respondents, for example, was raised by his mother because his parents separated when he was a young child. But his mother's eldest brother more or less took over the role of father and made a sizeable contribution to his nephew's upbringing.

Chapter Six

Children of Immigrants and Educational Mobility

Two studies on Surinamese youngsters were published in the 1990s. The first is the one by Sansone (1992) about lower-class Afro-Surinamese youths in Amsterdam. They grew up in Amsterdam, but they were born in Surinam. The second study, also conducted in Amsterdam, is the one by van Heelsum (1997) on the ethnic and cultural position of second-generation Surinamese youngsters. The picture Sansone presents of their socioeconomic position is an extremely grim one, whereas the youngsters in van Heelsum's study are not doing any worse than their native Dutch peers and are sometimes even doing better. Are we to conclude from these studies that there is a difference between the in-between generation and the second generation, and that the position of youngsters born in the Netherlands will automatically improve? This is precisely what remains to be seen. One important difference between the youngsters in the two studies is their socioeconomic background. Sansone focuses on average lower-class youngsters, whereas van Heelsum's respondents are from an earlier migration cohort in a more favorable socioeconomic position.[1]

In this chapter I examine how the socioeconomic position of the children of Afro-Surinamese and Indo-Surinamese immigrants has developed and how it compares to the position of their parents. For two reasons, I mainly focus on their educational level. First, not as much information is available on their labor market position. Second, their educational level will largely determine their future socioeconomic position. By the children of immigrants, I am referring here to the second generation and those who were not born in the Netherlands but did attend school full-time here. The latter belong to the "in-between" generation. The ages of these immigrant children in my research population range from seventeen to forty. The oldest respondents often came in the 1950s or 1960s with their parents and went to Dutch schools for a few years. The youngest ones are the children of later immigrants and most of them were born in the Netherlands.

Migration Factors and Family Background

First, I examine the importance of factors related to migration, namely, length of residence in the Netherlands, belonging to the in-between or second generation, the age at migration, and the age at entering the Dutch school system. How long have the respondents been in the Netherlands? Are they the in-between generation or the second generation? How old were they when they came? Did they get their entire education at Dutch schools or only part of it? Second, I examine the relative importance of these factors compared with the family background.

The Early and Late Second Generation

The children of the immigrants who came in the 1950s and 1960s are what I call the early second generation. I draw a distinction between this early second generation and the late second generation, the Dutch-born children of immigrants who came in the 1970s or later, because they differ in a number of senses. Before I go into these differences, I would like to give two typical illustrations of the early second generation. These are the stories of Denise, an Afro-Surinamese girl, and Carmelita, an Indo-Surinamese girl.

Denise (24) is the second daughter of Mrs. W., who came to the Netherlands in the 1950s. Denise was born in Amsterdam and grew up in one of the old urban districts. The way she talks says more about the excellent secondary school she attended in the best part of Amsterdam than about her childhood in a working-class district of the city or her Surinamese background. When I spoke to Denise for the first time, she was in her last year of business college.[2] She did not take a direct route to get her there. After primary school, first she attended a comprehensive five-year and six-year secondary school. After the two introductory years, she was advised to go on to the six-year branch, but she chose the five-year one instead, mainly because that was where her girlfriends were going. Almost all the pupils there were native Dutch, although more younger Surinamese pupils did enroll at the school later. After the five-year secondary school, she decided to go to a vocational junior college[3] because that was the school her older sister was attending and she had heard so many nice stories about it. After secondary school Denise could have gone straight to the vocational college, but she was not that ambitious at the time. She had been told it was a really big step and she was a bit intimidated by the idea of being surrounded by real college students. She didn't think it would be right for her. She felt much more attracted to the atmosphere at the junior college. "There were a lot of nice things about it. In fact I thought it was great. And I liked the fact that there were so many Surinamese kids there. If you had an hour off, you could play trump call [a Surinamese card game]." She had "two great years" at the junior college and after she graduated, she wanted to get a job rather than continue her studies. She was nineteen at the time and found a pleasant job with a good salary at a marketing agency, where she could take a course in marketing. She finished that too, but was having trouble with the job itself. Half a year later she decided to go back to school and get her college degree. While waiting for the school year to start, she got a temporary job as a secretary at Schiphol Airport. At business college, she chose Communication as her major. She got her degree a little more than four years later. In her last year, she worked as a trainee at a city district office, and afterward she worked there two days a week. But soon after she graduated, she got a job via an employment agency at a finance house. It was in the field she was specialized in and Denise was very enthusiastic about it. Maybe they would offer her a contract for a year. She is still thinking about going back to school part-time to study sociology, but first she wants to earn some money. She has just moved into her own place for the first time and she has to fix it up.

Denise's mother, who raised her two daughters on her own from the start, gave them ample freedom as regards what they wanted to study. She did encourage them but she did not pressure them to go in any specific direction. She did not object when Denise chose courses of study under her potential level on two different occasions, first when she did the five-year instead of the six-year secondary school, and then when she went to junior college instead of business college. She herself did not have any formal education past primary school (she dropped out of a four-year secondary school in Surinam), but she continued her education on her own. Her mother (Denise's grandmother) had completed a four-year secondary school and was employed as a civil servant in Surinam. Her father (Denise's grandfather) had also worked for the state as a bookkeeper.

Denise's father had not had much of an education. He worked on a ship and after an accident he was unable to continue working. He does not play much of a role in the stories Denise tells. Her parents split up when she was still at primary school. She has a great deal of respect for her mother, who was left to bring up her two daughters on her own. "She is the one who did everything for us, not him" is the way Denise summarizes the situation. Her mother started working again as soon as she thought the children were old enough. For almost fifteen years now, she has had a regular job at an office, the same kind of job her mother had before her.

Carmelita (24) was born in The Hague. Her parents came to the Netherlands in 1966, and soon got married and had two daughters; Carmelita is the youngest. Carmelita also speaks without even the slightest trace of a Surinamese accent, or even the local accent common in The Hague. She has a college education and majored in Labor and Organization. When I first met her, she had just gotten her degree.

She was tested at the end of primary school, and advised to go to a vocational school or at most a four-year commercial school. Her parents thought that was "utter nonsense." She may not have been as bright as her older sister, who was attending a six-year secondary school, but she still had more potential than that. They enrolled Carmelita at a comprehensive secondary school where she could chose from a four-year, five-year, or six-year course. She started with the four-year course and went on to complete the five-year one. Then she went to college and had now just graduated.

Her parents, who had to start helping out at home when they were still young, attach a great deal of importance to education. Alluding to the way things used to be in the past, they always told their daughters, "All you have to think about is doing your best at school. For the rest, you have got everything. You don't have to worry about money and you don't have to work on the side. You don't have to get up at four o'clock in the morning to go to work. You don't have to worry about anything at all, just concentrate on your homework." Carmelita's father is stimulating his older daughter to go back and finish her studies. She was studying economics in Rotterdam, got married, had two children, and now has a part-time job. She never did finish her studies. "Even if it takes you twenty years," he says to his daughter, "the important thing is to graduate."

Carmelita wants to find a job as soon as possible. The goal she has set for herself is to find a job at her level by the end of the year. Only if that does not work will she be willing to set her sights a bit lower. "But I don't want to just take anything I can get, that way you just keep circling around and never get to the level where you belong." Like her sister, Carmelita is married to a Dutch man. For the time being, she wants to keep working. Her husband also has a degree and they got married when they were both still studying. Her parents did not object to their daughters' choice of husbands, though they did object to the older daughter living with her boyfriend before they were married. Carmelita married a young man from a strict Protestant family that had the same objection to living together before marriage. In many ways, Carmelita felt quite comfortable with the small community and the close family ties in the circles her husband came from.

Both Carmelita's parents were teachers, her father at a higher vocational school and her mother at a lower one. They had both also been teachers in Surinam, but at a lower level. "People who wanted to make something of themselves," Carmelita says, "had to come to the Netherlands." Her father studied at Leiden University, her mother worked and studied. They came to the Netherlands with the idea of returning to Surinam after completing their studies. And that is the way it almost happened, Carmelita says. "All the arrangements had been made, they had given notice at the apartment where they were living and at their jobs. They had bought the airline tickets and sold the car. And then there was Bouterse and the December murders. That was two weeks before we were supposed to go. Everything was already gone, our winter clothes, our skates, our dolls. At school we had already said goodbye to everyone." Everything was changed back, her parents both got their old jobs back, they bought a house and settled in the Netherlands for good.

In both their families, Carmelita's parents are the ones who "made it." Her father has a university degree and a good job. Together with his youngest brother, a medical specialist, he has the best education. They both come from a background where every effort was made to allow at least some of the children to get a good education. His parents (Carmelita's grandparents) had a plot of land on the outskirts of Paramaribo, which had to support the whole family. Carmelita's mother's parents in Nickerie were better off; they had a sawmill and a rice field. Most of Carmelita's mother's relatives stayed in Suriname, while most of her father's family came to the Netherlands.

Despite the differences in the ambitions and aspirations that Denise's and Carmelita's parents passed on to them (I discuss this at length later), both of them completed college. Both their careers are typical of the early second generation, but they should not be viewed as representative since there is a wide variety, especially in the Afro-Surinamese early second generation. Their careers are even less representative of the entire second generation, since there are such sizeable differences between the early and late second generation. There are three differences to speak of. First, the early second generation consists of more Afro-Surinamese than Indo-Surinamese. This also means the Afro-Surinamese second generation is older and thus already contains more Afro-Surinamese adults (Martens and Verweij 1997: 14-73).

Second, there is a difference in the incidence of marriages or relationships with the native Dutch. Intermarriage was much more common among the early immigrants, especially the Afro-Surinamese. The early second generation thus consists of the children of mixed marriages to a large degree (van Heelsum 1997: 117). Most of them have a Surinamese father and a Dutch mother, since there were relatively large numbers of single Afro-Surinamese men, students and laborers, coming to the Netherlands at the time, at any rate to Amsterdam. Even in 1971, more Surinamese men than women still migrated to Amsterdam. Though the total number of Afro-Surinamese women who immigrated to the Netherlands was higher that year than the number of men, two to three times as many men as women came to Amsterdam (Zielhuis 1973: 27). Apart from this male predominance, the fact is that the Afro-Surinamese enter into mixed marriages or relationships more often than the Indo-Surinamese. This is still the case.[4] In my own study, the members of the early second generation are the children of Afro-Surinamese laborers who married Dutch women. As I note in the introduction, I have not included these children of mixed Surinamese and Dutch marriages or relationships in my study, but I did include the second-generation children of *two* Surinamese parents. Suffice it to note that in some senses, the children of mixed Surinamese and Dutch parentage do have an advantage over the children of two Surinamese parents in that they are better educated and less often unemployed (van Heelsum 1997: 120, 125).

A third difference between the early and late second generation is their composition as regards social class. There is a widely held but erroneous assumption that the Surinamese who came to the Netherlands in the 1950s and 1960s were all members of the elite. It is true that relatively large numbers of middle-class or upper-class immigrants came to the Netherlands at the time, but so did people from other segments of the Surinamese population. During the later exodus from Surinam, the number of people from the urban lower class and from the countryside increased sharply. This is why the later second generation includes many more people from these lower socioeconomic backgrounds than the early second generation.

All things considered, the early second generation had a more favorable starting position. The late second generation did not follow the positive trend evident among members of the early second generation. This changes the picture of the second generation as a whole, since the early second generation distorts it in a positive sense. Though the second generation will do better than the first, there are considerable differences as regards school performance within this generation. So it is premature to draw any optimistic conclusions about this second generation without taking into consideration the migration cohort the parents were part of.

The Relative Importance of Migration Factors
versus Family Background

It is true that the Surinamese still lag behind the native Dutch at school, but their educational level has exhibited a gradual rise in the course of time. This is related in part to the growing number of children entering the Dutch school system from the very start. It can even be observed within one and the same family, especially the frequently large Indo-Surinamese family.

> Mr. and Mrs. J. have eight children. Their youngest son is the only one still living with them. Mr. J. (61) only finished primary school, and his wife never had a chance to go to school at all and is illiterate. In Paramaribo, Mr. J. earned a living as a tailor. The oldest son (35) attended primary school in Surinam, and finished a junior commercial school in the Netherlands. The next two children, a son and a daughter, came to the Netherlands when they were halfway through primary school, and both also went on to complete a junior commercial school afterward. The next three children advanced further and finished a middle-level vocational and commercial school. The two youngest children, who had their entire education in the Netherlands, advanced the most. The youngest daughter (25) finished college and the youngest son (24) is now a college student.

This case clearly shows that the younger the children, the higher their educational level. The children's rising educational level is mainly related to the age when they enter the Dutch school system.

Of course the school performance of immigrant children is not only a question of how long they have been in the Netherlands and whether they entered the Dutch school system at the beginning or midway. There are youngsters in my study, some of them members of the second generation, who entered the Dutch school system at the start and were not any more successful there than youngsters who started their Dutch school career at a later age. In other words, some youngsters start their Dutch school career in the middle and are nonetheless quite successful. In these cases, their family background would seem to be of more decisive importance than how old they were when they entered the Dutch school system or whether they belong to the in-between or the second generation.

The importance of family background in explaining school performance is evident in the two cases described above of early second-generation youngsters. The children of the early immigrants were not only born and raised in the Netherlands, in comparison with the later immigrants they are also more frequently from a somewhat higher or more stable socioeconomic background. In addition to the favorable circumstance of having lived in the Netherlands their whole life, these youngsters also benefit from a favorable family background. So they have a double advantage, their family background and length of stay in the Netherlands. The case histories of the Afro-Surinamese Denise and the Indo-Surinamese Carmelita are good examples. Although Denise does not come from an upwardly mobile middle-class background like Carmelita, her mother's background can certainly be classified as upper lower class, also in view of her grandparents' educational level. In both these cases, it is hard to distinguish the effect of an entire school career in the Netherlands from the effect of family background.

The importance of family background is also clear from the cases of youngsters who did not attend Dutch schools from the start but are still quite successful. This is evident from the example of two Indo-Surinamese brothers.

Roy and Glenn came from Paramaribo to The Hague with their parents when they were eleven and twelve years old. Their father had been to the Netherlands in the early 1960s but went back to Surinam. He came to the Netherlands again in 1975, this time mainly to get a Dutch passport. Although he was from an extremely poor family, by working hard and studying he managed to work his way up and become a bookkeeper. In Surinam he worked for a trading company. His wife attended a four-year Catholic secondary school, where she also got her stenography and typing diplomas. The nuns helped her get a civil service job at a ministry.

The whole family moved to the Netherlands in 1980. They were hosted at first by a relative, but they soon purchased a home of their own in a quiet neighborhood not yet populated by many immigrants. Both parents found jobs in the

Netherlands, though it was not easy, and could more or less work in their own occupations. Roy and Glenn entered the Dutch school system midway. Roy came from the first class of secondary school, and Glenn from primary school. In the Netherlands they both went to a comprehensive school, where Roy did the four-year and Glenn the five-year course. Even after the death of their father, there was no question whether the boys were going to continue their education. They both stayed at the same school and ultimately finished the six-year course. Then Glenn enrolled at a commercial college, but he dropped out before he graduated. He got a job as a civil servant at a ministry and continued studying for his State Practical Business Administration Diploma. Roy went to the university and graduated with a degree in Business Administration.

Although Roy and Glenn had the disadvantage of entering the Dutch school system midway, both of them were successful there. In this case, family background was an important factor in their school performance and more than compensated for the fact that they had not been in the Dutch school system from the start. In other words, a favorable family background can make up for a relatively short period of residence in the Netherlands.

The importance of family background is also evident in the case of late second-generation youngsters, most of whom are from a low socioeconomic background. In Bijlmermeer, a district in Amsterdam largely populated by immigrants, I spoke to youngsters whose parents were poorly educated and had a hard time finding jobs in the Netherlands or were dependent on welfare. Some of them were the children of single mothers who did or had done unskilled work. Although these youngsters were born and raised in the Netherlands, they had not come much further than their parents. Even if they get a better diploma, due to the "diploma inflation" it is still no guarantee they will have a better position on the labor market than their parents.

Mrs. I. (37) came to the Netherlands in 1973 at the age of fourteen. Her parents sent her to live with an aunt. She admits herself that she was cutting classes a lot and giving her parents a hard time. She had not had much more than primary school when she came to the Netherlands. She did all kinds of unskilled work here, sorting at the post office, cleaning, working in the kitchen at a nursing home. At a given moment she started getting welfare. Since she had three children by then and had to take care of them on her own, she also worked off the books in addition to receiving a benefit. She was caught and had to pay back what she owed the Department of Social Services. A few years later, she had to go back to work and became a "neighborhood mother." She took a mandatory course in Child Care Supervision. This caused some problems with her children because she was away a lot.

Mrs. I. has five children with two different men. Gabriella (18) is the oldest. After completing a vocational school, she is now attending a junior college. She has always been the one her mother could rely on. The two other teenaged children are much more trouble. The oldest son (16) is attending a short vocational school but cuts classes a lot. The second oldest daughter (14) has a co-guardian appointed by the state and is attending a program combining school with didactic and psychological counseling at a special institute. The two youngest children are at primary school.

Here again, educational achievement would seem to be far more linked to family background than to migration-related factors. The children were born in the Netherlands, and their mother came to the country at a young age. Problems directly related to migration (e.g., adaptation or adjustment problems, housing or language problems) barely play a role any more, if at all. Just as the two successful boys described above had a favorable start because of their family background, these children had an unfavorable starting position because of their family background. But in both cases, migration-related factors were only of secondary importance.

These case histories help put the importance of immigration-related factors in the proper perspective. What is more, the assumption that the longer a family is in the Netherlands, the better it is for the children's educational career is not as simple as it sounds. Nor is it true that the youngsters of the second generation are always in a better position. In a number of cases, these factors can have quite the opposite effect on their school performance. That is sometimes the case with youngsters born and raised in the Netherlands who have barely had any experience with life in Surinam. Their parents think they have become "Dutchified" and are mainly interested in having a good time. It is okay to work hard now and then, as long as they have a good time at school and not too many demands are made on them. They have a hard time coping with any kind of setback and tend to opt for the easy way out.

Maureen (25) is the youngest of a family of four children. Her mother is of Indo-Surinamese and her father of mixed Afro-Surinamese and Chinese-Surinamese descent. Her parents came to the Netherlands in 1971 when Maureen was only a baby. She says she is less ambitious than her older brothers and sister. Although Maureen was advised to go to a six-year secondary school when she was tested at the end of primary school, she decided she would go to a five-year school. She had a good time there with her friends, but her school performance was poor. She was left back a few times, switched to another school, and dropped out before she graduated. Via a school for adult education and a short period at a junior college, she is now at a college studying to be a social worker. She says she was an unruly teenager when she was at school because her parents were never satisfied with anything she did. She still feels she has a problem disciplining herself. "I like the courses I am taking, but I am not the kind of student who goes home and studies every day, you know. I don't have that kind of regularity in my life. I am not really that career-oriented either." She has a boyfriend who earns a nice living, and she is not sure whether she is going to ever have a job herself. Maybe a part-time job or as a volunteer. "I don't necessarily have to earn anything, as long as I like the work. I am not that interested in having a career. As long as I can enjoy life."

These youngsters probably do not differ in this sense from their native Dutch peers, but they have a very different mind-set than their parents. The older generation knows from experience what it is like to be poor and what it means to be able to get an education. They realize how difficult it was for *their* parents to support a family. Their own children, however, are barely aware of it and do not want to be reminded all the time. Parents who want to give their children every opportunity to get an education have to stand by and watch them ignore or waste their chances. In one large Indo-Surinamese family, the children who arrived with their parents, the in-between generation, were still very ambitious and eager to meet their parents' high expectations by working very hard. However, some of the grandchildren no longer had this attitude at all and wound up with less of an education than their parents. In another Indo-Surinamese family, it was the youngest son (26) who threw in the towel, and he was the one the parents expected the most from. He was the only one of the children to study at the university, where he majored in chemistry, but he quit after the first year. He made friends with "the wrong crowd," his mother said. He got into debt and found himself in a lot of trouble. A trip to Surinam was the answer to the acute crisis, but he never did go back to the university.

In my research population, there are youngsters like him in both ethnic groups. Later in this book, I address the extent to which this pattern is more typical of one group than the other and the conditions that play a role. Here I would first like to examine the differences in educational mobility between the Afro-Surinamese and the Indo-Surinamese.

Patterns of Educational Mobility

Research conducted in the 1980s not only shows that Surinamese pupils did not do as well at primary school as their native Dutch peers, it also shows that the school performance of Indo-Surinamese pupils was considerably poorer than of Afro-Surinamese pupils (Koot et al. 1985; Tjon-A-Ten 1987). This contradicts the public image of the Indo-Surinamese to such an extent that there were doubts as to the reliability of the research results.[5] The transition from the Surinamese to the Dutch school system was sizeable, especially for Indo-Surinamese children who had language problems and sometimes transferred directly from a rural school in Surinam to a city school in the Netherlands. In itself, it is not so surprising that Indo-Surinamese children lagged behind at the time. The longer they were in the Netherlands and the higher the percentage of children born here, the better they did at school. The question thus is whether the fact that Indo-Surinamese children lagged behind Afro-Surinamese children at the time was mainly a matter of adjustment problems, and thus a temporary question, or something more lasting. How has the educational position of the two ethnic groups from Surinam developed since then?

Educational Mobility

The average Indo-Surinamese educational level is still lower than the Afro-Surinamese, but there have been a number of changes in the course of time. In this section I examine the quantitative research data to gain insight into the exact changes in educational mobility. Since no data is available on the educational mobility of parents and children, these are data at the group level. They give thus an indication of the trends over time and not necessarily of the intergenerational mobility.

Table 6.1 shows the educational level reached by various age categories. This gives an impression of the trends over time. In a certain sense, the data on the youngest age category (15-25) are distorted, since the information in the table only pertains to people who are no longer studying full-time and many youngsters in this age category still are. So the table only provides information about a certain selection of youngsters between fifteen and twenty-five. Even if we do not include this age category in the analysis, we can still draw a number of conclusions.

The younger they are, the more of an increase there is in the educational level of the Afro-Surinamese and Indo-Surinamese alike. The Indo-Surinamese pattern is linear; there is a decrease in the number of people who only attended primary school and a considerable increase in the number of people who attended secondary school. The increase is a bit less spectacular among the Afro-Surinamese. In the oldest age category, the Indo-Surinamese have reached a considerably lower educational level than the Afro-Surinamese. However, this difference is no longer nearly as sizeable for the twenty-five to thirty-five age category. So the educational levels of both groups are rising, but the Indo-Surinamese level is rising more rapidly. The percentage of Indo-Surinamese who did not go any further than primary school has decreased enormously. In addition, the percentage of Indo-Surinamese who attend four-year vocational or secondary schools has risen sharply. Although the Indo-Surinamese are still not very well educated in comparison with the native Dutch, the younger age categories are considerably better educated than the older ones. For the Indo-Surinamese, going from primary school to the lower forms of secondary school is still part of their upward mobility.

A comparison of tables 6.1 and 6.2 on the past and present levels of education gives another indication of the trends over time. Table 6.2 shows the schools Indo-Surinamese and Afro-Surinamese youngsters now attend. There are no sizeable differences between the two groups except at the highest level. No fewer than 23 percent of the Afro-Surinamese are attending a college or university, as compared with 13 percent of the Indo-Surinamese, which is still a high percentage compared with the older Indo-Surinamese.

Table 6.1 *Completed education (irrespective of country of education) of the Indo-Surinamese and Afro-Surinamese no longer studying full-time in 1994 according to age (in percentages)*

Indo-Surinamese	15-25	25-35	35-45	45-65
no more than primary school	21	32	45	64
four-year vocational or secondary school	54	40	31	20
five- or six-year vocational or secondary school	22	21	17	8
college or university	3	7	7	8
absolute total (=100%)	67	168	151	128

Afro-Surinamese	15-25	25-35	35-45	45-65
no more than primary school	31	24	26	29
four-year vocational or secondary school	28	38	38	40
five- or six-year vocational or secondary school	41	25	21	17
college or university	0	13	15	14
absolute total (=100%)	39	144	119	94

Source: SPVA-1994, ISEO/EUR.

Table 6.2 *Full-time schools attended by the Indo-Surinamese and Afro-Surinamese above the age of twelve in 1994 (in percentages)* [*]

	Indo-Surinamese	Afro-Surinamese
primary school	8	11
four-year vocational or secondary school	39	33
five- or six-year vocational or secondary school	39	33
college or university	13	23
absolute total (=100%)	158	70

Source: SPVA-1994, ISEO/EUR.
[*] After they are rounded off, the percentages do not always add up to exactly 100.

One final way to describe educational mobility is by comparing the first and second generations. Here again, the Indo-Surinamese are still lagging behind the Afro-Surinamese, but they are unmistakably in the process of catching up. The pattern described above is repeated in table 6.3. There is a sharp reduction in the percentage of Indo-Surinamese with no more than a primary school education and an increase in the percentage of Indo-Surinamese who have completed secondary school. It may still often not be the most advanced kind of secondary school, but at the higher level as well there are more graduates among the second than the first generation. The most striking thing about the Afro-Surinamese figures is the sharp rise in the number of higher (five- or six-year) secondary and vocational school graduates. In contrast, there are fewer Afro-Surinamese at the two lowest educational levels (no more than primary school, four-year secondary, or vocational school). Lastly, the findings at the highest educational level are striking. For both groups, the relation between the first and second generation is reversed—the first generation graduated from a college or university more often than the second generation. However, here again the people who are still studying full-time have not been included in the table. Since the members of the second generation are still relatively young, many have not yet reached their final level of education. This probably explains why the second generation has not yet completed a college or university education as often as the first generation.

Table 6.3 *Completed education of the Indo-Surinamese and Afro-Surinamese between the ages of fifteen and sixty-four no longer studying full-time in 1994 according to generation (in percentages)*

	first-generation Indo-Surinamese	*first-generation Afro-Surinamese*	*second-generation Indo-Surinamese*	*second-generation Afro-Surinamese*
– no more than primary school	44	28	26	21
– four-year vocational or secondary school	33	38	47	36
– five- or six-year vocational or secondary school	16	20	21	35
– college or university	7	14	5	8
absolute total (=100%)	456	311	57	84

Source: SPVA-1994, ISEO/EUR.

* After they are rounded off, the percentages do not always add up to exactly 100.

All things considered, the average Afro-Surinamese educational position is still better than the Indo-Surinamese, but the difference has become smaller. Both groups' educational levels are improving, but the Indo-Surinamese is improving more rapidly. The Indo-Surinamese exhibit consistent evidence of a steady advancement. The Afro-Surinamese trends are less linear.

Stagnation and Success

The trends over time indicate that the longer their length of stay in the Netherlands, the more upward mobility immigrants' school results exhibit. However, it is also clear that this advancement is occurring relatively rapidly among the Indo-Surinamese. What is not clear yet is the course of intergenerational educational mobility. The quantitative material does not suffice in this respect, since it does not provide insight into differences in the mobility of parents and children. My qualitative research sheds a bit of light on this aspect.

Certain patterns of intergenerational mobility emerge in my research population that demonstrate that, in addition to migration factors and family background, other circumstances influence school achievement levels. In the first place, there are children of early immigrants in my study whose family background gave them a favorable starting position but who nonetheless did poorly at school. In some cases, they even remained under the level of their parents, who gave them every opportunity to continue their studies. Despite a favorable starting position in two respects—the age of entering the Dutch school system and family background—they were less successful than their parents. This is illustrated in the following example.

Jeffrey (33, Afro-Surinamese) had not started school yet when he came to the Netherlands with his parents in the 1960s. His father mainly came to complete his studies and became an accountant. His mother had been trained as a primary school teacher, but she did not work as a teacher in the Netherlands. She did have a job though, which she kept for many years. In a material sense, with two working parents, the family was quite comfortable. Both parents wanted their children to get a good education. Jeffrey himself wanted to go to a technical school after he completed primary school, but his father insisted he go to a regular secondary school. He went to a four-year secondary school, where he was left back and had trouble graduating. After he finished, he went to a technical school for further training. He did not do well there. He loved sports and had friends whose pressure he could cope with, but they were engaged in criminal activities (stealing, breaking and entering). He dropped out of school and wanted to go into the Dutch army. While he was waiting to go into the army, his father insisted he complete a five-year secondary school in the evenings. He enrolled but never completed this course either. After a couple of years of working for employment agencies, and after he and his girlfriend decided to start living together, he decided he wanted a regular job and found one.

Apparently, entering Dutch schools at the start and having a favorable family background are not enough to guarantee a successful school career. Compared with their parents, there is even a certain degree of stagnation. Their peers can sometimes influence youngsters more than their parents at a crucial stage of their school career.

Educational stagnation is not uncommon among youngsters who, unlike Jeffrey in the example given above, are from a poor socioeconomic background. Jeffrey's favorable family background helped him finish school. In a sense, his parents were able to counteract the influence of his peers. Youngsters who do not have this kind of support at home have a much harder time dealing with this kind of pressure. This can result in the stagnation of their school career or in their taking an "alternative" route. This is something I observed among my Afro-Surinamese as well as Indo-Surinamese respondents, all of them boys or young men. Usually they have alternative careers of the kind described by Sansone (1992). They often start by cutting classes and dropping out of school, and then gambling, going into debt, selling drugs, sometimes resulting in semilegal activities or petty crime. Contrary to what is generally assumed, it is not only young Afro-Surinamese men who have alternative careers of this kind. The Indo-Surinamese families in my study also include boys who are viewed as "problems." One was temporarily sent to live with his relatives in Surinam, another wound up in prison, and a third cut off contact with his family and turned to illegal activities. In Indo-Surinamese circles, allusions are made to the growing "problems" with the youngsters and attention is focused on combating juvenile crime.[6]

My study does not enable me to specify the extent to which this kind of alternative career is more common among one ethnic group than the other. Quantitative research does, however, provide certain indirect indications, although data is not always available on men and women separately. If we first consider school dropout rates, there is no difference between the two ethnic groups (Martens and Verweij 1997: 80). There are, however, differences in other respects. At the age of nineteen, the school participation rate is twice as high among the Indo-Surinamese as the Afro-Surinamese (Martens and Verweij 1997: 29).[7] In other words, at this age Afro-Surinamese youngsters are far less apt to attend school full-time than Indo-Surinamese youngsters. The unemployment rate among Afro-Surinamese men up until the age of thirty-five is also much higher than among Indo-Surinamese men of the same age, especially among the poorly educated Afro-Surinamese men (Martens and Verweij 1997: 48, 82). Lastly, as I note in chapter 2, long-term unemployment is also more prevalent among the Afro-Surinamese. On the grounds of these data, one might expect alternative careers to be more common among young Afro-Surinamese than young Indo-Surinamese men.

But in fact another pattern in the educational careers of youngsters from a low socioeconomic background is their upward mobility as compared with their parents. A number of youngsters from the late second generation are quite successful despite the fact that their parents had so little schooling.

Judith (22, Afro-Surinamese) was three years old when she came to the Netherlands in 1975. She is the oldest in a family with three children. Her grandmother (69) worked in the informal sector in Paramaribo. One of her jobs was as a cook in the home of a middle-class family. She came to the Netherlands in 1977 and alternated between being here and in Surinam. Judith's mother (38) was still at a four-year secondary school when she got pregnant at the age of 15. She did unskilled work in the Netherlands, and at the moment she has a job in catering. Judith's father finished a four-year secondary school. He had a wide range of jobs in the Netherlands and is now working as a foreman at a flower auction hall. Judith herself completed a four-year and then a five-year secondary school and is now attending college.

Urmy (21, Indo-Surinamese) came to the Netherlands at the age of four in 1978. She is the middle child in a family with five children. Her father (47) is from a family of fifteen children that lived in the district of Saramacca. He was a tailor in Paramaribo. In the Netherlands he had various jobs via an employment agency, but has been classified as disabled for the past three years. Her mother had no schooling at all, married young, and had no paid employment either in Surinam or the Netherlands. The three oldest children completed a six-year secondary school, and the two youngest children are still attending one. Urmy is now studying law at the university. The two oldest children are also at the university; her oldest sister is studying biology and her brother is studying computer science.

Even children of parents with a low or extremely low educational level who never had a job in the Netherlands and have been on welfare ever since they arrived sometimes manage to complete their studies at the university. There are no data available on the extent to which this upward mobility is more common among either Surinamese group, but I have the impression this pattern is more typical of the Indo-Surinamese than the Afro-Surinamese.

The Afro-Surinamese are probably more apt to take a different route to a high educational level. This route is often a more gradual one, involving one course after the other. At any rate, the upwardly mobile Afro-Surinamese in my study tend to spread out their studies over a lengthier period of time and continue studying until a later age. This same observation can be made based on the SPVA figures. Relatively many Afro-Surinamese women complete their studies at a college or university (Martens and Verweij 1997: 77) and continue studying full-time until a relatively late age. It is striking at any rate that after the age of twenty-five, a higher percentage of Afro-Surinamese than Indo-Surinamese are still studying full-time. As I note above, the Indo-Surinamese school participation rate is higher at a younger age (19). This means that, on average, the Indo-Surinamese stop studying full-time at a younger age than the Afro-Surinamese. I have the impression, however, that the Indo-Surinamese who do continue to higher forms of education after that age complete their studies at a younger age than the Afro-Surinamese.

My qualitative research results thus suggest that in a subgroup of the Afro-Surinamese younger generation, there might be a tendency toward stagnation in the educational career, whereas among the Indo-Surinamese there is a subgroup of relatively rapid risers who come from a low socioeconomic background. Whatever the case may be, in comparison with Afro-Surinamese youngsters, Indo-Surinamese youngsters more frequently have parents with an extremely low educational level. It is clear from the SPVA data that twice as many Indo-Surinamese in the twelve to thirty-five age group have parents who attended no more than primary school, if that. In view of this family background (as measured by parents' educational level), the advances Indo-Surinamese youngsters are making at school are all the more striking. If the parents' educational level is the best predictor of school performance, as is often assumed in the sociology of education, then this finding is quite surprising. Apparently the role of family background in determining children's school performance does not solely lie in the parents' educational level. What is more, educational level alone is not adequate grounds for explaining differences in the educational mobility of Afro-Surinamese and Indo-Surinamese youngsters. There is obviously more to it.

Conclusion

The optimistic and the pessimistic pictures of the second generation presented at the beginning of this chapter both deserve to be addressed in greater detail because we are dealing with different migration cohorts in different socioeconomic positions. This is particularly true of the Afro-Surinamese, since their migration history exhibits greater variations. The arrival of the Afro-Surinamese in the Netherlands was spread out over a longer period of time and there were considerable social class differences between the various migration stages. The picture of the Afro-Surinamese as a whole is thus repeatedly "disturbed" by new migration flows. It is unclear, then, to what extent the position of the group changed as a result of the social mobility of earlier immigrants from this group or as a result of the continuing immigration. This issue plays less of a role with the Indo-Surinamese, who came to the Netherlands within a shorter period of time.

Although the Afro-Surinamese still have a head start in the field of education, the Indo-Surinamese are catching up at a relatively rapid rate. In part, this is only logical: the lower the starting point, the more of a rise there can be. There are nonetheless indications of a rapid intergenerational educational mobility among the Indo-Surinamese and a certain extent of stagnation in segments of the Afro-Surinamese population. At any rate, the average upward educational mobility is greater among the Indo-Surinamese than the Afro-Surinamese. Yet this is not what one would expect on the grounds of the two factors generally viewed as being crucial to educational achievement: length of stay and family background (as measured by parents' educational level). On average, after all the Indo-Surinamese have not been in the Netherlands as long as the Afro-Surinamese and the educational level of the first generation is considerably lower. The question is how to interpret these differences in educational mobility between the two ethnic groups. In the following chapters, I try to see exactly which conditions influence the differing mobility trajectories.

Notes

1. What is more, van Heelsum's respondents comprise a specific selection from this cohort. The youngsters in this study are relatively well educated compared with the national figures on the educational level of the second-generation Surinamese in the SPVA-1991 (van Heelsum 1997: 80).

2. Denise attended a HEAO, literally higher economic and administrative school, which is translated here as business college, the closest equivalent.

3. Denise first attended a MEAO, literally a middle-level economic and administrative school, which is translated here as junior college, the closest equivalent.

4. See chapter 8.

5. See the comments by Mungra on an article entitled "Een slecht rapport voor de overheid: Surinaamse kinderen op de basisschool" (A bad grade for the government: Surinamese children at primary school) in *Intermediair* (1982, nos. 24 and 25).

6. The Vedic Youth Netherlands Foundation (1997) devoted a special conference to this problem. Some of the delegates expressed words of caution, and others felt it was not wise to overstate the problem. No information is available on the juvenile crime rate among the Indo-Surinamese, but there is the general impression that it is lower than the juvenile crime rates of other immigrants groups (see also Kishoendajal 1997).

7. For the groups as a whole, the full-time school participation rate is also higher among the Indo-Surinamese (32 percent) than the Afro-Surinamese (22 percent) (Martens and Verweij 1997: 78).

Chapter Seven

Family Background

Unlike the situation in Surinam, in the Dutch welfare state the parents' income no longer plays a significant role in children's future position in society, at least not in a direct way. Educational sociologists largely agree that nowadays the parents' financial situation is less decisive for children's future occupational careers than in the past.[1] To a large extent, the influence of family background on the occupational careers of a younger generation is now exerted indirectly via education.

The parents' income similarly no longer plays the main role in the educational careers of children. Immaterial aspects of the children's upbringing in the parental home are more important to their school performance. These aspects are largely shaped by the parents' socioeconomic position. It has been repeatedly observed, however, that the socioeconomic position of immigrant parents does not explain everything about their children's school careers, and that ethnic-specific factors apparently play a role as well.[2] It is not clear though exactly what these factors are, and not everyone is completely convinced they even exist.

In this chapter, I examine these immaterial aspects of children's upbringing and the extent to which they are related to ethnic descent. I do not confine myself in advance to certain variables, as is often the case in research in the sociology of education.[3] I conceive of immaterial aspects of upbringing in the widest sense of the term in an effort to include whatever unexpected influences might prove relevant. In a general sense, I am interested in the "messages" children get from the parental home. Brinkgreve and van Stolk (1997) refer in this connection to *social legacies*: the transfer of values, views, and attitudes from one generation to the next.[4] I confine myself to whatever is relevant to the future educational and occupational careers of the following generation. I examine what parents pass on to their children and how the children add their own interpretations in changing circumstances.

Ambitions

The Afro-Surinamese and Indo-Surinamese both attach great importance to education as a route to advancement in society. In itself, this is not surprising, all the more since this conclusion is so frequently drawn in literature on immigrant families.[5] It is related in part to the opportunities people barely had if at all in the country of origin and do have in the Netherlands. First-generation immigrants who bring up their children in the Netherlands generally haven't had much of an opportunity to get an education themselves and want their children to have more of a chance to get ahead in society. They often express this wish by referring to high status professions such as medicine and law—professions they are familiar with from the country of origin. So the notions involved are very global ones. If researchers observe on the basis of these notions that immigrant parents have high aspirations for their children, in itself this observation is not that revealing. A lot more is required for good school performance than vague or abstract notions of upward social mobility. This is why it is important to know exactly what ambitions parents have for their children and, even more important, how these ambitions are put into practice.

Level of Ambition and Pressure to Succeed

I have noted above that for the Creoles in Surinam, education was traditionally the route to social advancement. However, for the East Indian immigrants in Surinam various forms of small-scale entrepreneurship constituted the main route to upward mobility in the beginning, and only in the second instance the school system. Whereas it was initially the elite and middle-class Creoles who were welleducated and worked in intellectual and high-status professions, some East Indians soon succeeded in rising from a low position in society to the same type of positions. Doctors and lawyers are widely held in high esteem in the Indo-Surinamese community. Unlike the rather abstract interest in high-status professions referred to above, this Indo-Surinamese interest has turned out to be more than wishful thinking. My research results do not enable me to make any statements about the incidence of specific professions, but I can indicate which ones I came across in my research population. There were repeated references to doctors in the family networks of my Indo-Surinamese research population, but not among the Afro-Surinamese respondents or their relatives. The fervent wish to see at least one of their children become a doctor was more typical of Indo-Surinamese than Afro-Surinamese parents. Other medical and paramedical professions were also in evidence among the Indo-Surinamese and not the Afro-Surinamese population. The same holds true for chemistry, laboratory technology, and other fields of science. Mungra (1993: 121) also observes a striking preference for medicine, law, economics, and technical fields among Indo-Surinamese youngsters. In addition to these "traditional choices," he mentions new fields of study such as information technology and econometrics.[6] The Indo-Surinamese tend to hold academic degrees in high esteem. In general, the Indo-Surinamese have high expectations of their children's education and there is a great deal of pressure to succeed.

Afro-Surinamese parents also tell their children how important it is for their future to have a diploma ("something on paper"). Their expectations are however not generally as high and the pressure they exert is not as great. Academic studies and professions are also held in high esteem by the Afro-Surinamese, but they do not look up to them as much as the Indo-Surinamese. Stated somewhat simplistically, Afro-Surinamese parents more often have a minimum requirement for their children, and Indo-Surinamese parents a maximum demand. Many Afro-Surinamese parents feel their children ought to *at least* graduate from secondary school. One single Afro-Surinamese mother with teenaged children said, "They ought to at least graduate from a four-year secondary school. Just to get a job, that is the least they ask for nowadays." Another Afro-Surinamese woman referred to a kind of minimum demand that her parents used to have. Her father (a mechanic) wanted his children to at least graduate from a four-year secondary school.

> Edmé (34, junior college graduate) says, "In our family, there was really no chance of doing less than the four-year secondary school. The primary aim at home was to graduate from the four-year secondary school; my father did not urge us to try to do the five-year school. It was not taken for granted that we would go on to college or the university, that we would become doctors or lawyers. It was just decided for you that you were going to go to the four-year secondary school and you had to graduate, that was the least you could do. For the rest, they were all happy as soon as we were finished with school."

The Afro-Surinamese often feel you can't force your children to do anything, and putting pressure on them just has the opposite effect. This does not necessarily mean they do not encourage them. On the contrary, it just means they put less pressure on them. Indo-Surinamese parents often want their children to strive for the highest goal and, as will become clear below, the circumstances are often such that they are able to impose their will upon their children.

One illustration of this difference is the description in chapter 6 of the lives of two young respondents, Denise (24, of Afro-Surinamese background) and Carmelita (24, of Indo-Surinamese background), both born in the Netherlands.[7] They both graduated from college, be it via different routes.

> Denise could have gone to the six-year secondary school, but preferred to attend the easier five-year secondary school because that is where her girlfriends were going. What is more, as she says herself, she wanted to be sure she could keep up

with the work. After secondary school, she once again chose an educational level that was lower than her potential, a junior college rather than a college. Once again, she had the same kind of reasons. Her sister was already attending the junior college, there were quite a few Surinamese students there, and it just seemed like a nice place to her. Denise's mother, Mrs. W., encouraged both of her daughters to continue their studies, but she did not pressure them. What she did demand of them was that they at least got some kind of diploma past secondary school, and after that they could do whatever they wanted. As Mrs. W. (51) says, "Look, studying is something you have to leave up to the children. I never pressured my children into anything. I did make sure they did their homework when they were at primary school. I do believe that as a mother you ought to encourage them. And at secondary school too. I said 'As long as you have some kind of secondary school diploma, I don't care which kind. So either from a four-year or a five-year secondary school.' I said, 'I don't care what you do after that, because whatever you decide to do, it is for your own future, not for me. But for me, you do have to finish secondary school.' After that, once they graduated, I let them do whatever they wanted. 'It is your life,' I said, 'You have to organize your life yourself. As far as I am concerned, you can get a job or you can go on with your education. It doesn't matter to me.'"

Mrs. W. says that she herself had not been very ambitious about studying at the time. It was her parents who felt she ought to go to the Netherlands to study at a hospital to be a nurse. Denise also describes herself as not being very ambitious. This is obvious from the fact that on two occasions, she opted for an educational level below her potential. She had various jobs in the meantime, since she was not consciously planning to continue her studies. But she did keep going further and further. For Denise, the most important thing is that she enjoys what she is doing. She didn't plan in advance to take the shortest route. She nonetheless gradually went further and further, and has a college degree and a job and is considering doing another part-time study at the university.

At the time, Carmelita's parents definitely did not agree with the CITO[8] test results. Based on these results, their daughter was advised to go to a four-year vocational or secondary school, and even though she was not as good a student as her sister, they still thought it was nonsense. Her parents enrolled her at a comprehensive school where she could attend a four-year, five-year, or six-year secondary school. It was the same school where her sister was attending the six-year secondary school. With the support of her parents and sister, Carmelita completed the four-year and then the five-year secondary school. She was expected to go on studying. The oldest daughter went to the university and Carmelita went to college, which she completed. She is now planning to look for a job at her level, and not to accept one at a lower level, "otherwise you just keep going around in circles." Only if it really does not work, is she willing to "lower her demands a little." Carmelita's sister is married and has two children, but her father is still encouraging her to complete her studies at the university. Carmelita is very grateful to her parents for always stimulating her to continue studying. She really would not have made it without them, she knows, and would never have come this far. She herself had the idea that she was not such a good student. "I always thought I would just go work in a shop somewhere, be a salesgirl, and that would be fine. That is what I used to think, that I just was not as good at studying as my sister."

It is evident from these two examples that the ambitions in the girls' homes were different. In the Afro-Surinamese family, there was no pressure to continue studying after secondary school, but there clearly was in the Indo-Surinamese family. On two separate occasions, Denise chose an educational option under her potential; Carmelita's parents chose a higher level than the school advised. Whereas Denise mainly planned her educational career herself and her mother barely exerted any pressure at all, the high expectation pattern of Carmelita's parents played an instrumental role in the educational route she ultimately took. Whereas Denise barely received or needed any help from her mother or sister, it was a great support for Carmelita. It is quite probable that Denise would have enrolled at the university right after secondary school if she had had parents like Carmelita's. And it is questionable whether Carmelita would have even finished college if she had grown up in Denise's family.

These examples show a difference in the ambitions and pressures families pass on to their children, a difference that is characteristic to a certain extent of Afro-Surinamese and Indo-Surinamese families. It is not true, however, that the one is more favorable than the other under all circumstances. If there is excessive pressure, high ambitions can have the reverse effect. I came across one concrete example of this pertaining to a six-year secondary school in The Hague. The school consulted an Indo-Surinamese social worker, because the Indo-Surinamese pupils were exhibiting so many symptoms of stress and were getting poorer grades than was normally the case. The parents' expectations and the pressure they were putting on their children to succeed were so high they were causing a fear of failure and the children's performance was only becoming poorer. I have no way of knowing whether this is an isolated case or a more widespread phenomenon, but other researchers also refer to this overpushing by Indo-Surinamese parents (Koot et al. 1985: 86). It is also clear how important "learning" is felt to be from the relatively strong relation Verkuyten (1988: 136-37) observed between self-esteem and school performance among Indo-Surinamese youths.

There are however two sides to the responsibility and freedom children are given. In Denise's case, it worked out well. The given circumstances enabled her to take her own route and still finish with a very good education. It is true that her mother did not push her in any specific direction, but she did support her daughter's ambitions. The circumstances are not always that favorable. As is illustrated below, some youngsters are less able to cope with the freedom they are given. In other words, they would have benefited from a more supportive family climate. The question is whether high ambitions are not also a question of social class.

A Question of Class?

In the sociology of education, parents' educational levels usually stand for multifarious other family factors, including their ambitions and expectations for their children.[9] Aren't the ambitions conveyed at home to children—including Afro-Surinamese and Indo-Surinamese children—also connected to their parents' educational level and to the related family climate?

In part of course this is the case. In Carmelita's case for example, both parents are well educated. They belong to the group of early Indo-Surinamese immigrants; her father came to the Netherlands to attend the university. He and his wife have high ambitions for their two daughters and support them any way they can in attaining these goals.

Well-educated parents generally stimulate their children to attend the more ambitious schools and choose the more ambitious courses of study. On the other hand, it is striking that parents who have not had much education themselves also have high ambitions for their children. This is most clearly evident among the Indo-Surinamese. The children of parents with an extremely low educational level and a poor mastery of the Dutch language (especially the mothers) have unexpectedly high ambitions. I give extensive accounts below of the situation of two Indo-Surinamese youngsters.

The parents of Vyay (30) came to the Netherlands in 1975 with his little sister. He and his brother arrived some time later. In Surinam they lived in the countryside, where his father worked as a truck driver for an agro-industrial company. The plot of land the family had inherited from his grandfather was too small to support the family. Moreover, Vyay's father was not the only one who had a claim to the land; so did Vyay's uncle (who drank up more money than he contributed to the family) and aunt (who was married but had returned to the family home) who both lived in or near his parental home. The family was in debt and Vyay's father was the only one bringing in any money. Shortly before Surinam became independent, he decided to emigrate.

Vyay's mother is from a large agrarian family with twelve children. Like her husband, she only finished primary school and that was all the education she had. She was a good student, but the family didn't have the money and the secondary school was far away. She did, however, learn to read "holy books" from her father, who was a pundit (a learned Hindu).

Both parents wanted their children to get a good education in the Netherlands. Vyay entered the Dutch school system in the middle of primary school, and then went on to a four-year secondary school. After he graduated, he got a five-year and then a six-year secondary school diploma and continued on to the university. First he studied information technology there and then economics, but without completing either of the studies. He had a hard time studying at the university level and at a given moment he decided he was too old. He got a college degree, found a job, and got married. Although Vyay himself does not view his educational career as a success ("it still bothers me that I didn't complete my studies at the university"), after a poor starting situation, he did manage to reach a high educational level, certainly in view of the educational level of his parents. At an early age, they both had to start working in the rice fields and engaging in other agrarian activities. They never had a job in the Netherlands and since their arrival, they have been living on welfare. They live in a state-subsidized flat in one of the postwar neighborhoods with a large concentration of immigrants. His mother has only a poor mastery of Dutch and Vyay himself started primary school with only a limited knowledge of the language. Although his parents never actually helped him with his homework, they stimulated him and did everything they could to enable him to go on with his studies.

Urmy (21) is from a family of five children. She came to the Netherlands in 1978 with her parents and her sister and brother. Her two youngest sisters were born in the Netherlands. The family is from Paramaribo, where her father earned a living as a tailor. Her father and mother are both from large agrarian families from the district of Saramacca. Her mother hardly attended school at all and her father only attended primary school. He learned to be a tailor on the job, but since he had no official certificate to show he was skilled, he could not work as a tailor in the Netherlands. He had various jobs here and there via an employment agency, but for the past few years he has been classified as disabled. Urmy's mother got married when she was seventeen, and never worked outside the home, either in Surinam or the Netherlands. She wanted her daughters to get a good education so they would always be able to support themselves. What she wanted most was for one of her children to study medicine and for one to study law. Urmy entered the Dutch school system in the middle of primary school. Then she went to a comprehensive school where, following obstacles and delays, in the end she got her six-year secondary school diploma. All three of the older children went to the university, where Urmy studied law, her sister studied biology because there was limited admission to the medical faculty, and her brother majored in information technology.

Urmy and her sister and brother were fortunate to have had the support at primary school of a teacher who meant a great deal to them. He helped them with problems, gave them private coaching if they needed it, and encouraged them. This teacher knew another teacher at the comprehensive school who more or less took over the role. So in addition to their parents' stimulating them, they also received concrete assistance from these teachers.

Without any problems, the two youngest sisters (15 and 13) went on to the six-year secondary school after primary school. They benefited from the experience and knowledge of their older sisters and brother. In other ways as well, the older children help make it easier for the younger ones to do well at school in an atmosphere that creates positive conditions for them. For example, the brother who is studying information technology helps his sisters with computer work and computer problems. And Urmy spends some of the money she earns on her younger sisters' school excursions. Thus a favorable family climate is not only created by the parents but also by the entire family.

The stories of Vyay and Urmy and their families illustrate that what is often viewed in the sociology of education as the best predictor of academic success, namely, the parents' educational level, apparently is not an important factor here. Among these immigrants, ambitions and the actual efforts to put them into effect are apparently much less related, if at all, to the parents' educational level. Even if both parents have had very little education and despite long-term welfare dependence, the children are still quite ambitious and successful. Even poorly educated parents appear to be quite capable of passing on high aspirations to their children. What is more, these parents can provide the kind of climate that stimulates education. They may not be able to help their children with their homework or other school-related activities because they lack the knowledge. But perhaps this is not the main aspect of educational support, at any rate it is not the only one. Numerous other elements of what can be called an education-supportive family climate clearly play a role: stimulating children, creating a place for them to do their homework, saving money and giving permission for school excursions, encouraging children to go on with their studies, expressing appreciation for good school performance, and so forth. Besides the fact that Vyay started in the middle of primary school and Urmy at the beginning, Urmy also had more and different resources than Vyay. The children in Urmy's family helped each other, the older ones helped each other, and joined to help the younger ones. Vyay did not have this kind of help, since his older brother dropped out of secondary school. Other studies show that the support of older brothers and sisters can be an important factor in the school performance of immigrant youngsters (Crul 2000). There also happened to be the teachers who made special efforts on Urmy's behalf in the form of private coaching and moral support. The difference between the two youngsters thus mainly lies in the additional resources that youngsters can have to help them put their ambitions into effect. What the two have in common is that their families instilled in them high ambitions even though they came from a background where, on the grounds of the common findings in the sociology of education, this would not have been considered very probable.

The ambitions of the native Dutch are closely related to the educational level of their parents. The way parents bring up their children in the Netherlands is also increasingly related to the parents' educational level (Meijnen and Riemersma 1992: 37). Among Surinamese immigrants, particularly the Indo-Surinamese, apparently this is not yet the case, or at any rate to much less of an extent. Obviously the parents' educational level does not play that much of a role in their aspirations and expectations as regards the school careers of their children. However, this does not hold true the other way around: not all Indo-Surinamese youngsters from a low socioeconomic background have high ambitions or experience a great deal of pressure from their parents to succeed. I will get back to this later. For the time being, I would like to address the fact that the high ambitions and great pressure to succeed on the part of parents, particularly Indo-Surinamese parents, can less easily be traced back to their socioeconomic position than in the case of native Dutch parents. In part, I feel the explanation might well be related to the educational situation in Surinam.

Educational Disadvantages and Educational Opportunities

In the course of time, people in the Netherlands have been continuing their studies longer and choosing courses appropriate to their own performance at school, which is why some authors speak of growing meritocratization (Meijnen and Riemersma 1992: 33).[10] This is feasible because nowadays there are barely any financial obstacles to studying in the Netherlands. In other words, parents' incomes now play only a very minor role in their children's school careers (Dronkers and de Graaf 1995). It was the case, though, up until the 1960s. Referring to Boudon and his concept of background-specific choice patterns, Meijnen and Riemersma note that higher status groups have a tendency to choose in accordance with their individual performance or higher, whereas lower status groups more often make choices under their potential (1992: 34). This is less and less the case in the Netherlands. The question, however, is whether this also holds true for immigrants, in this case from Surinam. After all, they do not come from a welfare state like the Netherlands and there were far more financial limitations in Surinam that kept people from lower socioeconomic groups from getting an education. This means there were more background-specific choice patterns in their school careers, To put it simply, there was greater inequality in Surinam than in the Netherlands as regards educational opportunities.

Financial obstacles to attending school involve actual expenses as well as loss of income. In addition to the purchase of school supplies, in Surinam children had to have shoes and a uniform. Parents experienced a loss of income if their children went to school instead of helping out in the family business or bringing in wages. The oldest children often had to go to work to augment the family income, and the younger children could go to school longer.

Mr. L. (73) and his wife (69) were farmers in the district of Wanica. Mr. L. only had three years of primary school. In his own opinion, this is why he does not speak such good Dutch. Since his oldest brother stayed behind at the parental home and cultivated the land adjoining it, Mr. L. leased a six-hectare plot of land somewhere else from the state. Together with his wife, he had to build up his farm from scratch. The two oldest of their nine children could not go to school; they had to help their parents at home. Earning some money came before going to school. To get to the school, the children had to go to the town, which was twenty kilometers away. First they had to bicycle for five kilometers, and then take the bus for another fifteen kilometers. So money was needed for the bus, and for shoes and clothes. The younger children, boys and girls, who were able to attend school, went there in the morning and helped out with the farm work in the afternoon.

Mrs. D. (69) was born and brought up in the center of Paramaribo. Her mother did all kinds of odd jobs to earn a living for the family, from selling at the market and doing laundry and ironing to working in a grocery store. She sold cassava and fruit, syrup and ginger beer on the market. She also made maize porridge and sold it to the workers during their break. Whatever was left over she would take home with her. Mrs. D. remembers that every week, if her mother had earned some money, she would have to pay the bill at the Chinese shop on the corner.

The children were able to go to primary school, but they also had to contribute to the family income. To Mrs. D. this meant she had to help her mother do the housework for a dentist's family. She would go to school in the morning, and she had to work in the afternoon washing clothes, mopping the floor, doing the dishes, making the beds. She earned seven and a half guilders a month. She gave the money to her mother, who gave her ten or fifteen cents. That was quite a bit in those days, but her grandchildren burst out laughing when she tells them about it today. After she finished primary school, Mrs. D. took sewing classes. Then she worked as the cook in the home where she had worked with her mother.

Mrs. D. has ten children. They could all go to primary school, and some of them went on to finish a three-year or four-year school after that.

Mrs. U. (51) was born in the district of Para and grew up in the city. Her mother pretty much had sole responsibility for her children and foster children. She did housekeeping work, for example, in a home for the aged and at a doctor's home. She hardly had any schooling; as a child she was already doing domestic work. The daughter of the family where her mother worked went to school and became a schoolteacher. Her mother, who was more or less the same age, did the housekeeping.

As a child, Mrs. U. earned her own tuition of eight guilders a month. From two to five in the afternoon and on Saturday, she did cleaning work and earned fifteen guilders a month. But she also had to save money for her *black-and-blues*, the mandatory two school uniforms. After primary school, she was able to go to a three-year school, which she completed. Then she had various jobs, one of which was in a home for the aged.

Financial considerations thus played a role in children's school attendance and the considerations that were involved. This held true for both the Creoles and the East Indians, but for various reasons, it was more the case for East Indians. As is noted above, there were extra obstacles to attending school for East Indians. This had to do with the quality and availability of schooling in the countryside. It was not always possible for children to attend school, and sometimes they had to travel long distances. What is more, this often required money to pay for transportation. One respondent who used to work at a district school told me there were children who had to travel three hours there and three hours back every day. They had to leave at five in the morning to get to school by eight when classes began. From school, first they had to walk to the boat that took them to the other side of the Saramacca River. Then they had to walk to the bus stop, take the bus, and then walk home. East Indian children often had to travel even farther to attend a secondary school, because there were even fewer secondary schools in the countryside. Another option was for children to stay with relatives or acquaintances in the city, or move into a boarding school. According to one respondent whose father had been to a boarding school, Catholic missionaries would knock on all the doors to recruit children for their schools. "The people were very poor and they offered them an opportunity to have their children go to a boarding school where they would get an education."

So East Indians in the countryside had to make quite a few sacrifices to send their children to school or have them continue their education after primary school.[11] In addition to living in the countryside, the fact that many East Indians were independent entrepreneurs often meant their children missed school or stopped going altogether. They had to start working on the family farm at a young age, or help out in the busy season.

As a rural population, East Indians had less easy access to schooling and in this sense, in actual fact they did not have equal educational opportunities. From a historical point of view, the East Indians in Surinam were still in the midst of an effort to catch up. They consequently had a greater educational disadvantage and, as was demonstrated earlier, this is still the case in the Netherlands.[12] This educational *disadvantage* was thus related to the lack of educational *opportunities*. This implies that among East Indians, family background in the sense of parents' educational level says even less about the children's expected school performance than among Creoles. Creoles had been living in the city much longer and had had access to schooling much longer. In their case it was mainly the family income that played an important role in whether or not they were able to go to school. We can thus assume that among Creoles there was more frequently a background-specific choice pattern in school careers. In other words, among Creoles the parents' educational level is (already) a better predictor of school performance than among East Indians.

There is another specific circumstance that applies to East Indians. In their case, a low educational level or lack of schooling does not necessarily mean they are illiterate. In fact quite a few East Indians who did not attend a regular school when they were children did have a religious education. They could not read or write Dutch, but they learned Hindi if they were Hindus or Urdu if they were Muslims. So the older generation was not always illiterate, even if they had not had any schooling in Dutch. Elsewhere as well, there are indications that regardless of the level of their formal education, elderly East Indians were not necessarily illiterate. Jadoenandansing notes, for example, that her grandfather liked to read in Hindi and even did the bookkeeping for his shop in Hindi (1992: 49). In this sense, there was more knowledge present in these circles than one might assume on the basis of the parent's formal educational level.

This explanation in terms of educational opportunities can nonetheless only be a partial explanation for the observed high Indo-Surinamese aspirations and pressure to succeed. Not all the Indo-Surinamese in the Netherlands came directly from the countryside, though the proportion of rural immigrants did increase in the migration around the time Surinam became independent. Historically, it is true that the presence of East Indians in Paramaribo was a more recent phenomenon, but many of the Indo-Surinamese in the Netherlands are from the city or its immediately vicinity, just as the Afro-Surinamese are. Here in the city, financial considerations as regards sending children to school played just as much of a role for Creole as for East Indian lower-class families. To put it simply, people who had no money could not send their children to school. The urban lower class, whether Creole or East Indian, had the same degree of access or lack of access to schooling. So differential educational opportunities cannot constitute the entire explanation for differences in the aspirations and pressure to succeed of the Afro-Surinamese and the Indo-Surinamese.

Trajectories to Success and the Belief in Progress

The way East Indians and Creoles made a living in Surinam before the migration to the Netherlands—their position in the Surinamese occupational structure and on the labor market—did exhibit certain similarities, but there were also sizeable differences. Their economic conduct and the related values, ideas, and attitudes held in premigration days were part and parcel of the baggage these immigrants brought with them to the Netherlands. What differences were there and how did they influence the following generation?

The Importance of Diplomas

I came across high aspirations and pressure to succeed relatively frequently among East Indian families. Does this necessarily mean East Indians attach greater value to schooling than Creoles? Creole parents also emphasize the importance of diplomas and make it clear to their children that, without some kind of a diploma, they will not get very far in society. But this statement needs to be put in the proper perspective.

Among Creoles, the striving for upward social mobility via education is not unambiguous. Two seemingly contradictory observations can be made about the value they attach to education. First, Creoles can be said to traditionally exhibit a great deal of interest in education. Compared with East Indians, they do indeed have a longer tradition of interest in education.[13] Diametrically opposed to this, there is the second observation that Creoles do not set much store by diplomas, and lean toward other ways to improve their position. Buschkens (1974: 163) observed these doubts about the value of education among the lower class Creoles in Paramaribo in the early 1970s. They were thought to believe upward social mobility could be achieved only by luck, for example, by gaining the patronage of influential people or winning the lottery. A defeatist attitude was thought to prevail with respect to the chances for advancement.[14] The observation was made in the Netherlands as well that some circles of Afro-Surinamese youth do not set much store by diplomas as entrance tickets to the labor market (Sansone 1992: 41-42).

These two extremes are less contradictory than they might seem at first. The differing value that is attributed to education can be largely explained on the basis of class differences within the Creole population. Even within the lower class, there are differences in this sense. It was noted earlier in this study that the tradition of educating children had been expanding ever since colonial times to wider and wider segments of the Creole population. Education became the most important route to advancement for the lower class in Paramaribo as well. The belief in education was nonetheless undermined by the persistent unemployment and poverty among a segment of the urban lower class. In part, this differentiation within the lower class coincides with the period of migration to the Netherlands. Among the early immigrants in my study, albeit few in number, the aspiration level and the family support for education were generally greater than among the later immigrants.

Thanks in part to the support she got from the nuns at school and from her father (shoemaker and shoe salesman), Mrs. E. was able to go on with her education at the time, even though it meant less of an income for the large family. Her husband came to the Netherlands to study (State Practical Business Administration Diploma) and their remaining in the Netherlands afterward was inspired in part by the educational opportunities there would be here for their children. Together they devoted a great deal of time and attention to the education of their children. Their oldest daughter enrolled at the university, although she did not complete her studies there. Their son Jeffrey had more problems at school than their daughters. He exhibited a combination of all the ingredients that made other boys drop out of school: he preferred sports and going out to doing his homework, and he had a circle of friends with a penchant for illegal activities. The pressure exerted by his parents, who were demanding and strict when it came to schoolwork, helped get him through the four-year secondary school.

These early immigrants were not always very well educated themselves and their parents certainly had not been, but they did come from families willing to make sacrifices to make sure the children got a good education. It was not taken for granted that the children would go to the university, but that was because of financial considerations—there was no doubt about the usefulness of diplomas.

In other families, I observed a combination of the two ideas cited above about the value of education, namely, that diplomas are important if you want to be a success, and that maybe they are no help at all. The value of diplomas is then a kind of abstract notion that does not have much concrete significance in daily practice. I nonetheless observed a less defeatist attitude and less doubt as to the value of diplomas among the late immigrants than Buschkens noted in Paramaribo or Sansone in Amsterdam. This can be for a variety of reasons, such as differences in the features of the research population. In part this is certainly the case: Sansone mainly focused on young men, and they are underrepresented in my study.[15] Compared with Sansone, I had more women among my Afro-Surinamese respondents and I focused more on families and the various generations within them.[16]

A sense of defeatism resulting in cutting classes and dropping out of school altogether is certainly in evidence among some Afro-Surinamese youngsters. It is particularly prevalent in certain urban districts such as Bijlmermeer in Amsterdam, where a number of unfavorable conditions converge. For the younger Afro-Surinamese generation as a whole, though, the dropout problem is not that widespread and seems to be on the decline.[17] I was struck by the difference between the importance people *say* they attach to education and diplomas and the way they actually act. In practice, parents who sincerely believe their children ought to do well at school and encourage them to succeed do not always provide the most adequate supportive climate for schoolchildren. Not only do I mean helping them with their homework, but also I mean supporting them in a wider sense, providing stimulation, creating an atmosphere of tranquility and discipline in the home and having special consideration for children who are doing their homework. The family Steve grew up in is a good example of what I mean. I give an extensive account of his story because it bears similarities to what I observed among a number of other families as well.

Steve (31) was seven when he came to the Netherlands with his grandmother and his two little brothers. His mother was already in the Netherlands and sent for them. The family lived in Bijlmermeer, and moved two or three years later to the Mercator neighborhood (Old West) and then to Osdorp (New West), all of them in Amsterdam. Steve went through primary school without getting left back, but in his own words, he was not a good pupil. After primary school, he was advised to go to the vocational school for bakers. He had once been there and thought it looked like a very nice school. But his mother did not agree at all. She wanted him to go to the four-year secondary school, so that is what he did. It went all right in the first year, but starting in the second year there were a lot of problems. He liked to hang out with his friends, "you do all kinds of fun things together, you don't know what is supposed to be your priority," is how he analyses the situation in retrospect. After two years at the secondary school, he switched to a vocational school where they taught office skills. But Steve's mother had her sights set on the four-year secondary school, and when she saw his report card, she decided to give it another try. Steve enrolled at another four-year secondary school, but this time it was one where the pupils received individual attention. His mother thought it was very important for him to go to a secondary school, but the conditions at home did not stimulate him to do his best. "It was a mess at home," Steve says now. Things were not going well with his two older brothers. One of them was a drug addict ("he was a junkie, he was aggressive"), and the other one got in trouble with the police for stealing. But Steve had his own agenda. Ever since he was a little boy, he wanted to be a policeman. A teacher once said to him, "That is the perfect thing for you," and he never forgot it.

The situation at home was not good. His mother was afraid he would follow in the footsteps of his two older brothers, and was very strict with him. After he came home from school, he had to stay home. His strict upbringing included some beatings. His mother was willing to do whatever it took to keep him out of trouble. He was given a lot of responsibility in the home. His mother and stepfather both had jobs, and when they weren't home he and he alone was responsible for the four younger children, even in the summer vacations. His mother had the youngest child stay with the grandmother; that would have been too much for Steve. So he spent a lot of time at home, and whenever he went out it led to a big fight with his parents.

Despite the individual attention there, he did not do well at the four-year secondary school. He himself cites three reasons why: his friends were pulling him in the "wrong" direction, his health was poor (bronchitis), and there was a lot of tension at home. When he went to school and was outside the home, he took advantage of his freedom to avoid his responsibilities at home. He never finished the secondary school. He dropped out, but when he was eighteen he decided to go back and finish by attending evening classes. He was still living with his parents, had a daytime job, and went to school after work. It was only after everyone was in bed and it was quiet at home—his stepfather often played the trumpet until eleven at night—that he had a chance to do his homework. "There was always a lot of noise at home, but if you didn't do well at school, they would blame it all on you!" He had passed his exams in three subjects by the time he left home. After he started living on his own, he went back and did his exams in another three subjects. So he finally had his secondary school diploma. He was twenty-four by then.

He had worked at a variety of jobs for employment agencies as a parking lot attendant, as an office clerk in the bookkeeping department at a bank, and as a stock clerk and archives clerk at a machinery business. After he finished secondary school he enrolled at a junior college. After teaching his favorite combat sport and tending bar at a community center, he started doing social and cultural work at a youth center. Then he got a job via an employment agency at the tax division of the Customs Department, and liked it so much that he stayed there for quite some time. They gave him references when he finally decided to leave and become a court officer for the state police. There was a Police Department reorganization, and he got an opportunity to do a special one-year training course to become a policeman. That is what he is doing now.

Steve still speaks of his school career with a touch of bitterness. "If I compare myself with other children whose mother or father would sit down and help them with their homework . . . I did not have that. They (his parents) always came first, they were the most important people in the house, but if you did not do well at school, they would really act like it was the end of the world."

In this case it is Steve himself who, unlike his two older brothers, achieved a certain extent of upward social mobility. He had not had much support at home. He managed to get ahead *despite* rather than *thanks to* his family background. There are, however, also youngsters from homes like that, like Steve's own brothers, who are not that successful. The unfavorable family climate does not result from the parents not thinking school is important. It is more a question of the *unintended* effects of certain acts and conditions, which in effect make it all the more difficult for youngsters to do well at school. In situations of this kind, it requires a great deal of perseverance and special efforts on the part of youngsters to complete their education. The ones who do not manage to do so can often make up for it by studying at a later age. They have ambitions, but they are not always passed on to them by their family. Either that, or the conditions at home were not such that they could put their ambitions into effect. So what is often involved are individual efforts later in life, as in the example of Steve. Getting one diploma after the other often means hard work, certainly if it is combined with a job and a family. This can be viewed as a traditional Creole pattern.[18] A pattern that coincides with the observation that Creoles traditionally attach a great deal of values to diplomas as a way to get ahead.

In the Netherlands, however, there is another specific aspect that influences the importance attached to diplomas. People's faith in the value of diplomas can be affected if they see obstacles they feel are beyond their power to control. On the average, the Afro-Surinamese are more apt than the Indo-Surinamese to attribute obstacles to their own career to discrimination. It is quite plausible that the Afro-Surinamese do indeed experience more discrimination, but there is no evidence of it here. At any rate in my study, the topic of discrimination did come up more frequently and more spontaneously in the talks with Afro-Surinamese respondents.[19] The Afro-Surinamese are more apt to see discrimination as an obstacle to their own position and career in Dutch society than whatever cultural difference there might be. Whether you have grown up in the Netherlands or not, it is still often the color of your skin that determines what people think of you.

> Jerryl (39) has three sons, the oldest is thirteen. He does not know the first thing about Surinam. If he went to Surinam, he would be viewed as a Dutch boy, Jerryl knows from experience. But in the Netherlands, where Jerryl's son was born and raised, he is a black boy. That is the second-generation problem, he feels, "the color of their skin makes them different, people expect them to be different."

So the perception of discrimination can give rise to a certain ambivalence. Whether you are assimilated or not, whether you do your best or not, you are still black and recognizable, and people tend to have certain expectations of you.[20]

The experience or perception of discrimination also generates a certain distrust of teachers and school. Parents experience what their children have to go through in this "white" society and are on guard for any conduct that can be interpreted as discrimination.

> The adult daughter of one of the early immigrants feels that many Dutch people —"though not all of them"—discriminate. "That is why I will teach my children that if a teacher says or does anything, they should immediately say what they think of it."

> Gina (32) adopts a comparable attitude. The school called her about the conduct of her son (13). He is in the first year of secondary school; his grades are good, but there are some complaints about his conduct. "He is a smart aleck," Gina says. When the principal of the school once called her to say her son had misbehaved, she did not even want to hear about it. She thinks they ought to solve that kind of problem at school. They can punish him as much as they want, but they don't have to call her about it, do they? "I thought he needs to learn a thing or two. I said, 'I don't go running to the Discrimination Bureau every time my son comes homes and says they called him this or that.' That shut him up."

Parents teach their children to be tough if they come up against any kind of negative treatment by the Dutch. They are aware of the obstacles their children are faced with, and they are quick to defend them against allegedly discriminatory conduct. This sensitivity to any traces of discrimination is something I came across more often among the Afro-Surinamese than the Indo-Surinamese. Children are sometimes taught beforehand how to defend themselves in these situations. No matter how much of a smart aleck Gina's son might be at school, his mother will still support him in a talk with the principal. I came across more conflicts involving children at school among the Afro-Surinamese than the Indo-Surinamese families. It is difficult for me to evaluate the relation between discrimination and conflicts at school, but I did observe a more hostile Afro-Surinamese attitude to school and teachers.

A Businesslike Mentality

There is much less of this kind of ambivalence in the Indo-Surinamese attitude and behavior toward the school system. The word many of them use is *progress*. It pertains to progress in an intellectual sense, but also in a material sense, that is, the accumulation of money and property. The importance the Indo-Surinamese attach to material progress is evident from their ownership of houses. Though the average Indo-Surinamese income is lower than the Afro-Surinamese, they are far more apt to own their own homes. This tendency is not unique to the Indo-Surinamese. The Afro-Surinamese are also sometimes homeowners, probably to the same growing extent as in the Netherlands in general, and they also purchase real estate in Surinam. But Afro-Surinamese property owners are more likely to be members of the up-and-coming middle class. Among my Afro-Surinamese respondents, it was the well-educated two-income families who bought their own homes. This saving and investing conduct would seem to be more a reflection of their social position than among the Indo-Surinamese.

Regardless of their social position, the Indo-Surinamese also need more money to pay for their children's weddings. Weddings are socioreligious events that it is hard to back out of even if one wants to. They are occasions that the family name is linked to and where social relations are reinforced. A "normal" wedding party is extremely expensive, and it is often paid for by the entire family. A separate East Indian style wedding and a wedding ceremony at City Hall and a reception are a costly matter. Mungra estimates the total costs of a wedding at more than 20,000 guilders or 8,000 dollars (1990: 125).[21] The Afro-Surinamese also have ceremonial get-togethers such as *wintipres* and *bigi jaris*, though this only holds true for a small part of the community and they are not nearly as much of a social obligation as the Indo-Surinamese weddings.

The importance the Indo-Surinamese attach to material advancement is also evident from their accumulation of various sources of income and their pooling of incomes. In its more classical form, this meant the joint incomes of all the members of the household were centrally managed. In its revised form, it still plays a role in some families in the solidarity the various members of the family exhibit in a financial sense.

Now that her older sister is married, Urmy (21), whose situation is described above, is the oldest child at home. In a financial sense, she is a big help for her parents, whose disability benefits are their main income. In addition to her student grant and loan, she has a part-time job that pays 400 guilders a month. She regularly foots the large family bills, which is very helpful since her parents have just paid for her sister's wedding and they are broke. They have to start saving all over again, because there are another three daughters who have to get married.

The desire for material property can perhaps be explained in part by the East Indian tradition of entrepreneurship. For East Indians, in the first instance the road to advancement and integration in Surinamese society went via independent entrepreneurship. Their diligence was often what enabled the parents of the first generation of adult immigrants to build up a life outside of farming. Bit by bit they saved some money and invested it in expanding the business. This gave East Indians the reputation of "being smart with money," as I was told in Surinam, and of "not being afraid of money."

The older generation is still very aware of its historical position as an immigrant group that was able to work its way up in Surinam. This is why they are less apt to automatically view their ethnic background as something that keeps them from getting ahead. After all, generations of experience in Surinam taught them that it was possible to make rapid progress as newcomers in a foreign society. Perhaps this is one reason why they are not quick to think in terms of discrimination. At any rate discrimination is not a topic that often came up spontaneously the way it did with the Afro-Surinamese. My Indo-Surinamese respondents repeatedly told me that how the Dutch treat you is largely your own doing. I often observed considerable faith on their part in the idea that you can shape your own career.

In the career trajectories of the Indo-Surinamese in Dutch society, this strong emphasis on the material aspects can still be observed among youngsters as well as their parents. The youngsters have been taught all their lives to work to attain property and "build something up for yourself." Having various jobs or incomes, buying private homes, and engaging in informal commerce all contribute to this end, as does getting a good education.

Vyay (30) is working via an employment agency as a financial comptroller for a housing corporation. He would prefer to have a permanent job, he says, because then you are independent and can build up something for yourself. "After all, you do want to get somewhere in life," Vyay says. Every so often he makes some effort to earn a little something in addition to his salary. Once he tried dealing in imported merchandise from India, clothing and jewelry, together with one of his relatives. They rented a space at Holiday Inn for four hours for 1,500 guilders and sold 10,000 guilders worth of merchandise there. On another occasion it did not go as well, and they just managed to earn back what they had invested. Vyay comes from an agrarian family and once studied at the university for a couple of years. He never completed his studies and never got the good job he was expecting. Earning money is very important to him (he wants to buy his own home), and if it does not work in a high status way (a university degree and a good regular job), then he will do it this way.

There are also many Indo-Surinamese with ambitions of an independent life with their own business ranging from vague desires to concrete plans. "Building up something for yourself" is a typical expression I often heard the Indo-Surinamese use. Some of them have even gotten it as an explicit message in life. Rick (27) for example, an independent entrepreneur himself, was taught the following by his grandfather: "Never work for anyone else. Always work for yourself, that is the most profitable."

This is even the reason why the brother of Mrs. R. (48) decided to go back to Surinam. He had a shop there, and rented it to someone else when he left for the Netherlands. He did shift work here but it was not for him. He went back to Surinam and started working in his shop again. "We are business people," Mrs. R. explains. "It is better to have your own business than to work for a boss, because he wasn't used to the life here. He did work, he worked shifts, but he couldn't get used to it."

Mr. B. has his own flourishing business where he employs a few of his relatives. His daughter works for the Post Office, but she is considering coming to work for her father too. She said to her father, "Dad, I sometimes give it my all, but it would be much nicer to do that in our own business."

The striking thing is that among the Indo-Surinamese, this business-like mentality is not very class specific. All the above-mentioned aspects of it can be observed among "ordinary" Indo-Surinamese families with a low socioeconomic position. What does occur though among the lower-class Indo-Surinamese is that going to school is easily exchanged for earning money. There are families where dropping out of school is not viewed as an unfortunate failure, but merely as a reason to steer the career in a different direction. It is not so important whether money is earned in one way or in another, as long as young people are earning it. Danny's family is a good example.

Danny (21) lives with his parents, two brothers (23 and 20) and sister (18) in a new flat in one of the old districts in The Hague. His father did not have much of an education because he had to help out in the family when he was very young. He was unemployed for years, and has now been officially classified as disabled and spends all his time at home. Danny's mother works caring for the ill. Danny thinks his mother is more modern than his father, and thinks this is because she has a job outside the home and he is home all day. "So he is not out there in society, there is not much happening in his life."

After primary school, Danny finished the five-year and then the six-year secondary school. Things went wrong in the last grade there. Not that he was a poor pupil. As he and his girlfriend recall, he hardly had to do anything for the science subjects, he just had to work hard for Dutch and English. But Danny was too fond of going out, drinking and gambling. He quit school about three months ago. After not doing anything for a while, now he has a temporary job as a delivery boy via an employment agency. He delivers the internal mail at a ministry. Danny has had part-time jobs before, but this is the first time in his life he has a "real" job. How does he like it? "I like the idea of being a civil servant. I will tell you very honestly, a civil servant has a good life. And it is fine as far as the work goes too. He gets his salary on time, he hardly has to do anything, and there isn't anyone to say anything about it!"

He says he does not regret his decision, and will "certainly" go back and finish school some day. Weren't his parents angry when he dropped out of school half way through the final year? No, they did not really mind, he thinks. But Danny thinks that was also because "my little brother is a criminal" (and was even in prison three years ago) and he was the first one to quit school. He hardly has any education at all. Then his oldest brother and his sister dropped out of school (a six-year and four-year secondary school, respectively). For a long time, Danny was even the example for the other children. What is more, he is the only one to have a diploma (from the five-year secondary school).

The parents encourage the children to "do something." "It is not that they don't stimulate us. 'If you don't want to go to school, then get a job. And if you can't find a job, then apply for welfare.'" The oldest son is now unemployed, the youngest son earns a living his own way, and the daughter worked for a while as a cashier in a supermarket but is now unemployed too. So compared to them, Danny is not doing that badly.

The whole family situation is such that it was not hard for Danny to drop out of school. Despite the criminal tendencies of his brother and the fact that he was the only one of the children still at school, now that he has dropped out, all his parents encourage him to do is make sure he has an income coming in. He has to either get a job or at least go on welfare. In the perception and mind-set of Danny's father, money is the most important thing; at any rate this is the implicit message he conveys to his children. Following from this mind-set, there is the more or less tolerated criminal career of his other son.

In Danny's own words, his younger brother (20) is "a petty criminal." He didn't finish school and never got any kind of diploma; he can barely read and write. He would come home with three or four thousand guilders. Once just as the whole family was about to go on holiday to Surinam, he was sent to prison. An older brother stayed behind to visit him in jail and give him some money now and then. That was what his father decided, even though he was very angry when this happened to his son. He told him that in the past they used to treat criminals very differently. His father's own brother had been whipped by his father when he caught him doing something he should not have been doing. At other moments though, Danny's father also seems to benefit from the money his son earned. His son even gives him his money for safekeeping, because it isn't money that you can just put in a bank account.

There are regularly father-and-son conflicts in this family, but at the same time the father conveys unintended messages that show his appreciation for his son's "earnings."

In short, the Indo-Surinamese would seem to have preserved their businesslike mentality in the Netherlands, though there are various routes that can be taken to success. Children are encouraged to "do something," but this can be interpreted in various ways.

Instrumental and Intrinsic Value of Education

The businesslike Indo-Surinamese mentality helps explain their instrumental attitude toward education. Indo-Surinamese parents also attach a great deal of importance to education. It is a means toward advancement in two senses, intellectual and material. Diplomas and degrees are viewed as status symbols that provide standing and income. The higher the degree, the higher the status and the higher the job and the income.

After a four-year secondary school, Geeta (25) wanted to go on with her studies and had to choose between a five-year secondary school or a junior college. Her brother advised her to go to a junior college. The five-year secondary school is not a vocational training, he knew, and with junior college you can get a job. So she went to junior college and was planning to get a job when she finished. Even before she finished she got married, but she and her husband both went on with their studies. After she finished the junior college she decided to continue studying at a college. She never would have thought of this herself, but her father-in-law thought it was a good idea since her husband was going to go on studying too. Some of the people in Geeta's family thought it was odd that she was going to go on studying for another four years. Her husband was going to an engineering college so he would be earning a nice income for them. Geeta has since gotten her college degree and wants to take advantage of it: "First I'll try and find a job, a good permanent job. And then we want to buy our own home and our own car. We had to do without those things all that time, it is what we worked so hard for, I hope we will be able to get them now."

This kind of instrumental attitude to education and work is generally more typical of poorly educated than well-educated people. Among the Indo-Surinamese however, it can also be observed in well-educated people. One of my key respondents, a social scientist himself, told me he does not know many people like himself: "The Indo-Surinamese are more interested in economics, law, medicine and technology, [laughs] the fields where they can earn a lot of money." A doctor he knew once told him that even his plumber earned twice as much as a social scientist. The high status of doctors, lawyers, and economists is not an isolated fact in itself, it has to do with the money people in these professions earn.

Whatever the case may be, a good education is one thing, a good job and income is something else. I repeatedly came across this emphasis on the material aspects among the Indo-Surinamese, and they themselves find it typically Indo-Surinamese. Of course earning money is an important part of a job for everyone, but there are differences in how the link is drawn with education. The Afro-Surinamese seem to be more frequently interested in the intrinsic value of education. They do not only choose a school or a subject to major in on the basis of how much money you can earn with it, at any rate not to the same extent. Their choice is also based on what seems like a nice school or an interesting subject to major in, or the kind of job or profession they want to have. Perhaps since relatively less pressure is put on them at home, Afro-Surinamese youngsters are more apt to choose an educational trajectory that is "more enjoyable." They choose the subjects they feel are the nicest and plan a trajectory they think will lead to a profession they will enjoy. The word "enjoy" recurs again and again in the descriptions some of the youngsters gave of their educational and occupational career. To get back to Denise and Carmelita, the two girls quoted at the beginning of this chapter, Denise thinks it is very important to enjoy school and work. On two separate occasions she chose a school under her potential and she interrupted her educational career because she felt more like getting a job. Carmelita's parents gave her much less of an opportunity to just do the things she felt like doing. She was encouraged to keep on going despite all the difficulties. Both the girls did nonetheless manage to get quite a good education. Apparently the decision to opt for one trajectory or the other does not necessarily exert that much of an influence on the final result.

Of course Indo-Surinamese youngsters also choose the educational career they think they will enjoy, but in their case there are also other considerations: the faith in progress, the pressure to succeed and ambitions conveyed to them by their parents, and the striving for material advancement. Among Afro-Surinamese youngsters there is more emphasis on the education itself, the school or the scholastic situation. Gibson (2000) draws a distinction in this connection between extrinsic and intrinsic educational motivation. Compared with Indo-Surinamese youngsters, there is less evidence among Afro-Surinamese youngsters of extrinsic reasons to do well at school, and sometimes there is even some doubt as to whether there is any point to it at all. The other side of this more intrinsic motivation is that Afro-Surinamese youngsters sometimes seem to choose the path of least resistance. That can mean being quick to switch schools if they don't like a school or if there is a conflict with a teacher, or choosing the easiest trajectories or subjects. This might in part explain the preference of some poorly educated Afro-Surinamese youngsters for careers in the world of fashion, popular music, or sports (Sansone 1992: 50). They think this means earning money fast and having a good time, and they do not realize this is only feasible for very few people. Sansone explains the interest of poorly educated Afro-Surinamese youngsters in these careers as being inspired by the poor prospects and discrimination on the regular labor market (1992: 49). From this perspective, it is a reactive choice. The question is to what extent this is only one side of the coin, since these clear preferences are barely in evidence if at all among poorly educated Indo-Surinamese youngsters. Their dropout and youth unemployment rates barely differ from those of Afro-Surinamese youngsters, but I barely observed any evidence of reactive choices in the career patterns of Indo-Surinamese youngsters. The preference of poorly educated Afro-Surinamese youngsters for what Sansone calls "spectacular careers" probably also has to do with their intrinsic motivation: first and foremost, school and work have to be enjoyable. Youngsters who feel they have few prospects for the future and have not experienced much pressure to succeed at home are more likely to develop this kind of attitude toward school.

Family Structure and Family Relations

The question of why the ambitions and pressure to succeed passed on at home are higher and the climate frequently more education-minded among the Indo-Surinamese than the Afro-Surinamese can be partially answered by referring to the history of the parents and more generally to the history of both population groups in their native country. The messages conveyed to children by their parents do play a role, but they do not explain everything. The family structure and family relations are also important. They not only constitute a context where ambitions emerge, in themselves they also stand for values that youngsters are given at home and that influence how far they will get in society.

The Importance of the Family

From a historical perspective, the collective behavior of the family is an important element in the economic success of the Indo-Surinamese.[22] Operating jointly as a family is much less of a necessity nowadays in the Netherlands, but the tendency certainly has not disappeared. It is not uncommon for unmarried children to still live with their parents, although this also has a practical advantage. It enables them to become eligible more quickly for subsidized housing since they are classified as "urgent." There are also still other traces of the joint family household, such as two-family homes shared by the families of two brothers or by a mother and her son's family. Large households consisting of a nuclear family and a number of other relatives are more common among the Indo-Surinamese than the Afro-Surinamese.

In other ways, concerted action as a family is also still in evidence. I still came across several more classical examples of this.

Soon after they were married, Mr. E. (75) and his wife moved away from the plot of land owned by his father, where he had worked the land up till then with his brothers. In the city, he got a job at a match factory before he built up a business of his own as a carpenter and building contractor. He had only had four years of primary school, because in a large family with eight children, they could not send him to school any longer. That is why he attached all the more importance to his own children's education. If necessary, he used his hands to make that clear to them. He delegated his authority in this connection to the oldest children, whose job it was to make sure the youngest children did their best at school and did their homework. If the younger children ever got an unsatisfactory grade at school, the older children were held accountable and were punished as if the failing grade was theirs. When the children came home with their report cards, there was a whole ritual. Father would look at the report cards one by one, starting with the oldest children. Anyone who had poor grades had to stand separately from others and he used a belt to punish them.

The first two children did not meet with Mr. E.'s expectations. The oldest daughter was taken out of school before graduation to get married, because she had secretly had contact with a boy. The second child, a son, did not get any further than primary school, and he started working as an apprentice to a tailor. His father wanted to set up a tailor shop for him and invested in it, but he could not make a success of it. His father was angry and disappointed and beat him. "My father was a tough man," one of his daughters recalls. "He insisted that we were successful and he could not take no for an answer. He always tried to be a success in his own life and it worked, so he wanted his children to do the same."

Mr. E. was extremely proud when his third child, a daughter, became a school-teacher. When she was twenty-one, she already earned a "fine salary" of 300 guilders. Her income and the incomes of the other children all went into the joint account, and the father bought a large house that he rented out. That brought in an extra income, so the younger children could continue their education. By the time that this daughter got married, a younger daughter completed her training as a teacher and started contributing her salary to the household income. After working for a year, she went to get her higher qualifications in the Netherlands, came back to Surinam, and got a better teaching job. She was earning more now. By the time she too got married, there was a son who had finished teachers' college.

He had a teaching job, and after that he would work for his father every day in the business. The following daughter also became a teacher, and then continued her studies at the university when the family moved to the Netherlands. The following children in the family had a lot of trouble with the transition to the Dutch school system and they did not all do as well as the older children. The youngest ones grew up in the Netherlands and got better grades at school.

In the Netherlands, there were still some vestiges of the old tradition of pooling incomes to finance the mortgage for the parental home. When the elderly parents only had a small income to live on, the children each contributed as much as they could at the time and jointly made sure that the mortgage was paid off and the house was renovated.

The picture presented above of the relations in this family is the traditional pattern that prevailed in Surinam.[23] The authority of the father or of the oldest children generated a certain order or discipline, and the younger children learned to accept authority and to conform. The relations in the family were hierarchic. The father was the main authority; the mother's position was subordinate to her husband's and her role was to make sacrifices for her children. The younger children were supposed to obey the older ones, especially the older brothers.

Relatively rapid changes are taking place in the Netherlands.[24] The case described above pertains to the situation of an older generation. The children in this example are the parents of this family's grandchildren who grew up in the Netherlands. The pattern of joining forces in the family is no longer as strong or as common among today's Indo-Surinamese families in the Netherlands. To varying extents, there are, however, still traces of it among many families. What is more, although the more immediately visible forms of the joint family have largely disappeared, the idea of the family as a collective unity with relatives having certain rights and obligations to each other is still very much a part of the Indo-Surinamese consciousness. In many joint families, there is still a great sense of loyalty among the various nuclear families and members of these families. Although the nuclear families of brothers and sisters do not necessarily live close to each other, they sometimes feel a great sense of responsibility toward each other's children. This is clear from the numerous forms of assistance: an uncle who houses a niece (his brother's daughter) when she comes to the Netherlands to complete her studies, an uncle who comes on a visit from Surinam and lectures the son of his deceased brother about his conduct, a problematic son who is sent to Surinam to spend an extended period of time with the family of his father's brother, a divorced woman who receives financial support from her family to pay her daughters' expenses at the university and so forth.

The importance of the family is still strongly emphasized by the Indo-Surinamese, including the younger generation. To the extent that the Indo-Surinamese family has partially preserved its more classical features, there are elements that can motivate children and stimulate them to perform well. The scholastic or other achievements of individual members of the family, for example, in business, are viewed as being in the interest of the whole family. Success radiates to the entire family. This makes it easier to understand the contributions and support that an entire family would give to one member of the family in the effort to advance as much as possible, as frequently occurred in the past.[25] Pooling the family incomes under the father's management was also a way to enable the younger children in a large family to continue their studies or at any rate enable one of them to advance in life. One successful member of a family means prestige for the entire family. An Indo-Surinamese daughter of extremely poorly educated parents who is now studying law at the university says, "My parents want the family to make a name." The Indo-Surinamese often describe themselves as people with a sense of status.

The hierarchic structure of the family and the respect for elderly people that is related to it are aspects that can motivate children to meet with their parents' expectations. The respect they feel makes them not want to disappoint their parents with their school performance. They are often aware—and are also often told—that the generation before them always had to work very hard and barely had a chance to get an education.

> In the words of Mr. D., "Youngsters here have wonderful opportunities. The only thing they have to think about and work on is their schoolwork. The only thing they have to do is go to school and do their homework. After school they either hang out at home or go out and play with their friends or something like that. So they never have to do the kind of hard work on the farm that we had to do in Surinam. Okay, I am not saying people do not work hard here, they work very hard in all the different sectors. But compared with Surinam . . . if you talked about working hard there, you were talking about farm work." His nephew Sunil (25) says, "If we had stayed there, I think we would have also become farmers."

In view of this hard work their parents had to do, the younger generation is very conscious of the opportunities they are getting in the Netherlands. Since the parents did not have the chances their children now have, they often set their hopes on their children, and the children do not want to disappoint them. Parents who did not have a chance to get an education themselves now seem to be projecting their frustrated ambitions on to their children. Children do not want to let their parents down, and with their support and encouragement, they are reaching an educational level their parents could only dream of.

> Joyce (22) knows her father was a good pupil and would have loved to continue his studies. But family circumstances were such that it was not feasible. Her grandfather was a farm worker and van driver. He had a van for transporting passengers and freight. Her father was the oldest in a family of seven children and had to help out a lot at home. It was often already nightfall by the time he could

start his homework. "He really had to do his homework under the worst kind of conditions," his daughter says. "He would work late at night and all he had was the light of a little candle. But he was very motivated, you know."

Geeta (25) comes from a family of eight children. Her father had very little schooling, and her mother none at all. Geeta is the first one in the family to get a college education. Her father is enormously proud of her. Her father-in-law encouraged her to continue studying after she got married. "Well, I did not want to disappoint him. But I was very happy about how my father felt. This was what he wanted all those years, and I like the fact that I was able to do that for my father."

The Indo-Surinamese view the parents' investment in their children's futures as something that distinguishes them from other groups. "The Indo-Surinamese really think about their children's future," is how they like to put it. In the past in Surinam, the important thing was the material inheritance parents could leave their children. Compared with Creoles, who often still leave undivided property, East Indians in Surinam always divide their money and property more clearly. This was a necessity, in cases of a family business, where the land and means of production had to be divided among the sons. I have heard a number of accounts of fathers making the arrangements before their death.

Mrs. S. (41) comes from a rather classic joint family. Her father divided all the family property before he died. "My father had already made plans for the grandchildren you see. He wanted to make sure the grandchildren would be able to succeed in life. He divided up all the plots of land, the inheritance. The boys each got five plots, the girls one. The girls got one so that if they ever need it, they will have something to fall back on. For the rest, women's property belongs to their husband's family, and they'll have a man to take care of them. But the boys got five plots of land to pass on to their children later."

Parents have become increasingly aware, however, that investing in their children's education is the best way to invest in their future. Nowadays children's education is viewed much more as something parents can give their children to enhance their chances in later life. In the case of girls, it is important that an education will enable them to take care of themselves if their marriage does not work out. Mothers often make it clear to their daughters that they are less dependent on their husbands if they are educated, and they have something to fall back on if they get divorced. A diploma is a kind of insurance policy in case of an emergency. This provides a different kind of motivation for a younger generation, in this case girls, to continue their education.

Of course, this does not hold true to the same extent in all Indo-Surinamese families. Nor is a close family favorable in every way. Youngsters in the process of getting an education sometimes perceive all the visits they have to pay to their various relatives as bothersome. Geeta, who is cited above, was already married when she started to go to college, and her husband was also studying. She comes from a large family and had a lot of trouble explaining to her parents and other relatives that she and her husband were not always free on the weekends because they had to study.

"From the very start," Geeta (25) says, "we made it clear to everyone that we were college students. Especially during the periods when we had our examinations, we told them all that we did not want to be disturbed. I have a very large family and so does he. So there is always someone dropping in for a visit. And usually they stay at our home the whole weekend, so you can forget all about studying until they have left. So we had to make all our relatives understand these things."

Other things are also changing. Some parents feel their children are not as motivated to get ahead in life as they were. In fact there was evidence of this in two classical joint families. Both these families have a "problem child" among the younger children. In one case it is a grandson in prison, in the other a son who does not want to either go to school or get a job. In addition to these more extreme examples, there are children who do not live up to their parents' expectations at school. Youngsters born and raised in the Netherlands who have no personal experience of what life was like in Surinam are much less aware of the obstacles their parents had to surmount to get ahead in life.

In any number of ways, the family system is under pressure in the Netherlands: the families are becoming smaller, family relations are changing, children are "Dutchifying" and are planning their own lives more independently. Some of them don't want to have anything to do with the values and ideas their parents want to teach them.

Shortly after she arrived in the Netherlands, Mrs. G. (49) realized she was alone and would have to bear sole responsibility for her three young children, two daughters and a son. She was faced with enormous financial problems. She did have a steady office job, but she wanted to buy a house because she was determined to leave the Schilderswijk, an old inner-city district where she was living. She had a job, worked as a seamstress, and dabbled a bit in stocks, which she had learned to do from a neighbor. Things went differently with her children than she had hoped. It was not so much their education as their lifestyle that she had wanted to be different. Her oldest daughter is living with her Dutch boyfriend, her son is living with his Dutch girlfriend, and the youngest daughter is living with her Indo-Surinamese boyfriend. Like many Afro-Surinamese single mothers, Mrs. G. feels her children's lives would have been very different if their father had been around to help raise them. The difference, however, is that she is frowned upon in the Indo-Surinamese community, and especially by her in-laws, because her children left home without getting married.

After having lived with her boyfriend for several years, her oldest daughter is now planning to get married. "Dutch style," Carla (21), the youngest daughter, tells me enthusiastically. She herself did not move in with her boyfriend until recently, and her mother is putting pressure on her to have some kind of an East Indian style celebration. But Carla told her mother that first it was going to be her brother's turn, "and it is the last thing on his mind."

The mother and children do not see each other very often, and that is another thing Mrs. G. is not at all happy about. They never have time and they are always busy. The three children do all come home on their mother's birthday, but for the rest they are rarely all at her house at the same time as a family. Carla and her brother rarely see each other, though she does see her sister slightly more frequently. "We have all got our own lives," she says, "it is a very different lifestyle."

Families like this are not that common in my Indo-Surinamese research population, but the less of an exception they are, the more the ideal of the family as a collective will presumably crumble. For the time being, though, many youngsters seem to be convinced of the importance of the family. In the Netherlands this is no longer of the same economic value as in Surinam, but it does inspire youngsters to achieve something in life, in whatever manner they choose, and often inspires the kind of behavior their parents hope to see in them.

Individual Responsibility

Afro-Surinamese family life is more individualized and more loosely structured, as is also clear from the composition of the households. The family is a less closed and less sharply delineated social unit than among the Indo-Surinamese. The Afro-Surinamese family structure is often more diffuse in the sense that nonrelatives are also considered members of the family and children of the same mother but different fathers grow up in one and the same family. The Afro-Surinamese often do not even know all their relatives. It can happen that total strangers unexpectedly turn out to be related.

There is often also a great deal of mutual support among the Afro-Surinamese in multifarious situations, but the extent varies to which they feel a shared responsibility or solidarity and make efforts on behalf of the family. Generally speaking, the Afro-Surinamese tend to think less in terms of a collective than the Indo-Surinamese. Whereas there is never any question about the mutual support to be provided within the Indo-Surinamese family, for the Afro-Surinamese it largely depends on the financial situation the family is in. Particularly in the case of financial difficulties and material needs, members of an Afro-Surinamese family are more apt to help each other than in situations where there are no such problems.

Edmé (34) told me her family is different from many other Surinamese families. "We don't have as much of that tendency to go to each other for help. That never happens in our family. I never had to do that. My brothers and sisters don't do that either. It is not a pattern of ours. You do see that sometimes in families, you know, I'll just borrow some money from so and so. We never do that. You get an education, you get a job, you are employed, you are independent, you don't bother anyone. The only thing you have to worry about is if your father needs something or your father has to go to Surinam or your father needs new false teeth or a new pair of glasses. Then you have to make sure he has what he needs. But there has never been an occasion when I went to my sister to ask her to lend me some money. I would not dream of it."

In Edmé's family, the children are all reasonably well educated (secondary school or junior college) and they all have a job, so there is not much need for them to depend on each other. At any rate, this holds true for the children, but they automatically help out if their elderly father needs anything. This is the case in virtually all Afro-Surinamese families; all the children chip in if their mother or father need money for a trip to Surinam, a *bigi jari*, or the purchase of durable consumer goods like a television or refrigerator. For the rest, though, it is mainly families in financial problems who call upon their relatives. Family networks can thus constitute an important safety net for people who are temporarily unable to cope with their problems or are in danger of getting into a socially marginal position.[26] Families like Edmé's lead a more independent life.

Studying also seems to be a more individual question for the Afro-Surinamese than the Indo-Surinamese in the sense that it is not so strongly viewed as a matter that involves the whole family and that, once a student is successful, enhances the status of the family. This greater individualism in educational matters also has to do with the family relations, which are less hierarchic and more egalitarian among the Afro-Surinamese than the Indo-Surinamese. This does not necessarily mean there never used to be strict discipline in the family. As was the case with East Indians, Creole children in Surinam were also expected to obey and respect their elders. In fact the parents were quite authoritarian. Decisions never used to be discussed with children and their opinions were not taken into consideration. Children were supposed to be obedient and otherwise there were sanctions. It was not that unusual to beat or whip them. This is not typically Afro-Surinamese; Indo-Surinamese respondents also told me children used to be accustomed to physical punishment. Parents from both groups repeatedly told me they preferred a strict school for their children. (In Paramaribo, Catholic schools were known as being strict.) A strict upbringing was viewed more as being "typically Surinamese" than as being characteristic of either of the two groups. The oldest members of the Afro-Surinamese community do, however, sometimes draw a link with the slavery era.

Mrs. C. (59) told me her mother was raised by an aunt who had lived in slavery as a child. The explanation for how her mother raised her was that she never learned to talk about anything. "Spare the rod and spoil the child" was her attitude.

A certain strictness can thus definitely be detected in the Afro-Surinamese attitude to bringing up children, but family relations are less hierarchically arranged under the authority of the head of the family. Children have a greater say in things and more individual responsibility.

Judith (22) tells me she was brought up quite strictly. Her parents also selected a strict school ("My parents felt that strict schools were good schools"). As the oldest daughter, she was not free to do nearly all the things she wanted to do, in fact she had less freedom than her younger brother. She had quite a few disagreements with her father about this. He didn't like the way she would answer him back. She in turn didn't like anyone bossing her around.

"One thing that bothers me," Judith remarks spontaneously, "is all the work I have to do around the house. My mother has a job, my father has a job. So I am the one who has to do everything. I am going to college and for a while I just was not able to devote enough time to my studies. They understand that I am studying, but they still somehow feel that since I am at home, they can just leave the housework to me." That is why she started studying somewhere else, either at the library or at her aunt's house. "I let them know how much it bothered me. 'Look Dad, you might have a job,' I said, 'but we are going to school. I am studying and if you want me to get an education, then you have to give me a chance to do my homework. Everyone lives here, so everyone has to help our here, not just us, Dad!'" She also told her brother and her younger sister "'You have to open your mouth and stand up for yourself.' Everyone has a job to do. So they shouldn't expect one person to do everything at home."

Afro-Surinamese youngsters have more of a tendency to disagree with their parents' decisions or want to discuss them and have a say. Indo-Surinamese and Afro-Surinamese youngsters alike see exactly how far they can go in this connection, but in Afro-Surinamese families the situation is a bit less confining because the relations are more egalitarian. A clear example of this is the view I came across repeatedly that mothers and daughters see each other more or less as equals, at any rate they would like to. When I asked Denise who her three best female friends were, she mentioned her sister, her cousin, and her mother. And Diana hopes that her children, who are still very young, will some day be able to talk about everything with her. "It ought to be like a relationship between two girlfriends." Judith even goes so far as to consider her grandmother a girlfriend.

"I really get along well with my grandmother on my mother's side. She is like my girlfriend, if you know what I mean. You can let your hair down and have a great time with her, you really can. She is not one of those grandmothers who sits there crocheting."

The greater responsibility or freedom that youngsters have in Afro-Surinamese families also extends to their scholastic and occupational choices.

Sandra (17) wanted to go to one specific secondary school because that is where all her girlfriends were going. This was not the school her mother would have chosen for her, but Sandra got her way. "I would not take no for an answer." In the end, her mother respected her choice. "My mother was not going to force me to do something I didn't want to do," Sandra says.

Mrs. U. (51) comments on the occupational choice made by her daughter (17): "I can't tell Monica what to do. She has to make her own decisions about what she wants to do." She does encourage her daughter to go on with her studies. "You have to get an education, because if you don't have any diplomas then you don't have a chance." But for the rest her daughter is free to make her own choices, "because if you force them and it doesn't work out."

Afro-Surinamese youngsters have more freedom to make their own decisions than Indo-Surinamese youngsters. In itself, this can be favorable. In a certain sense, it is a pattern that coincides with the expectations at school, where children are raised to be articulate and independent. Freedom can lead to well-considered choices and a strong motivation, as was illustrated in the case of Denise at the beginning of the chapter. The point, however, is that not all youngsters can cope with this freedom and responsibility. In addition to their own personal characteristics, whether they succeed or not also depends on the general climate in the family.[27]

A favorable climate is not necessarily linked to the family structure, but single-parent families are more apt to come up against a number of limitations than two-parent families. Single parents have to divide their time, attention, and energy among any number of matters, and are more likely to have family problems and financial difficulties. This does not hold true of all single parents to the same extent. A great deal depends on the socioeconomic position of the mother (education and income), and on the priorities she sets and the choices she makes.[28]

Ever since they were very young, Mrs. W. (51) raised her daughters on her own. "They always had respect for me, but I was very strict with them. I was not lenient with them in any way. That is how I had to be. I was the father and mother at the same time. Sometimes they say, 'You were so strict, you wouldn't let us do this or that.' But I couldn't tell them to go ask their father because he was not there."

Mrs. W. was not only aware she had sole responsibility for her daughters' upbringing, she also made a lot of sacrifices to make sure they had what they
needed in a material sense. She left her office job when her children were little so
she could stay home and take care of them. She was on welfare for a couple of
years, and had to live on a much lower income.

Her daughter Denise (24) realizes in retrospect that her mother must have had
to be very careful with money at the time. "Not that we had much money, but you
had to be careful with what little you had. When I look back now, I realize that as
children, we never wanted for anything. We could always go on the school trips.
I remember that one time I came home and my mother had even bought those
brand-name basketball shoes, well you know, that was so incredibly nice of her.
So we did have these luxuries now and then. When I look back, I think: How
could she have done that? She must have had to really scrimp and save and not
get anything for herself. Not that we had so many luxuries, but we were able to
do whatever we wanted."

When her children were a bit older, Mrs. W. got a job again. The summer vacations were a problem, but she made sure there was someone to take care of
them. "A couple of times I went to one of those day camps at the beach. My
mother did that so she could go to work. It was a lot of fun, but it is not till now
that I realize the sacrifices she must have made."

The large families of poorly educated mothers are in the worst position, especially in Bijlmermeer in Amsterdam. They often see it as a shortcoming that
they have to raise their children alone without the father. They themselves draw
a link with the lack of strictness in the children's upbringing and the lack of obe-
dience on the part of the children. They feel they have to play a double role,
which is very demanding. I observed the most problems with the children's upbringing and school performance in these families.[29]

Chronic financial difficulties can make life very hard for these families. It
does not take long for the oldest children to know all about their mother's
money problems and they feel responsible too or become involved. Some children are good at this and give their mother whatever support they can, others
seem to have a very hard time dealing with the chronic shortage of money. In
these families, children have to be very strong just to get by and keep up with
their schoolwork. At any rate it is clear how heavy the pressure is that these
family conditions can put on youngsters. I give a lengthy account below of the
family situations of one of the youngsters in my study.

Mrs. H. (37) lives with her five children in a four-room flat in Bijlmermeer. She
has not had much of an education, just a few years after primary school. She was
on welfare for a long time, but she was caught when she worked off the books, and
is now still paying off her debts. At the moment she works thirty-two hours a week
as a "neighborhood mother" in a state-subsidized job which she took a special

training course for. She earns 1,800 guilders (about 700 dollars) a month. The rent is more than 900 guilders, but she gets a 375 guilder monthly rent allowance. She could not manage without her daughter Audrey (18). Her son (16) often manages to evade her control. He stays out late at night, won't get up on time in the morning, and skips school. She describes one daughter (14) as a "problem child." A juvenile court judge has assigned a co-guardian to supervise her case. She lived with her father for a while, then came back to live with her mother, and is now staying with the family of a girlfriend until there is an opening for her at a boarding school. She also cuts classes at school. Audrey spends a lot of time taking care of her youngest sister (7) and brother (5). When I met her for the first time, she had not been to school that day because her little sister was sick. Her mother was still in the trial period at her new job and could not afford to take a day off.

Audrey is attending a junior college. For the time being, she is only getting a study grant of 91 guilders a month, because they are still checking to see how much her father contributes to her support. Audrey says she saves 30 guilders a month of this money for her little brother and sister so they will have a savings account later.

Audrey is used to having to do her share at home. "I was self-reliant at a very young age, essentially from the time I was six years old, because my mother has been alone for a long time. My father was gone and my mother had a job. I had to take care of my little brother and sister, not the two little ones, the middle ones. So I grew up playing the mother's role here at home. In addition, I always took care of my own business. I was eleven years old when I went out and got my own job, way under the minimum age. It was off the books, I worked at a shop, a supermarket. I worked at a dry cleaner's. I have had so many jobs. Also braiding people's hair, things like that. I still do that. But working at the supermarket and the dry cleaner's, those were my first real jobs." Now she works on Saturday and in the summer vacations.

When her mother was having serious financial trouble, was having problems with her second daughter, and was not working and was just sitting around the house, Audrey tried to talk to her and cheer her up. She has the feeling she is more or less on an equal footing with her mother, because she has so often given her advice about the other children and the problems they have and they cause. On the one hand, Audrey liked this situation, but she also sees the down side. "I missed out on my childhood," she says after a long monologue.

However, being a single mother is not always problematic. As is clear from the case of Mrs. W. and Denise described above, the socioeconomic position of the mother plays a significant role, as do the choices she makes, given all the limitations, and the priorities she sets.

All things considered, Afro-Surinamese family relations exhibit a rather modern and individualized pattern, which allows individuals a large amount of freedom to make their own decisions and take responsibility. There are, however, two sides to the coin. It can give youngsters a good preparation for what is expected of them in Dutch society, but under unfavorable conditions it can also have the opposite effect.

Conclusion

Based on the findings on school performance in the sociology of education, one might expect the family background of Afro-Surinamese youngsters to put them in a more favorable position than Indo-Surinamese youngsters. After all, on the average Afro-Surinamese parents are better educated than Indo-Surinamese parents, as a rule they speak better Dutch or at any rate more frequently speak Dutch with their children, most of them have an urban background and in Surinam they more often had occupations they could continue working in after they came to the Netherlands. Consequently, one might expect Afro-Surinamese youngsters to do better at school than Indo-Surinamese youngsters. In part this is indeed the case—on average their educational level is higher. Indo-Surinamese youngsters are, however, catching up relatively quickly, and there seems to be a certain degree of stagnation in a section of the Afro-Surinamese lower class.

The explanation for the relatively rapid scholastic success of the Indo-Surinamese has little to do with the parents' socioeconomic position (as measured by educational level). What is striking among the Indo-Surinamese is that poorly educated parents also pass on high educational and occupational aspirations to their children and exert a relatively large amount of pressure to succeed at school. I explain this in part on the basis of the history of East Indians in Surinam. First, the educational participation of the East Indians started later than that of the Creoles, so it is more common for the older generation to have had little opportunity to achieve their educational ambitions. Second, when they came to the Netherlands the Indo-Surinamese imported behavioral norms and ideas derived from the position of the group in Surinamese society, where independent entrepreneurship historically played such an important role. Third, the family structure and the behavioral patterns and values associated with it is also a contributing factor. All these aspects join to motivate the younger generation and to create a context that is relatively favorable for their educational and occupational careers.

There was also an educational lag among Creoles in Surinam, but in general they already exhibited a much longer education-minded tradition. This explains why the Afro-Surinamese are so apt to see education as an upward mobility route. Ambitions and the capacity to achieve them would seem, however, to be more related among the Afro-Surinamese than the Indo-Surinamese to the parents' socioeconomic position. As a result of the more modern and individualized Afro-Surinamese family pattern, youngsters are less pressured at home to achieve their educational and occupational ambitions. The family relations contain elements viewed in the Dutch school system as being "modern" and positive, such as individual responsibility and self-reliance, but under certain circumstances they can also have a detrimental effect. These circumstances are related in part to a weak socioeconomic position, often combined with single parenthood and the limitations it can entail.

Of course youngsters' success in society or at school does not completely adhere to ethnic boundaries. To varying degrees and in various combinations, the factors referred to above occur in Afro-Surinamese as well as Indo-Surinamese families. There is, nonetheless, also clear evidence of the influence of factors related to the history of the two ethnic groups in Surinam. Inherent to these specific circumstances is also the faith people have in the chance of getting ahead as immigrants in Dutch society. The Indo-Surinamese would seem to feel less impeded by their ethnic background. In part I view this as a legacy from the past, when East Indians managed to advance so rapidly as newcomers in Surinam. This historical experience might help explain why they are less apt to interpret obstacles to their upward mobility as indications of discrimination. For the time being, there are various upward mobility routes to be taken, but there is clear evidence of their faith in the possibilities and opportunities in the Netherlands.

Creoles have traditionally had great faith in the possibility of advancement via education, especially the ones who sought these educational opportunities in the Netherlands. Among the lower class in Paramaribo, this faith in advancement was less linear or unconditional. Back in Surinam there was already a certain ambivalence about education as a way to get ahead. In this sense, the doubts about the value of diplomas that are clear from their attitude and behavior toward the school system are part of the baggage they brought to the Netherlands. However, they are not just a legacy from the past. The experience and perception of discrimination in the Netherlands contributes toward this ambivalence and, in some cases, results in an oppositional attitude or doubts about the ideology of equal chances.

Notes

1. See, e.g., Dronkers and de Graaf (1995).
2. See chapter 2.
3. Teunissen and Matthijssen (1996: 93) are of the opinion, for example, that in quantitative research in the sociology of education, certain elements are never addressed for the simple reason that variables that have not been measured cannot be included in the analyses. According to these authors, the tradition of quantitative social inequality research has shortcomings where the problems of immigrants in the field of education are concerned because this research is trapped as it were in its limited choice of variables.

4. See also Brinkgreve et al. (1994).

5. See, e.g., Ledoux (1996: 123).

6. Mungra does not mention what he bases this information on. He does note that there are no separate figures on what specific groups of immigrants major in at the university.

7. See chapter 6.

8. CITO (Instituut voor Toetsontwikkeling) is the National Institute for Educational Measurement, which organizes the tests.

9. See Meijnen and Riemersma (1992).

10. Cf. Dronkers and Ultee (1995).

11. Haakmat relates his own personal experience of what a child from the countryside had to go through just to get an education. He also describes how children had to travel three hours to get to school and then three hours back at the end of the day. By piragua (a canoe made from a hollowed tree trunk), bus, or train, they had to go to the city every day, year in and year out. The fact that despite all these obstacles, many children from the countryside, most of them East Indian and Javanese, still managed to graduate from secondary school can solely be attributed to their superhuman perseverance (1996: 186).

12. Since then the East Indians in Surinam have more than made up for this educational disadvantage. An indication of this is the comment by Buddingh' (1995: 373) that at Anton de Kom University in Paramaribo, the number of students of Asian descent is disproportionately high. The question is, though, whether the Afro-Surinamese do not more frequently attend the universities in the Netherlands.

13. See chapter 3.

14. Cf. Kruijer (1977: 100).

15. See appendix 1.

16. Perhaps a certain extent of influence was also exerted by the difference in setting (the street and public space in Sansone's study) and the period of time. Sansone conducted his research in the 1980s, a period of increasing unemployment among the Surinamese. My study was conducted in the 1990s, when there was a considerable decrease in Surinamese unemployment.

17. In the younger age category (15-20 years old) the dropout rate is lower than in the older age categories, and it does not differ much from that of the native Dutch. Nor do the Afro-Surinamese differ much from the Indo-Surinamese in this respect.

18. Cf. van Amersfoort (1968); Buschkens (1974: 163).

19. A parallel can be found in a study on the experiences of immigrants with discrimination (Bouw and Nelissen 1988). As part of this study, the contents were analysed of a number of periodicals by and for immigrants. The Surinamese periodicals in the analysis were *Lalla Rookh* and *Span'noe*. Unlike *Span'noe*, *Lalla Rookh* is solely focused on the Indo-Surinamese; it addresses the topic of discrimination much less frequently. Moreover, the researchers conclude that there is a difference in how the topic of discrimination comes up. In *Lalla Rookh* the authors are very cautious about making any reference to discrimination or racism and tend to seek the cause of discrimination not only in the

native Dutch but also in themselves. In *Span'noe* there is much more of a tendency to address discrimination in terms of inequality and conflicts. In general, discrimination and racism are viewed as essential features of Dutch society. The articles in *Span'noe* are written much more clearly in the spirit of contestation, which is one of the reactions to discrimination that are cited in this study (1988: 125-28).

20. The Afro-Surinamese use the term *black* to refer to themselves far more frequently than the Indo-Surinamese, who usually use the term *brown*. Only the Indo-Surinamese employing a more politicized way of putting things, such as people who are active in self-help organizations, schoolteachers, or social workers, interpret their position in terms of black and white.

21. These are the estimated costs of a two-day wedding party as is traditionally customary among Hindus, and where two to four hundred guests are invited. The parents of the bride and bridegroom pay the bills together, but the parents of the bride pay most of them (see also Mungra 1990: 334).

22. See chapter 3.

23. Cf. Speckmann (1965).

24. See also Mungra (1990).

25. See also the section 'The First Indo-Surinamese Immigrants' in chapter 4.

26. Cf. Venema (1992); van Wetering (1987).

27. Cf. the case of Steve earlier in this chapter.

28. This also holds true of Indo-Surinamese single-parent families, but for reasons addressed in the following chapter, their situation is more favourable than that of Afro-Surinamese families. This is why I confine myself here to Afro-Surinamese families.

29. For whatever reason, school situations so problematic that children had to be sent to special child guidance agencies were something I observed more frequently among my Afro-Surinamese than my Indo-Surinamese respondents.

Chapter Eight

Social Environment and Networks

The book *Rosa Lee* by journalist Leon Dash (1998) gives a moving and authentic portrayal of a black "underclass" family in the United States. Rosa Lee is a middle-aged woman who lives with her eight children and her grandchildren in one of the ghettoes of Washington, D.C. She is illiterate and supports herself and her children with her welfare check and what she earns shoplifting and dealing drugs. Six of her children grow up in the neighborhood, barely get any education, and, like their mother, they turn to the world of drugs, crime, and prostitution. The same holds true of some of her grandchildren, for whom she is sometimes simultaneously the mother and grandmother. Two of her sons manage to escape ghetto life. Via a friend, one of them comes into contact with a middle-class family and learns at a young age that life can be very different. What is more, he meets a teacher who convinces him, for the first time in his life, that education is important. This son ultimately becomes a bus driver and is the only one of Rosa Lee's children to live with his family in a middle-class neighborhood. A second son begins attending school regularly only after he comes into contact with a teacher who encourages him and boosts his confidence. There is also a social worker he develops a personal relationship with who convinces him that he too can learn to read. After he finishes school, she continues to play an important role in his life. Both these brothers feel that without these adults, they would now be living the same kind of lives as the other people in the family.

This story shows that in itself, parental background is not a sufficient explanation for youngsters' success or failure at school or in their later careers. The social environment of the ghetto is so overpowering there is hardly any way for youngsters to escape. But these two of Rosa Lee's eight children did manage to find a way out. They came into contact with other circles and adults who gave them a whole new perspective and supported them in their efforts to find a way out of the ghetto. Of course, the Netherlands is not the United States, and there are no comparable ghettoes here, nor is there the kind of social isolation referred to by Wilson (1987 and 1996). I do not give this example to show any similarities between the Netherlands and the United States, I just want to make it clear that family background is not the only factor in youngsters' educational and occupational careers. In the Dutch situation as well, I think the notion should be taken seriously that the environment outside the parental home plays an important role.

The importance of social contacts outside the parental home lies in the access they provide to resources that can be instrumental for youngsters' educational and occupational careers.[1] These resources can involve direct assistance in the form of information, knowledge, and support, but they can also be a more implicit influence exerted by the circles youngsters move in: the ideas, norms, and role models they come across there. These influences from the surroundings can coincide with what youngsters experience at home and thus reinforce the influence of the parents, but they can also be different or diametrically opposed to it. Therefore, they are cultural influences exerted by the social contexts and networks youngsters are embedded in. These two aspects, the sociostructural and the cultural, are closely interwoven (Goody 1993).

In this chapter I focus on some of these sociocultural contexts. Depending on the freedom youngsters are given by their parents they also spend time in other settings such as the neighborhood and the social world of their peers. Sometimes via their parents, youngsters can also be embedded in social networks and frameworks inside or outside the ethnic community. I examine how these various social contexts and networks directly or indirectly influence the upward social mobility of Afro-Surinamese and Indo-Surinamese youngsters. I successively discuss the importance of the neighborhood, the influence of the interaction with their peers versus the ties with their relatives, and the degree of embeddedness in informal and formal social frameworks inside and outside the ethnic community. The central issue here is the extent to which the character of the ethnic community has advantages or disadvantages for the upward social mobility of the children of immigrants. More specifically, do ethnic ties promote or reduce social mobility?

The Neighborhood

In the postimmigration period, many Surinamese came to live in neighborhoods with large concentrations of immigrants (concentration districts). In the course of time, some moved to what they considered better areas, and some stayed there. This can influence how immigrant youngsters integrate into society. After all, the neighborhood partly determines whom they associate with and constitutes the social surroundings they adapt to. This section focuses on this influence from the immediate residential environment.

Concentration Districts

The problems that are so prevalent in concentration districts have to do with a set of interrelated aspects such as the concentration of immigrants, unemployed people and poorly educated people, schools with a largely immigrant pupil population, and high crime rates.[2] These aspects are widespread in districts like Bijlmermeer in Amsterdam and the Schilderswijk in The Hague, where many of the Surinamese immigrants settled at the time. They are well-known districts in the Netherlands and in a sense, rather extreme examples of phenomena that also occur elsewhere, albeit to a lesser extent or on a smaller scale. However, it is precisely these two districts that present a clear picture of how a neighborhood context can influence the careers of immigrant youngsters. What is more, relatively large numbers of Surinamese immigrants live in these two districts. Many of my respondents who now live in very different parts of The Hague once lived in the Schilderswijk, and some still do. The Surinamese in The Hague are strongly concentrated in this district and two adjacent ones (Kruythoff et al. 1997: 29). In Amsterdam, many of the Surinamese still live in Bijlmermeer. In 1994, 38 percent of all the Surinamese in Amsterdam lived there (Tesser et al. 1995: 67).

The "concentration problem" is not—as is sometimes suggested—merely a label attached to these districts from outside. Many of the Surinamese themselves see districts like the Schilderswijk in The Hague or Bijlmermeer in Amsterdam as environments where it is not easy to bring up children. This is one of the most important reasons why people want to leave these districts. Not everyone is able to do so though. Nor does everyone want to. For some people, the contacts in the neighborhood constitute their most important social network, as is the case for Mrs. U. (51), who lives in Bijlmermeer. She has an extensive social network based on all her informal economic activities and active social life. She plays cards at a club and often enters tournaments, she sings with a winti music group that has regular performances, and now and then she organizes soul music parties. Bijlmermeer is the site of most of the things she enjoys doing, so there is little reason for her to want to leave. The fact remains, though, that even the people who feel most at home in Bijlmermeer often agree that it is not easy to live there with children. "Bijlmermeer is a tough place to live," Mrs. U. says repeatedly when she tells me about her two teenaged daughters. That is why she is so strict about what time they have to be home and where they go when they go out. Her daughters have to be home exactly on time. "If they are late, I know there is something wrong. Because it is tough here in Bijlmermeer." This same impression is given by Mrs. J. (59), an early immigrant who did not move to Bijlmermeer until after her divorce. It was precisely in the period when so many Surinamese immigrants were moving there. Her son was happy to move from a town in the country to a district in Amsterdam with so many people from Surinam living there. But Mrs. J. kept a close eye on the friends he chose and taught him to watch out for the wrong kind of people.

"The kind of thing I taught my children is that you show other people you don't care what they think. You only do the things you want to do, that way they will have respect for you. You make them respect you. And that business with smoking and drinking. They used to bully my son, they would call him O.J. 'You will see,' I told him. 'As soon as they notice they aren't bothering you, they will stop. And they will respect you all the more for it.' And that is what happened."

The dangers parents watch out for have to do with the safety of their children and the contact they might have with the wrong friends. Another aspect parents generally have negative feelings about is the immigrant preponderance in the neighborhood and school population. Surinamese parents also often object to "black schools" because they think the concentration of Surinamese pupils will be an obstacle to their children's integration or are afraid the presence of other immigrant pupils will slow down their children's progress. The youngsters themselves also sometimes prefer to go to school somewhere else. During my study, I came across several youngsters who lived in Bijlmermeer but had made a deliberate decision to attend a school outside the district, either in downtown Amsterdam or in the nearby town of Weesp. The point is that even for the residents themselves, living in a concentration district often implies becoming integrated into a social environment where the members of their own ethnic group and other immigrants are in the majority for the simple reason that not many Dutch people live there any more. I noted objections of this kind among Afro-Surinamese and Indo-Surinamese parents alike. It is quite another matter when parents in concentration districts consciously choose to send their children to "their own school," which does not just happen to be in or near these districts. I get back to this later in the chapter.

The problems at black schools are closely related to the socioeconomic problems in the neighborhood. Children grow up in an atmosphere of unemployment and welfare dependence, where it is normal to have supplementary or alternative sources of income, one of them being the drug scene. Of course, not all school dropouts or unemployed people end up in the drug circuit, but in some neighborhoods the temptations of the drug scene as a source of income are very strong. The scene has a magnetic attraction for young people, including the ones who are still at school. They have to be very sure of themselves to be able to withstand the pressure if they can easily earn enough to afford the latest style in shoes or clothes just by selling some small packets of drugs in the immediate vicinity of their home or school. In this setting, schoolchildren already work as drug runners. One community worker who organizes athletic activities in Bijlmermeer—an early Surinamese immigrant himself—sees it happening right in front of him: dealers are recruiting schoolchildren, who cut classes and drop out of school to earn money, and mothers who let them because they themselves are having such a hard time making ends meet.

"Sometimes the mothers are on their own, the father is never home, or the kid doesn't even know the father. The mother has say eleven or twelve hundred guilders to live on. She has to pay the rent, buy food and everything else. She is never home, she is out there trying to earn a buck, you know, she sells cake or whatever. Just to earn a little something. And then you have these kids who are still at school, they just stop going. You have dealers who give them some small packets of drugs, ten or twelve packets to sell. If they sell them, they get a hundred or a hundred and fifty guilders. So they don't go to school any more. They walk around in the most expensive Nikes and all the rest. So their mother doesn't ask where they got the shoes. She is just happy she doesn't have to buy them."

The peer pressure in the neighborhood to "get with the program" is tremendous. Mike (30), who once lived in Bijlmermeer himself, has no trouble recalling the pressure that was put on him to engage in the same criminal activities as the other boys.

"They used to call me the seventh storey Grandpa because I lived on the seventh floor and because I didn't join in when they were breaking into houses, mugging, stealing bicycles, breaking windows. I wasn't one of the gang. I looked young, but I had the spirit of an old man."

The gang of boys that Mike was not part of and did not want to be part of legitimated their behavior by emphasizing how tough their lives were (having to live off welfare benefits) and how limited their chances were in society since they were black. Boys are more exposed than girls to the temptations of the street and the prevailing mentality there. So they are also more apt to develop a certain oppositional attitude to white society and Dutch agencies.[3]

The parents are aware of the peer pressure and the magnetic attraction of the drug scene. Afro-Surinamese parents in particular are afraid their sons will wind up in the drug scene and take measures to prevent it.

Jerryl (39) remembers how worried his parents were when he went back to the Netherlands on his own after the whole family returned to Surinam. He was twenty at the time and his parents were afraid he would wind up in the drug scene around Kruiskade in Rotterdam, where the family had lived. This is why his mother told an aunt in the Netherlands that her son was coming back to the Netherlands. She was at the airport to pick him up. But Jerryl had already arranged to rent the apartment of the mother of a good friend of his. In retrospect he understands his mother's fears very well. "I knew quite a few boys who got caught in that world. My girlfriend's brother-in-law was a drug dealer. So my mother and my aunt were afraid I would go in that direction too. That is why I had to go to my aunt's house for dinner every day."

The dangers of the drug scene are ever-present in neighborhoods of this kind and the perils seem to be greater for Afro-Surinamese than Indo-Surinamese boys. At any rate the Indo-Surinamese families I spoke to did not mention any boys who were drug dealers or addicts. This does not necessarily mean the Afro-Surinamese are more involved in the drug trade than the Indo-Surinamese (I cannot make any statements to this effect), but it does mean there are probably far fewer Indo-Surinamese boys selling drugs on the street.

For girls, the problem is more the neighborhood social network they are part of than the influence of the street culture. Parents feel the danger mainly lies in the boys they date, and thus the risk of getting pregnant and dropping out of school. In Bijlmermeer, teenage pregnancy is very much a topic of conversation among the girls. They know all about the girls in the neighborhood who have gotten pregnant, how old they were at the time, how much assistance their mothers were prepared to give them once the baby came, whether the girls were planning to move out or stay home with their mothers or go to a shelter, whether they were going to finish school or drop out after the baby was born, how much the welfare benefit is for girls with babies and so forth. The community sports worker quoted above noted that at a given moment the girls in a dance group got pregnant one after the other, girls who were sixteen and seventeen years old.

> "When one of them got pregnant, they all did. I think they were just trying to impress their girlfriends, to show them how grown-up they were. They don't always finish school unless they have someone to take care of the baby. They like being at home with the baby, playing with it, it is like a big doll."[4]

Becoming a teenaged mother not only makes it hard for girls to finish school, it also restricts what they can do in their leisure time. They can't go out the way they did before unless their mothers want to babysit for them.

> For Audrey (18), who is attending a junior college, this is a reason not to want children yet. "I don't want children until I have had my fill of partying. I like going out, I don't want to . . . You know, I don't want to have to leave my baby with someone every time I want to go out, what is the fun of that?"

> Gabriella (18), another junior college student, says "I know a lot of girls. So many of the girls I know are either pregnant or have just had a baby, sixteen, seventeen years old. Most of them do it to keep their boyfriend. I don't really see the point of that. If a guy loves you, he is going to stick around anyway. I don't need to have his baby. And even if you do get pregnant, they still leave."

Girls often disapprove of "children having children," which does not necessarily mean that if it happened to them they would not accept it. To most of them it is just a fact of life.

For the ones who are getting a better education like Judith, a college student, this is enough of a reason to postpone becoming a mother.

"It is also because what I see happening around me, all those girls having babies too soon, it is like a passing fad. But the baby is there to stay and he is the one who suffers. Because the mother wants to go out and she is going to pass the baby on to someone else. No, when I have a baby I want to be able to take care of him myself. But if I look around, I ought to have five children by now, you know, at my ripe old age of twenty-two. All my girlfriends already have children."

In other words, a certain normative influence is implicitly exerted by whatever behavior is prevalent in the neighborhood or social environment. Youngsters follow in the footsteps of the people near them who are a little bit older, especially if they have no other examples. In the background, their assessment of the job opportunities awaiting them and their faith in the value of diplomas play a role. Youngsters in a poor social position who mainly associate with others in the same position merely reinforce each other's conduct. They run more of a risk than youngsters who grow up in more heterogeneous surroundings. For reasons addressed below, this holds true more for Afro-Surinamese than Indo-Surinamese youngsters.

Of course, the immediate residential environment in the concentration districts does not have the same influence on all youngsters. Several youngsters are quoted above who were apparently able to avoid the negative influence of the neighborhood. One reason why is that youngsters' social contacts are not necessarily restricted to the neighborhood. Unlike the situation in the United States, in the Netherlands the physical distances are not that long between concentration districts and neighborhoods with a more heterogeneous or middle-class population.[5] In this sense, the residents are less isolated from other lifestyles and youngsters come into contact more easily with alternative role models. Even in concentration districts, the population is often still rather heterogeneous, especially in the old parts of the city (Anderiesen and Reijndorp 1991). In fact Bijlmermeer in Amsterdam is essentially an exception in the Netherlands, and perhaps the area that exhibits the greatest similarity to the ghettoes described in the American literature.[6] It is also where parents are most apt to see the risks of the social environment for their teenaged children. In general, though, many of the ideas related to concentration districts are not automatically applicable in the Netherlands.

Geographical Mobility

It is true that many Surinamese immigrants still live in the concentration districts of Amsterdam and The Hague, but quite a few have spread out to other parts of the cities. Many of the families in my study have left the neighborhoods they lived in when they first came to the Netherlands, some a very long time ago. Although there are certainly Surinamese residents who perceive living in a concentration district as something positive, many also acknowledge the problematic aspects. A number of them made a very conscious decision to leave these districts. There are Surinamese people who would rather not live in the middle of a lot of "foreigners" because they think it will keep their children back at school. A number of these parents do not wish to live among Surinamese people either. They feel Dutch people will look down on them if they do, and they think it will keep their children from integrating.

> This is how Mr. and Mrs. I. feel. They came to the Netherlands as young adults and both their children were born here. At the beginning they lived with Mrs. I.'s mother in the Schilderswijk in The Hague. They soon moved into their own flat and then bought a house "on the other side of The Hague." "I didn't want to be classified as one of the people in that group." Mr. I., who comes from Paramaribo himself, feels it is mainly Indo-Surinamese from the countryside who have a hard time assimilating in the Netherlands. In his own opinion, it was not that hard for him at all ("someone from Paramaribo assimilates in a different way than someone from Nickerie"), which is why he does not want to be put in the same category as rural Indo-Surinamese. What is more, he likes his privacy and feels you don't have much privacy if you live amidst people from the same place. But the neighborhood they moved to was also known as an "immigrant district." That is why they didn't want their youngest daughter to play on the street alone. Although they had renovated the house they bought very nicely and were quite fond of it, this is why they decided to sell it. Now they live in a new residential area in a suburb of The Hague.

This is a pattern I came across quite regularly. To a certain extent the Indo-Surinamese who have worked their way up in Dutch society don't want much to do with the Indo-Surinamese community, or at any rate with the "average" members of the community and their assumedly lower level of integration.

> Mrs. R. (48): "In Surinam when the big move started, you would hear people call The Hague a coolie compound. It was where the Indo-Surinamese settled. I am Indo-Surinamese myself and they are our own people, but still, you know [whispers now] I don't like that much. I don't like them at all. There is a time and a place for everything. They are nice enough. My folks [my relatives] are all Indo-Surinamese too, but still . . . I just can't accept the way they are. I really can't. I myself try to find a middle way. In this society, you have to adapt, don't you? I have been working at a ministry for about fifteen years now. So there is no way I can spend all my time being surrounded by those people. Where would it get me? Where would it get my children?"

Sometimes the picture people have of their own group, in this case the lower-class Indo-Surinamese who live in the Schilderswijk, is totally negative. Mrs. G. (49), who once very consciously decided to move out of the Schilderswijk herself, says it is "literally sickening" whenever she walks around the area. What her objections come down to is that the people there don't have a job and they live off welfare, they drink, they have a lot of children and live in tiny three or four-room flats, they always stick together and keep going to those Indo-Surinamese clubs.

Youngsters who have grown up in the neighborhood and now live in their own flats there also sometimes want to leave.

Like Sunil (25) and his wife Anita. Sunil grew up in the Schilderswijk in The Hague and some of his relatives still live there. When they first got married, he and Anita lived with his grandmother and uncle until they got their own flat just a few minutes' walk away. It is a flat in one of the many new parts of the neighborhood. They have a child and a second one on the way, but they do not feel the neighborhood is a good place to bring up their children. They think there are too many foreigners there. Their son can't even play outside because there are too many immigrant children at the nearby square and they are too rough. It isn't safe enough there.

Negative stories about Surinamese immigrants in Amsterdam often have to do with Bijlmermeer. In the public perception, it serves as the model as it were for everything that has gone wrong in the city with the Surinamese immigrants. The people who live there do not always experience it that way, but at the time it was not very popular with the people of Amsterdam. Anyone who did not absolutely have to go and live there preferred not to. Mrs. E. (60), one of the early immigrants, remembers that there were a lot of flats available in Bijlmermeer just when she was looking for a place to live. She could have moved there, but she didn't want to.

"When I am at work, I want to know that my children are safe. That is why I didn't take that flat in Bijlmermeer. And today I am very glad I didn't, because my children are all doing just fine. They all have good jobs, they went to good schools. And they grew up right here, on this street [in Amsterdam New-West]. We were the only people from Surinam, everyone else here was Dutch. But my neighbor always said 'Lovely children!' because I always told them 'If you are playing outside and the neighbor doesn't like the noise, then you come right upstairs!' They could only go play outside when I was home. Then I could keep an eye on them."

However, not everyone had this choice. Starting in the mid-1970s, more and more Surinamese moved to Bijlmermeer because it was relatively easy to get a flat there. As a result, they had much less contact with the native Dutch than the Surinamese who lived in town. For some of the Surinamese, Bijlmermeer was a good place to enter the Dutch housing market, but as soon as they had an opportunity to leave, they took it. A typical example of the Surinamese housing movements in Amsterdam is the history of the Indo-Surinamese family of Ronnie (23).

> In 1977 Ronnie and his family came to live in De Pijp, one of the nineteenth-century districts in Amsterdam. The whole family lived there in a cramped attic for a year. Ronnie went to kindergarten there. Then they got a flat in Bijlmermeer, where the family lived for five or six years and where Ronnie went to primary school. But his parents didn't want their children growing up there. "At a given moment, my father and mother started getting very concerned, because there were some very strange things going on there. So to make sure we didn't go bad ourselves, to get us out of there, we moved to a neighborhood called Slotervaart."

Many Surinamese left their first address to move to Bijlmermeer, and then went on to one of the post–World War II western suburbs like Slotervaart. Many of the native Dutch residents of the downtown area also moved to these new neighborhoods at the time. Just like them, Ronnie's parents saw the move as a step up. By the time he started secondary school, Ronnie was out of Bijlmermeer and had a group of friends who were largely native Amsterdammers. These friends were to play an important role in the choices he made in the course of his educational career. I return to this later.

The Surinamese who have since left the concentration districts are the ones who could afford to. In other words, geographical mobility is linked to socioeconomic mobility. It should be noted, though, that in the Dutch welfare state, the relation between people's position on the labor market and the housing market is not as strong as in countries like the United States. Despite their poor labor market position, many Surinamese have left the older districts to settle in newer ones (van Amersfoort 1992). Whatever the case may be, the changes in the residential environment had a favorable effect on the youngsters' educational careers. They grew up in a less dangerous environment and more often attended "white" schools, as in Ronnie's case cited above. However, the question remains: What is the cause and what is the effect? It is clear that Surinamese families in a somewhat better position were the ones who moved to better neighborhoods, but this still does not tell us whether the educational careers of their children were primarily influenced by the better neighborhood or the more favorable home environment.

Living in a concentration district implies certain risks for youngsters' educational careers. They are related to the circumstances described above in the immediate residential environment. Yet not all the youngsters from these districts get poor grades or drop out of school; in the same way, as not all the youngsters whose families have moved to "better" neighborhoods do well at school. Apparently there are also other factors that play a role. One of them is the composition of the social network regardless of its spatial component.[7] People can live in a concentration district and still be embedded in a varied social network, and people can live in a more heterogeneous neighborhood and still live in a limited social world shared only with other underprivileged people. So in itself, the neighborhood is not necessarily decisive. In the following sections I examine various other sociocultural contexts that youngsters move in, starting with the social world of their peers.

Peers and Relatives

Whether or not it is limited to the neighborhood, the social contact youngsters have can confront them with other social worlds and ideas. These ideas can be in line with what they have learned at home, or they can be very different or even contradictory to what they have been taught there. Here I focus first on the effects, positive as well as negative, of the contact with peers on youngsters' educational careers. Then I examine how the peer influence compares with the influence of the family network.

The Social World of Peers

The social world of peers can be confined to the immediate residential environment, but it can also include school and leisure time. The ethnic or class composition of this social world can be more or less mixed. If there is a marked social contact overlap between neighborhood, school, and leisure time, Surinamese youngsters move in less varied social circles than if there is no such overlap. Youngsters who leave the neighborhood every day to go to school somewhere else, where they come into contact with youngsters from different social circles, have a more heterogeneous social network than youngsters who go to school in the neighborhood and spend their leisure time there. Let me present the stories of two young Afro-Surinamese women as illustrations.

Denise (24)[8] lives in Amsterdam in a working-class district called De Pijp. After primary school, she went to a five-year secondary school at a comprehensive school in another neighborhood, where most of the pupils were Dutch. When she chose this type of school, she was not an exception in her parents' circle of friends and relatives, but she was compared with her girlfriends from the neighborhood, most of whom went to easier schools like the one specialized in domestic science. After she finished secondary school, Denise went to a junior college where there were a lot of students from Surinam. More than when she was at secondary school, she spent her leisure time with Surinamese youngsters, whom she knew from the neighborhood and from school. She entered a totally new world, though, when she graduated from junior college and went on to business college. Up until then, she had largely moved in Surinamese circles, "also because of the neighborhood I lived in. Somehow you always hang out with each other. That is very different nowadays. I don't think there is a single Surinamese student in any of my classes, so what can I do. . . . But I did grow up in the midst of Surinamese people."

With her Surinamese friends she would always go to Surinamese dances at halls or clubs. With her Dutch friends—college students—that changed. Going out meant going to a café or a film. She went to college parties with music she herself would never have listened to, but that was precisely what she liked about it. "It was suddenly just a totally different world." Denise can move comfortably in both worlds, and thinks the two ways of going out are different but both nice. She still enjoys spending time with her Surinamese girlfriends from the neighborhood, but she is well aware she is now living in a different world. Her girlfriends are not as well educated, have much less contact with Dutch peers, and already have children. "They don't do anything for themselves, they don't even finish the school they started, they quit everything half way." Denise feels that just like her mother, she does not want to be dependent on a man later. "I really got that idea from my mother, that in the first place you have to be able to take care of yourself, so you need to have a degree. A lot of girls I know, they have such a dependent attitude when it comes to guys, their boyfriend or, well, men." All these things make it clear to her that she is different now, and in a way she has outgrown the neighborhood. "I think if I had only been associating with my friends from the neighborhood, maybe things would have been very different for me." Not that she herself has a problem with it, "but I do think I have become more like a Dutch girl, even when I am with my Surinamese friends. But what can you expect?"

This example shows that the school environment can ultimately exert more influence than the neighborhood. Denise grew up in an old part of town, but outgrew this environment and integrated into the world of better educated youngsters with a different lifestyle than her girlfriends from the neighborhood. So the school and neighborhood are thus two separate environments, each with their own friends and ways to spend leisure time. The advantage is that Denise came to know both social worlds, the one of poorly educated youngsters in inner-city Amsterdam as well as the one of Dutch college students. This gave her a varied social network and more of an opportunity to move and look for a job in various worlds.

When she first came to the Netherlands in 1973, Marcia (30) lived at a boarding house in the fancy southern part of Amsterdam for two years. As she remembers it, she was the only Surinamese pupil at the school there. She didn't feel at home, it was "a school for rich kids." "The only friends I had there were Dutch and they all lived in the suburbs in Buitenveldert. If I went to their homes, it was like going to a castle. That was the only kind of friends I had at primary school." After primary school, Marcia went to the same comprehensive school in the neighborhood as many of the other children from her class. She did not do well there, her grades were poor, and she didn't like the atmosphere. "It was a very different world for me, where I did not feel comfortable. When I was at primary school, it all still seemed very normal, I would go visit my friends at home and they would come visit me. I didn't notice much discrimination at the time, I really didn't. It was also a question of the neighborhood where we lived, Beethovenstraat, Buitenveldert, and children from Amstelveen used to go to that school too. The truth is of course that they were all white people with money. A very different status than we had. We were living at a boarding house, they had real houses with front yards and back yards and cars. But that was not a problem at the time, not at all. I don't remember any signs of discrimination or anything like that, I just didn't feel comfortable there."

The family left the boarding house and moved from the south of Amsterdam to a working-class neighborhood. Shortly afterward, Marcia switched from the comprehensive school in the south of the city to a four-year secondary school closer to home. It was in the nineteenth-century Staatslieden district close to where she was now living. That was also where she spent much of her leisure time, taking part in organized activities and just hanging out. She had a group of girlfriends there, some of them Surinamese and some Dutch. The girls spent their time on the street and at the community centers there. Some girls even called their group of girls *the gang*. Together they explored the area and the teenage nightlife. The Surinamese girls learned a lot from the Dutch ones who had lived in the neighborhood all their lives; Marcia was also in the majorettes for a while. The Dutch girls were attracted in turn by the atmosphere of fun and excitement that the Surinamese girls knew how to generate.

The girls all went to the four-year secondary or vocational school. Not all their educational careers followed the beaten path as it were. Some of them, such as Marcia, switched from one school to the other because they were expelled, stayed away themselves, or just wanted to try a different school in the hope that things would go better there or that it would be more fun. Marcia once enrolled at a different school with one of her friends without telling her mother. At school Marcia and her friend were often thought to be loudmouths, but they in turn accused the teachers of discriminating against them. In retrospect, Marcia realizes she had trouble dealing with authority. "I couldn't stand it if the teacher told me what to do. And since I was always being a nuisance in the classroom, they did tell me a thing or two." Her parents felt at the time that their daughters, Marcia and her sister, were talking back because they got that from the Dutch kids. It was viewed as being un-Surinamese.

Marcia's story makes two things clear. First, if we examine the beginning of her educational career in the south of Amsterdam, we see a considerable discrepancy between her parental background and the background of the girls she was going to school with. This contact with a social world that was too far away from her own background does not seem to have exerted much influence on her. In other words, the discrepancy between the two backgrounds was so great that she could not easily identify with her peers there. In a situation like this, they do not serve as role models.[9]

If we go on to examine the continuation of Marcia's educational career in the Staatslieden district, it is clear that the social world of her peers there constituted a very specific cultural context. The neighborhood where she grew up as a teenager was largely populated at the time by lower-class residents and Surinamese immigrants. She integrated into a lower-class environment where she behaved in a way her parents considered un-Surinamese. Her parents were obviously no longer the only ones exerting influence on how their children behaved. The home background certainly does play an important role, but it is not the only environment to exert an influence on youngsters and their educational careers.

A comparison of the stories of the two respondents shows that the more of an overlap there is between the neighborhood and school friends who also spend much of their leisure time together, the more of an influence these friends exert. This overlap is more in evidence among pupils attending the lower kinds of schools. The neighborhood is less important for youngsters attending the higher kinds of schools; for them the school environment plays more of a role in their choice of friends.[10]

The importance of this sociocultural context is clear if we take a closer look at the role of peers in the course of youngsters' educational careers. Earlier in this chapter, a reference was made to the story of Ronnie, who lived, respectively, in De Pijp, Bijlmermeer, and Slotervaart in Amsterdam. His educational career is a good example.

Ronnie (23, Indo-Surinamese) spent his teens in Slotervaart. His friends exerted a great deal of influence on his choice of school. They were mostly native Amsterdam boys who he knew from the four-year secondary school. He was apparently so well adapted there that a teacher gave him speech lessons along with his friends to help him lose a bit of his Amsterdam accent. All his friends went on with their studies, and that was also what Ronnie wanted to do. After a short period at a junior college, the friends of his Dutch girlfriend told him about a college degree in Personnel and Labor. He successfully completed this study program, which made him the best educated person of his whole family. In Surinam his parents had not had any more than a primary school education, and since Ronnie was the oldest child in the family, his friends were all the more important to him where school-related questions were concerned. His parents also wanted him to get a good education, but his own motivation was just as great, "because all my friends were continuing their studies. I also had friends at the six-year secondary school who were going to the university. I really wanted to go to college, I thought it was a great idea. That was the direction all my friends were going." In his case, the importance of the role played by his friends is perhaps also clear from the fact that his brothers did not do nearly as well. His parents view the brother who is three years younger than Ronnie as "a real problem." He was expelled from a number of schools, he had all kinds of jobs and started any number of training courses (as cook, as security guard), but he didn't finish any of them. At the moment, he is a "flexi-worker," who does all kinds of different jobs at a company. But he never sticks with any one thing for long. Much to the distress of his parents, especially his mother, he spends a lot of time with Afro-Surinamese boys. They are boys like himself, who are not likely to encourage him in his occupational career.

Ronnie's friends exerted a positive, stimulating influence on his educational career, but in other cases quite the opposite happens.

Danny (21, Indo-Surinamese), for example, lives in the Schilderswijk in The Hague. His friends are very important to him. He went via the five-year to the six-year secondary school, but in the last year he quit school. He was staying out until all hours of the night with his friends, he liked to drink and gamble, he cut classes, and at a given moment he dropped out altogether. He spent a lot of time with friends who were out of work too. "And they didn't have anything to do all day," says Danny, "so what happened? We slept all day and went out at night. At about four or five in the afternoon I would get up. Go past the employment agency to see if they had a job. If they didn't, then that night we would party."

Danny was influenced by his friends who weren't going to school any more and were unemployed. More than is the case for girls, the activities boys engage in compete with school. This was the case with various of the boys in my study, Afro-Surinamese and Indo-Surinamese alike.

Sunil (25, Indo-Surinamese) went to a four-year secondary school after primary school. The first two years went well there, but not the third year. "I just didn't feel like it any more," Sunil explains. "I had other ideas. I was more interested in working and earning money. Maybe it was because I associated with the wrong kind of friends. That could have played a role in my suddenly not feeling like going to school any more. I would cut a lot of classes, you know. I never had any problems with my homework or with studying and all that. . . . But it was those friends, you know, and all that running around."

Jerryl (39, Afro-Surinamese) realizes it was more his own fault than his parents' fault that he never got any further than the four-year secondary school. "I was young, I looked at what my friends were doing. I just was not conscious of certain things, of certain consequences. All I thought about was having fun. I just wanted to do the things I enjoyed, go and have a good time with my friends."

Relations with peers can exert a great deal of influence on the course of youngsters' educational careers, but it can be in various directions. Depending on the kind of friends they have, young people can be positively or negatively affected. So the nature of the world the peers live in is important, their hobbies, ideas, and ambitions. Youngsters who do not receive much support at home and are not encouraged to fulfill any ambitions and, in addition, find themselves surrounded by friends who think much the same way are not likely to be stimulated by these friends to continue their studies. What is more, youngsters who remain inside homogenous networks of other poorly educated youngsters have little or no access to a more varied network that can help present more and different opportunities. Youngsters from a nonsupportive and nonambitious family background would clearly benefit from a circle of friends that exerts a stimulating influence. Via these friends, they can come into contact with other worlds and ideas, which can be advantageous for their further educational and occupational career in terms of information, encouragement, and skills. As regards these findings about the role of peers, I have not observed any systematic differences between Afro-Surinamese and Indo-Surinamese youngsters. However, these differences are in evidence if we look at the influence of parents and relatives on the interaction with peers.

Peers versus Relatives

How does the influence of peers compare with the influence of parents and relatives? Can parents counter the negative influence of the social circles their children associate with? To what extent can they monitor their children and exercise control over their educational career to make it more successful? And to what extent can they keep their children from dropping out of school and becoming involved in a subculture of the wrong friends?

I have noted above that the world of peers and the pressure to conform can be so great that there is little parents can do to counter these external influences. On the other hand, the situation at home can be so conflict-ridden and insecure or otherwise nonsupportive that children simply prefer to turn to their peers. For boys, the world of their male peers outside the family can have some very attractive sides. The less successful youngsters are at school or on the labor market, the more apt they are to think they can acquire more status or money somewhere else. This occurs among the Afro-Surinamese and Indo-Surinamese alike, but there are nonetheless important differences. First, family ties are stronger among the Indo-Surinamese, or at any rate different from those among the Afro-Surinamese, which has to do with family cohesion. The following is a good example.

Rick (27, Indo-Surinamese) grew up in the Schilderswijk in The Hague. He came to the Netherlands with his parents and sister at the age of four shortly before Surinam became independent. From the start the family lived in the Schilderswijk, where both children went to school. The four-year secondary school turned out to be too ambitious for Rick, and after two years he switched to a lower technical school, which he graduated from. After that, his educational career was less successful. He went to an intermediate technical school, but was no longer devoting much attention to his schoolwork. He spent a lot of time with his friends from the neighborhood and his parents no longer had much control over him. He and his friends were in a gang of about forty boys. Rick and a friend were heading the gang. They got into a lot of trouble in The Hague, he recalls, and in Rotterdam and Amsterdam as well. After they wreaked havoc in Zoetermeer, a court order was even issued forbidding him to be on the street. Those were his wild years, when he was fifteen, sixteen years old. Afterward he was one of the few boys in the group who was able to turn his life around; the other boys didn't change. One of them was recently sentenced to ten years in prison for a hold-up; he heard about it from the boy's brother. Another one had committed a murder. Rick himself didn't go in that direction, or he didn't have a chance to. He comes from a family where his lifestyle definitely was not tolerated. The first time he got into trouble with the police, it meant the end of his criminal activities. He went to a regional school part-time and got a job in the vegetable section at a supermarket. He went with his parents once to Surinam. His grandfather tried to convince him to come and help him run his rice business. Rick hesitated, but he decided in the end to stay in the Netherlands. He got married, and shortly before the wedding he went with his parents on a trip to the Far East. There he discovered the possibilities for importing inexpensive clothing. At the moment he is managing the family business, where his parents and sister also work.

This example shows that at a certain stage of life, friends from the neighborhood can exert more influence than parents. In his teens, Rick was totally out of his parents' control and developed a lifestyle that not only clashed with the mentality at school, but also was very different from what his parents had in mind for him. In this sense he did not differ from the other boys. The thing that was different in his case was the role his family played in changing his life. The reason they stepped in was that he had gotten in trouble with the police, but his family contributed toward all the changes that were to follow. His grandfather spoke to him and even asked him to become his partner in his business. His parents took him on a trip abroad and gave him their support and confidence in setting up his own business. They saw to it that he married the "right" girl. In the end, he was back on the customary path and conformed completely to what was expected of an adult Indo-Surinamese man in his circles, namely, to get married and earn a living.

This pattern is quite uncommon among the lower-class Afro-Surinamese. Getting married is not an important binding factor there that brings youngsters back to the family. Some parents manage to compensate for this by strict control and discipline in the home. Parents in a better socioeconomic position and two-parent families are better able to create a supportive environment in the home. They nonetheless also have a hard time keeping their sons from going astray because the outside world has such a magnetic attraction for them. They are at any rate aware of the dangers lurking there and explicitly state that the way they raise their children at home is designed to make their children strong enough to resist the pressure from their friends.

> It was his strict father's doing that made Jeffrey (33, Afro-Surinamese) finish the four-year secondary school he was attending. His father had come to the Netherlands in the late 1970s to work as a bookkeeper and continue his training in his occupation. An older daughter did better than Jeffrey at school and met with the parents' expectations more in this respect. "My father was always pushing me," Jeffrey recalls, "because I am not one of those people who likes to study. I am more someone who goes in for sports, that was what I liked." Jeffrey was, however, under a lot of pressure from his parents to finish school and resist the negative influence of his friends. "A lot of my friends would go out shoplifting or breaking into schools just for the fun of it. But I didn't do that kind of thing. Because I knew that if my father ever found out about it, I was in for it. In a way I would never forget!"

Once their children reach a certain age, Indo-Surinamese parents are often able to bring them back to the family norms and values, but this is not always so easy for Afro-Surinamese parents. At what can be viewed as the crucial age, the absence of a regulating mechanism comparable to marriage for the Indo-Surinamese is strongly felt. Afro-Surinamese parents have to make extra efforts if they want to keep their children from going astray. What is more, the magnetic attraction of their peer group is especially strong for the Afro-Surinamese. This has to do with the central role of the male peer group in at least some sections of the Afro-Surinamese lower class, and the alternative survival strategies that have been developed there. I give an example below of an Afro-Surinamese man in Amsterdam and his younger brothers who, unlike himself, sought alternative sources of income in the drug scene.

> Mike (30) and his two brothers are the youngest in a family with ten children from a poor neighborhood in Paramaribo. Their father, who was a lower-level civil servant, died when Mike was fourteen. Mike's mother went to work at a

hospital when her youngest daughter was two. Unlike some of the other brothers and sisters, Mike and his two younger brothers didn't go to school for long. In Surinam Mike just went to primary school. In their teens, he and his brothers no longer went to school, but they didn't have a job either. They were living in their mother's house and sometimes earned some money here and there with odd jobs. Mike left for the Netherlands at the age of eighteen and did a CBB training course there.[11] He took a roundabout route but in the end, he attended a part-time social service study program at a junior college. He is still receiving his welfare benefit while attending the program. One of his younger brothers has also been in the Netherlands for the past few years and is similarly attending a CBB study program. His other younger brother stayed behind in Surinam. He is twenty-four by now and earns a living selling drugs. Neither the talks with his mother nor his arrests by the police have been able to dissuade him from dealing drugs. Mike was also unable to exert any influence over him on his last visit to Surinam. To his distress, when he returned to the Netherlands he discovered that his other brother was now also involved in the drug trade.

In this case, the mother no longer has any control over her sons. The two youngest boys wound up in the drug trade, one in Surinam and the other in the Netherlands. They are poorly educated and were never able to find a regular job. Their lifestyle is typical of many young Afro-Surinamese men from the urban lower class. As adults, they continue to be part of the household of their mother, who works inside and outside the home to earn a living. They themselves earn only an irregular income with odd jobs. One of the two brothers continues this lifestyle after immigrating. The conditions of his life in the Netherlands are apparently not such that he can abandon his old lifestyle and build up a new life here.

The survival strategies of young Afro-Surinamese men are not simply generated in the Netherlands as a direct response to their opportunities here, or rather the lack of them. On the other hand, they should not be assumed to be merely a continuation of a traditional mode of survival. The question instead is why this Creole tradition, which once emerged in a context of urban poverty and unemployment, *continued* to exist after immigration to the Netherlands. The Indo-Surinamese did not bring any such tradition to the Netherlands. This does not mean they have not been faced with poverty and have not ever been involved in the drug trade. But their history in Surinam is much less linked to a tradition of survival on the edge of urban society.

This is also evident from the case of Rick, the Indo-Surinamese boy described above who grew up in the Schilderswijk in The Hague. His "deviant" lifestyle was stimulated far more by the neighborhood subculture of his peers than by Indo-Surinamese traditions. In fact it was the Indo-Surinamese traditions that steered him back to a regular way of life. It is important that his family gave him moral and financial support when he needed it most. In particular it is the parents' support in children's marriages that plays a decisive role. The role of this support is clear from the involvement of all the relatives in the marriage, and in financing and preparing for the wedding. Youngsters in turn are very dependent on their relatives, if not as regards the choice of their spouse, then at any rate for the organization of the whole wedding celebration. This support makes it all the more advantageous for youngsters not to break off relations with their family and to correct their "deviant" lifestyle in time.

This does not always hold true for young Afro-Surinamese men, at any rate not to the same extent. Under certain circumstances, the link with the peer group is apparently more advantageous for them than the link with their relatives. In terms of status and prestige, money and material earnings, the outside world can sometimes provide more than the kind of regular career their parents have in mind. The criteria for success that are used in certain circles of poorly educated boys are derived from the outside world of men rather than from their relatives.[12] What is more, there are parents who are quite lenient about the semilegal or illegal earnings of their sons. In view of their own poor socioeconomic position, they are sometimes apt to accept these earnings and thus implicitly grant their approval. In addition, the institute of marriage does not play a central role with the Afro-Surinamese and weddings are not the events of great social importance that they are to the Indo-Surinamese. In this sense, young Afro-Surinamese adults are not as dependent on their parents as their Indo-Surinamese peers. There is more at stake for Indo-Surinamese boys if they continue to pursue a "deviant" lifestyle.

There is a comparable difference for girls. The notion of girls having to be "protected" from the outside world is still widespread among the Indo-Surinamese and has to do with the family honor. If a girl gets a bad reputation, the family's good name is defiled, which is why her father and brothers have to protect a girl's purity. The family is a collective that requires the loyalty of its members, but they in turn can count on the protection and support of the entire family. At any rate, this is an idea many Indo-Surinamese take very seriously.

Urmy (21) is studying at the university and has to balance her desire to do the same things the other students do with her loyalty to her parents. She would like to rent a room and live on her own, but she knows her parents would not like it. She is not allowed to go to clubs or dances, and in fact she herself prefers to go to family parties. She does go out every so often with a group of students she is studying with. "I wouldn't want to be the only one who cannot go just because my parents don't want me to." But she does not cross the boundaries set by her parents. "I don't blame my parents for treating me this way. I like spending a lot of time at home. I am used to it. So it isn't a problem for me." She thinks it is logical that her parents are stricter with girls than boys. "You know how vulnerable girls are, that is usually where the problems are, or so they say. Because if something happens, it is the girl who disgraces the whole family."

There is indeed a high threshold for Indo-Surinamese youngsters when it comes to leaving the parental home in an appropriate way, and there is a high price to pay for breaking off contact with the family. This is true for boys, and even more so for girls. In Surinam, if a girl left home before she was married it used to be an awful disgrace for the family and could even lead to her being disowned.

Mrs. C. (49) came from a poor and problem-ridden family in the countryside. At a given moment, she simply could no longer stand the situation and ran away from home before she was married. In Paramaribo she stayed with acquaintances, was helped by a priest from school, and married a boy there who paid her last year's tuition. She realized her decision was final. "Once I left home, I knew I could never go back again." She did have contact with her younger brothers and sisters later (some of them came to live with her and her husband in Paramaribo to go to school there), but she was alienated from her older brothers.

In the Netherlands the traditional patterns are changing; not all Indo-Surinamese girls want to conform to their parents demands. Under the influence of their peers, they want more freedom of movement and leeway for making their own decisions.

Sharda (24) recalls what it was like when she was at a four-year secondary school. "I always had a group of Indo-Surinamese girlfriends and I also had a Dutch group. I was sort of somewhere in the middle. You know, the Indo-Surinamese couldn't do this and couldn't do that. I was always allowed to do more than the average Indo-Surinamese girl, that was true, but I still always felt it wasn't enough. At the five-year secondary school, I used to hang out a lot with Dutch kids. I would also go to the clubs. My father did always come and pick me up there, but still, I became a lot more free. If I had continued to just associate with other Indo-Surinamese girls, I would have just stayed in that same circle, and if someone else wasn't allowed to do something, well I wouldn't have done it either. At a given moment, I started really spending a lot of time with Dutch girls and boys, and they would go to the beach after school and do all kinds of things, and I would go with them. Well, when I got home, you can bet my parents gave me a piece of their mind!" Sharda got into more and more arguments with her parents and in the end, very much against her parents' will, she moved out.

There are differences in the extent to which parents accept this behavior. There are those who gradually adjust to the ideas and conduct of their daughters. This is what happened in Sharda's case. Once she was living on her own, her relationship with her parents gradually went back to normal. The more widespread these practices are becoming, the more the norms around them are changing, facilitating the parents' acceptance. But for the time being, there are definitely some conflicts. The desire for greater autonomy is one of the major reasons Indo-Surinamese girls leave home (Lalmahomed 1992b).

Afro-Surinamese girls leave home as well, but in their case it is not so much because they want greater autonomy. Compared with Indo-Surinamese girls, they already have more freedom of movement. They nonetheless often find their parents too strict. Afro-Surinamese girls leave home more often than Indo-Surinamese girls because they want to be "totally free," and they are barely willing to accept any rules at all (Josias 1992). Not that Afro-Surinamese girls do not have a reputation to lose. On the contrary, uninhibited Afro-Surinamese girls also get a bad name. But when they leave home, the parting is not as total as it is for Indo-Surinamese girls because they have less to lose.

From the youngsters' perspective, there are thus two social worlds they are more or less embedded in, the world of their peers and the world of their parents and relatives. The influence of their peers on their educational career can be either positive or negative, depending on the circumstances (neighborhood, educational level, leisure time). In principle, the influences exerted by the two worlds are not necessarily diametrically opposed. They can supplement each other in either a positive or a negative sense. If there is a clash and parents have something very different in mind from their children, a great deal depends on the assistance and support youngsters think they can expect from their peers or their parents. There are differences in this sense between Afro-Surinamese and Indo-Surinamese youngsters and between boys and girls. In the case of Indo-Surinamese girls, it is much less a question of negative peer influence on their careers. After all, they generally have less freedom of movement than Indo-Surinamese boys or Afro-Surinamese youngsters of both sexes. Afro-Surinamese boys are the other extreme; the male peer group and alternative survival strategies have a great attraction for them. As a result of the stronger family cohesion and the central importance of marriage, Indo-Surinamese parents are more frequently able to compensate for the negative influence of their children's peers or steer it in the desired direction. In the long run, for Indo-Surinamese youngsters the balance tips toward loyalty to their parents. However, the explanations for these differences also lie in the wider social networks parents and children are embedded in.

The Ethnic Community

The social networks individual families are part of can be situated inside or outside the ethnic community. They can be close knit or not, supportive or less supportive. In this section, I focus on this social embeddedness of individuals and families, and the way it is supportive or nonsupportive for the careers of the younger generation.[13] In this context, I examine the extent to which the two ethnic communities differ, what effects this has, and how advantageous or disadvantageous this is for upward social mobility. I am referring here to the openness or closedness of ethnic networks and to social cohesion. Social cohesion stands for the extent to which people have their social contacts inside or outside the ethnic group, and the extent to which ethnic boundaries are preserved. Cohesion and closedness can be examined at various levels of social organization.[14] Here, I focus on the informal social networks within the ethnic community, interethnic relations and marriages, and formal social contexts and symbolic ties.

Social Networks inside the Ethnic Community

Social networks can either promote or inhibit upward social mobility. One form of positive influence is the concrete support provided within family or other networks such as coaching and help with homework. Especially among the Indo-Surinamese, this includes the assistance of relatives outside of the nuclear family. They give younger members of the family coaching or help with their homework. Some of the youngsters were in the same class or at the same school as their cousins. Sheila (33), who comes from a large family, recalls that there was always some other member of her family in the class. "You looked out for each other and helped each other." Another respondent, Mr. N. (40), remembers that he and his brothers were coached by a cousin who was studying at the university in Wageningen. For hours on end, he would help them with their mathematics and chemistry assignments. Of course, not all the Indo-Surinamese youngsters have well-educated people in their family network. But it is striking that it is precisely the Indo-Surinamese youngsters who mention having had to do without anyone helping them with their homework. There is also support with schoolwork in Afro-Surinamese families, but Indo-Surinamese families are larger and the individual nuclear families within a family network have closer ties.

These direct forms of mutual assistance and support are not what I focus on here. In the rest of this section, I confine myself to the more implicit normative influence exerted by social networks. The extent to which this is feasible is related to the nature of the social networks. The more close-knit the networks are, the greater the social control over how individuals behave. And the more exclusive relations are with members of the group, the more effective the control over adherence to the prevailing moral code (de Vries 1990). Networks of this kind can function as moral communities since they provide role models and confirm norms and values. Especially in the Indo-Surinamese case, social networks are close-knit and can serve this kind of function.

Indo-Surinamese parents and children are often part of the exact same networks. They gather regularly for social, religious, and cultural events, especially weddings. Families are linked via marriages and these links are reinforced at weddings, which are often attended by hundreds of guests. For Indo-Surinamese youngsters, weddings are a fine opportunity for meeting other youngsters under the watchful eye of adult relatives. The frequent gatherings attended by various Indo-Surinamese generations also help youngsters develop a sense of the kind of status competition that prevails in the adult world and the gossip that accompanies it. This status competition pertains to material as well as nonmaterial issues. Showing off fancy clothes and expensive automobiles is at least as important as announcing what school you have graduated from and, far more important, what university you have graduated from. This is also communicated to a larger audience via local radio programs and local periodicals. Especially in The Hague, where there is a sizeable Indo-Surinamese community, there is strong status competition. Examples of this kind are also in evidence among the Afro-Surinamese, where the community is also the site of status competition (*stre libi*), rivalry and gossip, though they do seem to play a less compelling role and have less of a hold over the younger generation.

Status competition also occurs within the family network. In the field of education, there is an implicit pressure to achieve, especially since comparisons are so often made with the diplomas and degrees of other members of the family. This mainly occurs also among the Indo-Surinamese. When a member of a family gets a diploma and, even more so, a university degree, it enhances the status of the entire family, not just the individual. This is why families where education is scarce are particularly appreciative if one of the relatives gets a good education, since it boosts the status of the entire family in the Indo-Surinamese community. One respondent recalls how her father's family in Surinam used to act.

Mrs. E. (40) explains why her father felt it was extremely important for his children to go to school and get an education. He came from a farming family and after he was married he worked on the family plot of land. His eldest brother was a policeman and he was the boss at home. Mrs. E.'s father and his two other brothers would do all the work in the fields with their wives. He never had an opportunity to get much schooling, but his brother, the policeman, was widely respected. At a given moment he decided to go off to seek his fortune. He and his wife left for the city to build up a life of their own. What he wanted more than anything was for his children to gain the respect of the family. He wanted them to get an education so people would respect the family. In her father's family, everyone paid a lot of attention to who was going to what kind of school and how many of the children got a good education. "There was a kind of contest in the family to see who could get the best education."

Nowadays this kind of competition in the family network still plays a role for youngsters.

Greta (25) was the first in the family to finish college. Her father, who had barely had any education himself, was extremely proud of his daughter and regretted that his other children didn't do as well. "He thinks it is really a pity the others didn't go to college too. If he compares them with the other children in the family, he says, 'Look, all your cousins are going to college and the university, everyone except my children.' So he thinks that is really too bad."

Urmy (21): "In our family there was this extreme sense of competition because me and my cousin were always comparing to see who was doing better. We were at school together [six-year secondary school]. So it was like a real contest. His parents would say, 'Look what our son is doing, he is so great' while his own sister was just going to a four-year secondary school, there is nothing so special about that! All the youngest sister can think about is watching those silly Indian movies and singing songs and getting married, and she is only twelve years old. So there is nothing so special about her either!"

This is how ambitions and belief in progress are reinforced by the family and the wider network in the ethnic community. Social embeddedness in close networks of this kind is a supportive factor for the careers of the younger generation.

Family reputations in the Indo-Surinamese community are also related to the moral code. A central issue is that a family's good name and honor is linked to the reputation of the girls in the family. Many Indo-Surinamese still strongly feel that children, especially daughters, are not supposed to leave the home unmarried, the premarital conduct of girls should remain within certain boundaries, girls should get married before they reach a certain age, parents should be involved and approve of their children's choice of marriage partners, and there should be an Indo-Surinamese style wedding ceremony. Marriage is the endorsement as it were of the good reputation of the girl and her family. It can be viewed as an important ethnic marker; it marks the social boundaries between the people who do and do not belong to or want to belong to the ethnic group.

One of the effects is the pressure relatives exert on children, especially girls, to get married. As soon as girls reach a certain age, their whole family starts muttering or stating outright that it is time to get married. Girls who continue their studies are usually shielded by their parents from uncles and aunts whose children have not gone on with theirs.

Urmy (21) is studying law. Her older sister recently got married. "As a matter of fact, I ought to be getting married right about now. I have reached that age. All my older cousins are married, so now they look at me, at least that part of the family, as if to say: So what about you? Especially after my sister's wedding, they all asked 'When is your turn?' For the time being, Urmy is not planning on getting married. She wants to get her degree first. Her parents approve of her plans. Since they themselves did not have much education, they are extremely proud that their daughter is studying at the university.

Jeanine (25), the daughter of an Indo-Surinamese mother and Afro-Surinamese father (who are divorced): "A while back my mother and I went to visit an aunt, and the first thing she said when I came in was that she was going to look for someone for me."

Sharda (24): "There was a time when my parents kept telling me to do that [get married]. The pressure was mainly from the rest of the family though. Everyone is always pushing you."

In this sense, relatives can exert a negative influence on youngsters' educational careers, because if they marry young, they are not apt to continue their studies.

So there are two sides to the pressure exerted by the Indo-Surinamese family, and the signals can be contradictory: youngsters are supposed to get married by a certain age, but at the same time they are supposed to continue their studies. Some parents simply choose one option or the other. There are families where getting married is more important than studying, especially for girls, or where earning money is more important for boys. There are also parents who simply give a higher priority to studying than getting married young. The outside pressure is not as heavy for everyone. Individuals who are not strongly embedded in the family network or the wider networks in the ethnic community do not have to concern themselves much with the status competition or social control.

Other parents are, however, faced by a dilemma, since they want a successful career as well as an early marriage for their children. They would like their children to continue their studies and have good career prospects, but they also feel they ought to get married at the appropriate age. This puts more pressure on girls than boys, since the marriage age for boys is later, giving them more time to complete their studies first. The very fact however that there is this dilemma —marriage or a degree—is typical of the social change taking place within the Indo-Surinamese community. Not only is the proper age for marriage shifting, some youngsters find a creative solution to this dilemma by getting married and still continuing their studies.[15] In the Netherlands, a great deal is changing as regards the parents' role, the appropriate age for marriage, and how partners are chosen.[16] As is noted above, this mainly holds true of upwardly mobile individuals who are no longer completely willing or able to conform to the Indo-Surinamese code of conduct. Youngsters are also becoming increasingly critical and are no longer always willing to adhere to behavioral norms that inhibit their individual freedom.

Jenny (27) does not put much stock in any of the rules and commandments she was brought up with. She has only contempt for her family, who put a lot of pressure on her to get married because she had a boyfriend. "They are Muslims but they drink alcohol, they get divorced or run around with another woman. It is all one big farce."

Carla (21), who has quite an unusual lifestyle according to Indo-Surinamese standards, is very aware that many people, including the parents of a good girl-friend, frown on her conduct. She left her parents' home without getting married, lives on her own, looks quite modern, and realizes that people blame her mother for how she is acting. But she feels so far removed from the whole Indo-Surinamese community with all its rules that she could not care less. She is not interested in what people say there and does not worry about any harm to her reputation, and she certainly does not care about the status competition in the Indo-Surinamese community. At school she is not interested in the groups Indo-Surinamese girls form and how they stick together, and certainly she does not want to be part of it. She prefers public dances to wedding parties. "The difference between a wedding and a dance is that you are almost always with people your own age there. You don't take your parents along, so you do whatever you please. At a wedding party, all the parents are usually sitting right there, watching everything you do. You know how they like to keep an eye on everything."

The more the actual practice changes, the more the norms shift as to what is viewed as proper Indo-Surinamese conduct. In this sense, the changes have been very clear. I have the impression marriage is less and less of an obstruction to Indo-Surinamese youngsters' educational or occupational careers. Especially for girls, this change is taking place quite rapidly.

I did not observe the same normative pressure among the Afro-Surinamese as among the Indo-Surinamese, at any rate not in these fields and not to this extent. In the Afro-Surinamese mind-set, getting married and having children are not nearly as much of an obstacle to getting an education. On the other hand, there is also much less social pressure to achieve at school. Studying and graduating are also of very central importance to the Afro-Surinamese, but it is not something the whole family gets involved with and there is not such a competitive feeling about it in the family network. In this sense there is less pressure to conform to certain standards in the family. Another reason there seems to be less pressure to conform among the Afro-Surinamese is because the family network is more individualized and fragmented and less circumscribed.[17] Compared with the Indo-Surinamese, the Afro-Surinamese have fewer social mechanisms to reinforce the youngsters' ambitions at school. The Afro-Surinamese community not only exhibits less social cohesion but also it is less closed. In the following section I delve into this point in greater detail.

Interethnic Relations and Mixed Marriages

Earlier in this chapter I drew a link between social and geographical mobility and ethnic ties. It became clear that people are not always that fond of living amidst other people from Surinam or indeed of having that much to do with them. Families where the parents work outside the home and have advanced via their studies or job since their arrival in the Netherlands have less of a tendency to confine themselves to contacts within the ethnic community.[18] First-generation Surinamese immigrants without jobs come into less contact with Dutch people and more with other Surinamese immigrants. This is all the more so if they live in a concentration district, where there is ample opportunity for contact with other Surinamese immigrants.

There would thus seem to be a correlation between the social position and the degree of interethnic relations. There is, however, also a difference between the two ethnic groups. The Afro-Surinamese appear to have more contact with the Dutch than the Indo-Surinamese, especially in their leisure time and their private lives (Martens and Verweij 1997: 88-89). It is difficult to say to what extent this is because the social position of the Afro-Surinamese is somewhat better than that of the Indo-Surinamese. Part of the difference probably disappears if SES factors are controlled for. In part though the difference in interethnic relations can also be explained by the historical background of the two ethnic groups. The Afro-Surinamese are by definition a mixed group and have been more influenced by urban Western culture than the Indo-Surinamese. At the time, East Indians were relative newcomers to Surinamese society and also exhibited a relatively strong social cohesion there.

Of course the above-mentioned differences are averages for the groups as a whole. My research results demonstrate a wide range of variations and there are exceptions to the general pattern. What is more, relations inside the community do not necessarily exclude relations outside it. The Surinamese with a low social position who live in a concentration district can have strong ties with other Surinamese, but also be open to Dutch people or immigrants from other countries. One striking example is an Indo-Surinamese family in my study from the Schilderswijk in The Hague. This family adhered to a traditional Dutch working-class pattern when it accepted the Dutch neighbor's invitation to spend a weekend together at a camping site.

On the average though, the Afro-Surinamese have more interethnic relations than the Indo-Surinamese, and in this sense the Afro-Surinamese group is less closed. This holds true not only for the younger generation but for the older generation as well. One older respondent (69) told me she does not see anything strange about it if Dutch people come to the family parties. "Nowadays so many Surinamese people are married to Dutch people," she says, "and they all come to the parties, there is nothing out of the ordinary about that." A good example of this relative openness is a *kasmoni* group, a rotating credit association I came across in Bijlmermeer consisting of Afro-Surinamese and Dutch women. The Afro-Surinamese women had introduced this typically Afro-Surinamese lower-class practice to their Dutch colleagues at the home for the aged where they worked.

Together with five Surinamese and four Dutch women, Gina (34) is saving "cash money" (*kasmoni*). On the first of every month, they all take along a certain amount of cash to work, and each time a different woman gets the whole amount. Gina herself puts in 250 guilders a month, and after ten months she takes out ten times that amount. They have been doing this for years and it works out nicely.

There is a certain ambivalence among the Afro-Surinamese about having too much contact with other people of their own kind. They often say they would rather not live in a neighborhood with "too many" other Afro-Surinamese people or have their children attend a "black" school. What they seem to be saying is that if there are too many Afro-Surinamese (they themselves use the terms "Surinamese" or "negroes"), there are going to be problems, either arguments or problems at school or cliques.

The Afro-Surinamese exhibit a comparable ambivalence toward what is referred to as "acting Dutch." They acknowledge that it has positive as well as negative sides. The same holds true for "acting black." Afro-Surinamese parents are just as apt to tell their children not to "act so Dutch" as they are to say "Don't act so black." Used this way, both terms have negative connotations, though they do not necessarily express any approval or disapproval of contact with the Dutch or a high or low regard for Surinamese or Dutch culture. If parents do not want their children to speak Surinamese in certain situations, this does not imply a lack of appreciation for the Surinamese language. They simply feel it is not polite or desirable in certain situations. If parents use the term acting Dutch in a negative way, for example, when their children are fresh, this does not mean they disapprove of adaptation to Dutch society altogether. In general, Afro-Surinamese parents tend to see the Dutch social environment as less of a threat to their children's upbringing than Indo-Surinamese parents. Parents from both groups do have ambivalent feelings about their children acting Dutch, but Afro-Surinamese parents are not as concerned about their children's sexual morality as Indo-Surinamese parents. Many Indo-Surinamese parents have problems with what they see as the excessively free behavior of Dutch boys and girls.

The difference in interethnic contact between the Afro-Surinamese and the Indo-Surinamese is clearest from the partners they choose and in the tendency toward ethnically mixed marriages.[19] Mixed marriages and relationships are more common among the Afro-Surinamese than the Indo-Surinamese. This was also the case back in Surinam. In fact, historically speaking, the Creole population is the product of mixed relationships between Africans, Europeans, and mulattos. In the past, the ethnic hierarchy in Surinam was parallel to the hierarchy in social status. By marrying someone with a lighter skin, people would raise their own social status. In the Netherlands, there was never this kind of traditional social hierarchy based on physical appearance; the social distance to the Dutch seems to be determined more by culture and class (Oostindie 1996: 216).[20]

This does not mean, though, that the ideal of "coloring up" has disappeared. There are still clear traces of it.

Jerryl (39) recounts that his mother was not acknowledged by her father. Grandfather was light-skinned, grandmother dark-skinned. "My grandfather felt something like: she is not my child, she is black. Your color used to be really important. It was also important for the kind of job you could get in Surinam. Or if you were dark, your family would tell you to look for a wife who was lighter so you could make your color lighter. And you still see signs of that here. That business of light and dark. It has to do with status. A lot of guys I know still see a white woman as a status symbol. It is such a colonialist idea!"

This historical background makes it understandable why the Afro-Surinamese are more apt than the Indo-Surinamese to marry outside their group, although it is probably not the only explanation.[21] Sensitivity to color also plays a role among the Indo-Surinamese, but it is mainly an internal matter in that they would prefer a lighter-skinned Indo-Surinamese spouse to a darker-skinned one.[22]

Afro-Surinamese parents also approve more readily if their children decide to marry someone from outside their own ethnic group.[23] Indo-Surinamese parents have more trouble with this, but if their children do marry outside the community, they would prefer them to marry a Dutch rather than an Afro-Surinamese spouse.

Sharda (24): "The only kind of man I absolutely cannot come home with is an Afro-Surinamese man. My father says, "I would rather have a Dutch guy as a son-in-law than one of those Afro-Surinamese fellows." That is out of the question. All hell would break loose. It is because of that whole situation in Surinam . . . they think those people are lazy and good for nothing, they just hang out all day, you know. It is like they are our enemies. They really do not get along at all. But they would be more likely to accept a Dutchman than an Afro-Surinamese. Absolutely. No question about that. They would never accept it. There is no point even trying."

Youngsters themselves have much the same opinions as their parents when it comes to who would be an appropriate person to marry (Mungra 1990: 105). A mixed Afro-Surinamese and Indo-Surinamese relationship still gives rise to problems as is witnessed by the fact that it is a virtually classical theme in films, plays, and novels.[24] It is precisely in this area that so many ethnic prejudices are felt on both sides. The reluctance to mix is strongest on the part of the Indo-Surinamese. *Doglas*, people of mixed Afro-Surinamese and Indo-Surinamese descent, are generally viewed by the Indo-Surinamese as being Afro-Surinamese and are usually excluded (Dew 1978: 7).[25] It might be gradually less so among the younger generation, but for the time being there are still traces of this pattern.

Jeanine (25) is the daughter of an Indo-Surinamese mother and an Afro-Surinamese father, who are divorced. "Sometimes I really feel excluded for the simple reason that I come from two cultures. They [other Indo-Surinamese students] never totally accept me as being Indo-Surinamese, even though that is what I look like." One of the other students says on another occasion, "Jeanine is essentially totally Dutch. There isn't anything Indo-Surinamese about her." Jeanine: "For example that time we went to a temple, a *mandir*, with that Indo-Surinamese teacher. I was supposed to go too because I had never been in a temple before. But they said, 'Oh no, you can't come with us because you have eaten meat and all that kind of stuff.' I said, 'Why can't I come? A church is open to everyone, isn't it? Why should a temple only be open to Hindus? He [the teacher] is taking us inside, isn't he? It is supposed to be an open day?' So that is the kind of conflicts there are."

Not all youngsters of mixed Afro-Surinamese and Indo-Surinamese descent have this need to be accepted in the Indo-Surinamese community or feel excluded from it. Patrick (23), whose parents are divorced, grew up with his Afro-Surinamese mother and apparently feels just as at home with Afro-Surinamese or Indo-Surinamese as with Dutch people. The offspring of ethnically mixed marriages sometimes go through a stage where they don't know which friends to choose and switch from one circle of friends to the other.

In Surinamese terms, Maureen is what is called a *moksi*—her father is of Afro-Surinamese descent and her mother of mixed Chinese and Indo-Surinamese descent. Her first boyfriend was Dutch. "I found myself in the middle of a real Dutch family. He was from Amsterdam. I think I kind of became invisible, I acted like my own culture didn't exist, you know. After we broke up, there was a period when I went out a lot. I was associating with blacks and Indo-Surinamese kids, anything, as long as they were people of color. I was avoiding anything Dutch. I would go to Escape [a club], it was all real Surinamese. So I was headed more in that direction. I was kind of being a racist when it came to Dutch people, and I realized later how awful that was. It set me thinking. Nowadays I just sort of have a normal outlook. Not extreme in any way, I just like to have a good time. My friends are a little of everything." She is living with a Dutch boyfriend now.

So for these youngsters of ethnically mixed descent, social contacts do not occur as automatically as they do for the children of two parents with the same ethnic background. They are less unambiguously connected to a specific ethnic community and they can move more easily from one option to another.

The relative openness of the Afro-Surinamese community has definite advantages as regards the school and labor market participation of the younger generation. It can facilitate access to more formal fields because youngsters are more familiar with Dutch customs and habits. After all, many of the youngsters have Dutch relatives and have personal contact with them. What is more, an interethnic network generates access to knowledge and information that can be relevant to their educational and occupational careers. Afro-Surinamese youngsters also have more freedom of movement because less social control is exerted by the ethnic community. This has advantages, but at the same time it means the social environment outside their own ethnic circles can have more influence on youngsters, which, as has been noted repeatedly, can be favorable or unfavorable for their careers. Whether the youngsters' educational and occupational careers are affected in a positive or a negative way depends strongly on the nature of this "nonethnic" context they integrate into.

Social Relationships and Symbolic Ties

The ethnic social context is still important to the younger generation in various other ways. Here, I focus on two of these aspects. First, the formal social relationships people are involved in, the organizations or agencies in the ethnic community that directly or indirectly influence chances for upward social mobility in Dutch society. Second, the role of forms of popular culture and symbolic aspects of ethnicity. I am referring to what Anderson (1991) calls the "imagined community," namely, the community of people with whom individuals are not in a face-to-face relationship.

Both Surinamese ethnic groups have their own organizations and agencies, albeit the Indo-Surinamese ones have a more ethnically exclusive basis than the Afro-Surinamese ones.[26] For the Indo-Surinamese, language, culture, and religion constitute a more important basis for promoting their interests or improving their position in Dutch society than for the Afro-Surinamese. This is very clearly illustrated by the founding of their own Muslim and Hindu primary schools in Amsterdam and The Hague.[27] According to representatives of these schools, they have two aims: to teach children about their own religion, language, and culture and to improve their educational position.[28] Within this general goal, though, there are differences in emphasis: the Muslim school seems to put more emphasis on religion than culture. The one Afro-Surinamese school in Amsterdam was founded by the Church of the Moravian Brethren. More than at the other Surinamese schools, the emphasis there is on improving the educational position of the pupils and less on religion or culture. Second, there were far more obstacles to the founding of this school than the Muslim or Hindu schools, since the Church of the Moravian Brethren is a Protestant church and there are other Protestant schools the children could have gone to.

At all these schools, the reinforcement of the pupils' identity and the involvement of the parents are viewed as important subgoals that can contribute to improving the educational position of Surinamese pupils. The underlying idea is that the upbringing at school is an extension of the upbringing at home so the parents consequently become more involved in their children's school and this benefits their school performance. The school culture at these Surinamese schools is thought to have more of an appeal to the parents than the school culture at many of the Dutch schools in the neighborhood. The parents feel the children are given too much freedom there and there is not enough order and discipline. This is why parents prefer "their own" school to a Dutch neighborhood school.

This impression was reinforced in the interviews with parents. I did not conduct any systematic research on parents who consciously enroll their children at "ethnic" schools, but my respondents did happen to include several parents whose children attended these schools. One of them saw the Hindu school as an environment that could counter the negative influences of the neighborhood and as an alternative to the "black" neighborhood schools.

> Mrs. O. (43) lives in the Schilderswijk with her husband and children. She is satisfied with their home (a new house with a yard) but doesn't like the neighborhood "with all those foreigners." Their son (13) does not go out on the street in his leisure time. Their daughter (8) goes to the nearby Hindu school. First she was at an ordinary primary school in the neighborhood, but there were "just a lot of Turkish and Moroccan children there" and "the level was low."

Other parents are definitely not in favor of sending their children to "their own schools" since they feel it would keep them from adequately integrating into Dutch society. The question is indeed to what extent the possible negative effects of voluntary segregation counterbalance the anticipated positive effects of the community's own school. Very little is known about the effectiveness of these schools. For the time being, they would seem to deserve the benefit of the doubt.[29]

In addition to their own schools, the Surinamese have been able to take advantage of the policy based on the old pillarization idea in another field. Surinamese Hindus have their own radio and television broadcasting organization, the Organization of Hindu Media (OHM). The programs devote attention to current social themes as well as religious and cultural traditions, including those of Hindus in other parts of the world. The Afro-Surinamese do not have nearly as much of a need or possibility to organize separately within the broadcasting or school system. Most of the Afro-Surinamese are Christians, and this does not constitute grounds for state funding of ethnic religious institutions.[30]

Education in their original language and culture was never officially available for Surinamese schoolchildren.[31] The Indo-Surinamese community, however, took steps itself to teach Hindi and Urdu.[32] Unlike the case with *Sranan Tongo*, the classes are not solely focused on present-day language use, but also on the language the religious writings are in. My impression is that parents do attach a certain importance to their own Surinamese language or the language of their group, but they feel that teaching their own language should be secondary to teaching Dutch. After all, Dutch is the language that gives access to educational and job opportunities in the Netherlands. It is also the first language for more and more youngsters. Among the Indo-Surinamese, there are still quite a few older people who do not speak Dutch well, if at all, so that youngsters still do often hear their ethnic group language, *Sarnami*, in their home environment and can at least understand it. Children who have grown up in the Netherlands often have no choice but to communicate with their grandparents in *Sarnami*. The same holds true for children whose parents have a low educational level. *Sarnami* is often their first language, and it is spoken at home in conversations between the generations. Dutch plays a more important role for the Afro-Surinamese.

In addition to language and religion as the basis for promoting their interests and improving their position, Afro-Surinamese and even more so Indo-Surinamese organizations make efforts to preserve cultural traditions and pass on various forms of popular culture. In my study, there are children from Indo-Surinamese families who take lessons in classical Indian dancing or play classical Indian musical instruments. In The Hague there is a wide assortment of ethnic culture varying from Indian films to performances by music and dance groups from India. Numerous video rental shops feature a vast assortment of Indian films and the extremely popular soundtracks are widely available. Religious and cultural holidays such as Holi and Divali are publicly celebrated in some neighborhoods in The Hague. There is also the annual Milan festival, which is The Hague's equivalent of the Amsterdam Kwakoe festival in Bijlmermeer. Both these festivals have long become far more than local events and attract an audience from all across the Netherlands.

There are various organizations in Amsterdam that preserve the Creole winti and winti music traditions. However, they do not focus solely or largely on preserving these traditions, since winti is still very much a "living" culture that plays an important role in the day-to-day lives of many lower-class Afro-Surinamese.[33] The African dance groups of youngsters that I observed in Bijlmermeer in Amsterdam are of more recent origin. The youngsters, often born in the Netherlands, are thus exhibiting their interest in their cultural roots. Some Afro-Surinamese youngsters are very focused on American or international youth and music culture, and they also play an active role. They often perform and their renditions of this kind of music also attract a non-Surinamese audience. In the entertainment world in the large cities, they even play a vanguard role in many senses.

Indo-Surinamese youngsters are developing their own modern music style, Hindi-pop, a mixture of popular Indian film music and Caribbean musical elements.[34] They do not, however, perform much for the outside world. Unlike the music played by Indian youngsters in Great Britain, it is not as much of a mixture with new music styles (Kroon 1999). Hindi-pop is a music style that is more inward, more just for the Indo-Surinamese circuits of dances and parties.

In addition to the common consciousness of the Surinamese position in Dutch society, the two groups also exhibit a more specific awareness of their own roots and history. The awareness of the history of slavery is part and parcel of the Afro-Surinamese cultural heritage. The historical experience of slavery is engraved in the collective memory. Stories of what day-to-day life was like in days of yore are still passed on from generation to generation. They include not only the *Anansi tori* (fairy tales about the spider Anansi that slaves used to tell each other), which have since been recorded in writing, but also stories about the customs and habits at the time. Mothers tell their daughters, for example, how female slaves used to convey secret messages by tying their bandanas in a certain way. The term "house negro," which is still used in Surinamese circles today, also refers back to those days.[35] On the grounds of their own family history, many Surinamese feel they still know exactly how many generations back their forefathers were slaves. Mrs. U. (51) recounts for example that her grandmother's father was born on the boat from Ghana to Surinam. They often also know which plantation their family is from, and some Afro-Surinamese still have claims to the joint family inheritance, especially in the district of Para. In Surinam, there was also an oral tradition about the period of slavery, but it is reinforced perhaps by the migration to the former mother country or the increasing interest on the part of the younger generation. What is relatively new is the greater public focus on slavery, as is the political lobby for the recognition of this past and the construction of a memorial to commemorate the history of slavery.[36]

There is also growing interest from the Netherlands in the black diaspora, and social and symbolic ties have developed with black people elsewhere, for example, in the world of music.[37] For some time, there has been contact between the Surinamese and West Indians in Great Britain and African-Americans in the United States. An interest has developed in Africa and, following those made by African-Americans, there have also been Afro-Surinamese trips to Ghana.[38] Sometimes the aim is to investigate the family origins. Quite coincidentally, the link with Ghana is reinforced by the presence of a sizeable Ghanaian community in Bijlmermeer. There are Surinamese women who have a Ghanaian partner or—sometimes to get him a residence permit—marry a Ghanaian man.

Among the Indo-Surinamese, a stronger cultural focus on India and the Indian diaspora has emerged. Of course, the nearby presence of an Indian immigrant community in Great Britain also plays a role. The Indo-Surinamese in the Netherlands watch British Indian TV programs via the cable or saucers. One of my respondents attended a study program in Great Britain to become an imam. Immigration to the Netherlands also brought India itself closer. Immigrants often travel to India as tourists or to explore their family roots. Many Indo-Surinamese know exactly who in the family came to Surinam from India and which immigrant generation they belonged to. Some of them also know who went back to India from Surinam a long time ago. One informant told me his deceased father used to correspond with his relatives in India. For many East Indians in Surinam, the direct contact with India had been lost in the course of time, but efforts are now being made from the Netherlands to find the roots again.

Mrs. A. (51) thinks her family originally came from a poor district in Calcutta. As a boy of about seven or eight, her grandfather was lured to the boat and transported to Surinam. He died there when he was an estimated ninety-one years old. "Yeah, people were spirited away from those poor districts, they were promised all kinds of things."

Sheila (33) has an uncle who traced the family roots in India back to a poor little village. They had a funeral ceremony there at the time for a young man of twenty who suddenly disappeared and whom they assumed was dead.

Others travel to India with specific aims, for example, to learn to play the traditional musical instruments or acquire other cultural skills. Krish (32) was in India several times to enhance his expertise on his musical instrument, the tabla. Indra (25) spent two months with her mother in India as a junior college intern in fashion and clothing design. She learned to decorate material and do embroidery. Another respondent made a recording singing songs accompanied by Indian musicians at an Indian studio. The tapes were sold in the Netherlands and, via the Netherlands, one of them got to the family in Surinam. Others have commercial contacts and buy merchandise in India that they sell in the Netherlands. Ordinary tourists also often purchase clothing and jewelry in India and then sell it when they get back to the Netherlands. Some of my respondents have even been to India repeatedly and have relatives or friends there.

Youngsters who were born and raised in the Netherlands often barely have any first hand experience of Surinam and they do not know much about it. Some have never even been there on holiday, and they prefer to go to other places. Yet they are the ones who are often so interested in their own history and cultural traditions. Young parents, often born in Surinam themselves, lament the fact that their children have such an erroneous impression or know so little about Surinam. Sheila (33), for example, took her daughter to an exhibition on Surinam at the Museon in The Hague, and Marcia (30) took her son to the Tropical Museum in Amsterdam.

"My son had the idea we all lived in those little grass huts in Surinam. That was really awful. He thought we lived in little huts and climbed in the trees. And he said so in so many words! I thought, Oh my God! You can't imagine how I felt!

So I took him to the Tropical Museum. There is a Surinamese house there. I took him to see it, to show him where we used to live."

Modern means of communication are even more instrumental for finding out about the home countries and having contact with people there. They influence the ethnic identifications of immigrant youngsters from a distance and provide them with behavioral models different from the ones in their immediate social environment, varying from American rappers to Indian film stars. Cultural influences are less restricted than ever by geographical location. Present-day means of transportation and communication make transnational ties possible that influence the identity of immigrants and can reinforce them from afar (Anderson 1992; Gilroy 1993).

The social frameworks within the ethnic community that immigrants and their children take part in can thus be directly or indirectly focused on improving their position—directly in an effort to combat socioeconomic disadvantage, and indirectly to reinforce their cultural identity. The focus by the Indo-Surinamese on preserving their culture has led to a wide range of activities. It has also strengthened the cohesion of the ethnic community, albeit in an indirect and symbolic manner. There is less of a focus on preservation among the Afro-Surinamese, not that this necessarily means ethnic consciousness is any lower or that there is no desire to preserve various forms of culture. But the ethnic consciousness of the Afro-Surinamese is just as strongly linked, if not more so, to the shared history of slavery and deprivation as it is to culture. By definition, Creole culture is syncretic and strongly connected to Western urban culture. This is why Afro-Surinamese culture is less a basis for community forming and promoting interests. This also explains why there is less of a tendency to take the ethnic-specific as a point of departure for integration and upward social mobility.

Conclusion

In much of the literature on immigrant social mobility, the focus is on characteristics of the individual and his family background on the one hand, and on macrostructural conditions on the other. This is a somewhat sterile division that cannot adequately explain the social mobility of greatly differing groups of immigrants.[39] The nature of the social networks and social contexts individuals are embedded in are also important. In this chapter, I have addressed several of these aspects. I examined the extent to which being embedded in an ethnic community can be an advantage or disadvantage for upward social mobility. In other words, the extent to which ethnic ties can promote or inhibit advancement in society. It appeared that this has to do with the character of the ethnic community. The strong social cohesion of the Indo-Surinamese community serves to support youngsters in their educational and occupational careers because it reinforces their parents' expectations, aspirations, and values. Various social mechanisms (status competition and social control) intensify this. So being embedded in family and other networks within the ethnic community contributes toward giving the parents' and children's aspiration an extra stimulus. It also keeps youngsters from going too far astray. Indo-Surinamese youngsters are less apt to wind up in the world of drugs and street crime, and their tendencies to choose an "alternative" career are more likely to be steered back in the right direction. The more close-knit and closed ethnic networks protect youngsters as it were from the potentially negative influences exerted by the residential environment or the interaction with peers. For the time being, the advantages of the strong ethnic ties in the Indo-Surinamese community seem to be stronger than the disadvantages, which are also in evidence. After all, close-knit social networks and control mechanisms do imply a restriction of individual freedom.

The Afro-Surinamese community can be said to be more open to Dutch society and more individualized. Afro-Surinamese youngsters are more frequently rooted in ethnically mixed networks, and their social world is less frequently confined to the ethnic community. This has advantages for their social and cultural integration in Dutch society and gives them greater individual freedom. It depends, however, on the circumstances whether youngsters are able to fulfill their educational and occupational aspirations. Youngsters who come from a weak socioeconomic situation and have a residential environment and a circle of friends who do not stimulate them or who even have a negative effect lack the corrective mechanisms that play a role in the Indo-Surinamese community. The ties with the family and the ethnic community prompt Indo-Surinamese youngsters in the same weak situation to mend their ways more than they do Afro-Surinamese youngsters. In this context I observed a connection with the central importance of the institution of marriage among the Indo-Surinamese on the one hand, and the importance of the male peer group and survival traditions among the Afro-Surinamese on the other.

There is a certain convergence between the two groups in the case of upwardly mobile individuals. Social and geographical mobility usually go together, and this often means looser ties with the ethnic community. It is not always easy to distinguish the cause and effect. The cohesion and relatively closed nature of the Indo-Surinamese community gives the younger generation numerous advantages in their integration into Dutch society, but it can also act as an obstacle for individuals and as a reason to dissociate themselves from the ethnic community. The opposite would seem to be the case for the Afro-Surinamese: the limited cohesion and open nature of the ethnic community leaves room for individual freedom, but it is less supportive for the younger generation. So both forms of integration have positive and negative aspects. However, for the time being, the strong ethnic ties among the Indo-Surinamese would seem to provide the younger generation with important resources.

Notes

1. See, e.g., Fernández Kelly (1995); te Grotenhuis (1993); Zhou (1997).

2. See Tesser et al. (1995). Opinions differ as regards the connection between the spatial concentration of immigrants and their social integration. For a discussion on this question, see the special issue of *Migrantenstudies* (Migrant Studies) "Concentratie en segregatie" (Concentration and segregation) (van Niekerk and Rath 1996).

3. See also Sansone on "Het vertoog van de hosselaar" (The discourse of the hustler) (1992: 135-42).

4. Cf. Anderson (1990: 123ff.), who refers in this connection to the "baby club."

5. Cf. van Amersfoort and Cortie (1996).

6. Cf. Quispel (1997).

7. Cf. de Klerk (1996: 83-84).

8. Part of her story was already told in chapter 6.

9. Cf. te Grotenhuis (1993: 109ff.).

10. Cf. van Niekerk (1990 and 1991).

11. CBB stands for the Center for Vocational Training and Vocational Counseling.

12. Cf. Sansone (1992).

13. Cf. Coleman (1988).

14. Cf. Vermeulen (1984: 16).

15. See chapter 5.

16. See also chapter 5; cf. Lalmahomed (1992a); Mungra (1990).

17. Cf. Venema (1992).

18. This is also illustrated by earlier quantitative research. In general, the Surinamese who have had a good education and earn a good living have less contact with other Surinamese people and relatively more contact with Dutch people (CBS/UvA 1988). Reubsaet et al. arrived at comparable conclusions (1982: 283ff.).

19. Whenever I use the term marriage, I am referring to common-law as well as official marriage.

20. Oostindie suggests, and quite rightly in my opinion, that "class and culture" explain why Caribbean immigrants in the Netherlands are more apt to marry partners from ethnic groups other than Turkish or Moroccan immigrants (1996: 216). It is striking in this connection that in her study on the acceptance of mixed marriages in the Netherlands, Hondius (1999) nonetheless puts a strong emphasis on color differences in the case of Caribbean immigrants.

21. Zenner (1991: 89ff.) suggests for example that there might be a relation between the caste system and the low incidence of interracial marriages among South Asians overseas. After all, endogamy was the rule there. He also notes, however, that the caste system is relatively weak among the creolized East Indian population of the Caribbean region (cf. van der Burg and van der Veer 1986). However, at the time of the study by Speckmann, ethnically mixed marriages were very rare among East Indians in Surinam (1965: 116-17).

22. Mungra draws a link between this preference for lighter-skinned spouses and the *warna* consciousness (color or caste consciousness) that is still thought to play a role in

the choice of spouses in the Netherlands (1990: 118). The Indo-Surinamese do not have the same kind of historical tradition of mixed marriages with whites as the Afro-Surinamese.

23. Cf. Martens and Verweij (1997: 92).

24. Pim de la Parra's film *Wan Pipel* is the best known example. Radjindre Ramdhani wrote a novel on this theme based on a true story called *Zielcontact: Een Hindoestaan—een Creoolse: Een verboden liefde* (Soul contact: An East Indian man—A Creole woman: A forbidden love) (Utrecht: Kismeth, 1998).

25. East Indians traditionally exclude anyone of ethnically mixed descent from their community, especially in the countryside. This has gradually changed in the city (Speckmann 1965: 118). Dew (1978: 6-7) nonetheless notes that people of mixed Creole and East Indian or Creole and Chinese descent are viewed by East Indians and Chinese as being Creoles. This is quite different in the case of people of mixed Creole and Javanese or Creole and native Indian descent, who are viewed by the Javanese as being Javanese and by the native Indians as being Indian if they respect the cultural practices of these groups.

26. Cf. Bloemberg (1995).

27. Schools of this kind have also been founded elsewhere in the Netherlands. See Bloemberg and Nijhuis (1993) on Hindu schools, Rath et al. (1996) on Muslim schools, and Teunissen (1990) on both types of schools. The Muslim schools are far more numerous than the Hindu schools, which is understandable since there are so many more Muslims than Hindus in the Netherlands (Prins 1994).

28. I interviewed five individuals who played a role in founding or who teach at one of the Hindu schools in The Hague and one in Amsterdam, one Muslim school in Amsterdam and the Church of the Moravian Brethren school in Amsterdam.

29. See Bloemberg and Nijhuis (1993); Driessen (1996).

30. Only certain health care facilities have been set up based on winti, the religious and cultural complex of the Afro-Surinamese lower class (van Wetering 1990).

31. Only very recently were pilot projects launched to teach Hindi and *Sranan Tongo* in the framework of Education in Original Languages (*Bulletin Surinaams Inspraak Orgaan*, November 1999).

32. See also Bloemberg (1995).

33. Cf. Venema (1992).

34. See for the development of Hindi-pop Weltak (1990).

35. It is a term comparable to "bounty" or "fake negro," words the Afro-Surinamese use to indicate that they think someone is acting too Dutch in a certain situation.

36. Cf. Oostindie (1999).

37. Cf. Gilroy (1993).

38. Cf. Kroon and Wiggers (1997).

39. See, e.g., Portes (1995); Portes and Rumbaut (1996). Portes et al. were neither the first nor the only ones to point this out; see, e.g., also Gans (1992); Perlmann (1988); Waldinger et al. (1990).

Chapter Nine

Premigration Legacies and Immigrant Social Mobility

In this study I have made an effort to demonstrate how social mobility differences between Indo-Surinamese and Afro-Surinamese immigrants are related to their premigration history and the intangible baggage they brought with them. I started from the assumption that this intangible baggage was not the only, or the most important, explanation for success in their careers in the Netherlands. In fact it might have played only a very minor role in the total range of factors that can influence the success of immigrants and their children. In any case the structural context in the host society also plays an important role, as does the place immigrant groups occupy within it. Economic and political factors (such as the state of the economy at the moment, the labor market situation, and government policy) cannot, however, completely explain why some immigrant groups occupy a better position on the labor market or in education than others. This unexplained residual is generally ascribed to two complexes of factors that can be summarized under the headings of racism or discrimination and culture.

In this study, the social context for both the groups was more or less constant so that the emphasis came to be on additional explanations for differential social mobility. Given this social context, the question was how the history of the two immigrant groups influences their position in the host society. I have tried to show how the intangible baggage Indo-Surinamese and Afro-Surinamese immigrants brought with them was connected to their position in Surinamese society, and how it influenced the improvement of their own and their children's position in Dutch society.

The findings presented here on these two Surinamese groups are the result of anthropological study combined with existing quantitative data. The qualitative research provided the empirical material that constitutes the core of this study. It was conducted in Amsterdam and The Hague and focused on lower-class immigrants and their children. Whereas the quantitative material gives a total picture of the two ethnic groups in the Netherlands, my empirical research only pertains to a segment of both Surinamese populations, namely, immigrants from the lower socioeconomic class. The aim was not to make the qualitative research quantitatively representative. Instead the aim was to detect connections that barely emerge if at all in quantitative research and to interpret them theoretically. In this last chapter, I summarize my findings. Then I discuss several of my conclusions in greater detail and place them in a broader theoretical context.

Indo-Surinamese and Afro-Surinamese Social Mobility: Ethnic Myths and Reality

The East Indians rose rapidly from their position as immigrants in Surinamese society. This striking social mobility gave them the reputation of being hard workers who were diligent and frugal. In the Netherlands as well, they are known for being successful. This image is frequently contrasted with that of the Afro-Surinamese, whose position was always more controversial and is more often associated with social deprivation. Is this a matter of ethnic stereotyping or of what Steinberg (1989) calls an ethnic myth? Is there any reality to it? Are the Indo-Surinamese indeed more successful than the Afro-Surinamese?

My quantitative data do not show the Indo-Surinamese to be a more successful immigrant group than the Indo-Surinamese. In fact in a number of respects they lag behind. One place this is clear is on the labor market. The labor participation of the Afro-Surinamese is higher and, contrary to what is often thought, their unemployment rates are no higher than those of the Indo-Surinamese. What is more, the employed Afro-Surinamese often work at a higher level and earn a higher income than the Indo-Surinamese. This difference in labor market position reflects the difference in the educational levels of the two groups; the Afro-Surinamese are generally better educated. So in terms of their occupational and educational levels, the Afro-Surinamese are doing better than the Indo-Surinamese. This is contrary to the customary views of the two groups, which hold that the Indo-Surinamese are the successful immigrants and the Afro-Surinamese the ones who are lagging behind.

The question is where these images of successful Indo-Surinamese and unsuccessful Afro-Surinamese come from. In part they probably have to do with the images of the two groups in Surinam. As newcomers in Surinamese society, the East Indians worked their way up in only a few generations. This gave them a reputation for being hard workers who climbed the social ladder by taking initiative and setting up little businesses. Whatever class division and poverty were also in evidence among the East Indians were much less clearly visible. The image of the Creoles, however, was largely shaped by the unemployed segment of the lower class in Paramaribo, especially the men. Something similar would seem to be occurring in the Netherlands: the image of both Surinamese immigrant groups is mainly shaped by their most visible segments. As to the Afro-

Surinamese, media and research attention mainly focuses on the unemployed young men of the lower class in the large cities.[1]

The Indo-Surinamese, however, are more conspicuous as tradesmen whose trades are immediately visible in the large cities. The Indo-Surinamese themselves sometimes confirm this image of success by referring to "the Asian success" elsewhere in the world. The striking thing about this ethnic stereotyping is, first that it is apparently not entirely a Dutch invention, since it was also in evidence in Surinam. Second, the image of the whole group is apparently shaped by a segment of it. So the image is not separate from reality, but it constitutes a distortion of it.[2]

Contrary to what their image would lead us to assume, the Indo-Surinamese are not doing better in the Netherlands than the Afro-Surinamese. How can this be explained? Part of the explanation can be found in the history of the two groups in Surinam. Creoles traditionally occupied a dominant position in Surinamese society. Historically speaking, the Creole population is extremely heterogeneous in the sense of social class and ethnic background. It consists of descendants of the Dutch colonial elite as well as descendants of slaves. So if the average social position of the Afro-Surinamese in the Netherlands is higher than of the Indo-Surinamese, in part at any rate this is a reflection of the premigration class structure of the Creole population. It is true that the Indo-Surinamese also exhibit social segmentation, but this is historically a more recent phenomenon. When they came to Surinam from the former British India around 1900, they were a less heterogeneous population as regards social class than the Creoles in the same period. In present-day Surinam, there are virtually no longer any differences between the social positions of the two groups. There are even signs that the East Indians, partly as a consequence of the economic recession, are overtaking the Creoles.[3] The question, however, is whether this was the case at the time of the mass migration in the 1970s. Had the East Indians already caught up with or even passed the Creoles as regards their social position? Or did this only happen later in the 1980s and 1990s? In other words, could a comparable class division among the Indo-Surinamese have already emerged in the Netherlands? Or should we not exclude the possibility that the higher middle class and elite are more strongly represented among the Afro-Surinamese in the Netherlands? These are questions to which there are still no exact answers. But if the upper class is indeed more strongly represented among the Afro-Surinamese in the Netherlands, it would mean they have a favorable influence on the average figures pertaining to their social position.

It is clear at any rate that the starting positions of the two groups in the Netherlands were not the same. The quantitative material presented in chapter 1 shows that the Afro-Surinamese had a better average starting position than the Indo-Surinamese. They had a better chance of succeeding on the Dutch labor market and at Dutch schools. On the labor market, the Afro-Surinamese also had the advantage of being from an urban background: on the average they were better educated, spoke better Dutch, and more often had occupations or job experience that were useful on the Dutch labor market. Many Indo-Surinamese also came from the city, but they had moved there much more recently, and in fact some had come directly from the countryside to the Netherlands. The average educational level of the Indo-Surinamese immigrants was lower when they arrived in the Netherlands and their mastery of the Dutch language was poorer, especially among the older generation. In addition, their occupational history and job experience were not as suited to the requirements on the Dutch labor market. People who had plied various trades in Surinam often lacked the required qualification to continue doing so in the Netherlands. The Indo-Surinamese were thus unable to take direct advantage of their tradition of self-employment. They witnessed a process of proletarization: for some Indo-Surinamese, immigration meant a transition from small-scale entrepreneuring to wage or welfare dependence.

Despite their better average starting position, many Afro-Surinamese nonetheless did not have immediate access to the Dutch labor market. The early immigrants arrived in a period when there was a labor shortage, but this was no longer the case for the ones who came in such large numbers starting in the mid-1970s. There were relatively large numbers of poorly educated people among them, and less and less of a need for them on the Dutch labor market. In this sense, the situation was no different for the Afro-Surinamese than the Indo-Surinamese. Regardless of their occupations or job experience in Surinam, many unskilled workers from both groups wound up in similar positions. In this sense, migration had a leveling effect on the differences between the two groups. Many immigrants worked in sectors where unemployment was growing, became unemployed, or never had jobs at all and became dependent on welfare benefits, sometimes on a long-term basis. What is more, many of these immigrants lived in concentration districts where the schools were gradually transformed into black schools. So even though the two groups came to the Netherlands with very different backgrounds, after they arrived a certain convergence occurred.

In addition to this convergence in the positions of the two groups, there were also some divergent developments. I have already referred to the greater occupational continuity that was possible for the Afro-Surinamese and the fall in status that was more frequent among the Indo-Surinamese. There was also a striking difference in what I refer to as the accumulation of resources. The Afro-Surinamese "accumulate" one diploma after the other, often attending evening school while working in the daytime. It is more common for the Indo-Surinamese to accumulate different sources of income by engaging in various economic activities, formal as well as informal, at the same time. Although entrepreneurship was an important route of advancement for the East Indians in Surinam, this is not the case in the Netherlands. At any rate there is no evidence of it in the figures. The percentage of the self-employed is no higher among the

Indo-Surinamese than the Afro-Surinamese working population. I do note, however, in chapter 3 that the economic activities of the Indo-Surinamese are much more comprehensive than the formal figures show. Perhaps the relatively high Indo-Surinamese inactivity on the formal labor market is compensated by informal economic activities. In this sense, the Indo-Surinamese would seem to have preserved their business-like mentality.

Even in situations where the Indo-Surinamese and Afro-Surinamese were faced with very similar conditions after their migration to the Netherlands, there are still differences. They do not always perceive a situation of long-term unemployment and welfare dependence in the same way, nor do they always cope with it the same way. Welfare dependence is frequently accompanied by efforts to earn an extra income. This holds true for the unemployed and other people dependent on welfare in both groups, and indeed for the native Dutch as well. No strict distinction can be observed between what the Surinamese call *hustling* and what I refer to above as engaging in informal economic activities. The difference mainly lies in the ideas and behavioral norms associated with it. Whereas the Indo-Surinamese acquisition of an informal income fits into their tradition of self-employment, for the Afro-Surinamese it is more linked to a situation of economic instability and urban marginality. The imported skills and mind-sets connected to both their traditions influence their economic conduct and the nature of their economic activities. This is why the same situation does not necessarily have the same effect on the following generation. This is most evident among the men. As I note above, it is mainly the young Afro-Surinamese men from the lower class in the large cities who attracted attention. They were not only the most visible, Afro-Surinamese men also have relatively high unemployment rates compared to Afro-Surinamese women. This makes it easier to understand why there has been the kind of Afro-Surinamese stereotyping that I refer to above.

In other ways as well, differences between the two ethnic groups are more marked if men and women are taken separately. Gender differences are mainly visible in the labor market participation of women, where the levels are far lower among Indo-Surinamese than Afro-Surinamese women. Indo-Surinamese women also have lower employment rates than Indo-Surinamese men. I have sought the explanation for this difference in the position of women in the family and the division of labor between men and women there as well as in the ethnic division of labor in Surinam (where for a long time they predominantly earned a living in the farming sector or small-scale entrepreneuring). The cultural ideal of the male breadwinner has since lost much of its importance, though it still does play a role in the Netherlands. In the fields of education as well as labor, the Afro-Surinamese differences between men and women are smaller than the Indo-Surinamese. In other words, in a number of senses, Afro-Surinamese men and women occupy a more equal position. In some senses, Afro-Surinamese women are even making more progress; there has been a relatively sharp rise in the percentage of working women, and unemployment is lower among Afro-Surinamese women than men. The rather independent and economically active role lower-class Afro-Surinamese women play similarly derives from premigration conditions. I have related this to the matrifocal family structure, where women are often the head of a household, in combination with the economic instability of the urban lower class that has gone on for generations. Although in some ways, Indo-Surinamese men occupy a better position than Indo-Surinamese women, it is precisely the women who are now also making rapid progress. Generally speaking, gender relations are changing more rapidly among the Indo-Surinamese than the Afro-Surinamese, where there was always less of a difference between the labor market participation of men and women. In this sense, there is greater continuity among the Afro-Surinamese.

Another divergent tendency is evident in the field of education. In both ethnic groups, parents see it as a great advantage that their children have better educational opportunities in the Netherlands than in Surinam. In the Dutch welfare state, the parents' income no longer plays a major role in the younger generation's educational opportunities. Nor does the parents' economic position determine the course of the children's educational career. It is far more the social and cultural resources of the parental home that influence children's success, or lack of it, at school, and this is where the difference in ethnic background manifests itself most clearly.

The transition to the Dutch school system was sizeable, particularly for Indo-Surinamese children. They were initially faced with more problems and obstacles than Afro-Surinamese children and their results were poorer. They have nonetheless since made a great deal of progress. The general educational position of the Indo-Surinamese is still poorer than the Afro-Surinamese, but the difference is getting smaller. This is not what the parents' educational level would have led us to expect. Apparently the low educational level of Indo-Surinamese parents is not that much of an obstacle to the progress of the younger generation at school. Clear advancement has also been observed among the Afro-Surinamese, but it is less consistent. In part this has been a result of the specific migration history, which transpired over a longer period of time and followed a less regular course in their case. This was evident, for example, from the difference in the educational achievement levels of the early and the late second generation. In any case, there is a certain stagnation among some subgroups of the Afro-Surinamese lower class in the sense that the children barely do any better, if at all, than their parents. I have sought the explanation for the Indo-Surinamese educational mobility and the continuing lag among certain Afro-Surinamese subgroups in a combination of conditions that are addressed in chapters 6 and 7. I summarize them here in four clusters of factors.

First, the Indo-Surinamese are engaged in a *continuing* passing maneuver that was already going on in Surinam. Their educational lag can partly be explained by a lack of educational opportunities. This was much more the case in

Surinam than the Netherlands, and more for the East Indians than the Creoles. For both groups, the parents' income played an important role in the children's education, but there were extra obstacles for the East Indians. They lived in the countryside where the quality of the schools was poorer and they were not as easily accessible. In the Netherlands, children are now getting more chances than their parents ever had, and the older generation has convinced the younger generation to take advantage of them. Parents are often able to inspire and motivate their children to get a good education. The aspirations exhibited by the Indo-Surinamese children of extremely poorly educated parents are thus partially and indirectly derived from the greater educational lag that was experienced in Surinam.

A second cluster of factors is related to what I call "belief in progress" and the value people attach in practice to diplomas. Differences between the Afro-Surinamese and the Indo-Surinamese in this sense date back to the period before migration to the Netherlands, where we are now witnessing the sequel. The historical experience of East Indian upward mobility in Surinamese society has inspired great faith in the possibility of getting ahead despite severe obstacles. This belief is nourished and supported by what I call the "businesslike mentality" of the Indo-Surinamese and their striving for material advancement. However, for generations on end the Afro-Surinamese lower class, at any rate part of it, has been confronted with economic instability due to a strongly fluctuating employment situation. So for many of them, the value of diplomas was not that indisputable. Informal survival styles were sometimes more useful than the formal social advancement routes. Just as the Indo-Surinamese imported their belief in progress as it were, part of the Afro-Surinamese lower class brought its ambivalence and survival strategies to the Netherlands. Faced with the large-scale unemployment in the Netherlands, these strategies did not disappear, they were merely adapted to survival in a Dutch urban context. So there are differences in the attitudes and ideas of the lower class Afro-Surinamese and Indo-Surinamese even though they objectively find themselves in much the same socioeconomic position.

Third, in addition to the above-mentioned influences of the parental home, the family structure also appears to play a role. The family hierarchy and control over the children, the pressure to achieve, the central importance of the institution of marriage, the mutual support within the extended family network, and, in a more general sense, the cultural ideal of the family as a collective all exert a favorable influence on the educational and occupational careers of Indo-Surinamese youngsters. Negative influences exerted by the social environment outside the parental home seem to have less of an effect on Indo-Surinamese youngsters. The regime in Afro-Surinamese families is generally not as strict, and youngsters have more freedom of movement. This can be an advantage, but under certain conditions it can also put parents at risk of losing control over their children. This can be due to a combination of conditions: single parenthood, a precarious socioeconomic position, the attraction of peers, and the drug scene. This kind of pattern is also in evidence among the Indo-Surinamese, but lower-class Indo-Surinamese families generally seem to be better able to keep control of their children under these conditions.

The fourth and last factor is the nature of the ethnic community. The strong social cohesion of the Indo-Surinamese community is accompanied by a relatively closed stance toward outsiders. More than the Afro-Surinamese, the Indo-Surinamese strive to shield the younger generation from what they perceive as negative Dutch influences. Moreover, the value they attach to the preservation of their culture imbues the younger generation with an awareness of their rich cultural tradition. The Afro-Surinamese community exhibits less cohesion and is less closed, as is witnessed by the large number of interethnic marriages and relationships and their social contact with the Dutch. There are two sides to this lack of cohesion and greater openness. Whereas the Afro-Surinamese have greater individual freedom and integrate relatively quickly in social and cultural fields, the Indo-Surinamese have less individual freedom and are less integrated socially and culturally. As a consequence, the Indo-Surinamese have more control over their younger generation than the Afro-Surinamese and are more successful at directing them. For the time being, this would seem to be having a favorable effect on the educational and occupational careers of Indo-Surinamese youngsters.

Ethnic Background and Social Mobility

What conclusions can be drawn on the basis of this study on the central issue of the relation between ethnic background and social mobility? Immigrants' success is generally interpreted in terms of "structure" or "culture" or a combination of the two.[4] Structure thus pertains to the opportunity structure in the host society and the structural locations of immigrants within it. This opportunity structure contains chances as well as obstacles to upward mobility. The importance of this postmigration social context to the social mobility of immigrants —the structural side of the explanation—is usually not a controversial issue. Precisely what culture implies in this connection and how culture is related to the structural context and the class position of immigrants is much less clear and is sometimes the subject of heated debates. One topic of discussion is: which is of primary importance, structure or culture? Some authors emphasize culture (Sowell 1981), others stress structure (Steinberg 1989). In essence, though, most of the discussions, and the most interesting ones, are not about *whether* the two play a role but *how*, and especially about the extent to which this dichotomy is satisfactory.[5] People too often think in terms of a polarity between structure and culture. It might be more useful to work from approaches that do not focus on a polarity but try instead to unravel the interrelation between the two. In the light of this discussion, in this section I examine several conclusions on the relation between ethnic background and social mobility.

Premigration History and Opportunity Structure

In this study an effort is made to explain the Indo-Surinamese and Afro-Surinamese social mobility patterns in the Netherlands. Given the shared social context of the two groups in Dutch society, I have examined the relation with factors that go back to their premigration history. To what extent does the premigration heritage, in other words the intangible baggage the immigrants brought with them, play a role in shaping their social position in Dutch society? How relevant is this premigration heritage to their differential socioeconomic success?

As I note above, there is generally not much disagreement about the importance of the postmigration structural context. In the Surinamese case as well, it is very clear that at the start, the economic recession and rising unemployment rates affected their position on the labor market. For many Surinamese immigrants, the "historical timing" (Steinberg 1989) was extremely poor. The early immigrants had the advantage of arriving in a period of labor shortage, but this was no longer the case at the time of the mass immigration. The two oil crises and their aftermath more or less coincided with the two largest peaks of immigration. Not only did the labor supply now exceed the demand, there was a mismatch on the labor market in terms of the educational levels required. Precisely when numerous poorly educated immigrants were arriving there was less and less of a need for poorly educated people in the traditional sectors of the economy. Diploma inflation and replacement by better educated workers affected the Surinamese as well.[6] The moment of immigration in a period when the labor market and indeed the whole economy were changing gave the Surinamese immigrants an extremely unfortunate start. To a large extent, this explains the rising unemployment rates in the 1980s among Surinamese immigrants of both ethnic groups. Most of them settled in the Randstad, particularly in the large cities, and this only reinforced this effect since this was the area most severely affected by the recession.

Nonetheless, neither the historical timing nor the mismatch can explain the differences between the Afro-Surinamese and the Indo-Surinamese labor market positions. Features of the labor supply also played a role. What intangible baggage did the immigrants bring with them, not only in terms of their educational level but also in terms of their occupations and job experience? The premigration history shows that the specific position in the ethnic division of labor in Surinam generated advantages for both groups after they arrived in the Netherlands, albeit in totally different ways. The Afro-Surinamese had a "competitive advantage" over the Indo-Surinamese because their education, occupations, job experience, urban background, and orientation toward a European lifestyle put them higher on the social ladder at an earlier moment in history. All this also constituted the basis for their more favorable starting point in Dutch society. It facilitated their adjustment to the school system and their participation in the labor market. So at any rate in the short term, the Afro-Surinamese were at an advantage. At the time, the East Indians had been on their way to catching up as an immigrant group in Surinam. Their "competitive advantage" in the fields of farming and small-scale entrepreneuring served as the basis for their further social rise in Surinamese society. This very same background, however, proved to be an obstacle to their adjustment to Dutch society. At the start, their education, occupations, job experience, rural background, and lack of familiarity with Dutch culture put them in a less favorable starting position in the school system as well as on the labor market.

The postmigration history shows, however, that despite the lag they still exhibit, the Indo-Surinamese are making rapid progress. The changes are less consistent among the Afro-Surinamese. Some of them apparently benefited from the more favorable starting position and are quickly improving their position, but a segment of the lower class is exhibiting only very negligible improvements or a certain extent of stagnation. These differences in the social mobility of the two ethnic groups cannot be completely explained by structural conditions in Dutch society. This is clear if we examine specific aspects of their labor market positions. The Indo-Surinamese are not more frequently unemployed than the Afro-Surinamese, though this might be expected on the grounds of their less favorable starting position in the Netherlands. What is more, the Afro-Surinamese more often experience long-term unemployment. In addition to these differences between the two groups, there are gender differences that are hard to explain on the basis of the opportunity structure on the Dutch labor market. The most striking example is the labor market participation of women, which is considerably higher among the Afro-Surinamese than the Indo-Surinamese. There is another gender difference within the Afro-Surinamese group: men are more frequently unemployed than women. The explanation for these gender differences lies more in the premigration history than in the opportunity structure of the host society.[7]

Why is it that, despite their more unfavorable starting position, the Indo-Surinamese are not more frequently unemployed than the Afro-Surinamese? Why is there more long-term unemployment among the Afro-Surinamese, and why are Afro-Surinamese men more frequently unemployed than women? These differences can hardly be explained by the mismatch in the labor supply and demand. One supplementary explanation might have to do with the discrimination the two groups experience on the labor market.

Discrimination as Explanation?

Some authors feel an explanation in terms of a mismatch fails to acknowledge the existence of discrimination on the labor market. Wilson (1987 and

1996) argues that the rapidly rising black unemployment rates in the United States are mainly due to the disappearance of unskilled industrial jobs from the inner cities. The blacks who remained behind did not meet the growing demand for highly qualified labor in the expanding service sector. Wilson argues that, in itself, race is less and less of a factor in shaping the labor market position, but others feel he is underestimating the existence of racism on the labor market.[8] In Dutch studies that make an effort to explain the labor market position of immigrants, questions are also regularly posed as to the relation between educational level and other features relevant to the labor market and discrimination.[9]

The existence of discrimination on the labor market has been repeatedly demonstrated in Dutch studies.[10] We do not know, however, whether discrimination has different effects on the labor market positions of the Afro-Surinamese and Indo-Surinamese, or of men and women. Might one group experience more discrimination than another? In other words, can differences in the labor market position, in this case unemployment, be attributed in part to differential treatment? Little empirical data are available on this point, and the information we do have is extremely fragmentary or only pertains to the perception of discrimination. The rare studies using an unorthodox approach with minority members testing for discrimination (Bovenkerk and Breuning-van Leeuwen 1978; Gras et al. 1995) are one exception. Educational level appears to play an important role (better educated people experience less discrimination), as does gender (women experience less discrimination). Although these studies are not explicit about ethnic background, one can conclude from the context that poorly educated Afro-Surinamese men experience the most discrimination on the labor market.[11]

The suggestion that the negative image the Dutch have of the Surinamese mainly has to do with lower-class Afro-Surinamese men is also formulated by Schuster (1999). He refers to the "criminalization" of the Surinamese immigration that took place in the dominant discourse in the period when the inflow from Surinam was expanding. In this discourse, the behavior (crime and sexual activity) of a minority of the Surinamese immigrants, namely, lower-class Afro-Surinamese men, was magnified. In other words, the combination of ethnic background, class, and gender is central to this discourse.

Having duly noted this negative image of lower-class Afro-Surinamese men, we still do not know anything about whether they are treated differently than Indo-Surinamese men. Based on the study by Choenni (1995), we do know that young Afro-Surinamese men report more discrimination than young Indo-Surinamese men. So what is involved is the perception of discrimination and not necessarily an actual difference in treatment. But even if we were to assume there is indeed differential treatment, and that poorly educated Afro-Surinamese men experience more discrimination on the labor market than poorly educated Indo-Surinamese men, we still cannot say what the explanatory force is of this discrimination. Because why should this kind of distinction be drawn? Is it inherent to what Hoetink calls the somatic norm image, that is, the complex of physical (somatic) features accepted by a group as being the norm and ideal (1967: 120)? According to Oostindie (1996: 216) this concept, which Hoetink developed in the context of race relations in the Caribbean, is not very applicable in the Netherlands. According to Oostindie, it is more class and culture that shape the relations with the native Dutch.

The issue is perhaps easier to comprehend if we examine the role ethnic imaging and discrimination play in shaping people's social position. It is clear from the historical overview of the development of the Creole and East Indian positions in Surinam (chapter 3) that the ethnic ideology dominant in colonial times was a reflection of the positions the two groups had long occupied in the ethnic division of labor there, but that this same ideology simultaneously contributed toward the preservation of these social positions. In the Netherlands as well, processes of stigmatizing and discriminating the Surinamese would seem to play an intermediary role (Vermeulen 1984). Stigmatization and discrimination influence the social position, but in turn the social position also influences ethnic imaging and ideology. The relation between ethnic imaging and social position is also clear from the findings of Hagendoorn and Hraba (1989) about the ethnic hierarchy. In the Dutch perception, the Surinamese occupy an intermediate position between the Turks and Moroccans on the one hand and the native Dutch on the other. This parallels the rankings of the social positions of these immigrant groups. A similar finding emerged from a qualitative neighborhood study (van Niekerk et al. 1989).

In the interrelation between social position and processes of imaging or discrimination, the perception of the parties involved plays a central role. After all, it is this perception that shapes their response. The research by Ogbu and his concept of the folk theory of success are important in this connection (Ogbu 1987; Ogbu and Simons 1998). It is true that Ogbu's theory pertains to the educational position of immigrant groups, but the basic idea behind it is also relevant to their labor market position. He feels that not all groups respond in the same way to discrimination, stigmatization, or in general to the treatment they receive in society. Some groups do well at school despite the discrimination they experience. For other groups, discrimination or a negative approach at school is too great a barrier. In response to this negative approach, they develop an oppositional frame of reference that is even more of an obstacle to their success at school. From this perspective, it is the *perception* of the structural obstacles that is thus decisive for the attitude to education and work. In Ogbu's opinion this difference in responses has to do with the group's mode of incorporation into society, that is, the origin of its minority status. African-Americans came to the United States as slaves, and this is a crucial difference with the immigrants who came of their own accord.

In Dutch studies, Ogbu's theory is often refuted because this distinction is not applicable in the Netherlands, since all the immigrants came voluntarily. For various reasons, however, this does not completely negate the value of his folk theory of success. First, comparable ideas have been developed that are unrelated to the immigration issue. The concept Willis (1977) formulates of the antischool culture bears similarities to the folk theory of success, but pertains to British working-class youngsters. These youngsters develop an oppositional cultural style that ultimately leads to their acceptance of the same status their fathers had before them. In other words, the question is how important this element of voluntary or involuntary incorporation in Ogbu's theory really is. Second, even if Surinamese immigrants did come voluntarily to the Netherlands, in the past there was an involuntary incorporation into Surinamese society. The question is whether this historical experience of slavery and racism did not leave traces, particularly on the Afro-Surinamese. As is noted above, ideas and attitudes regarding progress are in part brought along upon migration to the Netherlands. So there is good reason to assume the earlier involuntary incorporation into Surinamese society still affects the present. Based on both arguments, it would seem unwise to completely discard Ogbu's ideas just because of his distinction between voluntary and involuntary immigration.

It is clear from my study that part of the Afro-Surinamese lower class exhibits a certain ambivalence as to the mainstream routes to social advancement. This is evident from the values the Afro-Surinamese attribute in practice to education and from the men's alternative survival strategies. Here too, the perception of the opportunities and obstacles in Dutch society plays a role. The experience and perception of discrimination and stigmatization evoke a response that in turn influences the behavior and attitude to socioeconomic progress. The study shows, for example, that without it being intentional, in some Afro-Surinamese families the messages conveyed to children at home are not unambiguous. Parents also sometimes have certain reservations about the school their children attend. They are on the alert for possible discrimination, which they want to shield their children from. This oppositional attitude is even clearer among poorly educated young men, who turn to alternative survival strategies because they do not feel the regular routes to social advancement are likely to get them anywhere.

In addition to the objectively observable discrimination on the labor market, this subjective element thus plays a role. For reasons I have explained in part on the basis of their history, this is different for the Afro-Surinamese than the Indo-Surinamese. I did not observe any reservations or ambivalence toward the school system on the part of Indo-Surinamese parents. On the contrary, although they had to overcome greater cultural barriers, they have great faith in progress. The reservations Indo-Surinamese parents sometimes have are more in the normative field and pertain to morality, not socioeconomic progress. To put it somewhat schematically, whereas for the Afro-Surinamese it is not cultural difference but discrimination and stigmatization that play the most important role in their perception of progress and their belief in it, for the Indo-Surinamese the opposite would seem to be the case—their perception of discrimination plays less of a role than cultural difference.

This would seem to coincide with Ogbu's idea that, despite the discrimination they experience, some immigrant groups do not lose their faith in progress. Modood (1991) suggests something similar with respect to Indian immigrants in Great Britain. He holds that they are successful *despite* the discrimination they experience. With approval, he quotes Banton (1979: 242), who notes that the British initially exhibited more hostility toward West Indians because they wanted greater acceptance than the British were willing to concede. Later though, there was thought to be greater hostility toward the Asians because they did not have enough of a tendency to adapt to British customs. In *Ethnic Minorities in Britain* by Modood et al. (1997), the conclusion is confirmed that Asian immigrants experience as much or even more discrimination than Caribbean immigrants, and that this is also increasingly related to the growing antipathy to Muslims.[12] It is also clear that there is not necessarily any relation between the extent to which people perceive discrimination and the actual socioeconomic disadvantage. Caribbean immigrants occupy a middle position on the labor market between various Asian groups, but they report the most discrimination. Pakistanis and Bengalis have a greater socioeconomic disadvantage than Caribbeans, but they report less discrimination.

In short, the connection between discrimination and socioeconomic disadvantage is complex. Judging from the British study cited above, there is no simple linear connection between the two. This does not contradict Ogbu, nor does it contradict my own finding that the subjective perspective has an intermediary function. It is not only the discrimination itself that counts in this connection but also the perception of discrimination and the response to it. It is probably no coincidence that West Indians in Great Britain and the Afro-Surinamese in the Netherlands both put more emphasis on discrimination than either Asians in Great Britain or the Indo-Surinamese in the Netherlands. This would seem to confirm the idea I expressed above that the folk theory of success is largely a product of the historical experience. Actual experiences of discrimination reinforce or reproduce this folk theory in the Dutch context.

Once we assume discrimination to be part of the explanation for differential social mobility, we cannot confine ourselves to unequal treatment as such. We also have to take into account the shared experiences of the parties involved and how they influence their response to discrimination and their assessment of their chances. These responses and chance assessments would seem to have developed historically and have become part of the immigrants' cultural repertoire. This implies that the "unexplained residual" that is left after their labor market position is explained in terms of a mismatch cannot be simply attributed to discrimination.

Sociocultural Context

In addition to the explanations referred to above, which are apparently incomplete or have no independent explanatory power, I have examined another aspect of the premigration heritage: the cultural transmission or, quite simply, the messages conveyed to children at home. I have repeatedly observed that certain aspects of social mobility seem to be less related to the socioeconomic status of Indo-Surinamese than Afro-Surinamese parents. This holds true, for example, for the motivation or pressure to achieve conveyed to youngsters at home, the businesslike mentality, and the belief in progress. However, a class difference (within the broadly defined "lower class") repeatedly emerged between the Afro-Surinamese with a better or stable socioeconomic position (including the early immigrants) and the Afro-Surinamese with a poorer socioeconomic position. In practice, the parents in the former category were better able than those in the latter category to convey to their children the importance the Afro-Surinamese traditionally attach to education. In summarizing, the conclusion that can be drawn is quite a striking one: certain features are more clearly related to the socioeconomic position of Afro-Surinamese than Indo-Surinamese parents. How can this be explained?

In the first instance, this would seem to confirm the explanations that directly link socioeconomic success to the Indo-Surinamese culture or religion.[13] This is an explanation the Indo-Surinamese themselves also formulate, sometimes alluding to the success of East Indians elsewhere in the world or even of Asians in general. Some of my respondents almost saw the Indo-Surinamese desire for progress as an inherited trait "in their blood." An explanation in terms of cultural tradition or religion contains, however, too much of an implication of internal homogeneity. It can hardly help us understand why there are such great socioeconomic differences among the Indo-Surinamese (in Surinam as well as the Netherlands).

I would rather seek an explanation in the history of the East Indians in Surinam and the specific economic niche they occupied there. Many East Indian peasants began to trade in farm products and played an important intermediary role between the city and the countryside. They gradually moved into transport and other branches of economic activity. This does not mean all the East Indians were entrepreneurs, nor does it mean they all prospered, but it does mean that as an ethnic group in Surinam, they played an active role in the commercial sector and in entrepreneurship. These activities constituted the basis for their upward mobility and status as a group in Surinamese society.

This history implies that the Indo-Surinamese brought with them quite a firm belief in progress when they came from Surinam. They view education as a means toward further advancement and the Netherlands as providing opportunities for it. This kind of historically shaped optimism is also witnessed among the more established native Dutch middle class (Kuipers 1994). The premigration history also means that, although first-generation Indo-Surinamese immigrants might have very little formal education, they have more informal knowledge and skills than is evident from diplomas. In part this has to do with their tradition of self-employment. I have observed the continued existence of a business-like mentality that manifests itself in various ways, for instance, in a striving to accumulate sources of income. For that matter, frugality and a focus on achievement and on the future are features often attributed to middlemen minorities.[14] Orientations of this kind can also be observed among Indo-Surinamese who are not or are no longer small-scale entrepreneurs themselves. There were also a number of older Indo-Surinamese respondents without much formal education who did, however, have ample religious knowledge and had mastered the relevant language, whether it be Hindi or Urdu. In this sense as well, there is a certain parallel to be drawn with earlier middlemen minorities.[15] Whatever the case may be, on the grounds of their religious knowledge and entrepreneurial knowhow, older people do have more social and cultural resources (such as status and authority in their own circles, knowledge, and skills) than one might expect judging from their educational or occupational level.

The Afro-Surinamese exhibit less evidence of this kind of discrepancy between their formal education and social or cultural resources. More than in the Indo-Surinamese case, the educational level of Afro-Surinamese parents reflects their social and cultural resources. With their urban background, the Afro-Surinamese, even the lower classes, generally had higher educational attendance. It is plausible that class differences in educational participation had already crystallized to a greater degree among them.[16] In the Netherlands there is indeed a clearer relation between the socioeconomic position of the Afro-Surinamese and their attitudes, views, and aspirations as regards education. There would seem to be a certain division within the lower class.[17] A segment of the Afro-Surinamese lower class clearly takes the traditional route of gradual social advancement via education (accumulating diplomas or combining studying and working). In practice, another segment exhibits a certain ambivalence toward school or doubt as to the value of diplomas. There is nothing new about this, since it was already observed in Paramaribo (Buschkens 1974; Kruijer 1977).[18] The striking thing though is that this ambivalence did not disappear in the Netherlands, where there are far more educational opportunities. One way to explain this is by examining the perception of discrimination at school and the high Surinamese unemployment rates, particularly among poorly educated Afro-Surinamese men.

Different though their backgrounds might have been, when the Indo-Surinamese and Afro-Surinamese came to the Netherlands in the 1970s, many of them were unemployed or dependent on welfare. So in this sense, their immigration had a leveling effect. Does this mean the two groups were in the same situation? It does as regards their social position, but the worldview that went with welfare dependence was different for each of the two groups. The Indo-Surinamese were drawing on a different cultural repertoire than the Afro-Surinamese to cope with the situation they found themselves in. To many lower-class Afro-Surinamese, long-term unemployment was nothing new, and they were able to fall back on old survival strategies. The corresponding folk theory on making ends meet is based in part on experiences back in Surinam and in part on new experiences in the Netherlands. The Indo-Surinamese, however, had not had generations of experience with periodical or long-term unemployment in an urban context. This is why the Dutch experiences did not have such a discouraging effect on them, at least not on the first generation. For the time being, they have not lost their belief in the possibility of progress and are still able to motivate the next generation to reach a higher achievement level.

Two conclusions can be drawn from what has been said above. First, the formal social position of the Indo-Surinamese does not say that much about the family climate or the messages conveyed to youngsters at home. These messages are less class-specific than in the Afro-Surinamese case. Second, in practice the Indo-Surinamese and Afro-Surinamese who are in a similarly poor social position differ in the messages they convey to the next generation as regards their educational and occupational careers. The cultural transmission would seem to be less class-specific among the Indo-Surinamese than the Afro-Surinamese.

The motivation and pressure to achieve that are conveyed to children at home differ for boys and girls; in other words they are gender-specific. Afro-Surinamese women traditionally have more of a mainstream orientation than Afro-Surinamese men, a difference that is also expressed in the twin concepts of "respectability" and "reputation" (Wilson 1973). In this sense there is a certain continuity in Afro-Surinamese gender roles, which I have explained by the economic, social, and cultural context in the Netherlands.[19] In this respect there is more flux in the Indo-Surinamese community and the old messages seem to be less adequate in the new context.

The very different histories and socioeconomic backgrounds can thus explain the different messages that are conveyed to youngsters—boys and girls alike—at home. It is still unclear though to what extent these legacies of the past are preserved and continue to make sense in a new context. There are any number of influences from outside the parental home. In addition to the macrostructural context (economic and employment situation), there is the youngsters' direct social environment: the world of their peers, the neighborhood, the school, and the ethnic community. Youngsters move in various social circles and come into contact with a wide variety of behavioral norms, ideas, and role models. As a result, their adaptation to Dutch society takes a different course than that taken by their parents. The factors affecting this adaptation include their ethnic background, gender, educational level, and immigrant generation. This implies social and cultural change and heterogeneity. Behavior is not only influenced directly though by changing circumstances and social contact, it is also influenced indirectly and symbolically.[20] Modern-day means of communication introduce youngsters to other behavioral models than the ones in their own immediate environment. They come into contact with forms of popular culture from the diaspora or from the regions their forefathers came from (India or Africa), and take part in an international youth culture. In the following section, I focus special attention on the ethnic community as specific context.

Ethnic Community: Two Forms of Integration

Research on the position of immigrants often starts from the notion of a linear process of cultural integration or assimilation as a prerequisite for upward mobility.[21] In American and Dutch studies alike, the assumption is frequently made that one follows the other, and that assimilation or adaptation to the mainstream society thus lead to social mobility. My study demonstrates that this is not always exactly the case.

My study shows that globally speaking, the Afro-Surinamese and Indo-Surinamese exhibit two modes of sociocultural integration. The Afro-Surinamese mode of integration is characterized more than the Indo-Surinamese by ethnic "mixing" as regards marriage partners and other social relationships. In a social sense, the Afro-Surinamese are thus a less closed ethnic group and also exhibit less social cohesion. In terms of language and culture, they do not come up against many obstacles to integration. Like all Afro-Caribbean cultures, by definition the Afro-Surinamese culture is a mixed one, uniting Western and African elements and exhibiting flexibility, creativity, and a great absorption capacity.[22]

As a group, the Indo-Surinamese are more closed in terms of interethnic contacts and marriages. The network of relatives and the wider social networks largely consist of other Indo-Surinamese, and outsiders are not as easily included as in the Afro-Surinamese community. This is mainly illustrated by a strong preference for Indo-Surinamese marriage partners. Parents want to shield their children from what they see as the negative aspects of becoming all too Dutch. Steps to preserve their culture are supported by their own organizations and utilized as an instrument to improve the younger generation's position.

It is not easy to say exactly what the underlying reason is for this difference in ethnic cohesion. Some authors suggest a connection with the social and moral resources the family and other ethnic networks provide the younger generation with (Portes 1995; Portes and Rumbaut 1996). In other words, there seems to be a link with the available resources in the ethnic community, which some authors refer to as "ethnic resources." The approach taken by Todd (1994) is a totally different one. He holds that ideologies, such as the ones on the assimilation and integration of immigrants, can ultimately be traced back to long-lasting traditions related to family structure, the status of women, and inheritance laws. In societies where family relations are patriarchal and hierarchic and inheritance laws do not treat male and female children equally, the emphasis is on the acceptance of differences. Simply put, he holds that it is this acceptance of differences that leads to the exclusion of outsiders. However, in societies with less hierarchic family relations and inheritance laws that treat male and female children equally, he feels a worldview is dominant that centers around the principle of equality. There is less emphasis on differences and exclusion. To Todd, the prime criterion is the intermarriage rate; it is the ultimate measure for assimilation. I will leave aside the issue of whether Todd's analysis is plausible. It is clear, though, that the two patterns described here do clearly resemble the ones exhibited by the Indo-Surinamese and Afro-Surinamese. In light of processes of inclusion and exclusion, it is striking that the Surinamese category exhibiting the largest extent of ethnic "mixing," the Afro-Surinamese, is also the category that feels the most excluded or discriminated. Whatever the underlying reasons, it is clear at any rate that the Afro-Surinamese enter interethnic relationships with relative ease, at least compared with the Indo-Surinamese (and, for example, Turks or Moroccans).[23] If we compare the two forms of integration of Afro-Surinamese and Indo-Surinamese immigrants, the Indo-Surinamese would be at a disadvantage in terms of the linear assimilation referred to above, and the Afro-Surinamese at an advantage in their striving for upward mobility. After all, the model does assume that assimilation precedes social advancement. Yet this is not what the research findings suggest. On the contrary, on the grounds of the social structural features of the Indo-Surinamese community, the Indo-Surinamese would seem to be at an advantage. The older generation is better able to keep the younger one under control and provide social and moral support for the youngsters' educational and occupational careers. Apparently a low level of sociocultural integration is not an obstacle for upward mobility. This also refutes the notion that individualization has to precede economic success. Under the influence of Weberian thinking, it has often been assumed that individualism was a necessary prerequisite for modernization and that extensive family ties only served as an obstacle. This definitely does not always hold true, as Goody (1996) argues with regard to India. Patriarchal family relations there prove instead to have been an important resource for economic success. For certain Asian immigrant groups in the United States as well, the preservation of extensive family ties with a large extent of mutual solidarity and trust has proved to be a favorable condition for upward mobility.[24]

The ethnic social context Indo-Surinamese youngsters frequently move in also means that the messages conveyed to them at home are being reinforced. Although not all Indo-Surinamese have had personal experience with entrepreneuring or have a "middle-class orientation," the ethnic community's relative closedness and strong cohesion do mean it also serves as a moral community. For many Indo-Surinamese, the ethnic group and the success stories told there serve as the frame of reference. Social mechanisms such as status competition reinforce this, and they stimulate members of the community to reach a higher level of achievement. In this sense, ethnic cohesion seems to reinforce the motivation for upward mobility.[25]

The other way around, the more diffuse and open nature of Afro-Surinamese networks of relatives and other social networks does not always seem to have been an advantage as regards their socioeconomic participation in Dutch society. The weaker family and other ethnic ties generally mean Afro-Surinamese youngsters are more exposed to the influence of social contexts outside the ethnic community than Indo-Surinamese youngsters. These influences can have positive or negative effects on their careers. In other words, what the effect is of greater integration largely depends on the context.[26] Afro-Surinamese cultural openness and flexibility do, however, also make for easier access to the institutions of Dutch society. From the start, many of them have indeed been able to benefit from their greater familiarity with the Dutch language and culture. In the beginning, it facilitated the transition to the Dutch school system. It is also true, though, that for people in the poorest socioeconomic position, this kind of adaptation does not necessarily lead to greater socioeconomic participation or upward mobility via education. One might reason that particularly in this segment of the lower class, there was a category of immigrants that was less Dutchified upon migration to the Netherlands. This is certainly the case, but on the average these Afro-Surinamese also have a relatively strong focus on the Dutch world around them. In the second instance, here too a cultural difference can be observed, but this has more to do with the folk theory of success referred to above and the alternative survival strategies. It refers more to what Ogbu calls secondary cultural differences: cultural differences that have mainly developed in response to the circumstances and in opposition to the mainstream society. Other theories refer instead to subcultural differences (Hannerz 1969: 177ff.) or ghetto-specific behavior (Wilson 1996: 51ff.).

In discussions on the differential success of immigrant groups in the United States, this conception of the context of integration plays an important role. Portes distinguishes three patterns of assimilation.[27] The first is the classical assimilation model. The second pertains to rapid economic progress on the basis of a strong ethnic community with the preservation of important values and mutual solidarity. This includes integration into an ethnic enclave where self-employment is an important route for upward mobility. The third form of assimilation is the adjustment to the subculture of American inner cities, with immigrants assimilating downward. In this option, the younger generation of immigrants does not adjust to the American middle class but to what is referred to as the underclass.[28] Based on these three different patterns of assimilation, Portes speaks of segmented assimilation. In the second pattern, the ethnic context is more important to the social mobility of the second generation than the American context. The conclusion is that a strong ethnic cohesion and preservation of the ethnic culture can be favorable conditions for academic success and economic advancement.[29]

These three patterns are not observed among Surinamese immigrants in the Netherlands in their pure forms. The classic assimilation route among segments of both the Surinamese communities is perhaps the most prevalent. Adaptation to an underclass presumes the existence of an underclass, and this is not the case in the Netherlands, at least not to the same extent and in the same form as in the United States. But a segment of the Afro-Surinamese lower class does exhibit certain underclass-like features, especially in some concentration districts.[30] This, however, similarly appears to be a legacy from the past as a result of adaptation to the Dutch context. The question is to what extent the more favorable economic situation of the 1990s and the greater job opportunities can alter these processes in the course of time. For now it is still not at all certain whether this pattern constitutes a final state or only a passing phase in a longer process.[31]

Nor is there much evidence of rapid economic incorporation via self-employment. In the description of the Indo-Surinamese social position in the Netherlands, several aspects emerge that are indicative of rapid progress, and there are relatively few indications of stagnation or of deviant careers or alternative survival strategies like those of the Afro-Surinamese. This relatively strong potential for upward mobility among the Indo-Surinamese does not seem to be directly connected to the entrepreneurial activities in the Indo-Surinamese community in the Netherlands. Compared with the situation in Surinam, formal entrepreneurship is relatively insignificant in the Netherlands. The power of the Indo-Surinamese community does not lie as much in its economic potential or the formation of an ethnic enclave as in its strong motivation regarding upward mobility. The cultural messages conveyed to children at home seem to be more significant than the economic capital or entrepreneurial experience of the first generation.

There are various conceivable reasons why the forms of assimilation Portes refers to are not observed as such in the Netherlands.[32] They mainly have to do with the nature of the Dutch welfare state.[33] Various authors have noted that an underclass is not expected to emerge in the Netherlands, at any rate not to the same extent as in the United States, because the mismatch hypothesis is only partially valid in the Netherlands (Kloosterman 1994) and there is no evidence of a spatial mismatch between the labor supply and demand (van Amersfoort and Cortie 1996). Another aspect is related to the more favorable social benefits in the Netherlands as compared to the United States. In the Netherlands the severest ramifications of economic restructuring and unemployment are mitigated, which can help prevent or reduce the emergence of an underclass. On the other hand, references have been made to welfare dependence as a factor in the development of an underclass. The lack of any prospects of improvement in one's position in the future combined with long-term welfare dependence can ultimately cause people to adjust their expectations and aspirations accordingly. In this connection, references are made to the "trap of the welfare state" (Musterd and Ostendorf 1993: 478).[34]

An effect of a totally different type is evident in the political and legislative context in the Netherlands, which turns many economic activities into informal ones. This can lead us to underestimate the role of Indo-Surinamese self-employment. We should not exclude the possibility of the Indo-Surinamese economic potential being greater than it would formally seem to be. For the time being though, in the Dutch welfare state parents' economic capital has less influence on their children's educational and occupational careers than their social and cultural resources.

The Relevance of History

In closing, I would like to go back to the central question of this study. What influence do the premigration history and the intangible baggage of immigrants have on their social mobility in Dutch society? What exactly does the premigration heritage consist of? In my option, it consists of three interrelated aspects. To start with there are the occupational skills.[35] Closely related to people's occupations and the place the group occupies in the economic structure of the country of origin or, in the Surinamese case, its place in the ethnic division of labor, they involve the knowledge and skills that can be summarized in terms of educational level, occupation, and job experience. Economic behavior in a wider sense can also be included. A second aspect of the premigration heritage is what I refer to as the faith in progress, which is somewhat comparable with what others call the folk theory of success (Ogbu 1987; Ogbu and Simons 1998). It includes the values, ideas, and attitudes people have to socioeconomic progress. It is the immigrants' cultural repertoire that can be traced back directly or indirectly to their present or former position in the economic structure of society. Third, the premigration heritage also includes social structural elements, in this case the family structure and division of labor between men and women related to it.

These three notions of premigration heritage are closely related and in practice it is difficult to separate them. Economic behavior (e.g., a sober lifestyle and frugality) are closely linked to people's occupation and livelihood, but they also have to do with the belief in progress or the folk theory of success. The same holds true of gender roles, which result in part from features of the ethnic division of labor in Surinam, the family structure, and the division of labor between men and women, and which are not unrelated to the folk theory of success either.[36]

In this study, I have repeatedly observed that among the Indo-Surinamese, certain success factors are not very class-specific. In the first instance, this seems to be a confirmation of a cultural explanation in terms of a collective historical heritage. Explanations in terms of cultural tradition are also often given for Indian immigrants elsewhere, particularly in the United States.[37] The legacy of the past is frequently accepted as a given without devoting much attention to the premigration class position and without empirical evidence that draws a link between this tradition and socioeconomic success. Helweg and Helweg (1990), for example, explain the success of Indian immigrants on the basis of various cultural aspects without making any explicit reference to their class position. On the grounds of their education and occupation, these immigrants already belonged to the middle class in India. So it was not that much of a matter of social advancement after immigration as of a continuation of their middle-class position. I am not denying that cultural heritage plays a role, I simply note that at least part of this success is shaped by the premigration class position.

This is something Steinberg (1989) devotes quite a bit of attention to. In the interpretations referred to above, culture is mainly viewed as a tradition from the past that has every appearance of being immutable. I agree with Steinberg's rejection of this kind of culturalist interpretation of, for example, the Jewish success in the United States. He holds that the Jews came to the United States with the right industrial skills at the right time. He thus puts the role of the cultural and religious Jewish tradition in the immigrants' social mobility into a different perspective. He backs this line of reasoning by referring to modern-day Israel. Recent Jewish immigrants from North Africa not only lack the educational and occupational qualifications of the earlier immigrants but also the present labor market makes different demands than in the past. Despite the shared religion, the more recent immigrants occupy the lowest positions in Israeli society (Steinberg 1989: 103).

Although Steinberg is thus adding a significant correction to the culturalist approaches and does indeed present an alternative, there is a weakness to his line of reasoning. By reducing cultural values completely to class or socioeconomic conditions, in essence Steinberg is ignoring culture or explaining it away. Values apparently cease to be values once they can be related to socioeconomic conditions that are either linked to them or precede them (Vermeulen 1992: 20). Steinberg finds it quite understandable that peasants in semifeudal societies do not have the same values as an urban proletariat (1989: 103); he just no longer calls it culture. In essence Steinberg is using a materialist and determinist concept of culture; culture has its origins in class and in concrete socioeconomic conditions.

It is not that this notion is erroneous, it is merely one-sided. In a widely used anthropological definition, culture is not only a reflection of social and material conditions, but culture also refers to the collective body of values, norms, and knowledge that can attain a certain autonomy vis-à-vis whatever social context it might have come from.[38] As such, in part it is culture that steers behavior, and this is the aspect Steinberg overlooks in his analysis. His criticism is completely focused on an understanding of culture in which it is attributed with an autonomous, independent role or is reified. His statement that culture cannot be the finishing point of analysis is accurate, but his criticism seems to be so one-sided that the point is lost. Portes and Rumbaut (1996) use a comparable line of reasoning. In an effort to explain why some immigrant groups more frequently earn a living in independent entrepreneurship than others, they quite understandably reject interpretations in terms of national or religious culture.[39] They rightly conclude that this is not a satisfactory explanation. For these reasons, they hold, sociologists have turned away from cultural interpretations in their efforts to find the key to economic behavior in the situational features of immigrant groups (1996: 76). This is accurate but, as I have noted, quite one-sided.[40]

If we do not take culture as our starting point but do not wish to explain it away either, the question is what approach to take to culture. I have concisely defined culture as collective or shared knowledge, skills, and values. I take culture to be the result of an adaptation to the present on the basis of a heritage from the past.[41] I did not take culture as the starting point in this study because it would overly presume a model that all people share and that emerges in their everyday lives in much the same way. This denies the wide range of conditions people find themselves in, conditions that differ according to their socioeconomic position, gender, age, generation, and so forth. If culture does play a role, it should be evident from their concrete actions, otherwise there is no way to demonstrate that it affects their social position. As Lindo (1996) rightly notes, research that takes ideational constructions as its starting point runs the risk of solely examining how people *ought* to act and not how they actually *do* act. Like Lindo, I have examined people's conduct, but that is not all. As I have observed, the social heritage or messages conveyed to children at home exert an important influence—in addition to other influences—on their behavior.[42] Youngsters do not reproduce this heritage in precisely the same form; they adapt it on the basis of their own experiences. This is characteristic of the dual nature of culture; it is acquired as well as situationally determined. So people's behavior is not a direct response to the conditions, it is mediated by their worldview—their expectations, attitudes, ideas, and aspirations.

This kind of concept of culture assumes an intertwining of class and culture. Strikingly enough, despite their explicit rejection of cultural explanations, authors like Steinberg and Portes implicitly start from this assumption. What they are in essence primarily rejecting is culture as an autonomous factor, and this is precisely what happens in culturalist approaches: culture is reified. If culture is, however, viewed as an adaptation to present conditions and if this adaptation occurs on the basis of experiences from the past, it would be difficult to speak of a separate cultural or ethnic factor. Culture is interwoven with people's position in the social structure of a society, and this differs according to class, gender, age, generation, and other social divisions. Does this mean that it is enough to know the position of individuals and groups, and that culture is thus no more than something derived from it? That is not the case. I have noted above that culture also has a relative autonomy—certain aspects of culture can temporarily continue to exist despite altered conditions. This poses the question as to the rate of change. To what extent are aspects of culture preserved after migration or do they change under the influence of the new social context?

Cultural patterns do not change at the same rate or to the same extent and in the same way for all immigrant groups. I would like to cite two aspects in this connection that emerged in my study. One is the belief in progress as part of the cultural baggage immigrants brought with them. The extent to which ideas, aspirations, and attitudes to social progress change in altered conditions is one of the core questions in a debate that has been repeatedly held in the United States under multifarious titles. A few decades ago it was the debate on the "culture of poverty," and more recently the discussions on the "underclass" or "ghetto poor." Under new titles, the old controversies come up again. But in essence, they all bear upon the issue of whether the poor have a different pattern of norms and values than mainstream society. Is it this pattern of norms and values that keeps them imprisoned in poverty, or is this cultural pattern merely a result of poverty and will it change if conditions improve? On the other hand, there is the question as to whether successful immigrants will be able to continue to imbue the younger generation with the aims that guided them in their migration. Will strong social cohesion and preservation of their culture enable them to keep the younger generation from assimilating to American norms and values (in this case of the underclass) that are contrary to their own aspirations?[43] The contrasts are not as sharp in the Netherlands as in the United States, but in essence the same questions are relevant.

The second point pertains to the different forms of integration. From the perspective of Portes and Rumbaut (1996), the answer to the above-mentioned questions depends on the context of integration. They mainly refer in this connection to the postmigration history; the social context in the host country is decisive for the mode of assimilation and the extent of economic and educational success. With this approach, these authors hope to supplement the structural explanations that use a rather sterile divide between individual characteristics and macrostructural factors. The question however is whether Portes and Rumbaut (1996) are not overlooking the cultural orientations immigrants brought with them when they came, such as their aspirations and expectations of social progress and their belief in it. They only devote general and superficial attention to them and conclude that there is not much difference between the aspirations of various second-generation groups (1996: 264). My study demonstrates that the subjective perspective, people's motivation and perception, cannot be overlooked because it influences their behavior.[44] Perlmann (2000) voices comparable criticism. In part the problem is that quantitative research only includes variables that can easily be measured. After measuring structural or SES variables and several easily measurable cultural variables, it might be feasible to interpret the unexplained residual in terms of social context. Perlmann doubts that this is the case, or at any rate feels it has not been demonstrated. Differences in social context as explanation for differential socioeconomic success can be indicative of structural as well as cultural factors.[45] In other words, precisely because the two are so strongly interwoven, the social context can not be isolated from culture, and vice versa.

Lastly, migration and the settlement of immigrants are long-term processes.[46] From this perspective, the Surinamese have been in the Netherlands for a relatively short period of time—it is only now that a sizeable segment of the second generation is reaching adulthood. It is difficult to predict which of the paths to social and cultural integration described here for the Indo-Surinamese and Afro-Surinamese will ultimately be more conducive to upward mobility.[47] One might wonder whether, over time, a strong ethnic cohesion will be preserved, or whether it will ultimately turn out to have been only a temporary stage in the adaptation process of immigrants.

Notes

1. Cf. Biervliet (1975); Buiks (1983); Sansone (1992).

2. In this connection, Zenner (1991: 47) notes "the kernel of truth in stereotypes." People can evaluate the same behavior in very different ways even though they give the same description of it. What one person sees as frugality, someone else might see as stinginess. Situational factors (such as animosity between a shopkeeper and a customer) also influence these judgments. Nonetheless, quite apart from the concrete interaction, someone's judgment about the group as a whole will influence the image of it.

3. See, e.g., Egger (1955); Hassankhan et al. (1995).

4. See, e.g., Boissevain and Grotenbreg (1986); Metcalf et al. (1996); Penninx (1988a); Waldinger et al. (1990).

5. See, e.g., Ogbu (1987); Perlmann (1988); Portes 1995; Portes and Rumbaut (1996); Vermeulen and Perlmann (2000); Wilson (1987 and 1991); DeWind et al. (1997).

6. As regards these changes on the Dutch labor market, see Godschalk (1999), in particular the contributions by Wolbers and Dronkers, Doomernik and Penninx, and de Beer.

7. West Indians in Great Britain and the United States exhibit comparable gender differences in their labor market position (Model 1991 and 1999; Modood et al. 1997).

8. See, e.g., Fainstein (1992).

9. See, e.g., Bovenkerk et al. (1991); Dagevos (1998); van der Meer and Wielers (1997).

10. See for an overview Penninx (1988a: 79-86); Veenman (1994: 90-92).

11. See also chapter 1. Wilson (1996: 111ff.) arrives at a comparable conclusion. He demonstrates that discrimination is most prevalent against poorly educated African-American men from the inner city. There is also evidence, though, of this same discrimination on the part of black employers (1996: 129-30).

12. In a certain sense this coincides with findings from the study cited above on the ethnic status hierarchy in the Netherlands. The findings show that ex-colonial groups like the Surinamese are attributed a lower status than European groups, but a higher status than Muslim groups such as Turks and Moroccans (Hagendoorn and Hraba 1989: 449).

13. See, e.g., Mungra (1993).

14. In a number of other senses, the earlier position of East Indians in Surinam seems to resemble that of the middlemen minorities. In addition to the relatively large percentage of East Indians in the commercial sector, this pertains to their position at the time as foreigners in Surinamese society, the patriarchal family relations, their secondary economic activities as artisans, and, later, their preference for medical professions (see Vermeulen 1991). Judging from what Zenner (1991: 88-89) says about a somewhat comparable group, the East Indians in the former British Guiana, the East Indians in Surinam, however, cannot be viewed as a middlemen minority.

15. Cf. Gellner (1983: 101-9).

16. An indication of this is the class background of Afro-Surinamese and Indo-Surinamese students in the Netherlands in the 1960s. As I note in chapter 3 (based on Sedoc-Dahlberg 1971), Afro-Surinamese students in the Netherlands at the time were frequently from the middle class and elite, whereas among the Indo-Surinamese students, the lower class was also amply represented.

17. There are striking similarities in this connection between the Afro-Surinamese and West Indians in the United States (Waters 1994) and Great Britain (Modood et al. 1997).

18. See also chapter 6, "The Importance of Diplomas."

19. Cf. van Niekerk (1992 and 1993a).

20. Cf. Hannerz (1996); Rumbaut (1997: 948-49).

21. See, e.g., Rumbaut (1997).

22. Cf. Gilroy (1993); Mintz and Price (1992).

23. The interesting thing though about Todd's analysis is that it is applicable to immigrant groups themselves as well as to the host society. This makes Todd's analysis less one-sided than approaches that solely view assimilation processes in terms of the inclusion and exclusion of immigrants by the host society (cf. Schuster 1999).

24. Cf., e.g., Fukuyama (1995); Light and Gold (2000).

25. Cf. Zhou (1997).

26. Cf. Waters (1994).

27. See especially Portes (1995); Portes and Rumbaut (1996); Zhou (1997).

28. Cf. Gans (1992).

29. Cf. Zhou (1997).

30. Cf. Sansone (1992).

31. Cf. Perlmann and Waldinger (1997).

32. Portes's theory of segmented assimilation is not, however, undisputed in the United States either. See especially DeWind et al. (1997).

33. Cf. Wilson (1996: 155ff.).

34. Cf. Wilson (1987: 93-106).

35. See, e.g., Perlmann (1988); Steinberg (1989).

36. See also van Niekerk (1999).

37. See, e.g., Gibson and Bacchu (1988); Helweg and Helweg (1990).

38. Cf. Abbink (1992: 100).

39. Alluding to Light (1984), Portes and Rumbaut (1996: 75) hold that cultural explanations of this kind all go back to Weber's theory about the connection between Protestant ethics and the influence it had on the emergence and development of capitalism.

40. Cf. Perlmann (1988 and 2000).

41. Cf. Barth (1994); Hannerz (1969 and 1996).

42. Cf. Kuipers (1994).

43. Cf. Rumbaut (1997).

44. Cf. Ogbu (1987); Ogbu and Simons (1998); Roosens (1989b).

45. What is more, Perlmann leaves the possibility open of cultural factors such as religious traditions and values that are not directly related to the structural position.

46. See, e.g., Lieberson (1980); Lucassen and Penninx (1994); Perlmann (1988).

47. Cf. Vermeulen and Penninx (2000); see also Alba and Nee (1997); DeWind and Kasinitz (1997).

Appendix One

The Research Population

In this appendix I describe a number of the relevant features of the research population in the qualitative study. As I have argued earlier, the study is focused on Surinamese immigrants who belonged to the lower socioeconomic groups when they arrived in the Netherlands and their descendants. In view of the aim of my study, it was also necessary to examine a research population consisting of Afro-Surinamese as well as Indo-Surinamese, men as well as women, and people of various ages and generations. This was an absolute necessity. For the rest, I wanted a research population as varied as possible.

The actual research population consists of 102 respondents from 64 nuclear or extended families. Via these respondents, I have gathered information about a total of 288 individuals who are part of these families. The respondents are divided into ethnic groups as follows (see table 1).

Table 1   *Research population*

	nuclear or extended families	*respondents*	*individuals including respondents*
Indo-Surinamese	30	57	159
Afro-Surinamese	28	39	113
mixed	6	6[*]	16
total	64	102	288

[*]   These are children of ethnically mixed marriages or relationships. If applicable, their parents are categorized as Indo-Surinamese or Afro-Surinamese.

Although there is not much difference between the number of Indo-Surinamese and Afro-Surinamese families, there are more Indo-Surinamese than Afro-Surinamese respondents. The Indo-Surinamese respondents have the largest families, as do the Indo-Surinamese in the total population.[1] The Indo-Surinamese research population more frequently contains various families from one and the same family network than the Afro-Surinamese research population.

The research population that more data and more in-depth data were gathered about consists of a smaller core of twenty-five families. Table 2 gives the same information as table 1, but pertaining to what I refer to as the core cases. In total, data were collected about 129 individuals via 61 respondents within these core cases.

Table 2   *Core cases*

	nuclear or extended families	*respondents*	*individuals including respondents*
Indo-Surinamese	10	35	75
Afro-Surinamese	13	24	48
mixed	2	2	6
total	25	61	129

The core cases pertain to (a) respondents who were interviewed at least twice or (b) families with at least two members involved in the study or (c) families with relatives in Surinam who were interviewed or (d) respondents who were involved in an earlier study of mine.

In the following sections of this appendix, I give information about the actual research population, that is, the 102 respondents.

The Respondents

First, I would like to give some information about their gender and age and how long they have been in the Netherlands. Then I give an impression of their socioeconomic position based on their educational level, economic roles, and several background features of the people with and without jobs.

It is clear that Afro-Surinamese men are underrepresented.[2] For the rest, the research population is evenly divided as regards gender: Afro-Surinamese women and Indo-Surinamese men and women are represented virtually to the same extent (see table 3).

Table 3   *Gender*

	men	women	total
Indo-Surinamese	28	29	57
Afro-Surinamese	11	28	39
mixed	4	2	6
total	43	59	102

As is clear from table 4, all the age groups are represented in the research population. I had 18 in mind as the minimum age, but in practice it turned out to be 17. The underlying idea for this minimum age was that there already ought to be some impression of the career prospects. In comparison with the total population, the 25-35 and 45-65 age groups are overrepresented, which is mainly because of the Indo-Surinamese.[3]

Table 4   *Age*

	17-25	*25-35*	*35-45*	*45-65*	*65+*	*total*
Indo-Surinamese	9	20	9	17	2	57
Afro-Surinamese	7	12	9	7	4	39
mixed	2	3	1	-	-	6
total	18	35	19	24	6	102

The respondents had been in the Netherlands for various lengths of time (see table 5), as had the entire Surinamese population in the Netherlands. There is clear evidence in table 5 of the two largest waves of immigration in 1974-75 and 1979-80, especially—as in the total population—among the Indo-Surinamese. The Afro-Surinamese arrived in the Netherlands more widely distributed over various periods.

A number of respondents (9) are members of the second generation. As in the total population, the Afro-Surinamese second generation is somewhat older than the Indo-Surinamese (Martens and Verweij 1997: 14).

Table 5 *Periods of arrival in the Netherlands*

	Indo-Surinamese	Afro-Surinamese	mixed	total
before 1960	-	2	-	2
1960-1970	4	6	-	10
1970-1973	4	7	1	12
1974-1975	24	4	1	29
1976-1978	3	2	-	5
1979-1980	13	4	1	18
1981-1985	-	2	-	2
1986-1990	5	1	1	7
after 1990	2	4	2	8
born in the Netherlands	2	7	-	9
total	57	39	6	102

I take the respondents' most recent diploma as a measure of their educational level. Table 6 shows the educational levels most recently completed by all the respondents including the ones who are still attending school full-time. For this category I take their last diploma, but it is clear that their educational level can still rise. The classification into educational levels is the same one that is used in the SPVA so that the data can easily be compared.[4] Table 7 only gives information on the respondents who no longer attend school full-time.

Table 6 *Educational level of all the respondents*

	Indo-Surinamese	Afro-Surinamese	mixed	total
– no more than primary school	15	5	-	20
– four-year vocational or secondary school	12	18	2	32
– five- or six-year vocational or secondary school	12	6	2	20
– college or university	18	10	2	30
total	57	39	6	102

Table 7   *Educational levels of respondents no longer attending school full-time*

	Indo-Surinamese	Afro-Surinamese	mixed	total
– no more than primary school	15	5	-	20
– four-year vocational or secondary school	11	14	2	27
– five- or six-year vocational or secondary school	7	5	-	12
– college or university	17	10	2	29
total	50	34	4	88

Both these tables on educational levels show that the research population includes relatively large numbers of well-educated people. They are overrepresented in comparison with the average educational level of the total population.[5] In view of my research aim, however, it is important that all the educational levels be reasonably well represented.

Table 8 shows the respondents' main economic status. By "nonworking" I mean people who do not have a job and are not looking for one. People who do not have a job but are looking for one are in the "job-seekers" category. This group is overrepresented, at any rate if I compare their percentage in the research population with the percentage of the *registered* unemployed in the total population.[6] I do not exclude the possibility that some of the respondents I categorize as "nonworking" are officially registered as looking for a job.

Table 8   *Main economic status*

	Indo-Surinamese	Afro-Surinamese	mixed	total
working	35	20	2	57
student	7	5	2	14
nonworking	12	14	1	27
job-seeker	3	-	1	4
total	57	39	6	102

In table 9 the focus is on the "nonworking" category of table 8, which is divided into subcategories. The "other" category contains people who are probably officially registered as unemployed. However, they are not looking for a job. In practice, they are not available for the labor market, for example, because they work off the books or are studying.

Table 9   *Nonworking persons (not including job-seekers and students)*

	Indo-Surinamese	Afro-Surinamese	mixed	total
housewives*	3	-	-	3
welfare mothers**	-	3	-	3
disabled	3	4	-	7
retired/retired early	3	5	-	8
other	3	2	1	6
total	12	14	1	27

*   Nonworking women who live with male breadwinners.
**   Nonworking female heads of households.

Tables 10 and 11 present a picture of the working people in the research population categorized according to their educational and job levels.

Table 10   *Working respondents' educational levels*

	Indo-Surinamese	Afro-Surinamese	mixed	total
– no more than primary school	8	2	-	10
– four-year vocational or secondary school	9	5	1	15
– five- or six-year vocational or secondary school	6	4	-	10
– college or university	12	9	1	22
total	35	20	2	57

Table 11   *Working respondents' job levels*

	Indo-Surinamese	Afro-Surinamese	mixed	total
elementary level	2	1	1	4
low level	15	4	-	19
middle level	9	10	1	20
high level	8	5	-	13
academic level	1	-	-	1
total	35	20	2	57

The division into job levels is based on the 1992 Statistics Netherlands Occupational Classification (CBS 1992). This classification was also used in the SPVA-1994, so that the data are comparable.

If I compare the data presented here with the socioeconomic position of the Surinamese in the Netherlands as described in chapter 2, in some respects the socioeconomic profile of the research population differs from it. On the average, the socioeconomic level of the research population is a bit higher. To a certain extent this distortion is corrected if I take the research population in a wider sense, that is, the 288 individuals I may not have all interviewed myself but did collect data on. This group includes individuals who do clearly find themselves at the lowest levels of the socioeconomic hierarchy: people with little or no education, the long-term unemployed, and young men pursuing an "alternative" or criminal career. In other words, the families represented in the study nonetheless probably constitute a reasonably good sample of the Surinamese population in the Netherlands. Wherever possible, I refer to this wider research population in my analysis.

Notes

1. Cf. Martens and Verweij (1997: 75).
2. See also my comments about this in the section entitled "The Research Population" in chapter 1.
3. See Martens and Verweij (1997: 72).
4. See chapter 2.
5. See Martens and Verweij (1997: 77).
6. See chapter 2.

Appendix Two

The SPVA-1994 and Ethnic Origin

In this appendix I present information about how the Surinamese are classified in the 1994 survey *The Social Position and Use of Provisions by Ethnic Minorities* (SPVA) according to their ethnic origin. For general information on the aim and design of the SPVA, I refer the reader to Martens (1995: 15-30).

The SPVA includes everyone either born in Surinam or with at least one parent born in Surinam in the Surinamese category. Of course the "place of birth" criterion cannot be used to divide the Surinamese population by ethnic origin. This is why a second-best solution was sought. The combination of two criteria, a subjective and an objective one, turned out to be relatively successful. The subjective criterion is the ethnic self-identification of the respondents. A number of stepped questions were posed to the respondents. Before asking which ethnic category they feel they belong to, the interviewers asked the respondents if they view themselves as Surinamese. A total of 639 (77 percent) of the 837 heads of households identify themselves as Surinamese, and 192 (23 percent) do not (see table 1).

Table 1   *Self-identification of Surinamese heads of households in 1994 (in percentages)*

identify themselves as Surinamese	23
do not identify themselves as Surinamese	77
total	100
	(n=831)

Source: SPVA-1994, ISEO/EUR.

In the second instance, both these categories (i.e., the ones who do and the ones who do not view themselves as Surinamese) were asked to identify themselves as "Afro-Surinamese," "Indo-Surinamese," or "other." Only the respondents

257

who did not identify themselves as Surinamese also had the option of filling in "Dutch." Of the category who do *not* identify themselves as Surinamese, 60 percent fill in Dutch. This is 14 percent of the total population. In other words, this is the percentage of Surinamese heads of households who (1) do not identify themselves as Surinamese and (2) subsequently indicate that they identify themselves as Dutch. Most respondents who do identify themselves as Surinamese see themselves as either Indo-Surinamese (46 percent) or Afro-Surinamese (37 percent) (see table 2).

Table 2   *Surinamese (heads of households) who do or do not identify themselves as Surinamese by self-identification in 1994 (in percentages)*

	identify themselves as Surinamese	do not identify themselves as Surinamese
Indo-Surinamese	46	13
Afro-Surinamese	37	5
Dutch	n.a.	60
other/unknown	18	23
total	100*	100*
	(n=639)	(n=192)

Source: SPVA-1994, ISEO/EUR.
*   Percentages do not add up to 100 because they have been rounded off.

If we combine these two categories (those who do and those who do not identify themselves as Surinamese), a total of 560 of the 837 heads of households do include themselves in either the Afro-Surinamese (242) or Indo-Surinamese category (318). In other words, 29 percent of the total population identify themselves as Afro-Surinamese and 38 percent as Indo-Surinamese. As I note above, 14 percent of the total population identify themselves as Dutch (see table 3).

Table 3   *Surinamese (heads of households) by self-identification in 1994 (in percentages)*

Indo-Surinamese	38
Afro-Surinamese	29
Dutch	14
other/unknown	20
total	100*
	(n=837)

Source: SPVA-1994, ISEO/EUR.
*   Percentages do not add up to 100 because they have been rounded off.

There is still a relatively large segment of the Surinamese population that can not be categorized by ethnic origin. This pertains at any rate to the "Dutch" category (14 percent) and to part of the "other/unknown" category (20 percent). This is why in the second instance, another criterion was added to determine as much as possible of their ethnic origin. This was done on the basis of an objective criterion, that is, language. The respondents were asked what their mother language is and what language *other than Dutch* they speak with their friends and relatives. This made it possible to determine the ethnic origin of more of the respondents.

Now the Afro-Surinamese and Indo-Surinamese percentages are higher: almost half the Surinamese heads of households are Indo-Surinamese (47 percent) and somewhat fewer are Afro-Surinamese (42 percent) (see table 4).

Table 4   *Surinamese (heads of households) by ethnic origin based on self-identification and language use in 1994 (in percentages)*

Indo-Surinamese	47
Afro-Surinamese	42
Javanese	7
other Surinamese groups	4
total	100
	(n=735)

Source: SPVA-1994, ISEO/EUR.

These categories only pertain, however, to the heads of households. It is possible to also count the other household members in this ethnic origin classification, in other words the partners and children and anyone else living in the household. This does not take into consideration partners who are Dutch. It does count the children of ethnically mixed marriages or relationships. All these household members (except the Dutch partners) are then classified in the same ethnic category as the head of the household. The results are shown in table 5.

The percentages now exhibit a change; more than half (53 percent) are Indo-Surinamese and more than a third (38 percent) are Afro-Surinamese. These differences, as compared with table 4, probably have to do with the fact that Indo-Surinamese households tend to be larger than Afro-Surinamese ones.

Table 5   *Surinamese (heads of households, partners*, children and other
              household members) by ethnic origin based on heads of households'
              self-identification and language use in 1994 (in percentages)*

Indo-Surinamese	53
Afro-Surinamese	38
Javanese	7
other Surinamese groups	3
total	100**
	(n=1.987)

Source: SPVA-1994, ISEO/EUR.
*   Not including Dutch spouses and partners.
**   Percentages do not add up to 100 because they have been rounded off.

All things considered, the successive use of a subjective and objective criterion
made it possible to determine the ethnic origin of the large majority of the Surinamese. For the sake of completeness, I should state that use was made of a subjective criterion (self-definition) to determine objective information (ethnic origin). There are objections to this, but it could not be avoided. The method used
did nonetheless seem to overcome some of the objections. First, the interviewers
did not confine themselves to a one-time question whereby respondents could
choose from a wide range of ethnic categories or fill in various categories simultaneously. This might be a good way to find out something about ethnic identity,
but not to determine ethnic origin. Instead, the respondents were presented with
a limited number of choices, and the routing of the questions was such that in
the second instance, they were asked about their specific ethnic origin. It is not
plausible that Afro-Surinamese would identify themselves as Indo-Surinamese or
vice versa. So in many cases, ethnic self-definition and ethnic origin will indeed
coincide. Adding a second criterion, an objective one (language), considerably
reduced the percentage of respondents whose ethnic origin could not yet be determined (for example, because they had defined themselves as Dutch). Although
there can also have been a certain extent of distortion here (for example, regarding the Indo-Surinamese who speak *Sranan* rather than *Sarnami* in addition to
Dutch), the problems have thus largely been overcome.

A second comment pertains to the classification of household members in
the ethnic category of the head of the household (table 5). These are their partners, children, and anyone else living in the household. This can be an objection
as regards partners who have a different ethnic origin from that of the head of
the household. (It should be noted once again that Dutch partners have not been
included.) Surinamese partners of different ethnic origins are thus rightly or
wrongly classified in the same ethnic category as the head of the household. The
same holds true for the other people living in the household, who are usually

members of the immediate family (brothers, sisters, or parents). The problem as to the children in the household is approximately the same if the (Surinamese) partner of the head of the household is of a different ethnic origin from that of the head.[1] If that is not the case (both parents have the same ethnic origin), there is no objection to classifying the children in the same ethnic category as the head of the household. Of course, this would be inadmissible for someone who examines ethnic identity, but for someone who wants to know people's ethnic origin, it is quite an appropriate method.[2]

Notes

1. Berthoud et al. (1997: 14) note that this is a tricky problem no matter what method is used to classify ethnic groups.

2. See also the section entitled "Ethnic Origin and Ethnic Identity" in chapter 1.

Appendix Three

Afro-Surinamese and Indo-Surinamese Socioeconomic Positions

Table 1 *Labor market participation of the Indo-Surinamese, Afro-Surinamese, total Surinamese, and native Dutch populations in 1994, in total numbers and by gender (in percentages)*

	Indo-Surinamese (n=637)	Afro-Surinamese (n=463)	Surinamese (n=1,380)	native Dutch (n=1,598)
total	51	69	60	63
men	60	77	69	72
women	43	63	52	53

Source: SPVA-1994, ISEO/EUR and Martens (1995: 56).

Table 2 *Registered unemployment* of the Indo-Surinamese, Afro-Surinamese, and the total Surinamese population in 1994, in total numbers and by gender (in percentages)*

	Indo-Surinamese (n=325)	Afro-Surinamese (n=321)	Surinamese (n=726)
total	20	21	20
men	21	25	23
women	20	17	18

Source: SPVA-1994, ISEO/EUR.
*   Percentage of nonworking individuals in the labor force registered at an employment bureau.

Table 3   *Main sources of income of the Indo-Surinamese and Afro-Surinamese by*
              gender in 1994 (15-64 age group) (in percentages)[*]

	Indo-Surinamese		Afro-Surinamese	
	men	*women*	*men*	*women*
no personal income	17	27	17	15
employment	49	37	59	52
welfare benefit	10	16	6	16
unemployment benefit	7	6	9	9
disability benefit	8	6	4	2
pension, old age pension, early retirement pension	1	1	1	1
student grant	8	7	3	4
other	0	1	1	2
absolute total (=100%)	299	323	209	249

Source: SPVA-1994, ISEO/EUR.
[*]   The percentages in this table and some of the other tables in this appendix
             do not always add up to 100 because they have been rounded off.

Table 4   *Main economic status of the Indo-Surinamese and Afro-Surinamese by*
              gender in 1994 (in percentages)

	Indo-Surinamese		Afro-Surinamese	
	men	*women*	*men*	*women*
employed >18 hours	46	31	59	50
unemployed/job-seeker	19	12	22	15
housewife/houseman	1	36	1	20
disabled	9	4	4	3
schoolchild/student	21	16	12	11
retired/retired early	2	1	2	0
other	2	0	1	0
absolute total (=100%)	293	318	203	240

Source: SPVA-1994, ISEO/EUR.

Table 5   *Job levels of the Indo-Surinamese and Afro-Surinamese in the Netherlands in 1994 of (a) last job in Surinam (b) first job in the Netherlands, and (c) present job (in percentages)*

	last job in Surinam		first job in the Netherlands		present job	
	I-S	*A-S*	*I-S*	*A-S*	*I-S*	*A-S*
elementary level	12	16	34	21	27	12
low level	39	29	34	38	33	39
middle level	38	45	24	31	29	38
high level	10	8	6	9	11	9
academic level	1	2	-	1	-	2
absolute total (=100%)	134	137	270	258	260	246

Source: SPVA-1994, ISEO/EUR.

Table 6   *Levels of last jobs in the Netherlands by levels of first jobs in the Netherlands of the Indo-Surinamese and Afro-Surinamese in 1994 (in absolute numbers)**

Indo-Surinamese	*first job*				
	elementary level	*low level*	*middle level*	*high and academic level*	*total*
last job					
elementary level	62	9	7	1	79
low level	11	71	5	1	88
middle level	17	10	49	2	78
high and academic level	2	2	4	14	22
total	92	92	65	18	267

Afro-Surinamese	*first job*				
	elementary level	*low level*	*middle level*	*high and academic level*	*total*
last job					
elementary level	32	9	3	-	44
low level	9	71	8	2	90
middle level	12	14	65	-	91
high and academic level	2	3	2	21	28
total	55	97	78	23	253

Source: SPVA-1994, ISEO/EUR.
* Unlike the other tables in this appendix, this one shows absolute numbers instead of percentages because many of the numbers are too small to be expressed as percentages.

Table 7 *Educational levels (regardless of where diploma was issued) of the Indo-Surinamese and Afro-Surinamese no longer attending school full-time in 1994 (in percentages)*

	Indo-Surinamese	Afro-Surinamese
no more than primary school	42	26
four-year vocational or secondary school	34	38
five- or six-year vocational or secondary school	17	24
college or university	7	13
absolute total (=100%)	514	396

Source: SPVA-1994, ISEO/EUR.

Table 8 *Total net monthly income of the Indo-Surinamese and Afro-Surinamese in 1994 (in percentages)*

	Indo-Surinamese	Afro-Surinamese
less than NLG 1,100	24	15
NLG 1,100 to NLG 1,500	19	16
NLG 1,500 to NLG 1,900	28	26
NLG 1,900 to NLG 2,300	12	15
NLG 2,300 to NLG 2,700	9	13
more than NLG 2,700	8	16
absolute total (=100%)	363	276

Source: SPVA-1994, ISEO/EUR.

Table 9 *Duration of unemployment of the Indo-Surinamese and Afro-Surinamese registered as unemployed in 1994 (in percentages)*

	Indo-Surinamese	Afro-Surinamese
0-6 months	27	24
6-12 months	23	5
1-2 years	22	20
2-5 years	22	29
5 years or longer	6	23
absolute total (=100%)	64	66

Source: SPVA-1994, ISEO/EUR.

Table 10   *Indo-Surinamese and Afro-Surinamese household composition in 1994 (in percentages)*

	Indo-Surinamese	Afro-Surinamese	native Dutch
one single person	17	33	36
husband and wife	13	14	29
man and woman and children (and others)	39	27	28
single-parent family	24	22	3
other	7	4	4
absolute total (=100%)	345	309	1.062

Source: SPVA-1994, ISEO/EUR; Martens and Verweij (1997: 74).

References

Abbink, J. 1992. "Epilogue." Pp. 95-106 in *History and Culture: Essays on the Work of Eric Wolf*, edited by J. Abbink and H. Vermeulen. Amsterdam: Het Spinhuis.

Alba, R., and V. Nee. 1997. "Rethinking Assimilation Theory for a New Era of Immigration." *International Migration Review* 31: 826-74.

Amersfoort, H. van. 1968. *Surinamers in de lage landen*. The Hague: Staatsuitgeverij.

———. 1970. "Hindostaanse Surinamers in Amsterdam." *Nieuwe West-Indische Gids* 47: 109-38.

———. 1987. "Van William Kegge tot Ruud Gullit: De Surinaamse migratie naar Nederland: Realiteit, beeldvorming en beleid." *Tijdschrift voor Geschiedenis* 100: 475-90.

———. 1992. "Ethnic Residential Patterns in a Welfare State: Lessons from Amsterdam, 1970-1990." *New Community* 18, no. 3: 439-56.

Amersfoort, H. van, and C. Cortie. 1996. "Social Polarisation in a Welfare State? Immigrants in the Amsterdam Region." *New Community* 22, no. 4: 671-87.

Amersfoort, H. van, and R. Penninx. 1993. "Migratieontwikkeling en migratiebeheersing." Pp. 57-84 in *Migratie, bevolking en politiek*, edited by H. van Amersfoort. Amsterdam: Institute for Social Geography, University of Amsterdam.

Anderiesen, G., and A. Reijndorp. 1991. "Op zoek naar de onderklasse: Heterogeniteit en sociaal isolement in stadsvernieuwingswijken." *Migrantenstudies* 7, no. 3: 49-63.

Anderson, B. 1991. *Imagined Communities: Reflections on the Origin and Spread of Nationalism*. London: Verso. [1983]

———. 1992. *Long-Distance Nationalism: World Capitalism and the Rise of Identity Politics*. Amsterdam: Center for Asia Studies Amsterdam (CASA).

Anderson, E. 1990. *Street Wise: Race, Class, and Change in an Urban Community*. Chicago: University of Chicago Press.

Autar, K. 1990. "Uitstoting van leerlingen uit etnische minderheidsgroepen." Pp. 101-20 in *Schoolloopbaanverbetering van Surinaamse leerlingen*, edited by V. Tjon-A-Ten and K. Autar. Amsterdam/Lisse: Swets and Zeitlinger.

Banton, M. 1979. "It's Our Country." Pp. 223-46 in *Racism and Political Action in Britain*, edited by R. Miles and A. Phizacklea. London: Routledge and Kegan Paul.

Barth, F. 1986. "The Analysis of Culture in Complex Societies." *Ethnos* 54: 120-42.

―――. 1994. "Enduring and Emerging Issues in the Analysis of Ethnicity." Pp. 11-32 in *The Anthropology of Ethnicity: Beyond "Ethnic Groups and Boundaries,"* edited by H. Vermeulen and C. Govers. Amsterdam: Het Spinhuis.

Bayer, A. 1965. *Surinaamse arbeiders in Nederland.* Assen: Van Gorcum.

Beer, P. de. 1999. Book review of Dagevos, "Begrensde mobiliteit" (1998). *Migrantenstudies* 15, no. 3: 208-9.

Benedict, B. 1979. "Family Firms and Firm Families: A Comparison of Indian, Chinese, and Creole Firms in Seychelles." Pp. 305-26 in *Entrepreneurs in Cultural Context,* edited by S. Greenfield, A. Strickon, and R. Aubrey. Albuquerque: University of New Mexico Press.

Bertaux, D. and P. Thompson, eds. 1997. *Pathways to Social Class: A Qualitative Approach to Social Mobility.* Oxford: Clarendon Press.

Berthoud, R., T. Modood, and P. Smith. 1997. "Introduction." Pp. 1-17 in T. Modood et al., *Ethnic Minorities in Britain: Diversity and Disadvantage.* London: Policy Studies Institute.

Biervliet, W. 1975. "The Hustler Culture of Young Unemployed Surinamers." Pp. 191-201 in *Adaption of Migrants from the Caribbean in the European and American Metropolis,* edited by H. Lamur and J. Speckmann. Amsterdam/Leiden: KITLV/ ASC.

Bloemberg, L. 1995. *Tussen traditie en verandering: Hindostaanse zelforganisaties in Nederland.* Utrecht/Amsterdam: Royal Dutch Geography Society/Institute for Social Geography.

Bloemberg, L., and D. Nijhuis. 1993. "Hindoebasisscholen in Nederland." *Migrantenstudies* 9, no. 3: 35-51.

Boissevain, J., A. Choenni, and H. Grotenbreg. 1984. *Een kleine baas is altijd beter dan een grote knecht: Surinaamse kleine zelfstandige ondernemers in Amsterdam.* Amsterdam: Antropology-Sociology Center, University of Amsterdam.

Boissevain, J., and H. Grotenbreg. 1986. "Culture, Structure and Ethnic Enterprise: The Surinamese of Amsterdam." *Ethnic and Racial Studies* 9, no. 1: 1-23.

Bouw, C., and C. Nelissen. 1988. *Gevoelige kwesties: Ervaringen van migranten met discriminatie.* Leiden: COMT, University of Leiden.

Bovenkerk, F. 1973. *Terug naar Suriname? Over de opname-capaciteit van de Surinaamse arbeidsmarkt voor Surinaamse retourmigratie uit Nederland.* Amsterdam: Antropology-Sociology Center, University of Amsterdam.

―――. 1975. *Emigratie uit Suriname.* Amsterdam: Antropology-Sociology Center, University of Amsterdam.

―――. 1976. *Wie gaat er terug naar Suriname? Een onderzoek naar de retourmigratie van Surinamers uit Nederland 1972-1973.* Amsterdam: Antropology-Sociology Center, University of Amsterdam.

―――. 1983. "De vlucht: Migratie in de jaren zeventig." Pp. 152-81 in *Suriname: De schele onafhankelijkheid,* edited by G. Willemsen. Amsterdam: De Arbeiderspers.

Bovenkerk, F., and E. Breuning-van Leeuwen. 1978. "Rasdiscriminatie en rasvooroordeel op de Amsterdamse arbeidsmarkt." Pp. 31-77 in *Omdat zij anders zijn: Patronen van rasdiscriminatie in Nederland*, edited by F. Bovenkerk. Amsterdam/Meppel: Boom.

Bovenkerk, F., B. den Brok, and L. Ruland. 1991. "Meer of minder gelijk? Over de arbeidskansen van hoog opgeleide leden van etnische groepen." *Sociologische Gids* 38, no. 3: 174-86.

Brana Shute, G. 1979. *On the Corner: Male Social Life in a Paramaribo Creole Neighborhood*. Assen: Van Gorcum.

Brinkgreve, C. et al., ed. 1994. "Overdragen en eigen maken: Over sociale erfenissen." Book issue of *Amsterdams Sociologisch Tijdschrift* 21, no. 1.

Brinkgreve, C., and B. van Stolk. 1997. *Van huis uit: Wat ouders hun kinderen willen meegeven*. Amsterdam: Meulenhoff.

Bruijne, A. de, and A. Schalkwijk. 1994. *Kondreman en P'tata: Nederland als referentiekader voor Surinamers*. Amsterdam: Institute for Social Geography, University of Amsterdam.

Bruijne, G. de. 1976. *Paramaribo: Stadsgeografische studies van een ontwikkelingsland*. Bussum: Romen.

———. 1995. "Suriname's benarde positie." *Geografie* 4, no. 6: 5-10.

Buddingh', H. 1995 *Geschiedenis van Suriname*. Utrecht: Het Spectrum.

Buiks, P. 1983. *Surinaamse jongeren op de Kruiskade: Overleven in een etnische randgroep*. Deventer: Van Loghum Slaterus.

Burg, C. van der, and P. van der Veer. 1986. "Ver van India, ver van Suriname: Hindoestaanse Surinamers in Nederland." Pp. 23-36 in *Surinaamse religies in Nederland*, edited by C. van der Burg. Amsterdam: VU Uitgeverij.

Burgers, J., and G. Engbersen. 1996. "Globalisation, Migration, and Undocumented immigrants." *New Community* 22, no. 4: 619-35.

Buschkens, W. 1974. *The Family System of the Paramaribo Creoles*. The Hague: Martinus Nijhoff.

CBS (Statistics Netherlands). 1992. *Standaard beroepenclassificatie 1992*. The Hague: SDU.

———. 1999. "Allochtonen, 1 januari 1999." *Maandstatistiek van de Bevolking* 12: 48-115.

CBS/UvA (Statistics Netherlands/University of Amsterdam). 1988. *De leefsituatie van Surinamers en Antillianen in Nederland 1985: Deel 2: Kerncijfers*. The Hague: Staatsuitgeverij.

Choenni, A. 1997. *Veelsoortig assortiment: Allochtoon ondernemerschap in Amsterdam als incorporatietraject 1965-1995*. Amsterdam: Het Spinhuis.

Choenni, C. 1995. *Kleur in de krijgsmacht: De integratie van Surinaamse jongemannen in Nederland*. Utrecht: Social Science Faculty, University of Utrecht.

Coleman, J. 1988. "Social Capital in the Creation of Human Capital." *American Journal of Sociology* 94: 95-120.

Cottaar, A. 1998. *Ik had een neef in Den Haag: Nieuwkomers in de twintigste eeuw*. Zwolle: Waanders.

Crul, M. 2000. *De sleutel tot succes: Over hulp, keuzes en kansen in de schoolloopbanen van Turkse en Marokkaanse jongeren van de tweede generatie.* Amsterdam: Het Spinhuis.

Dagevos, J. 1995. "Allochtonen bij de rijksoverheid: Oorzaken en falen van voorkeursbeleid." *Tijdschrift voor Arbeidsvraagstukken* 11, no. 2: 143-53.

———. 1998. *Begrensde mobiliteit: Over allochtone werkenden in Nederland.* Assen: Van Gorcum.

Dagevos J., E. Martens, and J. Veenman. 1996. *Scheef verdeeld: Minderheden en hun maatschappelijke positie.* Assen: Van Gorcum.

Dash, L. 1998. *Rosa Lee.* London: Profile Books. [1996]

Despres, L. 1967. *Cultural Pluralism and Nationalist Politics in British Guiana.* Chicago: Rand McNally.

———. 1970. "Differential Adaptations and Micro-cultural Evolution in Guyana." Pp. 263-87 in *Afro-American Anthropology: Contemporary perspectives,* edited by N. Whitten, and J. Szwed. New York: The Free Press.

Dew, E. 1978. *The Difficult Flowering of Surinam: Ethnicity and Politics in a Plural Society.* The Hague: Martinus Nijhoff.

DeWind, J., C. Hirschman, and P. Kasinitz, eds. 1997. "Immigrant Adaptation and Native-Born Responses in the Making of Americans." Special issue *International Migration Review* 31, no. 4.

DeWind, J., and P. Kasinitz. 1997. "Everything Old Is New Again: Processes and Theories of Immigrant Incorporation." *International Migration Review* 31, no. 4: 1096-111.

Dors, H., S. Karsten, G. Ledoux, and A. Steen. 1991. *Etnische segregatie in het onderwijs: Beleidsaspecten.* Amsterdam: Center for Educational Research Foundation, University of Amsterdam.

Dors, H., and K. Sietaram. 1989. *De onderwijssituatie van Surinaamse leerlingen.* Utrecht: Stichting Surinaams Inspraakorgaan.

Driessen, G. 1995. "Het relatieve belang van sociaal milieu en etnische herkomst voor de verklaring van onderwijsachterstanden." *Tijdschrift voor onderwijsresearch* 20, no. 4: 341-62.

———. 1996. "Prestaties, gedrag en houding van leerlingen op islamitische basisscholen." *Migrantenstudies* 12, no. 3: 136-51.

Dronkers, J., and P. de Graaf. 1995. "Ouders en het onderwijs van hun kinderen." Pp. 46-66 in *Verschuivende ongelijkheid in Nederland: Sociale gelaagdheid en mobiliteit,* edited by J. Dronkers and W. Ultee. Assen: Van Gorcum.

Dronkers, J., and W. Ultee, eds. 1995. *Verschuivende ongelijkheid in Nederland: Sociale gelaagdheid en mobiliteit.* Assen: Van Gorcum.

Dusseldorp, D. van. 1963. "Geografische mobiliteit en de ontwikkeling van Suriname." *Bijdragen tot de Taal-, Land- en Volkenkunde* 119: 18-55.

Egger, J. 1995. "Sociaal-economische ontwikkeling van de Creolen na 1940." Pp. 172-205 in *De erfenis van de slavernij,* edited by L. Gobardhan-Rambocus et al. Paramaribo: Anton de Kom University.

Eldering, L., and J. Borm. 1996. *Alleenstaande Hindostaanse moeders.* Utrecht: Van Arkel.

Engbersen, G. 1990. *Publieke bijstandsgeheimen: Het ontstaan van een onderklasse in Nederland.* Leiden: Stenfert Kroese.

Eriksen, Th. 1992. *Us and Them in Modern Societies: Ethnicity and Nationalism in Mauritius, Trinidad and Beyond.* Oslo: Scandinavian University Press.

Fainstein, N. 1992. "The Urban Underclass and Mismatch Theory Re-examined." Pp. 276-312 in *Ethnic Minorities and Industrial Change in Europe and North America,* edited by M. Cross. Cambridge: Cambridge University Press.

Fase, W. 1994. *Ethnic Divisions in Western European Education.* Münster: Waxmann.

Fase, W., and H. Kleijer, eds. 1996. "Onderwijs en etniciteit." Theme issue *Sociologische Gids* 43, no. 2.

Fernández Kelly, M. 1995. "Social and Cultural Capital in the Urban Ghetto: Implications for the Economic Sociology of Immigration." Pp. 213-47 in *The Economic Sociology of Immigration: Essays on Networks, Ethnicity, and Entrepreneurship,* edited by A. Portes. New York: Russell Sage Foundation.

Fukuyama, F. 1995. *Trust: The Social Virtues and the Creation of Prosperity.* London: Penguin Books.

Gans, H. 1990. "Deconstructing the Underclass: The Term's Danger as a Planning Concept." *Journal of the American Planning Association* (summer): 271-77.

———. 1992. "Second Generation Decline: Scenarios for the Economic and Ethnic Futures of the Post-1965 American Immigrants." *Ethnic and Racial Studies* 15, no. 2: 173-92.

Gelder, P. van. 1985. *Werken onder de boom: Dynamiek en informele sector: De situatie in Groot-Paramaribo.* Dordrecht: Foris Publications.

———. 1990. "Het Surinaamse begrip 'hosselen.'" *Migrantenstudies* 6, no. 3: 31-43.

Gellner, E. 1983. *Nations and Nationalism.* Oxford: Blackwell.

Gibson, M. 2000. "Situational and Structural Rationales for the School Performance of Immigrant Youth: Three Cases." Pp. 72-102 in *Immigrants, Schooling and Social Mobility: Does Culture Make a Difference?* edited by H. Vermeulen and J. Perlmann. London: Macmillan.

Gibson, M., and P. Bacchu. 1988. "Ethnicity and School Performance: A Comparative Study of South Asian Pupils in Britain and America." *Ethnic and Racial Studies* 11, no. 3: 239-62.

Gilroy, P. 1993. *The Black Atlantic: Modernity and Double Consciousness.* London: Verso.

Godschalk, J., ed. 1999. *Die tijd komt nooit meer terug: De arbeidsmarkt aan het eind van de eeuw.* Amsterdam: Het Spinhuis.

Goody, J. 1993. "Culture and Its Boundaries: A European View." *Social Anthropology* 1, no. 1A: 9-32.

———. 1996. *The East in the West.* Cambridge: Cambridge University Press.

Gooskens, I., J. Hooff, and M. Freeman. 1979a. *Surinamers en Antillianen in Amsterdam: Deel I: Analyse.* Amsterdam: City of Amsterdam.

———. 1979b. *Surinamers en Antillianen in Amsterdam: Deel II: Tabellen.* Amsterdam: City of Amsterdam.

Gras, M., F. Bovenkerk, K. Gorter, P. Kruiswijk, and D. Ramsoedh. 1995. *Een schijn van kans: Twee empirische onderzoeken naar discriminatie op grond van handicap en etnische afkomst*. Arnhem: Gouda Quint.

Grotenhuis, H. te. 1993. *Bijstandskinderen: Opgroeien aan de rand van de verzorgingsstaat*. Amsterdam: Amsterdam University Press.

Haakmat, A. 1996. *Herinneringen aan de toekomst van Suriname*. Amsterdam: De Arbeiderspers.

Hagendoorn, L., and J. Hraba. 1989. "Foreign, Different, Deviant, Seclusive and Working Class: Anchors to an Ethnic Hierarchy in the Netherlands." *Ethnic and Racial Studies* 12, 4: 441-68.

Hannerz, U. 1969. *Soulside: Inquiries into Ghetto Culture and Community*. New York: Columbia University Press.

———. 1992. *Cultural Complexities: Studies in the Social Organization of Meaning*. New York: Columbia University Press.

———. 1996. "When Culture Is Everywhere: Reflections on a Favorite Concept." Pp. 30-43 in U. Hannerz, *Transnational Connections: Culture, People, Places*. London: Routledge.

Hassankhan, M., M. Liegon, and P. Scheepers. 1995. "Sociaal-economische verschillen tussen Creolen, Hindoestanen en Javanen: 130 jaar na afschaffing van de slavernij." Pp. 249-74 in *De erfenis van de slavernij*, edited by L. Gobardhan-Rambocus et al. Paramaribo: Anton de Kom University.

Heelsum, A. van. 1997. *De etnisch-culturele positie van de tweede generatie Surinamers*. Amsterdam: Het Spinhuis.

Heijdt, J. van der. 1995. "Twintig jaar na de Surinaamse onafhankelijkheid: Surinamers in Nederland." *Maandstatistiek van de Bevolking* 10: 19-21.

Heilbron, W. 1982. "Kleine boeren in de schaduw van de plantage: De politieke ekonomie van de na-slavernijperiode in Suriname." Dissertation University of Amsterdam.

Helweg, A., and U. Helweg. 1990. *An Immigrant Success Story: East Indians in America*. London: Hurst.

Hira, S. 1982. *Van Priary tot en met De Kom: De geschiedenis van het verzet in Suriname 1630-1940*. Rotterdam: Futile.

Hoetink, H. 1961. "Gezinsvormen in het Caribisch gebied." *Mens en Maatschappij* 36, no. 2: 81-93.

———. 1967. *Caribbean Race Relations: A Study of Two Variants*. London: Oxford University Press.

Hof, L. van 't, and J. Dronkers. 1993. "Onderwijsachterstanden van allochtonen: Klasse, gezin of etnische cultuur?" *Migrantenstudies* 9, no. 1: 2-25.

Hondius, D. 1999. *Gemengde huwelijken, gemengde gevoelens: Aanvaarding en ontwijking van etnisch en religieus verschil sinds 1945*. The Hague: SDU.

Jadoenandansing, S. 1992. "Wonen aan de Leidingen." *OSO, Tijdschrift voor Surinaamse taalkunde, letterkunde, cultuur en geschiedenis* 11, no. 1: 46-52.

Josias, H. 1992. "Creoolse wegloopsters." Pp. 263-331 in *Andere tijden, andere meiden: Een onderzoek naar het weglopen van Marokkaanse, Turkse, Hindostaanse en Creoolse meisjes*, edited by L. Brouwer et al. Utrecht: Jan van Arkel.

Juglall, W. 1963. "Het onderwijs aan nakomelingen van Brits-Indische immigranten in Suriname." Pp. 83-89 in *Van Brits-Indisch emigrant tot burger van Suriname*, edited by E. Azumullah et al. The Hague: Surinaamse Jongeren Vereniging Manan.

Kagie, R. 1989. *De eerste neger: Herinneringen aan de komst van een bevolkingsgroep*. Houten: Het Wereldvenster.

Kishoendajal, M. 1997. "Op het randje van de criminaliteit." *Contrast* 4, no. 14: 1, 4.

Klerk, C. de. 1953. *De immigratie der Hindostanen in Suriname*. Amsterdam: Urbi et orbi.

Klerk, L. de. 1996. "Concentratie en segregatie: Meer dan een volkshuisvestingsprobleem?" *Migrantenstudies* 12, no. 2: 79-85.

Klerk, L. de, and H. van Amersfoort. 1988. "Surinamese Settlement in Amsterdam 1973-1983." Pp. 221-49 in *Lost Illusions: Caribbean Minorities in Britain and the Netherlands*, edited by M. Cross and H. Entzinger. London: Routledge.

Kloosterman, R. 1994. "Amsterdamned: The Rise of Unemployment in Amsterdam in the 1980s." *Urban Studies* 31, no. 8: 1325-44.

Kloosterman, R., and T. Elfring. 1991. *Werken in Nederland*. Schoonhoven: Academic Service.

Kloosterman, R., J. van der Leun, and J. Rath. 1997. *Over grenzen: Immigranten en de informele economie*. Amsterdam: Het Spinhuis.

Koot, W., V. Tjon-A-Ten, and P. Uniken Venema. 1985. *Surinaamse kinderen op school*. Muiderberg: Countinho.

Koot, W., and P. Uniken Venema. 1988. "Education: The Way up for Surinamese in the Netherlands." Pp. 185-203 in *Lost Illusions: Caribbean Minorities in Britain and the Netherlands*, edited by M. Cross and H. Entzinger. London: Routledge.

Kroon, H. 1999. "Asian Underground." *Onze Wereld* (March): 46-50.

Kroon, H., and P. Wiggers. 1997. "Op pelgrimage in Afrika." *Onze Wereld* (November): 8-13.

Kruijer, G. 1951. "Urbanisme in Suriname." *Tijdschrift van het Koninklijk Nederlandsch Aardrijkskundig Genootschap* LXVIII: 31-63.

———. 1968. *Suriname en zijn buren: Landen in ontwikkeling*. Meppel: Boom.

———. 1977. *Suriname: De problemen en hun oplossingen*. Utrecht: Het Spectrum.

Kruythoff, H. et al. 1997. *Towards Undivided Cities in Western Europe: New Challenges for Urban Policy: Part 1: The Hague*. Delft: Delft University Press.

Kuipers, L. 1994. "Zorg dat je later niet een ander z'n hok hoeft schoon te maken: Klasse- en seksespecifieke boodschappen van ouders aan kinderen." *Amsterdams Sociologisch Tijdschrift* 21, no. 1: 85-99.

Lalmahomed, B. 1992a. *Hindostaanse vrouwen: De geschiedenis van zes generaties*. Utrecht: Jan van Arkel.

———. 1992b. "Hindostaans-Surinaamse wegloopsters." Pp. 155-260 in L. Brouwer et al., *Andere tijden, andere meiden: Een onderzoek naar het weglopen van Marokkaanse, Turkse, Hindostaanse en Creoolse meisjes*. Utrecht: Jan van Arkel.

Lamur, H. 1973. *The Demographic Evolution of Surinam 1920-1970*. The Hague: Martinus Nijhoff. [1971]

Langbroek, J., and P. Muus. 1991. *De Surinaamse beroepsbevolking in Nederland*. The Hague: Vuga.

Leacock, E., ed. 1971. *The Culture of Poverty: A Critique*. New York: Simon and Schuster.

Ledoux, G. 1996. "De invloed van 'sociaal milieu' bij Turkse, Marokkaanse en Nederlandse sociale stijgers." *Sociologische Gids* 43, no. 2: 114-30.

Lenders, M., and M. van Vlijmen-van de Rhoer. 1983. *Mijn god, hoe ga ik doen? De positie van Creoolse alleenstaande moeders in Amsterdam*. Amsterdam: Antropology-Sociology Center, University of Amsterdam.

Lewis, O. 1966. "The Culture of Poverty." Pp. 67-80 in O. Lewis, *Anthropological Essays*. New York: Random House.

Lieberson, S. 1980. *A Piece of the Pie: Black and White Immigrants since 1880*. Berkeley: University of California Press.

Lier, R. van. 1971. *Frontier Society: A Social Analysis of the History of Surinam*. The Hague: Martinus Nijhof. [1949]

Light, I. 1984. "Immigrant and Ethnic Enterprise in North America." *Ethnic and Racial Studies* 7, no. 2: 195-216.

Light, I., and S. Gold. 2000. *Ethnic Economies*. New York: Academic Press.

Lindo, F. 1996. *Maakt cultuur verschil? De invloed van groepsspecifieke gedragspatronen op de onderwijsloopbaan van Turkse en Iberische migrantenjongeren*. Amsterdam: Het Spinhuis.

Lippe, T. van der, and J. van Doorne-Huiskes. 1995. "Veranderingen in stratificatie tussen mannen en vrouwen?" Pp. 104-24 in *Verschuivende ongelijkheid in Nederland: Sociale gelaagdheid en mobiliteit*, edited by J. Dronkers and W. Ultee. Assen: Van Gorcum.

Lowenthal, D. 1960. "The Range and Variation of Caribbean Societies." In *Social and Cultural Pluralism in the Caribbean*, edited by V. Rubin. Annals of the New York Academy of Sciences 83: 786-95.

Lucassen, J., and R. Penninx. 1994. *Nieuwkomers, nakomelingen, Nederlanders: Immigranten in Nederland 1550-1993*. Amsterdam: Het Spinhuis.

Martens, E. 1995. *Minderheden in beeld: Kerncijfers van de survey Sociale Positie en Voorzieningengebruik Allochtonen 1994*. Rotterdam: ISEO/EUR.

———. 1999. *Minderheden in beeld: SPVA-1998*. Rotterdam: ISEO/EUR.

Martens, E., T. Roelandt, and J. Veenman. 1992. *Minderheden in Nederland: Sociale positie en voorzieningengebruik van autochtonen en allochtonen 1991*. Rotterdam: ISEO/EUR.

Martens, E., and A. Verweij. 1997. *Surinamers in Nederland: Kerncijfers 1996*. Rotterdam: ISEO/EUR.

Martens, E., and Y. Weijers. 2000. *Integratiemonitor 2000*. Rotterdam: ISEO/EUR.

Meer, P. van der, and R. Wielers. 1997. "Hoe belangrijk is opleiding voor de arbeidsmarktpositie van allochtonen?" *Mens en Maatschappij* 72, no. 1: 40-47.

Meijnen, G., and F. Riemersma. 1992. *Schoolcarrières: Een klassekwestie? Een literatuurstudie*. Amsterdam: Swets and Zeitlinger.

Metcalf, H., T. Modood, and S. Virdee. 1996. *Asian Self-employment: The Interaction of Culture and Economics in England*. London: Policy Studies Institute.

Mintz, S., and R. Price. 1992. *The Birth of African-American Culture: An Anthropological Perspective*. Boston: Beacon Press. [1976]

Model, S. 1991. "Caribbean Immigrants: A Black Success Story?" *International Migration Review* 25, no. 2: 248-76.

———. 1999. "Ethnic Inequality in England: An Analysis Based on the 1991 Census." *Ethnic and Racial Studies* 22, no. 6: 966-90.

Modood, T. 1991. "The Indian Economic Success: A Challenge to Some Race Relations Assumptions." *Policy and Politics* 19: 177-89.

Modood, T., R. Berthoud, J. Lakey, J. Nazroo, P. Smith, S. Virdee, and S. Beishon. 1997. *Ethnic Minorities in Britain: Diversity and Disadvantage*. Londen: Policy Studies Institute.

Mungra, B. 1990. *Hindoestaanse gezinnen in Nederland*. Leiden: COMT, University of Leiden.

———. 1993. "Hindostanen in de lift." Pp. 113-25 in *Binnen de grenzen: Immigratie, etniciteit en integratie in Nederland*, edited by R. Gowricharn. Utrecht: De Tijdstroom.

Musterd, S., and W. Ostendorf. 1993. "Stedelijke armoede en etniciteit in de verzorgingsstaat: Amsterdam als voorbeeld." *Sociologische Gids* 40, no. 6: 466-81.

Niekerk, M. van. 1984. "Surinaamse meisjes doen het in stijl: Etnische identiteit van Creoolse meisjes in Amsterdam." MA thesis, Cultural Anthropology, University of Amsterdam.

———. 1990. "Etniciteit: Surinaamse, Turkse en Nederlandse jongeren in een naoorlogse wijk." *Migrantenstudies* 6, no. 1: 18-30.

———. 1991. "Allochtone meisjes: Surinaamse en Turkse meisjes in Nederland." Pp. 177-92 in *Het is meisjes menens: Inleiding meisjesstudies*, edited by I. van der Zande. Amsterdam/Leuven: Acco.

———. 1992. "Armoede en cultuur: Caraïbische vrouwen en meisjes in Nederland." *Migrantenstudies* 8, no. 3: 18-33.

———. 1993a. *Kansarmoede: Reacties van allochtonen op achterstand*. Amsterdam: Het Spinhuis.

———. 1993b. "Ethnic Studies in the Netherlands: An Outline of Research Issues." *Research Notes from the Netherlands* (SISWO) 1: 2-14.

———. 1994. "Zorg en Hoop: Surinamers in Nederland nu." Pp. 45-79 in *Het democratisch ongeduld: De emancipatie en integratie van zes doelgroepen van het minderhedenbeleid*, edited by H. Vermeulen and R. Penninx. Amsterdam: Het Spinhuis.

———. 1995. "A Historical Approach to Ethnic Differences in Social Mobility: Creoles and Hindustanis in Surinam." Pp. 118-43 in *Post-migration Ethnicity: Cohesion, Commitments, Comparison*, edited by G. Baumann and T. Sunier. Amsterdam: Het Spinhuis.

———. 1996. "Differentieel maatschappelijk succes: Creolen en Hindostanen in Suriname." *OSO, Tijdschrift voor Surinaamse taalkunde, letterkunde, cultuur en geschiedenis* 15, no. 1: 5-17.

————. 1997. "Surinaamse Nederlanders: Dilemma's van integratie." *Justitiële Verkenningen* 23, no. 6: 36-48.

————. 1999. "Culture and Gender: Male and Female Careers among Surinamese Creoles and Hindustanis in the Netherlands." Pp. 112-29 in *Culture, Structure and Beyond: Changing Identities and Social Positions of Immigrants and Their Children*, edited by M. Crul, F. Lindo, and C. L. Pang. Amsterdam: Het Spinhuis.

————. 2000a. "Paradoxes in Paradise: Integration and Social Mobility of the Surinamese in the Netherlands." Pp. 64-93 in *Immigrant Integration: The Dutch Case*, edited by H. Vermeulen and R. Penninx. Amsterdam: Het Spinhuis.

————. 2000b. "Creoles and Hindustanis: Patterns of Social Mobility in Two Surinamese Immigrant Groups in the Netherlands." Pp. 184-205 in *Immigrants, Schooling and Social Mobility: Does Culture Make a Difference?* edited by H. Vermeulen and J. Perlmann. London: Macmillan.

Niekerk, M. van, and J. Rath, eds. 1996. "Concentratie en segregatie." Theme issue *Migrantenstudies* 12, no. 2: 57-116.

Niekerk, M. van, T. Sunier, and H. Vermeulen. 1987. *Onderzoek interetnische relaties: Literatuurstudie*. Rijswijk: Ministry of Welfare, Public Health and Culture.

Niekerk, M. van, T. Sunier, and H. Vermeulen, 1989. *Bekende vreemden: Surinamers, Turken en Nederlanders in een naoorlogse wijk*. Amsterdam: Het Spinhuis.

Niekerk, M. van, and H. Vermeulen. 1989. "Ethnicity and Leisure Time: Surinamese Girls in Amsterdam." Pp. 138-52 in *Dutch Dilemmas: Anthropologists Look at the Netherlands*, edited by J. Boissevain and J. Verrips. Assen/Maastricht: Van Gorcum.

Ogbu, J. 1987. "Variability in Minority School Performance: A Problem in Search of an Explanation." *Anthropology and Education Quarterly* 18: 312-34.

Ogbu, J. 1991. "Immigrant and Involuntary Minorities in Comparative Perspective." Pp. 3-33 in *Minority Status and Schooling: A Comparative Study of Immigrant and Involuntary Minorities*, edited by J. Ogbu and M. Gibson. NewYork: Garland Press.

Ogbu, J., and H. Simons. 1998. "Voluntary and Involuntary Minorities: A Cultural-ecological Theory of School Performance with Some Implications for Education." *Anthropology and Education Quarterly* 29: 155-88.

Oostindie, G. 1986. "Kondreman in Bakrakondre/Surinamers in Nederland." Pp. 3-131 in G. Oostindie and L. Maduro, *In het land van de overheerser II: Antillianen en Surinamers in Nederland 1634/1667-1954*. Dordrecht: Foris.

————. 1996. "Ethnicity, Nationalism and the Exodus: The Dutch Caribbean Predicament." Pp. 206-31 in *Ethnicity in the Caribbean: Essays in Honour of Harry Hoetink*, edited by G. Oostindie. London: Macmillan.

Oostindie, G., ed. 1999. *Het verleden onder ogen: Herdenking van de slavernij*. The Hague: Uitgeverij Arena.

Openneer, H. 1995. *Kid Dynamite: De legende leeft*. Amsterdam: Jan Mets.

Penninx, R. 1988a. *Minderheidsvorming en emancipatie: Balans van kennisverwerving ten aanzien van immigranten en woonwagenbewoners*. Alphen on Rhine: Samsom.

————. 1988b. *Wie betaalt, bepaalt?* Amsterdam: Institute for Social Geography, University of Amsterdam.

Perlmann, J. 1988. *Ethnic Differences: Schooling and Social Structure among the Irish, Italians, Jews and Blacks in an American City, 1880-1935.* Cambridge: Cambridge University Press.

———. 2000. "Introduction: The Persistence of Culture versus Structure in Recent Work: The Case of Modes of Incorporation." Pp. 22-33 in *Immigrants, Schooling and Social Mobility: Does Culture Make a Difference?* edited by H. Vermeulen and J. Perlmann. London: Macmillan.

Perlmann, J., and R. Waldinger. 1997. "Second Generation Decline? Children of Immigrants, Past and Present." *International Migration Review* 31, no. 4: 893-923.

Pierce, B. 1973. "Status Competition and Personal Networks: Informal Social Organisation among the Negroes of Paramaribo." *Man* 8, no. 4: 580-91.

Portes, A. 1995. "Children of Immigrants: Segmented Assimilation and Its Determinants." Pp. 248-80 in *The Economic Sociology of Immigration: Essays on Networks, Ethnicity, and Entrepreneurship,* edited by A. Portes. New York: Russell Sage Foundation.

Portes, A., and R. Rumbaut. 1996. *Immigrant America: A Portrait.* Berkeley: University of California Press.

Prins, C. 1994. "Islamieten en Hindoes in Nederland: Herziening van de tijdreeks." *Maandstatistiek van de Bevolking* 42, no. 2: 22-28.

Quispel, G. 1997. "Getto's en concentratiewijken: Segregatie in Nederland en de Verenigde Staten." *Justitiële Verkenningen* 23, no. 6: 150-60.

Ramdas, A. 1996. "Apache-Indian." Pp. 141-44 in A. Ramdas, *De beroepsherinneraar en andere verhalen.* Amsterdam: De Bezige Bij.

Rath, J., R. Penninx, K. Groenendijk, and A. Meyer. 1996. *Nederland en zijn islam: Een ontzuilende samenleving reageert op het ontstaan van een geloofsgemeenschap.* Amsterdam: Het Spinhuis.

Renselaar, H. van. 1963a. "Het sociaal-economisch vermogen van de Creolen in Suriname." *Tijdschrift van het Koninklijk Nederlandsch Aardrijkskundig Genootschap* 80: 474-81.

———. 1963b. "De houding van de Creoolse bevolkingsgroep in Suriname ten opzichte van de andere bevolkingsgroepen." *Bijdragen tot de Taal-, Land- en Volkenkunde* 119: 93-105.

Reubsaet, T., and R. Geerts. 1983. *Surinaamse migranten in Nederland: Het beleid in enkele Nederlandse steden.* Nijmegen: Institute for Applied Sociology.

Reubsaet, T., and J. Kropman. 1983. *Beter opgeleide Antillianen op de Nederlandse arbeidsmarkt.* Nijmegen: Institute for Applied Sociology.

Reubsaet, T., J. Kropman, and L. van Mulier. 1982. *Surinaamse migranten in Nederland: De positie van Surinamers in de Nederlandse samenleving.* Nijmegen: Institute for Applied Sociology.

Robinson, V. 1990. "Roots to Mobility: The Social Mobility of Britain's Black Population, 1971-87." *Ethnic and Racial Studies* 13, no. 2: 274-86.

Roosens, E. 1989a. *Creating Ethnicity: The Process of Ethnogenesis.* Newbury Park, Calif.: Sage Publications.

————. 1989b. "Cultural Ecology and Achievement Motivation." Pp. 85-106 in *Different Cultures Same School*, edited by L. Eldering and J. Kloprogge. Amsterdam: Swets and Zeitlinger.

Rumbaut, R. 1997. "Assimilation and Its Discontents: Between Rhetoric and Reality." *International Migration Review* 31, no. 4: 923-60.

Sansone, L. 1992. *Schitteren in de schaduw: Overlevingsstrategieën, subcultuur en etniciteit van Creoolse jongeren uit de lagere klasse in Amsterdam 1981-1990*. Amsterdam: Het Spinhuis.

Savage, M. 1997. "Social Mobility and the Survey Method: A Critical Analysis." Pp. 299-326 in *Pathways to Social Class: A Qualitative Approach to Social Mobility*, edited by D. Bertaux and P. Thompson. Oxford: Clarendon Press.

Schalkwijk, A., and A. de Bruijne. 1997. *Van Mon Plaisir tot Ephraimzegen: Welstand, etniciteit en woonpatronen in Paramaribo*. Amsterdam/Paramaribo: Institute for Social Geography (UvA)/Leo Victor.

Schuster, J. 1999. *Poortwachters over immigranten: Het debat over immigratie in het naoorlogse Groot-Brittannië en Nederland*. Amsterdam: Het Spinhuis.

SCP/CBS (Social and Cultural Planning Bureau/Statistics Netherlands). 1999. *Armoedemonitor*. The Hague: SCP/CBS.

Sedoc-Dahlberg, B. 1971. "Surinaamse studenten in Nederland." Dissertation, University of Amsterdam.

Sowell, Th. 1981. *Ethnic America: A History*. New York: Basic Books.

Speckmann, J. 1962/63. "Enkele uitkomsten van een sociologisch onderzoek onder Hindostaanse leerlingen van de Mulo-school in Nieuw Nickerie." *Nieuwe West Indische Gids* 42: 208-11.

————. 1963a. "De positie van de Hindostaanse bevolkingsgroep in de sociale en ekonomische struktuur van Suriname." *Tijdschrift van het Koninklijk Nederlandsch Aardrijkskundig Genootschap* 80: 459-66.

————. 1963b. "De houding van de Hindostaanse bevolkingsgroep in Suriname ten opzichte van de Creolen." *Bijdragen tot de Taal-, Land- en Volkenkunde* 119: 76-91.

————. 1965. *Marriage and Kinship among the Indians in Surinam*. Assen: Van Gorcum.

Sprangers, A. 1994. "Gezinsherenigende en gezinsvormende migratie 1987-1991." *Maandstatistiek van de Bevolking* 10: 11-17.

Steinberg, S. 1989. *The Ethnic Myth: Race, Ethnicity and Class in America*. Boston: Bacon Press. [1981]

————. 1997. "Science and Politics in the Work of William Julius Wilson." *New Politics* (winter): 108-20.

Tas, R. 1994. "Surinaamse en Antilliaanse bevolking in Nederland, 1 januari 1994." *Maandstatistiek van de Bevolking* 10: 6-9.

Tesser, P. 1993. *Rapportage minderheden 1993*. Rijswijk: SCP.

Tesser, P., F. van Dugteren, and A. Merens. 1996. *Rapportage minderheden 1996: Bevolking, arbeid, onderwijs, huisvesting*. Rijswijk: SCP.

Tesser, P., C. van Praag, F. van Dugteren, L. Herweijer, and H. van der Wouden. 1995. *Rapportage minderheden 1995: Concentratie en segregatie*. Rijswijk: SCP.

Teunissen, J. 1990. "Basisscholen op islamitische en hindoeïstische grondslag." *Migrantenstudies* 6, no. 2: 45-57.

———. 1996. "Etnische segregatie in het basisonderwijs: Een onderwijskundige benadering." Pp. 23-43 in C. Tazelaar, A. Joachim-Ruis, J. Rutten, and J. Teunissen, *Kleur van de school: Etnische segregatie in het onderwijs*. Houten: Bohn Stafleu Van Loghum.

Teunissen, J., and M. Matthijssen. 1996. "Stagnatie in onderwijsonderzoek naar de etnische factor bij allochtone leerlingen: Een pleidooi voor theoretische en methodologische vernieuwing." In "Onderwijs en etniciteit." Theme issue *Sociologische Gids* 43, no. 2: 87-99, edited by W. Fase and H. Kleijer.

Tillaart, H. van den, and E. Poutsma. 1998. *Een factor van betekenis: Zelfstandig ondernemerschap van allochtonen in Nederland*. Nijmegen: ITS.

Tjon-A-Ten, V. 1987. "Creoolse en Hindoestaanse kinderen in het Nederlandse lager onderwijs." Dissertation, University of Utrecht.

Todd, E. 1994. *Le destin des immigrés: Assimilation et ségrégation dans les démocraties occidentales*. Paris: Éditions du Seuil.

Valentine, C. 1968. *Culture and Poverty: Critique and Counterproposals*. Chicago: University of Chicago Press.

Vedic Youth Netherlands Foundation. 1997. "Problemen van en problemen met Hindoestaanse jongeren: Criminaliteit en preventie." Report of Conference on 19 April, The Hague.

Veenman, J. 1994. *Participatie in perspectief*. Houten: Bohn Stafleu Van Loghum.

Venema, T. 1992. *Famiri nanga kulturu: Creoolse sociale verhoudingen en Winti in Amsterdam*. Amsterdam: Het Spinhuis.

Verkuyten, M. 1988. *Zelfbeleving en identiteit van jongeren uit etnische minderheden*. Arnhem: Gouda Quint.

Vermeulen, H. 1984. *Etnische groepen en grenzen: Surinamers, Chinezen en Turken*. Weesp: Het Wereldvenster.

———. 1991. "Handelsminderheden: Een inleiding." *Focaal* 15: 7-28.

———. 1992. "De Cultura: Een verhandeling over het cultuurbegrip in de studie van allochtone etnische groepen." *Migrantenstudies* 8, no. 2: 14-30.

———. 2000. "Introduction: The Role of Culture in Explanations of Social Mobility." Pp. 1-21 in *Immigrants, Schooling and Social Mobility: Does Culture Make a Difference?* edited by H. Vermeulen and J. Perlmann. London: Macmillan.

Vermeulen, H., and R. Penninx, eds. 2000. *Immigrant Integration: The Dutch Case*. Amsterdam: Het Spinhuis.

Vermeulen, H., and J. Perlmann, eds. 2000. *Immigrants, Schooling and Social Mobility: Does Culture Make a Difference?* London: Macmillan.

Verweij, A. 1997. *Vaststelling van etnische herkomst in Nederland: De BIZA-methode nader bekeken*. Rotterdam: ISEO/EUR.

Vocking, J. 1994. "Achtergronden van de immigratie van Surinamers vanaf 1980." *Maandstatistiek van de Bevolking* 8: 6-14.

Volkstelling (Census) 1971/1972, 1978. *4e Algemene Volkstelling 1971/1972 (geheel Suriname)*. Paramaribo: Algemeen Bureau voor de Statistiek.

Vries, G. de. 1994. *Nederland verandert: Sociale problemen in de jaren tachtig en negentig*. Amsterdam: Het Spinhuis.

Vries, M. de. 1990. *Roddel nader beschouwd*. Leiden: COMT.

Waldinger, R. 1996. *Still the Promised City? African-Americans and New Immigrants in Postindustrial New York*. Cambridge, Mass.: Harvard University Press.

Waldinger, R., H. Aldrich, and R. Ward. 1990. *Ethnic Entrepreneurs: Immigrant Business in Industrial Societies*. London: Sage Publications.

Warrier, S. 1994. "Gujarati Prajapatis in London: Family Roles and Sociability Networks." Pp. 191-212 in *Desh Pardesh: The South Asian Presence in London*, edited by R. Ballard. London: Hurst.

Waters, M. 1994. "Ethnic and Racial Identities of Second-Generation Black Immigrants in New York City." *International Migration Review* 28, no. 4: 795-820.

Weltak, M., 1990. *Surinaamse muziek in Nederland*. Utrecht: Uitgeverij Kosmos.

Werbner, P. 2000. "What Colour Success? Distorting Values in Studies of Ethnic Entrepreneurs." Pp. 34-60 in *Immigrants, Schooling and Social Mobility: Does Culture Make a Difference?* edited by H. Vermeulen and J. Perlmann. London: Macmillan.

Wetering, W. van. 1987. "Informal Supportive Networks: Quasi-kin Groups, Religion and Social Order among Surinamese Creoles in the Netherlands." *Netherlands Journal of Sociology* 23, no. 2: 92-101.

———. 1990. "Dissonance in Discourse: The Politics of Afro-Surinamese Culture in the Netherlands." Pp. 291-307 in *Resistance and Rebellion in Suriname: Old and New*, edited by G. Brana Shute. Williamsburg, Va.: Department of Anthropology, College of William and Mary.

Willemsen, G. 1980. "Koloniale politiek en transformatie-processen in een plantage-economie: Suriname 1873-1940." Dissertation, Erasmus University, Rotterdam.

Williams, B. 1991. *Stains on My Name, War in My Veins: Guyana and the Politics of Cultural Struggle*. Durham, N.C.: Duke University Press.

Willis, P. 1977. *Learning to Labour: How Working-Class Kids Get Working-Class Jobs*. Westmead, U.K.: Saxon House.

Wilson, P. 1973. *Crab Antics*. New Haven, Conn.: Yale University Press.

Wilson, W. 1987. *The Truly Disadvantaged: The Inner City, the Underclass, and Public Policy*. Chicago: University of Chicago Press.

———. 1991. "Studying Inner-City Dislocations: The Challenge of Public Agenda Research." *American Sociological Review* 56: 1-14.

———. 1996. *When Work Disappears: The World of the New Urban Poor*. New York: Vintage Books.

———. 1999. "When Work Disappears: New Implications for Race and Urban Poverty in the Global Economy." *Ethnic and Racial Studies* 22, no. 3: 479-99.

Wolf, E., 1994. "Perilous Ideas: Race, Culture, People." *Current Anthropology* 35, no. 1: 1-12.

Zenner, W. 1991. *Minorities in the Middle: A Cross Cultural Analysis*. New York: State University of New York Press.

Zhou, M. 1997. "Segmented Assimilation: Issues, Controversies and Recent Research on the New Second Generation." *International Migration Review* 31, no. 4: 975-1008.

Zielhuis, L. 1973. *Buitenlandse migratie van Suriname in 1971*. Paramaribo: Ministry of Social Affairs.

Index

285

About the Author

Mies van Niekerk is a senior researcher at the Institute for Migration and Ethnic Studies (IMES) at the University of Amsterdam. She received her MA degree in cultural anthropology and a PhD from the University of Amsterdam. She previously held academic posts in the Department of Anthropology and Sociology at the same university, where she carried out research on immigrants in the Netherlands. Her main focus has been on immigrants from the Caribbean (Surinam or the former Dutch Guiana and the Netherlands Antilles). She has published on a variety of topics including ethnic identity and youth culture, interethnic relations in a postwar urban neighborhood, immigrant elderly, and urban poverty. In 2000 she published *'The Grashopper and the Ant.' Fables and Facts about the Social Mobility of Surinamese Creoles and Hindustanis in the Netherlands* (in Dutch), of which the present book is an English version. Her main areas of interest include the relation between the socioeconomic integration of immigrants, their premigration history and postmigratory processes. Currently she is participating in an interuniversity research program on immigrant entrepreneurship and informal economic activities in the Dutch multicultural city. She is a member of the editorial staff of the Dutch sociological journal *Sociologische Gids* and editor of the IMES Book Series *Migratie- en Etnische Studies*.